P9-DNB-056

psychology
the science of behavior

Under the editorship of Wayne Holtzman

Harper & Row, Publishers
New York, Evanston, San Francisco, London

psychology

the science of behavior

second edition

ROBERT L. ISAACSON
University of Florida

MAX L. HUTT
University of Detroit

Psychology: The Science of Behavior, Second Edition

Standard Book Number: 06-043233-0
Library of Congress Catalog Card Number: 71-148454

Contents

Preface

This edition of *Psychology: The Science of Behavior* has been written with the students of the 1970s in mind. One characteristic of today's college undergraduates is their greater ability to master the abundant supply of facts about the world and about people. This second edition of the book has incorporated a large amount of new material, much of which has been generated since the first edition of the book was published six years ago. Scientific knowledge expands at almost a geometric progression year by year, and it is fortunate that the educational processes are becoming more effective in preparing students to cope with this ever-increasing body of knowledge.

In this revision we have not only added new material but streamlined our presentation of the information. The student is more readily able to progress from the early considerations of genetic inheritance (Chapter 2) to the behavioral phenomena called learning, memory, motivation, and emotion. We have eliminated that material in the previous edition which was predominantly related to psychology as a social science. We have emphasized psychology as a natural and a biological science to a much greater extent, hoping that this would allow for a greater integration of the materials presented in the book.

College students interested in doing their part to improve the lot of mankind will probably derive much useful and needed background information about the behavior of people from this book. A few students may feel that this is not the kind of information that can lead to the changes needed in our highly organized and technologically advanced society. We disagree completely. Real advancement of the cause of mankind must be based upon the appraisal of all available knowledge about the phenomenon under study, which in this case is man himself. We do not believe that significant progress, or any progress, can be made merely from a casual and incompetent rejection of the present state of man's affairs. In this sense we dedicate the book to the serious and careful student of behavior.

Psychology is the study of man, his mental activities, and his behavior. There is no higher region to study. It is worth the best in all of us to advance this investigation and thus to provide the means whereby improvements in the quality of life will be made.

ROBERT L. ISAACSON
MAX L. HUTT

psychology
the science of behavior

1
Definition and historical roots

Psychology is the study of the mind and of behavior. Simply put, psychologists study the mental experiences and behavior of people and other animals. For the most part the emphasis is on the study of an individual during his lifetime. The study of large groups of people and the changes occurring in animals over successive generations is left to other sciences.

In a very real sense, there is no one psychology, there are many. Perhaps the name of the field should be changed to "psychological sciences" to describe more adequately the diversity of approaches and interests found among psychologists.

Looking at the kinds of things psychologists do will give further insight into the diversity that is psychology. Some psychologists investigate the neural mechanisms underlying sensation and perception by studying the structure and function of the eye or the ear. Their methods and their background usually are similar to those of physiologists interested in the sensory processes. Some psychologists work with emotionally disturbed people or with patients in hospitals or clinics, and their training is often similar to that of psychiatrists. Psychologists also try to discover techniques for designing and operating machines that will most efficiently take advantage of the special characteristics of man. Others study the man at his job, as an individual in a group or society. They may consider the effect of union membership or participation in various kinds of company programs on morale and attitudes. Psychologists also work on the development of testing programs ranging from intelligence tests, with which all of us have had experience, to measurements of specific kinds of aptitudes or abilities. Although many psychologists are concerned with applied problems such as these, there are also many others who are entirely involved with the development of theories of behavior. These people are relatively removed from immediate and practical applications.

In this book we will be concerned almost entirely with the experimental studies of behavior that have a natural science or biological science approach. These approaches try to understand how behavior originates, develops, and is changed throughout life, using ideas and theories that "fit in" with ideas and theories found in other natural and biological sciences.

This book does not cover all of the psychological sciences; it is restricted in scope. Our companion book, *Psychology: The Science of Interpersonal Behavior,* approaches the study of psychology quite differently. It attempts to describe behavior using ideas and theories concerning the development and change of the individual personality. Neither orientation is better nor worse than the other. They are different and each represents a valid and interesting approach to the understanding of behavior.

WHAT PSYCHOLOGY IS NOT

Psychology is often confused with a number of rather similar words. The two words most commonly confused with it are *psychiatry* and *psychoanalysis.* Psychiatry is a medical specialty area concerned with mental and behavioral disorders. Psychiatrists are physicians who have taken additional work, after obtaining their M.D. degrees, in the care and treatment of patients suffering from many varieties of mental and physical problems that have produced a severe impairment in their ability to function in, or cope with, society. The psychiatrist seeks to alleviate the problems of his patients with behavioral disorders. Some psychologists, often called clinical psychologists or psychotherapists, attempt to help people with behavioral problems.

They do not use medical methods of treatment and often treat less severe disorders. Clinical psychologists go through a graduate program in psychology directed toward a Ph.D. degree with special training in techniques used to help patients singly or in groups.

Psychoanalysts are psychiatrists or psychotherapists who use a specific type of treatment called *psychoanalysis*. This procedure is based upon the belief that it is important to uncover a person's memories of past events while helping him resolve the difficulties of the present. This technique was the one made popular by Sigmund Freud.

THE HISTORICAL DEVELOPMENT OF PSYCHOLOGY

The present-day activities of psychologists are derived historically from at least four different streams of influence: philosophy, clinical studies, physiology, and mental testing.

Philosophy

Man has always been curious about himself. Where does he come from? Where is he going? What is his purpose in life? Is he born with a knowledge of right and wrong? How does he find his real identity? Is the mind or the body more real? Does man exist, or is he merely an idea in the mind of God? Questions such as these have persisted throughout history, yet their answers have not been found and are not likely to be found. At least you will not learn such answers from this book.

Nonetheless, one of the most prominent historical roots of psychology comes from the philosophers and their attempts to understand the nature of man through reason, logic, and argument. The most important philosophical roots of psychology come from the Greeks, especially Plato and Aristotle. The Eastern philosophies (Zen Buddhism, Hinduism, Confucianism) have contributed little to our modern view of behavior. Somewhat more recently, the school of philosophy called British associationism and some German philosophy, as developed by writers such as Leibniz and Kant, have been influential. More will be said of the contributions of the British associationists in Chapter 7, on learning (see pp. 243-245). The greatest influence of these philosophical ideas can be found in the areas of learning and perception. For example, when we speak of learning as an "association" between a stimulus and a response we are using a concept of association not very different from that propounded by the British philosophers several hundred years ago.

In the United States, the contributions of William James (1842–1910) of Harvard were influential in establishing psychology as an academic discipline separate from philosophy. His book *Principles of Psychology* (1890) is an early landmark in psychology and still is well worth reading today. It shows his belief that a strong background in biology is important for the understanding of human behavior. Soon after writing *Principles of Psychology,* James turned to philosophy and is known as a leading proponent of the pragmatic theory of truth, which holds that if a theory or belief works then it is true. William James is recognized as the founder of American psychology and made contributions to science and philosophy comparable to those his brother (Henry James) made to literature.

Physiology

The investigations of physiology, in many ways, represent the most direct contribution to modern psychology. Our knowledge of the functions of the brain, its sensory systems, and the anatomical substrates of behavior comes almost wholly from physiology. The indirect effects of physiological investigations can be seen in theories of learning and motivation. For example, the ideas of the Russian physiologist Ivan Petrovich Pavlov (1849–1936) are clearly reflected in our current theories of learning. The work of modern physiologists is now affecting our theories of motivation and emotion, and there is much general cross-fertilization between physiological and psychological investigations. In one sense, the behavioral study of the organism defines the problems that may someday be solved through understanding of the physiological functions of the body.

Probably the most important physiologist to contribute to modern psychology was Hermann von Helmholtz (1821–1894). His work on the anatomy of the eye and the ear as well as on color vision remains classic. Experimental psychology started in the laboratory of Wilhelm Wundt (1832–1920), a German physiologist and former assistant of von Helmholtz. Another German scientist, Gustav Fechner (1801–1887), was the first to study the relation between physical stimulation and received sensation (*psychophysics*).

Clinical studies

The antecedents of modern attempts to treat the mentally ill can be traced directly to Sigmund Freud (1856–1939). Freud was an Austrian physician who founded a new method of treating the mentally ill and developed a new theory of personality. Both the method of treatment and the personality theory are called *psychoanalysis.* Freud emphasized the role of unconscious impulses (wishes, desires, drives, or motives). The behavior of the individual, and especially that of the emotionally disturbed individual, is thought to reflect his unconscious motives, which are always active even though unknown to him. The contributions of Freud relating to the development and organization of personality are discussed at length in our companion volume, *Psychology: The Science of Interpersonal Behavior,* and therefore are only briefly touched upon here.

Freud's influence is pervasive throughout all psychology. While crediting Sigmund Freud we should note, however, that the assumption of continually active unconscious impulses had been suggested many times before. In particular, the German philosopher Johann Herbart (1776–1841) proposed a theory of unconscious impulses that was remarkably similar to Freud's. Freud's major contribution was to make explicit the sexual nature of the unconscious impulses. We speak of Freud's contribution as *clinical,* because it is based on the clinical study of persons with mental disorders.

Modern clinical psychologists are active in research contributing to our understanding of personality, the emotions, mental retardation, and a host of related fields. Today clinical psychologists draw upon information derived from many fields. Principles of *behavior modification*—which arise from the application of basic principles of learning to the behavior of disturbed people—have become an increasingly effective tool in the hands of clinical psychologists. Team approaches that include the combined efforts of psychiatrists, clinical psychologists, social workers, and educational specialists also are becoming more common.

Mental testing

The fourth historical root of psychology comes from France, where Alfred Binet (1857–1911) developed the first standardized method of mental testing. He was commissioned to develop a method for identifying mentally retarded children so that they could be educated more economically and effectively in special programs. Even today one of the most important tests of intelligence, the Stanford-Binet, still bears his name.

Mental tests have been useful in predicting success in school and in industrial and military programs. Some people have argued that there has been too much reliance on objective testing of mental capacities, especially in the United States. If this is so, it is because the tests *do* predict many aspects of human behavior.

Current trends

Today we find psychologists striving to understand man directly along the lines of the four historical approaches broadly outlined above. Psychologists work toward understanding the physiological mechanisms supporting behavior, they work in mental testing, they work to understand the rules governing learning and memory, and they work toward helping those who are mentally disturbed. But each of these historical roots has extended beyond its own domains. The psychologists working to understand the basic laws of learning know and use concepts derived from mental testing; those working with mentally disturbed patients know the many facets of intelligence that have been reported from mental-measurement efforts, and this information helps them to understand the potential abilities of their patients. There is a constant process of cross-fertilization among all areas of psychology.

THE ANIMAL IN BEHAVIORAL EXPERIMENTS

For many practical reasons, animals must be used in psychological experiments even though the ultimate goal is to understand man. Only by using animals is it possible to control the genetic background and day-to-day environments of the subjects adequately. Often it is possible to attain precise control of training conditions only with animals. When the factors of complete control over background, environment, or training are important in the study of an experimental problem, animals must be used.

Animals are used in psychological studies whenever the need arises to do things that for ethical or practical reasons cannot be done with people. Beyond this, however, animal behavior has fascinated people in many sciences for centuries. Patterns of animal behavior are incredibly complex and often beautiful in their execution. More important, what we learn about animal behavior can lead to new insights and hypotheses about human behavior.

COMPARISON OF SPECIES

In the 1930s, American psychologists were greatly interested in comparing the behavior and intellectual capacities of animals of different species. Animals were trained in different types of problems, each of which was designed to test the limits of some specific intellectual ability of the species. This method of the comparative study of behavior has for the most part been abandoned, however, mainly because of the impossibility of delineating the connection between specific behaviors of various animals and their intellectual abilities.

In the 1940s and early 1950s many American psychologists undertook systematic studies of learning and memory based largely upon experiments performed with rats. Laboratory rats are highly inbred, docile animals which are relatively easy to maintain in large colonies. Both students and teachers can handle them easily. They can readily be trained to do a great number of tasks. Because they are small, the machines used for training them need not be large. Also, it is easy and fairly inexpensive to control the rats' environment and diet so that precise training conditions can be maintained. Many modern theories of learning and memory are based upon studies made of the laboratory rodent. These theories should be considered as tentative proposals for theories of human learning, which may or may not be supported by further investigations.

Today, as a result of the extensive use of rats in the 1940s and 1950s, more is known about the behavior of the laboratory rat in different training situations than is known about the behavioral capacities of any other species, including man. In most cases, however, since comparative studies are no longer popular, the findings concerning rats are seldom contrasted with the behavior of other species.

Indeed, it serves little purpose to compare the behaviors of different species chosen randomly from commonly available animals. Comparison for the sake of comparison among species could go on endlessly and would accomplish very little. A far better approach is to make comparisons among species that represent a given class of animals. Today, for example, comparative psychologists select animals for behavioral comparisons on the basis of their position on the *phylogenetic* or *phyletic* scale. The concept of a phylogenetic scale comes from Aristotle, who proposed that animals exist on a single line of development from man at the top to formless creatures like sponges at the bottom. Later, religious philosophers replaced man at the top of the scale with God, and all animals, moving downward on the scale, were less and less perfect images of God.

If we believed in a scale such as Aristotle's, we might think that fish, snakes, birds, rats, cats, and monkeys could be arranged in order, like rungs on a ladder ascending toward man (the top rung). In reality, however, the phylogenetic scale is more like a widely branching tree (see Figure 1-1). Indeed, the line of fish from which amphibians evolved is quite separate from other fish. No teleost (bony) fish, and this includes most living specimens, ever gave rise to amphibians, reptiles, birds, or mammals. Birds are also a specialized line of animal development and are not ancestors of higher forms. At the mammalian level, rats were not

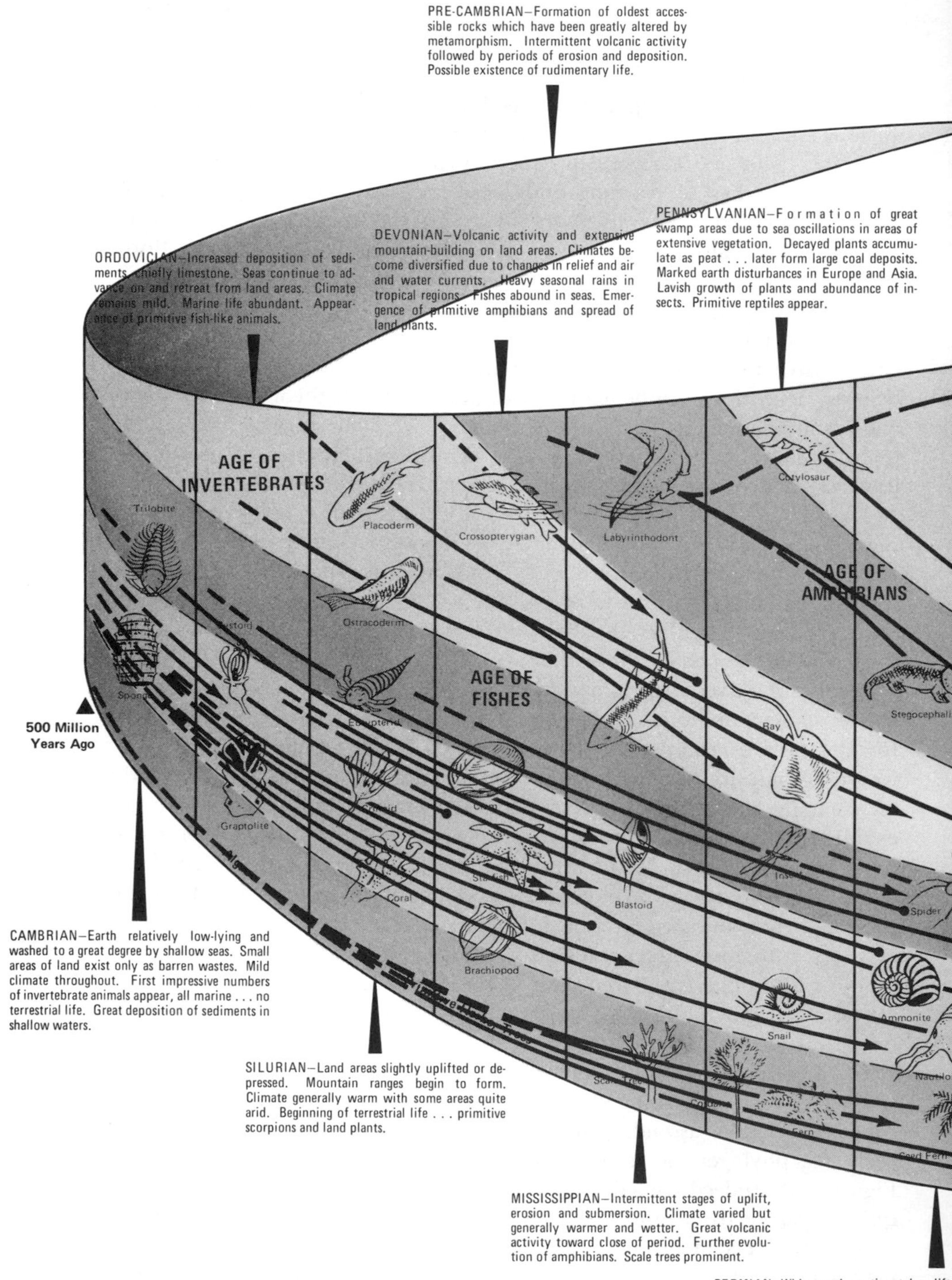

Figure 1-1 *The geologic record.*
(© Copyright 1967, Hammond Incorporated #10367.)

MESOZOIC ERA CENOZOIC ERA

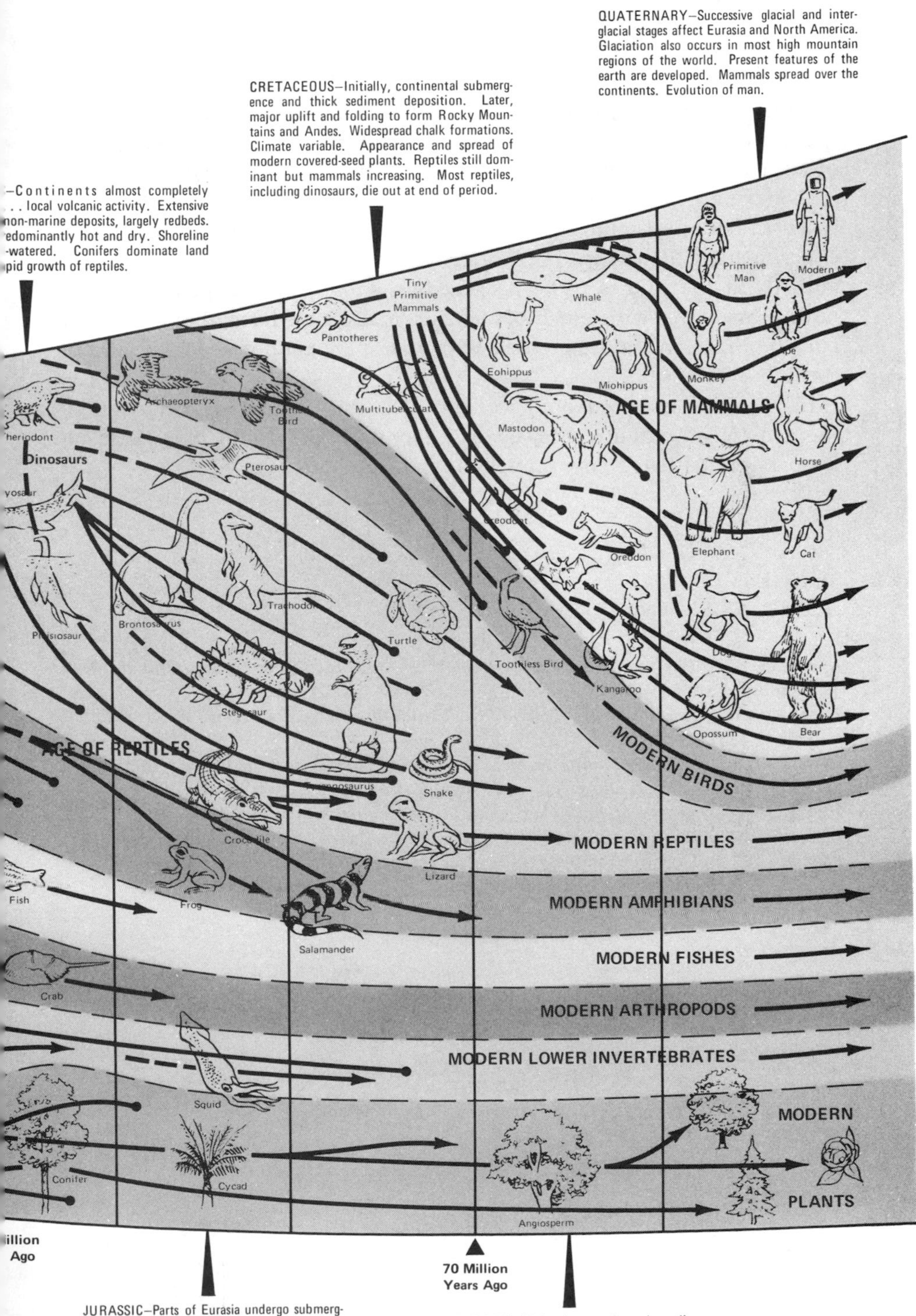

illion Ago

70 Million Years Ago

JURASSIC—Parts of Eurasia undergo submergence and deposition. Western United States altered by subsurface heat and pressure. Widespread erosion in Eastern United States. Climate humid. Coal beds accumulate in lowlands. Cycad-like plants dominant. Dinosaurs chief land animals. First bird appears. Mammals established but primitive.

TERTIARY—Distinctive continental outlines begin to form. Moderate submergences in Europe. North America flooding restricted to present lowland areas. Further elevation of existing North American mountains and formation of Alps and other European ranges. Formation of Himalayas. Climate varied. Mammals become dominant.

the forebears of cats, nor did cats lead to monkeys. Each represents a specialized, end-product of a distinct evolutionary line. Comparisons of animals at these end branches tell us little about evolutionary trends of behavioral development.

These few words and warnings about the use of animals in behavioral experiments will prepare the reader for examination of the wide use of animals in the studies to be discussed in subsequent chapters. Animals have provided us with much of the information we have about behavior and the brain. We must proceed with them; we cannot proceed without them.

In the following chapter we consider the origins of behavior in the genetic inheritance received by every individual and how these influences act with the environment to produce behavior.

SUGGESTED READINGS

Anderson, B. F. *The psychological experiment: An introduction to the scientific method.* Belmont, Calif.: Wadsworth, 1966.

Bachrach, A. J. *Psychological research: An introduction* (2nd ed.). New York: Random House, 1965.

Conant, J. B. *On understanding science.* New York: New American Library, 1951.

Eysenck, H. J. *Uses and abuses in psychology.* Baltimore: Penguin Books, 1953

Havemann, E. *The age of psychology.* New York: Simon & Schuster, 1957.

James, W. *The principles of psychology.* New York: Dover, 1950. 2 vols.

Pavlov, I. P. (C. V. Anrep, trans.) *Conditioned reflexes.* New York: Dover, 1960.

Watson, J. B. *Behaviorism.* Chicago: University of Chicago Press (Phoenix), 1935.

2
Genetics and psychology

Both the similarities and differences among people can be seen in any family, group, or nation. In the past, many psychologists have attempted to explain these similarities and differences by stressing the contribution of environmental influences and minimizing the contributions of heredity. Others have naïvely assumed heredity to be the sole factor determining one's behavior as well as appearance. Yet there is no doubt that both heredity and environment contribute to the development of each person.

Consequently, a basic understanding of behavior involves a knowledge of heredity and, therefore, of genetics. Genetics and psychology are interrelated sciences in that psychologists strive to understand how and to what extent each person's genes do affect his behavior.

On the other hand, we know that every mature person also has had a considerable degree of cultural training. Twenty or more years of almost constant interaction between the individual and his surroundings produces a person whose behavior is, in many respects, largely predictable from the social demands of his culture. The best predictors of behavior are often merely the expectations of society and one's peer group. Think of your own behavior: What you wear, what and when you eat, and what you say in practically every situation from the classroom to an intimate conversation are all predictable by our current social customs. Anyone who reaches maturity has had his behavior shaped and molded by the various environmental factors that go with being reared and educated in groups.

Environmental factors act to determine behavior at all levels of development. Parents try to establish desired behavior patterns in their children by punishment or praise. These techniques are used for transmitting the prominent social values of the culture. There are also other kinds of environmental influences that may affect the child even before his birth. For example, the amount of oxygen or other vital substances available to the developing fetus will have a great deal to do with its ultimate adult characteristics.

With the meeting of the sperm and egg, the genetic information from the father and mother are joined; from this point on, the rest of the individual's development is up to the environment. Nevertheless, the genetic traits passed down to us from our ancestors are significant factors in influencing our behavior. How much of our adult behavior is determined at fertilization? How great is the effect of heredity on behavior? How do genetic influences control behavior? It is to these questions that we turn in this chapter.

EARLY BEHAVIORISM AND GENETICS

The leading proponent of the behavioristic school of psychology, John B. Watson, offered the following challenge to those who believed that behavior was significantly determined by heredity:

> I should like to go one step further now and say, give me a dozen healthy infants, well-formed, and my own specified world to bring them up in and I'll guarantee to take any one at random and train him to be any type of specialist I might suggest—doctor, lawyer, artist, merchant-chief and, yes, even beggar-man and thief, regardless of his talents, penchants, tendencies, abilities, vocations, and the race of his ancestors. I am going beyond my facts and I admit it, but so have the advocates of the contrary and they have been doing it for many thousands of years (Watson, 1924, p. 104).

Watson directly and unequivocally denied the importance of genetic factors in determining the behavior of the individual person. He believed that heredity does not matter, because any type of person can be produced through subsequent socialization and training. This statement, unusual in its strength as well as its argument, needs to be set against the background of psychology as it existed prior to 1930 and against the social and political atmosphere of the culture.

Watson was attacking both *introspective psychology* and *instinct psychology*. The term *introspection* refers to an individual's attempt to see within himself, to become aware of his own conscious experiences. Introspective psychology attempted to build theories of sensation and perception based upon an individual's analysis of his own mental experiences. At the time of Watson's statement, psychology was just beginning to free itself from being restricted to "the study of mental experience"—a study that had created an endless series of controversies and debates without hope of adequate empirical resolution. Watson was seeking less subjectivity and more objectivity.

Instinct psychology, on the other hand, placed great emphasis on behavior that was primarily instinctive. It considered most human behavior to be influenced by innate psychological dispositions; in fact, instincts were the fundamental source of all human activity and the determinants of the ends of all behavior. Although instincts were conceded to be modifiable, the original behavior form was considered to be innate. Here again, the theory was subjective rather than empirical in nature.

Watson's desire to study human behavior more objectively evolved into the study of animal behavior. He was aware of the work of Pavlov, the Russian physiologist, and became firmly committed to the Pavlovian view that the relation between stimulus and response (both of which could be objectively measured) was the proper study for scientists interested in behavior. Soon Watson argued that *all* behavior was merely the product of conditioning and was no different from Pavlov's dogs learning to salivate at the sound of a bell after both the bell and food had been presented to them together many times.

Reviewing the history of modern psychology, we find a steady progression away from introspective and instinct psychology, toward the new view of behaviorism. Consciousness was first attacked as inconsequential to psychology and later rejected as being illusory. The influence of heredity upon behavior declined in Watson's writings until he reached the categorical denial of genetic influences expressed in the quotation given above.

On the positive side it must be said that behaviorism stressed the view that all we can know about another person is what we can observe of his behavior; we can never directly know another's perceptions or thoughts. If we accept this position, and if we recognize that psychology attempts to provide theories to explain observable behavior, then we have come to the behavioristic position widely accepted by many present-day psychologists.

The denial of the importance of heredity in influencing behavior is supported by our social and political assumptions. Our Declaration of Independence reads, "All men are created equal." Of course, the Declaration of Independence referred to a political equality, in terms of rights and responsibilities, among all men and was not a denial of obvious differences based upon inherited abilities. Nevertheless, many political leaders have assumed a more general equality among men and emphasized the effects of environmental influences upon behavior. Doesn't Watson's view seem to agree more with an equalitarian philosophy than with a theory that holds that intellectual abilities are determined by heredity, and therefore men are not equal? If some men are smarter than others, shouldn't the wiser men be rulers? Is a view of behavior that stresses the importance of genetic inheritance undemocratic? Of course it is not—but it should be remembered that social and political factors have always influenced prevailing opinions concerning the extent of genetic influences. The challenge presented by Watson was in part a product of the political and social beliefs of his time.

The resistance among psychologists to crediting genetic influences with determining behavior also comes from another quarter. Clinical psychologists, psychiatrists, psychoanalysts, and others who attempt to evaluate and treat personality disorders have tended to minimize the importance of hereditary influences in such disorders. An extreme reliance upon heredity as the cause of all such disturbances would negate the effectiveness of traditional clinical methods of psychological treatment, and clinicians believe that most mental disturbances can be helped by treatment. Yet we know that hereditary factors may contribute to tendencies toward more or less disintegrated behavior. Some psychologists believe that schizophrenia is fundamentally a neurological disease of genetic origin. The manner in which the disease is expressed may depend upon the person's environment and his past experiences. Nevertheless, a tendency to react to situations of stress and strain with schizophrenic behavior probably has a genetic base.

To a considerable degree, the antiheredity attitude made explicit by Watson has prevailed in psychology. Only in recent years have psychologists begun to pay attention to the relation between behavior and heredity, and it is likely that there will be an increasing interrelationship between the sciences of genetics and psychology. This reconciliation is one that promises to help in understanding behavior and to serve as a counterbalance to the excesses of early behaviorism.

GENETIC MATERIAL

When the human sperm and egg unite, each provides 23 chromosomes. *Chromosomes* are bodies of material in the nucleus of a cell that are darker than the other cellular material. Because of their dark appearance after staining, they are called *chromosomes,* or "colored bodies." It is these bodies which carry the hereditary traits to the potential baby. Every cell in the body contains the same number of chromosomes. All normal human cells have 46 chromosomes, half from the mother and half from the father (see Figure 2-1). Each species has its own special number of chromosomes in each cell, and some have fewer than 46. Figure 2-2 shows the appearance of chromosomes as examined by the scanning electron microscope.

Since several species may have the same number of chromosomes, the number of chromosomes found in an animal does not provide an exact method of determining to which species it belongs.

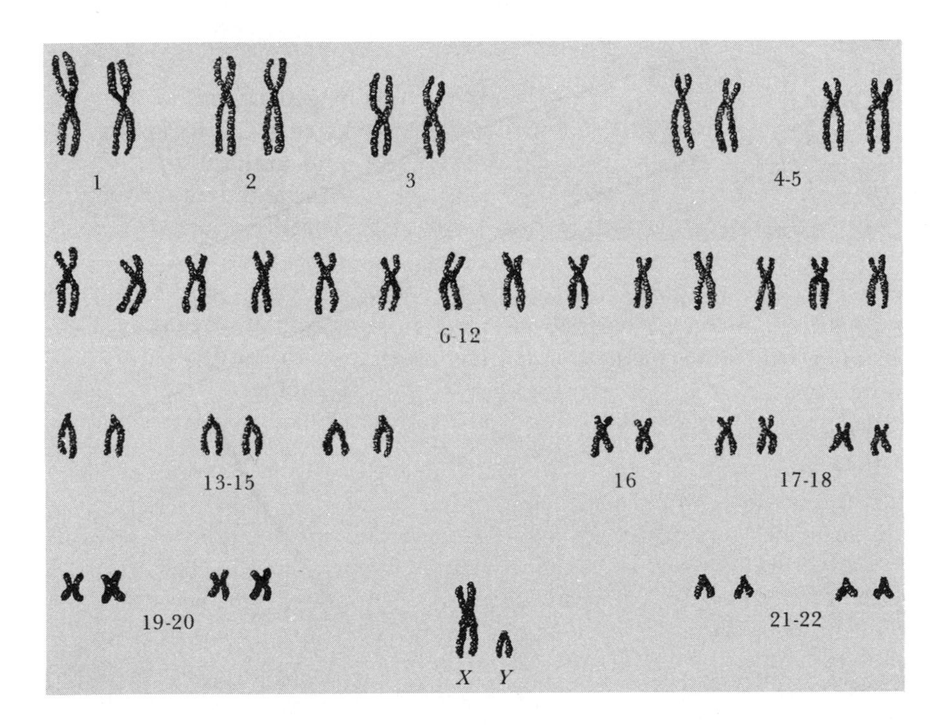

Figure 2-1 *Normal male chromosomes. (Courtesy of M. Neil Macintyre, Western Reserve University, School of Medicine.)*

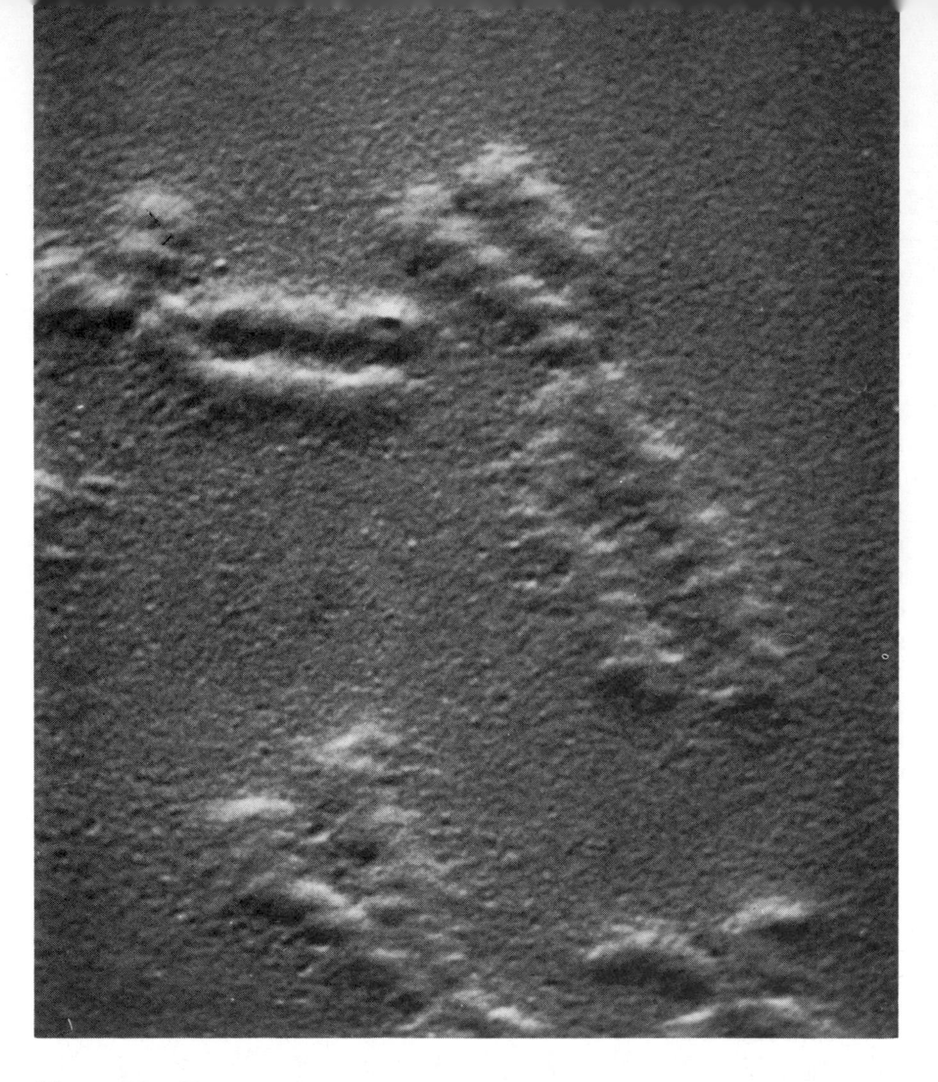

Figure 2-2 *Chromosomes as examined by the scanning electron microscope at magnification of about 4370. (Courtesy of P. W. Neuragh and M. E. Burns, New England Medical Center Hospital.)*

Through the genetic inheritance contained in the chromosomes, each cell becomes a specialist in the body. Some cells become nerve cells, some blood cells, some muscle cells, and so on. In fact, the information in the chromosomes determines not only the structure and function of each cell but also, through these cells, the individual's general bodily characteristics such as hair color, eye color, and the number of muscle and nerve cells. In the horse and dog, selective breeding has isolated pure strains with special characteristics especially suitable for hunting, running, and jumping.

There also is evidence that some genetic information can be carried by unknown mechanisms outside the nucleus, in the cytoplasm of the cells. The cytoplasm of a cell is the fluid inside the cell membrane; it contains many miniature organs and systems concerned with the metabolic activities of the cell. When a cell divides, each of the resulting cells receives the same chromosome content as the original cell but different amounts and regions of the original cytoplasm. This differential distribution of cytoplasm may account for the fact that identical twins (which originate from the same fertilized egg) can have somewhat different physical characteristics and, in some cases, different abnormalities. Nevertheless, most genetic information probably is transmitted by the material found in the chromosomes.

Just how is hereditary information stored in the chromosomes, and how does this information exert such a powerful influence upon the development of the individual? For the answers to these questions, we must look at the genetic code.

The genetic code

In 1962 the Nobel Prize for Medicine and Physiology was awarded to Francis Harry Compton Crick, James Dewey Watson, and Maurice Hugh Frederick Wilkins for their discoveries concerning the structure of the material of heredity. Their investigations have provided important insights into the composition of the chromosomes and, more important, into how the genetic information is encoded within the chromosomes.

Chromosomes consist primarily of two chemical compounds: deoxyribonucleic acid (DNA) and ribonucleic acid (RNA). There is relatively little RNA, and the amount varies according to the metabolic activity of the cell in which it is found. Cells in more active physiological organs have more RNA in their chromosomes than do the cells of less active organs. Most of the RNA in a cell's nucleus acts as a messenger system that conveys genetic information from the DNA to enzyme- and protein-manufacturing sites in the cytoplasm of the cell. The DNA is the primary substance in which the genetic information is stored.

The DNA is found in the chromosomes as two long strands connected at intervals by chemical bonds. These connecting bonds are composed of four organic compounds called *bases:* adenine, thymine, guanine, and cytosine. The two strands of DNA are curled in the form of a *helix,* a configuration similar to a spiral except that it does not come to a point (see Figure 2-3).

In normal cell division, or *mitosis,* DNA material, which usually is spread diffusely throughout the nucleus, gathers together with other nuclear materials to form the chromosomes. Subsequently, each chromosome reproduces itself exactly, so that the two cells resulting from the division will have precisely the same chromosome composition.

The most constant feature of genetic material, after many cell divisions,

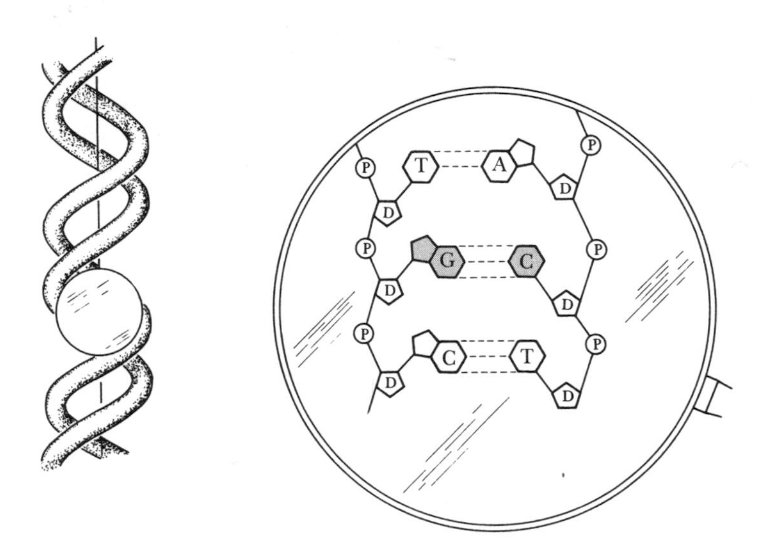

Figure 2-3 *Highly schematic reconstruction of double helix formed by DNA molecule. Lower part of helix is enlarged to show bases adenine (*A*), thymine (*T*), guanine (*G*), and cytosine (*C*), and how these are linked with deoxyribose (*D*) and phosphoric acid (*P*).*

is the order of the four base compounds connecting the two strands of DNA. The genetic information of the chromosomes is encoded into the order of the four connecting compounds, and therefore, the order, like the genetic information itself, must be constant throughout normal cell division. Our hereditary information is not in the long strands of DNA itself nor in the four connecting compounds per se. It is in the *order* of appearance of the four compounds between the two strands of the DNA helix.

Actually there is a simpler way of viewing the genetic code. Since an A (the adenine base) will under normal circumstances be associated with a T (the thymine base) and a G (the guanine base) will be associated with a C (the cytosine base), there are only two possible bonds: A–T and G–C. If we let the A–T bond be designated "0" and the G–C bond be designated "1," then the genetic message can be considered as written as an order of 0's and 1's, which represent a simple binary (two-element) code.

The list of 0's and 1's is quite long. No one knows the number of possible 1's and 0's in a human chromosome; but the bacterium *E Coli* has only one chromosome, and scientists have estimated that the one chromosome has places for over three million 1's and 0's. To give some idea of the length of DNA that makes up a human chromosome, if the base-pair were a yard wide, the DNA would stretch from the earth to the moon.

Although all the cells in the human body have 46 chromosomes, unfertilized eggs and sperm contain only half as many, or 23. In a stage of cell division in the ovaries of the female and the testes of the male, a special type of cell division, *meiosis,* takes place. During meiosis the normal number of chromosomes is reduced to half. This reduction in chromosomes prepares the way for the meeting of the egg and the sperm, each of which will have 23 chromosomes. During meiosis, the regular process of chromosome duplication and regrouping is altered. In this case cell division occurs without duplication of chromosomes, and one member of each pair of chromosomes goes into each of the two new sex cells.

Determination of Sex

In the human being, the sex of the offspring resulting from the union of sperm and egg is determined by the composition of one pair of chromosomes. Females have two similar chromosomes called X chromosomes, while males have an X and a (smaller) Y chromosome (see Figure 2-1). Since the female has two X chromosomes, her egg, which carries half the normal number of chromosomes, will always have one X chromosome; the pair of sexual chromosomes (like all other chromosome pairs) divides during meiosis, and only one of the two is passed on to the egg. The same process takes place in the male, except that since he has one X and one Y chromosome, a sperm may receive either the X or the Y chromosome. If a sperm carrying an X chromosome unites with the egg, the fertilized egg will contain the XX chromosome pair, and the offspring will be female. If a sperm carrying a Y chromosome fertilizes the egg, the offspring will be male because it will carry the XY chromosome pair.

Under rare circumstances, sex chromosomal abnormalities occur. It may happen that a sperm or an egg has more than two sex chromosomes. The offspring then will have 47 or more chromosomes in his genetic constitution instead of the normal 46.

The gene

The early anatomists who used microscopes thought that the lumps which appear on the chromosomes in histological preparations were genes, but they are not. Originally, genes were inferred by tracing lines of inheritance in both people and animals. Through analyzing parents and offspring, rules of inheritance were discovered for certain bodily characteristics such as eye color. When these traits are passed on from parent to progeny in a regular fashion, they are said to result from a certain gene in the chromosomes. A *gene* is a packet of information determining a specific hereditary trait in the species.

Genes may act singly or in combination with several genes to determine a particular trait or characteristic. The gene is the irreducible, minimal unit of genetic inheritance. Since all genetic information is in the chromosomal material of the nucleus, the gene must be represented by the coding of information using the four basic organic compounds occurring over a limited area of the long double-stranded DNA molecule. The fundamental code unit is a sequence of three bases, and more than a thousand such code units act together to convey the information of a single gene.

How genes work

Genetic information determines heredity by controlling the production, or *synthesis,* of proteins. A messenger substance called *messenger RNA* (mRNA) carries the protein-forming information in the DNA of the cell nucleus to the *ribosomes,* the protein-manufacturing sites in the cytoplasm. Messenger RNA is a compound very similar to DNA, except that RNA (ribonucleic acid) picks up information contained in the configuration of nuclear DNA and transports this information to the ribosomes, which are also made of RNA (see Figure 2-4). Several ribosomes will attach themselves to the mRNA and begin building up *protein* according to the chemical message of the RNA. The amino acids (the building blocks of protein) come to the ribosome surface attached to another kind of ribonucleic acid called *transfer RNA* (tRNA). There is a specific tRNA for every amino acid. The various amino acids that will be combined into the specific protein demanded by the mRNA coding arrive at the ribosome accompanied by the tRNA. Then, at the ribosome surface, the amino acids combine to form protein.

As mentioned before, the fundamental code unit is written in terms of pairs of the four base compounds connecting the DNA strands. Certain sets of these are used as starting signals for the construction of a protein molecule, while others are used to signal that the chain of amino acids is complete. Without the appropriate starting and ending signals, protein formation is impossible or abortive, since either the chains would not exist or they would continue forming randomly or perhaps even endlessly.

The human being starts as a single fertilized cell. Through subsequent cell divisions, millions of additional cells are produced. Each has es-

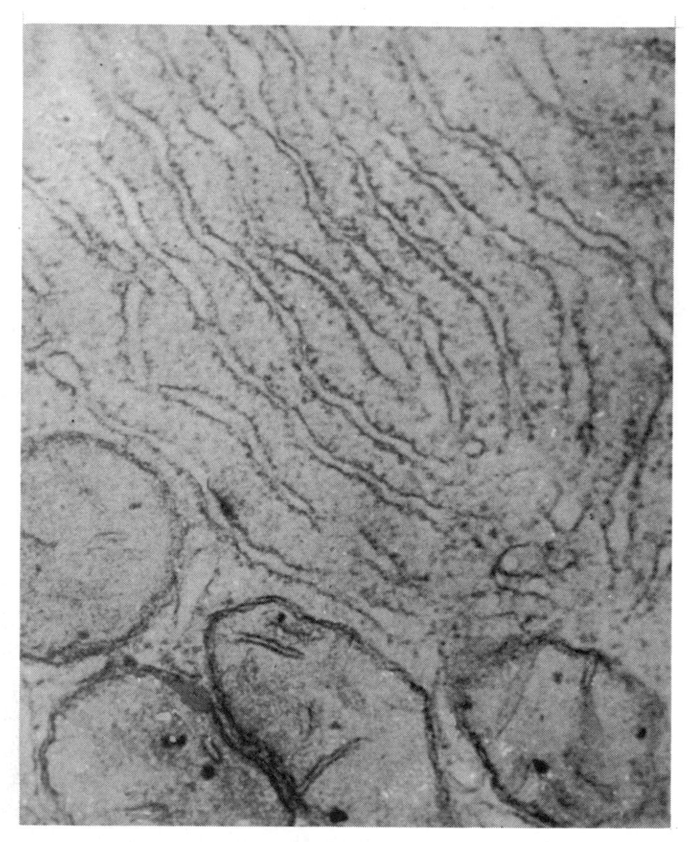

Figure 2-4 *Ribosomes, the dark granules on the tube-like structures, are the sites of protein synthesis. The large irregular spheres are mitochondria. The photograph was taken using an electron microscope at 50,000 diameters. (Figure 18-7 from J. A. Moore,* Heredity and development. *Copyright © 1963 by Oxford University Press, Inc.; reprinted by permission.)*

sentially the same DNA inheritance as the others. Why is it then that some cells develop into one type of cell (e.g., into neurons in the brain), while others develop entirely differently (e.g., as muscle cells)? Not only must there be a way to determine the nature of cellular development, but there must be a way to control the development of new cells at appropriate times. Scientists are just beginning to understand the mechanisms that control cell development.

In most cases, the genes responsible for the formation of any particular protein are probably in a quiescent state; that is, they are "turned off" until their proteins are needed by the cell. A gene is turned off by a repressor protein, which blocks the formation of mRNA on the DNA molecule at the place where the gene is expressed. This place at which a repressor protein can turn off a gene is called the *promotor region.* Repressor proteins are activated by a signal arising at another gene location called the *regulator gene site.* In short, the manufacture of any protein prescribed by a gene is controlled by a different gene region, the promotor region. This can be affected by a protein called a *repressor,* arising from yet another DNA location, the regulator gene site.

These very complicated relationships that govern the quality and quantity of every cell in the body are currently becoming the subject of fruitful investigation with lower organisms. If these complicated controlling mechanisms for genetic expression can be determined, then the way will be paved for "genetic engineering." The fundamental code words of genetics could be understood, changed, and even manufactured. If genetic deviations could be corrected, many diseases could be eliminated. Three genetic diseases that would certainly not be overlooked are hemophilia, Down's syndrome (trisomy 21), and sickle-cell anemia.

One point cannot be overemphasized: Heredity supplies the DNA of the fertilized egg and, perhaps, any extrachromosomal hereditary influences. All events occurring thereafter are due to environmental influences. The environment can produce its effects by influencing any and all of the steps between the DNA and the finished cellular proteins.

Rules of heredity

Gregor Mendel, in 1866, published the conclusions of his years of painstaking observations on the crossbreeding of strains of plants. Mendel discovered the rules of inheritance through the study of hybrid peas growing in an Austrian monastery garden. His principles of inheritance are applicable to both plants and animals when the particular characteristic under study is determined by a single gene. In several varieties of peas he found a number of differentiating characteristics, for example, flower color. He then studied the progeny that resulted from crossbreeding plants with different characteristics. He designed his experiments to study the inheritance of one characteristic at a time.

When Mendel developed purebred strains of pea plants, one with red flowers and one with white, he crossbred them. All of the first generation plants bore red flowers. From this he concluded that the gene for red was *dominant* over the gene for white, which was termed *recessive.* Before the turn of the last century and well into this one, the word "gene" was a hypothetical term used to describe a unit of heredity in a descriptive sense. In Mendel's time, chromosomes were still undiscovered. When the first generation plants were inbred with each other, three-fourths of the plants were red and one-fourth were white.

Further experiments showed that one-third of the red plants were purebred reds and two-thirds had both red and white genes, with the red gaining expression because of their dominance.

The Mendelian scheme is well known today, but it was a striking innovation when first presented. Mendel's contributions were overlooked until more than 20 years after his death. From his experiments we recognize that genes tend to exist in pairs for each characteristic. If both members of a pair dictate the same characteristic, the condition is called *homozygous.* If the two genes dictate different characteristics, the condition is *heterozygous.* In the case of the pea plants, if both color genes called for either red or white flowers, the plant would be purebred; it would be homozygous for this characteristic. If the plant had one gene for red and another for white, it would be crossbred and heterozygous for color.

The concept of dominant and recessive characteristics also resulted from Mendel's work. Some genes for animal characteristics and behaviors can be described as dominant or recessive. In pea plants, red flower color is dominant and white recessive. The only way a pea plant can have white flowers is to inherit two recessive white genes. Any red gene will produce a plant with red flowers.

If a man who is homozygous for blue eyes marries a woman homozygous for brown eyes, the children of this couple will have only brown eyes, since brown is dominant over blue. Let us call the genes determining this characteristic eye color BB (brown) and bb (blue), the capital letters designating the dominant characteristic and the small letters the recessive one. The children of the homozygous couple will have one gene for brown eyes (B) and another for blue eyes (b). Now what happens if a heterozygous man marries a heterozygous woman? Figure 2-5 shows the outcome of this union. The distribution of children from this marriage will be one-fourth homozygous for brown eyes (BB), one-half heterozygous (Bb), and one-fourth homozygous for blue eyes (bb). Thus, three-fourths will have brown eyes, and one-fourth will have blue eyes. Note that blue-eyed children can result even though both parents were brown-eyed.

Mendel's contribution has great significance because it points out that all genetic information is conveyed to future generations in units rather than in graduated amounts. In other words, the genes we inherit from our ancestors control the development of specific unitary characteristics.

The Mendelian view that genetic inheritance comes in gene packages is at odds with a long-prevalent notion of biometricians (those who study the characteristics of various kinds of biological populations).

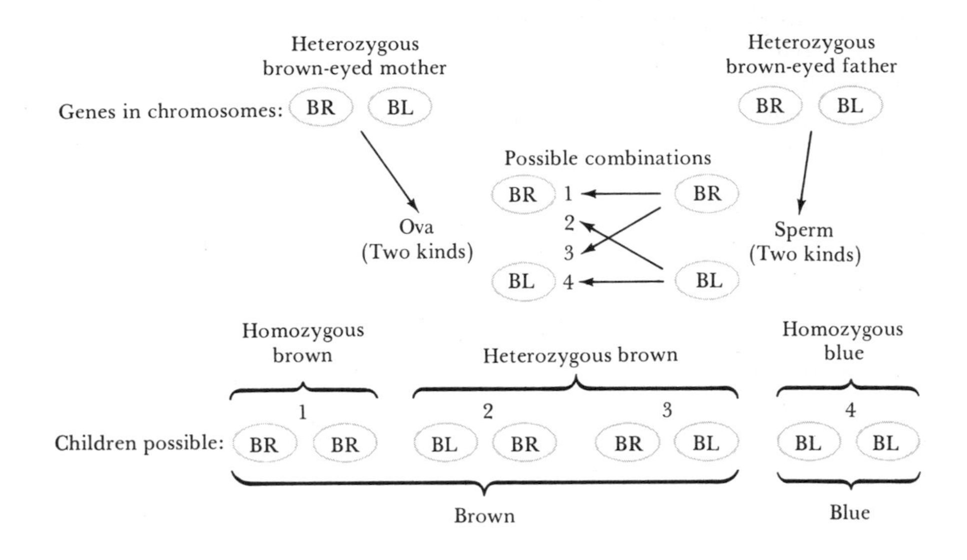

Figure 2-5 *Probable eye colors from brown-eyed heterozygous parents. Gene for brown-eye color (*BR*) is dominant. Gene for blue-eye color (*BL*) is recessive.*

Characteristics of men and animals tend to vary continuously along a dimension as, for example, does intelligence. We do not find a cluster of bright people and a cluster of stupid people, but rather we find intelligence to be distributed in an apparently "normal distribution" (see Appendix B). If our genetic inheritance comes in units, as Mendel suggests, then why do we find a continuously varying measurement of population characteristics, as we do with intelligence?

One answer to this question was suggested by Mendel himself. He suggested that some characteristics might be determined by two or three elements (genes) acting together. In the early 1900s it was shown that if a certain characteristic were determined by several genes that had small but cumulative effects on it, the result would be a population that was continuous in that characteristic. Gradually the idea of continuous genetic inheritance was discarded, and the rules offered by Mendel to explain genetic inheritance became generally accepted rules for all inheritances.

The term *polygenic inheritance* describes the fact that some characteristics are determined by genes at more than one location in the chromosomes. No doubt many characteristics of the individual result from the interaction of several genes, each of which participates in determining the functions of many kinds of organic systems. If two or more genes influencing a characteristic are located on the same chromosome, they are linked together and will be passed on to subsequent offspring at the same time. If they are located on different chromosomes, they will be passed along together or separately, depending upon whether the chromosomes accidentally reach the egg or sperm together after meiosis.

Some structural or functional characteristics of the body seem to be especially prominent in one sex rather than the other. This is because the gene concerned with the development of the characteristic is associated with the X or the Y chromosome. Baldness is one sex-linked characteristic. Color blindness of the red-green variety is another. The incidence of color blindness is much higher among men than women. Perhaps as much as 8 percent of the male population suffers from a red-green defect in color perception, but only a fraction of 1 percent of the female population has this condition. The reason for this is that the gene for normal red-green vision is located on the X chromosome; when defective, it acts as a recessive. Since women have two X chromosomes, and the gene for normal color vision is dominant, a woman could be color blind only if she is homozygous with the defective gene. A man, on the other hand, would be much more likely to be color blind because, in the absence of a color vision gene in his Y chromosome, he needs only one defective color gene in his X chromosome to produce the imperfection in vision. A diagram of the inheritance of red-green visual defects is shown in Figure 2-6.

Other than baldness and red-green color blindness, few sex-linked characteristics have been identified. However, certain deficiencies in blood-cell conditions and a few other characteristics are now known to be sex-linked, and surely many more characteristics will be found in the future.

Genotypes and phenotypes

The effects of genes upon behavior, as well as on the structure and function of the body, are difficult to appreciate fully for several reasons. One of the reasons is that environment often acts to blur the differences found among individuals that are the result of various genetic backgrounds. Often environmental factors can mimic the effects of genes in the characteristics under study. Radical changes in the physiological environment can alter development of organic structures of the body. For example, lack of oxygen in the environment of a very young fetus produces marked changes in the final structure of those organ systems undergoing the

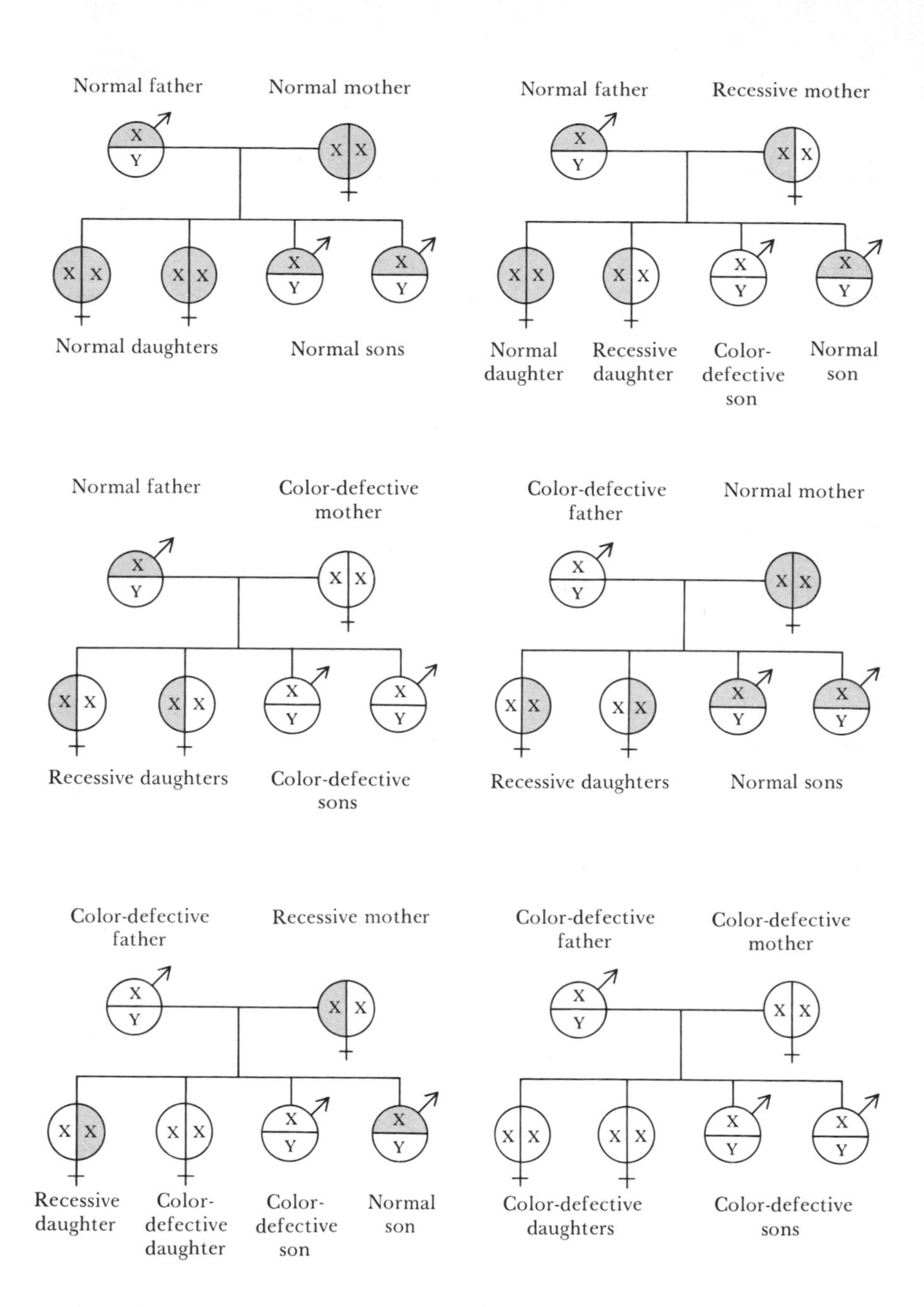

Figure 2-6 *A diagram of the inheritance of red-green color deficiency. The shaded portion of each figure represents the presence of the gene that makes red-green color vision possible. A "recessive mother" refers to a woman with one normal color gene and one defective color gene. The defective gene is recessive and thus her genetic defect would be hidden. (From W. A. H. Rushton, "O Say Can You See?,"* Psychology today, *1969, 3, 49; copyright 1969 by Communications Research Machines, Inc.)*

greatest degree of development during the period of oxygen privation. Less drastic alterations in the environment produce smaller changes in the developing fetus, but such changes tend to make the genetic inheritance less evident. For these reasons it is important to distinguish between the appearance of an organism and its genetic structure. Often the terms *phenotype* and *genotype* are used to make this distinction. Genotype is the total genetic endowment of an individual. Phenotype is the observable appearance, structure, and behavior. Owing to differential actions of the environment, similar phenotypes can result from dissimilar genotypes and, conversely, very dissimilar phenotypes can result from similar genotypes.

The great diversity of individuals is sometimes a cause for confusion among beginning students who wonder how such diversity can exist in families or among siblings in view of the fact that each inherits only one of a pair of chromosomes and there are only 23 pairs contributed by each parent. However, the number of possible combinations of these 23 pairs of chromosomes is 2^{23}. This is the number of possible combinations from each parent. The number of possible combinations from two parents is the square of this number, or 2^{46}. The chance of two offspring of the same parents having an identical chromosomal constitution is less than 1 in 70 trillion!

In addition, we tend to think of a particular trait as being one of two possibilities. Pea plants can produce either red or white flowers; people have brown or blue eyes. However, genes for many characteristics come in more than two forms, and this can add to the possible genetic combinations in a population.

It should also be noted that there must be a complex interaction between genes at practically all gene locations. In principle, this means that every gene can influence the effects of all other genes in governing the developing cell. This makes the study of the genetic influences upon behavior difficult. At the same time this principle recognizes the fact that one gene affects bodily development or function only in concert with the many other genes inherited by the organism.

Mutations

From time to time changes occur in the structure of the genetic materials. Ultimately these must be reflected in changes in the order of the base-pairs connecting the DNA strands of the chromosomes, that is, in the genetic code. These changes can arise from improper replication of the base-pairs or from the effects of specific chemical or physical changes within the body. From whatever cause, mutations frequently occur in individuals of all species. Even though all of the factors influencing the rate with which mutations occur are not known, certain environmental conditions tend to increase it. Atomic radiation is one prominent factor that speeds up mutation rates, probably by direct alteration of the base-pairs.

When mutations occur in cells destined to be eggs or sperm, they will be passed on to subsequent generations. However, many mutations are lethal and the union of an altered egg or sperm with its normal complement will not result in a live offspring. This failure of a mutated individual to live at all is an extreme case of a negative outcome of a mutation. Over-all, one of three things may happen: Mutations may have a positive outcome and result in individuals having an improved ability to cope with their environment; a negative outcome is one in which the progeny are less able to cope with their environment (the extreme being when the progeny are unable to develop at all); and neutral outcomes would be those which do not alter the animal's survival chances.

Most mutations produce "negative" effects on the progeny inheriting the mutation. Many mutations do not allow the offspring to survive at all, and others place the offspring at a disadvantage with its environment. Some positive results do occur, however, and are passed along from generation to generation.

The successful mutations that have occurred over the course of life on this planet have been the cause of the differences found among the animals and plants. Time and again, one line of animals broke away from a previously existing one because of a mutation that occurred and was perpetuated. Those animals which exist today are ones whose mutations have made them better suited for the environment than animals which have become extinct.

In the next chapter, we will discuss behaviors characteristic of all members of a species. Each member of the species, and the behaviors shared by members of a species, has arisen from mutations with a positive outcome that have been passed along from generation to generation. The differences found among species are strong testimony to the influence of heredity upon behavior.

Mutations are not a thing of the past. They occur today and every day, and perhaps even more frequently now than in the past, as a result of higher levels of radiation in the atmosphere. The question might be asked, Why don't we see more new forms of animal life? One reason is that most mutations are negative and the mutants fail to survive or perpetuate themselves. On the other hand, there may be mutant individuals occurring with positive outcomes that will pass along their favorable changes. The time scale required to see these changes, however, may be measured in the thousands of years, making observation difficult for man whose lifespan is but a small fraction of this period.

BEHAVIORAL GENETICS

Behavioral genetics represents one facet of the attempt to relate the study of behavior to studies in other domains of biology. Historically, behavioral genetics directed its attention to demonstrating the genetic foundations of behaviors—that is, to demonstrating the "hereditability" of given behaviors. The extreme example of this approach would be to trace behavior of some kind to a single gene, thus providing a clear-cut case of a genetic contribution to behavior—one that even follows Mendel's rules.

The most commonly used technique for studying the effects of genetic endowment on behavior has been the selective breeding of animals. This technique takes advantage of behavioral differences that occur in a population. Animals which exhibit a similar behavioral characteristic are mated together for many generations. For example, fast horses are inbred with other fast horses. If there is a genetic foundation to running speed, after several generations of such inbreeding in which only the fastest are bred with the fastest, a strain of horses should emerge that is made up of very speedy animals. If, on the other hand, there is no genetic inheritance underlying the ability to run fast, this inbreeding technique should not work; horses inbred for speed for many generations should be no faster than randomly bred horses. The obvious fact is that horses and other animals can be successfully inbred for speed in running, as well as for other characteristics, and this provides a foundation for a belief in the genetic inheritance of these characteristics.

Bright and dull rats

By means of selective inbreeding, strains of rats have been isolated that have considerably greater maze-learning abilities than animals randomly mated. By the seventh generation of inbreeding there was little overlap between the bright and the dull maze-learners.

Once two strains of animals which differed in the maze abilities had been isolated, the question remained whether the genetic effects were due to a single gene or whether they were polygenic. If their behavior were due to a single dominant gene, then crossbreeding the bright with the dull animals would produce a type of animal reflecting the dominant gene of the pair. If the strains were distinguished polygenically, the animals resulting from inbreeding of the bright and the dull ones would instead have a level of intelligence intermediate between the two strains. When this experiment was performed, the progeny of the bright and the dull animals fell into an intermediate position with respect to ability. This indicates that the maze skill is polygenic.

Further research on bright and dull animals has indicated that the maze-learning abilities were only one manifestation of many differences between the strains. The bright animals were really not smarter than the dull animals after all. The dull animals tended to respond to *visual* cues of the inside of the maze, whereas the bright animals responded more to *spatial* cues of the situation. The dull animals were superior to the bright animals in a situation that required them to escape from water. The bright animals were more active in mazes but less active in an activity wheel, an apparatus that measures spontaneous running, than dull animals. Moreover, the superiority of the maze-bright animals in their mazes is found only when the training trials are spaced close together. If the training trials are separated by several minutes, the differences between the strains of animals vanish.

There is much more to the story than this, however. Several times during the inbreeding of the maze-dull and maze-bright animals, some of the animals in each category were selected and crossbred with each other. The offspring of this mating were then inbred among themselves. According to the rules of Mendelian theory, the offspring of this second inbreeding should have been much more variable as a group than the first generation offspring resulting from the crossbreeding of the original maze-bright and maze-dull animals. However, this was not found to be true. This failure to find greater variability in the second breeding phase has become known as the "Tyron effect" and assumes importance because similar results have been found in many other inbreeding experiments. It means that our expectations about the results of inbreeding experiments have been based on much too naïve ideas concerning the role of genetic mechanisms in behavior.

A frequent error is to assume that inbreeding for a particular behavior has produced a group of rats (or other animals) with identical endowments. How wrong this assumption is can easily be shown. Think of the chromosomal structure of the rat. It has 21 pairs of chromosomes. From this number of chromosomes more than two million combinations can be generated in a sperm or egg. Combinations of sperm and egg chromosomes would number in excess of four trillion. Inbreeding members of this potential population of animals, even for 20 or 30 generations, could never produce a reasonably similar genotype within a strain. Remember that the expression of behavior depends not only upon the genes important to a particular behavioral tendency but also upon the entire genetic endowment of the individual. Expression of an inherited behavior is also conditioned by the environment and by the reactions of other genes to the environment.

Hirsch (1967) has pointed out all of these difficulties and more, and summarized the potential of the behavioral genetic approach as follows: "We can study the behavior of *an* organism, the genetics of *a* population, and individual differences in the expression of some behavior by the members of that population" (p. 121). He tried to point out that geneticists study the inheritance of traits within a *population,* not within a particular individual of a population. In experiments in which attempts were made to inbreed toward particular behaviors each subject began with a unique genetic package, and the sum of all the genetically unique individuals is the total population. There always will be a wide spectrum of individual differences, because the inbreeding method is applied to a richly diverse population at all stages.

Selection for other characteristics

Inbreeding experiments have been used to separate strains of animals according to many characteristics other than maze-learning ability. Strain differences in emotionality, vigor, wildness, aggressive initiative, and the ability to win fights have been reported in mice. In fact, the number of different types of behavior among mice and rats that can be shown through inbreeding experiments to have a genetic base is enormous. Of particular interest are strains of animals that inherit physiological or biochemical abnormalities. These animals can be thought of as a new breed of subjects that may be useful for special kinds of research problems. Some mouse and rat strains are particularly prone to convulsions early in life when subjected to strong, shrill noises. Other strains are prone to have seizures in the presence of certain odors. These animals can be used to study the behavioral correlations of seizure activity by using closely related strains that are not prone to seizures.

The demonstration of the heredity of avoidance learning in the mouse is of special importance to psychologists interested in learning. Mice of different strains were trained to avoid electric shocks by running from one side of a small box to the other when presented with a signal. The behavior of a group of genetically rather diverse Swiss mice showed a wide range of performance. Three homogeneous mouse strains performed in a consistent manner (see Figure 2-7). The performance of animals within each of the strains is similar but the behavior of the different strains is quite distinct. This information can provide a useful tool for behavioral studies. If one were to test the effect of a drug on learning in this avoidance task using the Swiss strain, the effects could be more or less obscured by the wide variations in performance found in the population. By using one of the more homogeneous strains, the test could be made with a group of animals behaving consistently. In addition, by using all three groups, it would be possible to test the drug effects on good, medium, and poor learners. Studies like this have already been undertaken. The administration of nicotine generally improves avoidance performance, but the effect is most pronounced in poorly performing strains. It might be expected that other drugs could improve the learning of poorly performing strains and impair the performance of those animals which normally learn rapidly. Such results could easily be lost if genetically mixed strains of rats were to be used.

NATURAL SELECTION

The theory of biological evolution had been advanced by the early 1800s. It had been accepted by some scientists but rejected by others. The idea of a progressive change in the nature of animal life from lower to higher forms had a number of champions, even though the views of many established religious and ethical organizations were set against it. Many famous scientists did not accept the evolutionary view of man's development from the mainstream of animal life on the grounds that there was too little evidence for or against the theory. Erasmus Darwin, Charles Darwin's grandfather, was one of the early proponents of evolutionary theory, and the famous zoologist, Lamarck, argued for a doctrine of transmutation of species in the course of evolutionary development. Today, however, the name of Charles Darwin is most closely associated with the establishment of evolution as a principle of biological life.

Darwin's contribution stems from the fact that he recognized the need for more evidence on which to decide the acceptability of the evolutionary view. He sailed as a naturalist on a ship making explorations in many parts of the world from 1831 to 1835 in order to study

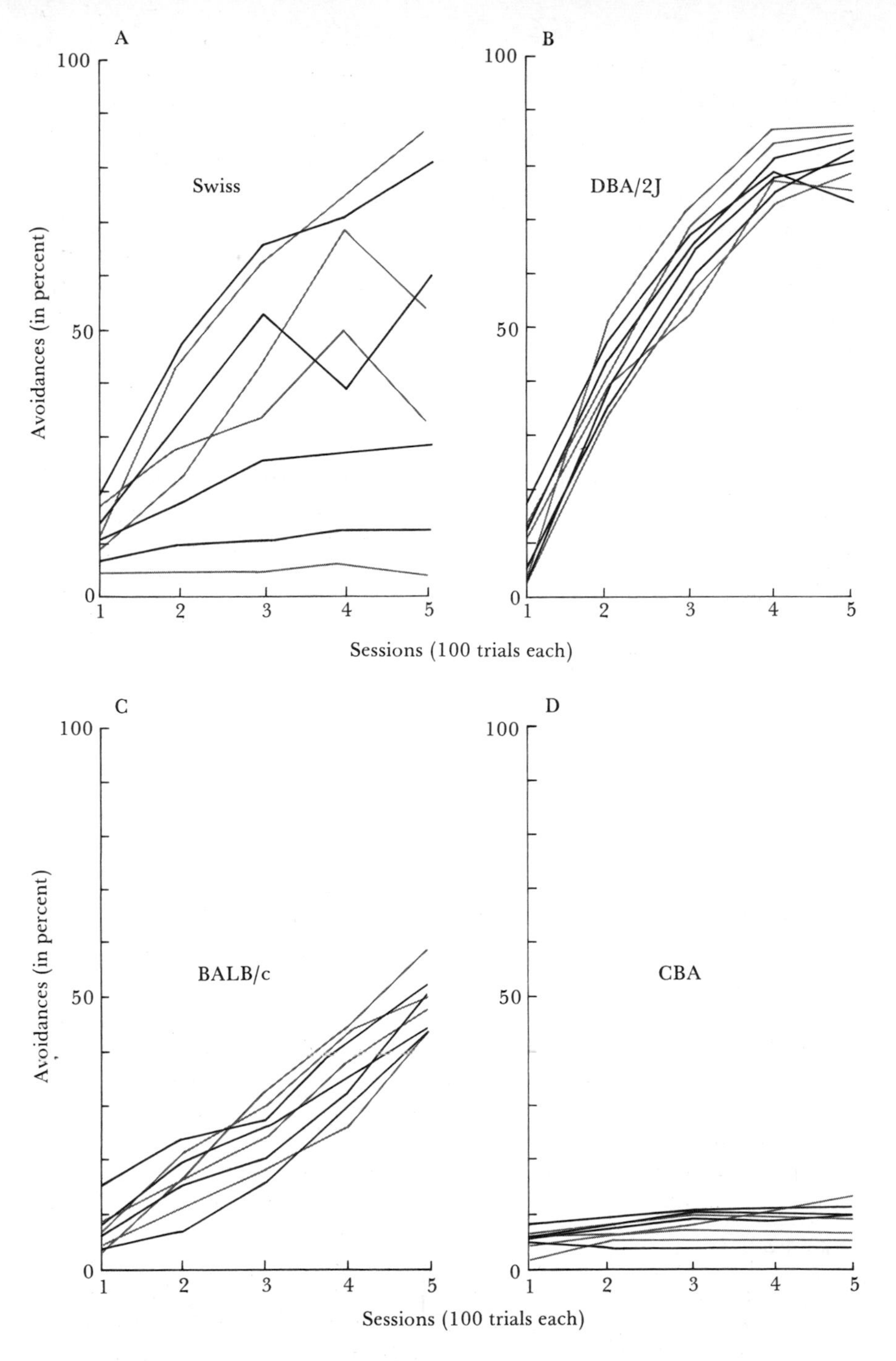

Figure 2-7. *Avoidance learning charted in* (A) *is by a heterogeneous population of Swiss mice; in* (B), DBA/2J *mice; in* (C), BALB/c *mice; in* (D), CBA *mice. Each curve represents the individual performance of a mouse during five avoidance sessions of 100 trials each. (From Bouet, Bouet-Nitti and Oliverio, Genetic aspects of learning and memory in mice.* Science, *1969,* 163, *139–149.)*

the records from earlier geological periods and the forms of life then existing and to give attention to the ways nature "chose" which animals were to survive in their environments. In 1859, almost 25 years later, his famous book *The Origin of the Species through Natural Selection* was finally published. Keeping in mind that the evolutionary theory was not new, we should recognize that the importance of the work was due to its massive documentation of the theory with the result that the evolutionary view became more persuasive to scientists.

The idea proposed to account for the survival of certain forms of animals and the loss of others is the theory of natural selection. In this theory Darwin argued that the genetic variations which occur from time to time may be either a help or a hindrance to the preservation of the animal in its never-ending battle against the environment and changes in the environment. Variations in animals of a species reflect mutations of the genetic material. If the mutation is of positive survival value, then the animal will tend to survive and perpetuate the mutated characteristic. When an animal survives, its progeny have a chance to survive. In natural settings the survival rate among offspring of a species is rather low. Mutations that hinder animals in their struggle for survival will result in decreased survival chances for the mutant animal; fewer progeny will occur, and the progeny will be less likely to survive. We can think of natural selection as describing the "survival of the fittest." Variations that make an animal better fit to survive tend to be promulgated through later generations by the ever-increasing numbers of progeny arising from the mutations. Variations that make an animal less fit tend to be extinguished.

The effect of natural selection is to act as a "control" on mutations of genetic material. It does not originate new genetic messages, it edits them. If the mutations make the animal better suited for survival, the mutation will tend to be propagated to offspring. Most mutations are *not* adaptive, however, and tend to be eliminated from the population.

SEXUAL SELECTION

Darwin also proposed a second principle for survival, the law of sexual selection. He recognized that certain mutations occurred which might be of no direct consequence to the animal's immediate survival chances. The colorful variety in the plumage of birds is a case in point. These nonfunctional variations of feathers might have no direct influence upon the question of immediate survival, but they could affect the sexual attractiveness of the birds. If less sexual attractiveness means fewer progeny, then there is a likelihood that the variation will be extinguished—and the converse is also true, with sexual attractiveness ensuring the perpetuation or survival of the species.

Nature selects animals that are best suited for survival through the principle of natural selection, and selects animals for increased reproduction rates through secondary and indirect characteristics explained by the principle of sexual selection. But what are the effects of the development of human societies and their cultural institutions on selection of the fittest human beings?

When populations of animals leave their natural settings, selection for survival is based on different standards. In the laboratory situation animals are often maintained for countless generations. The principles that are important for their survival are quite different from those needed in the natural state. Laboratory rats are favored for maintenance if they have a calm disposition—that is, if they do not bite their handler's fingers. The mildness of laboratory animals would not serve them very well in nature!

Strains of laboratory rats and wild rats have been compared. Several apparent differences were found between them that would be predictable on the basis of our current knowledge of physiology. Laboratory animals have smaller adrenal glands, for example. These glands serve the body's mechanisms for emergency reactions, including aggression. The sexual organs of laboratory animals also mature more rapidly than those of wild animals, because in the laboratory a high fertility rate is desirable. This is an artificial selection criterion imposed by the laboratory caretakers, one that would favor the selection and breeding of animals with such characteristics. Like the laboratory, man's artificial environment imposes artificial rules of selection; they effect the survival and perpetuation of human beings with characteristics quite different from those favoring survival in the wild.

In man's earliest stages of development, the laws of natural and sexual selection played a more important role than they do today. One of the effects of culture is to protect those who might otherwise be eliminated in a struggle for survival. With mercy, society acts to protect the weaker members from extinction through natural selection. People with genetic backgrounds that produce rather drastic and unfavorable bodily problems can be cared for by social institutions, and deficiencies can often be overcome by the use of medical know-how. Even Darwin's law of sexual selection is circumvented by the use of plastic surgery, cosmetics, and the effective use of clothes. From time to time certain objections have been raised against this role of society. People have pleaded that conditions which favor undesirable mutations will ultimately result in a population of people too weak to survive despite all the remedial activities that can be undertaken. In general, eugenicists (who argue for the controlled breeding of humans) have not found a favorable reception among either laymen or scientists. There are too many unknown factors determining the structure of man to make the eugenic movement a forceful one. Even more important, it is man's compassion and kindness for his fellow men that makes his perpetuation worthwhile.

LAMARCKIAN INHERITANCE

The zoologist Lamarck (1744–1829) developed a theory of *transmutation* of genetic material. He believed that changes in behavior acquired through constant use or disuse and those demanded by changes in the environment could be passed on to subsequent generations through heredity mechanisms. Even Darwin suggested that this might be so. *Lamarckian inheritance,* the doctrine of the inheritance of acquired (learned) characteristics, is still prominent in some circles, despite the fact that scientific data to support such a theory are quite lacking.

It is not quite clear why the theory of *Lamarckian inheritance* survives at all, since with a few doubtful exceptions, all of the evidence bearing on the Lamarckian hypothesis has been negative. For many generations animals have learned various kinds of behavioral discriminations and been mated with other animals with similar training without any evidence that the experience of earlier generations had any effect upon later ones.

A related misconception in thinking about evolution arises when we assume that an animal's environment shapes its heredity. A typical example is the belief that giraffes developed long necks because they needed to stretch in order to eat the leaves and branches at the tops of trees. It may be that giraffes actually do eat the tops of trees and by doing so survive when other animals have eaten all of the leaves from lower branches, but the long neck developed as a chance *mutation,* which coincidentally happened to provide a better survival rate than that of similar animals with shorter necks. Today neither Lamarck's views nor the opinion that environment can influence genetic materials is commonly accepted in scientific circles.

GENETIC INFLUENCES IN MAN

Although some genetic defects are tragically obvious in human beings, most predominant behavioral influences of genes (those with slight or unknown physiological correlates) have been difficult to establish. This probably arises from the fact that our knowledge of genetics is more advanced than our knowledge of behavior.

Psychologists concentrate on investigations aimed at elaborating the contributions of inheritance along lines most related to studies of the inherited behavioral characteristics.

It should be pointed out that the direct study of the genetic make-up of human cells became possible only recently through advances in techniques and methods. It is likely that the study of human genetics will advance in the immediate future even more rapidly than before. Only in the past few years, for example, has it been possible to show that mongolism, a condition of mental retardation associated with specific abnormalities of bodily development, results from the pressence of an extra chromosome of the smaller variety.

Early studies of human inheritance

The modern study of the inheritance of behavioral characteristics can be said to have originated with another grandson of Erasmus Darwin, Sir Francis Galton (1822–1911). Galton was a man of many interests: an explorer, anthropologist, and statistician, as well as a psychologist. In his imaginative study of various topics in the area of psychology, Galton attempted a number of approaches to the study of man, many of which are still being used today. At the moment, we are concerned with his study of the nature and extent of genetic inheritance in man.

Observing that genius seemed to run in families, Galton was convinced that strong genetic influences underlie behavior. He was not satisfied with merely pointing out the many instances in which this seemed to be true, but proceeded to collect data to support his position. In this way he was much like his cousin, Charles Darwin, who became famous for prolific, detailed support of the evolutionary point of view.

Galton suggested ways to discover men who could truly be called eminent, that is, men whose talents were found only about once in every four thousand men. Galton discovered that many more than one in four thousand eminent men were found in families that had already at least one eminent member. Furthermore, he found fewer instances of eminence as the degree of relationship to the eminent man decreased. These data, however, are not conclusive for his hypothesis, and this fact was recognized by Galton himself. The similarity among members of a family could result from common environmental conditions rather than from a common genetic inheritance.

Galton considered other kinds of evidence to substantiate his claim of the importance of genetics for creating men of eminence. He pointed out that the proportion of eminent men was no greater in the United States than in England, despite the greater range of educational opportunities in the United States. More directly, he compared the incidence of eminence in the adopted relatives of Roman Catholic Popes, who were granted many of the finest social and environmental advantages. But Galton found that this background gave rise to fewer cases of eminence than were found among the sons of eminent men.

Another one of Galton's innovations was the study of genetic inheritance through the use of twins. Although he recognized the existence of similar and dissimilar twins, he did not distinguish between them in his analyses. Today we know that most of the "similar twins" are identical twins, whereas the majority of the "dissimilar twins" are fraternal. He reported that twins who were dissimilar at birth did not tend to become more similar even though their environments were almost identical. As we shall see later in the chapter, the use of twins for the study of human genetics is now an established procedure despite the difficulties underlying this method.

Gross genetic abnormalities

As we indicated earlier, it is now well established that mongolism, today better known as trisomy 21 or Down's syndrome, is the result of the presence of three chromosomes of size "21" rather than the normal complement of two. This extra chromosome can be attached to another chromosome or be floating "free" in the nucleus of the cells. A karyotype of the chromosomes found in a patient with Down's syndrome is shown in Figure 2-8.

The condition of trisomy 21 is always associated with severe mental retardation. Other characteristics include a prominent epicanthal fold across the corner of the eye, a short neck, flaccid muscles, hyperflexibility of the joints, and certain characteristic patterns of folds in the skin, especially on the hands and feet. Children suffering from trisomy 21 tend to age prematurely. As with most genetic diseases, we know more about the genetic configurations themselves than about how these configurations act to produce the mental and physical abnormalities.

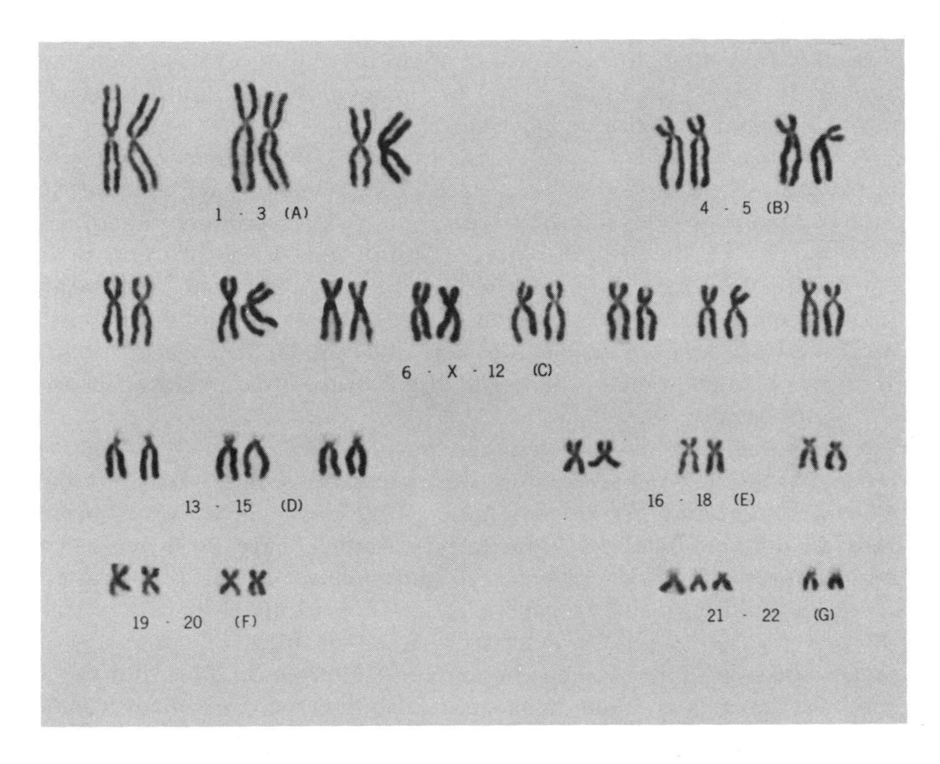

Figure 2-8 *Down's syndrome karyotype. (From C. B. Francisco, Genetics investigations and family counseling in mental retardation.* Mod. treatm., *1967, 4, 837.)*

While the condition trisomy 21 is probably the most common genetic anomaly involving an additional chromosome, another fairly common genetic misfunction arises when a male inherits an extra female sex chromosome (XXY). The baby often looks completely normal but fails to mature sexually. This condition is called Klinefelter's syndrome. The other possible extra-chromosome condition is the inheritance of an additional male chromosome (XYY). This configuration of chromosomes is estimated to occur in about two-tenths of one percent of the male population. It brings about deleterious effects of a different sort. There are many issues about this condition that are not completely settled, but men with an XYY inheritance are generally taller than men of a normal chromosome inheritance and they may be more disposed toward aggressive actions against society or other people than most men. Once again, it is important to recognize that statements like this are statements about *populations* of subjects and not about individuals. Even though an individual might inherit an XYY chromosome pattern, its expression in his stature or behavior is conditioned by other factors of his unique genetic inheritance.

A person might inherit more than three sex chromosomes, and patterns like XYYY or more complicated arrangements are occasionally found. Among women, Turner's syndrome, which produces abnormal development of the ovaries, short stature, and other physical signs along with mild mental retardation, results when only one X chromosome is inherited. When additional chromosomes of the larger sizes are inherited, severe forms of physical and mental deficiencies occur. If an extra chromosome of the largest size is transmitted to the offspring, the fetus usually aborts.

Some forms of genetic disease can be identified only by the occurrence of the disorders running through family lines—that is, the genetic error is less severe than that of an extra chromosome. More than 20 different kinds of biochemical disorders have been associated with improper genetic inheritance, and about one-half of deafness found in children is due to genetic causes. Unfortunately, many people do not realize that their defects—whether deafness or an error of metabolism—arise from their hereditary endowment. This illustrates the need for greater numbers of genetic counselors, since many conditions respond to treatment if discovered early in life. Probably the greatest contribution that could be made by genetic counselors would be the determination of carrier conditions for potential parents. Unfortunately there are few genetic counselors available in most parts of the country. It is a field of service that needs to be encouraged, since at least 2 percent of all babies born have serious, life-threatening genetic defects.

The inheritance of intelligence

Galton began the study of the genetic influence on the development of intelligence with his analyses of the families of eminent men. Many other studies have followed this line of investigation. Generally, positive correlations have been found among members of the same family. The correlations have been less than perfect, as would be expected from our discussion concerning the effects of the total genetic endowment upon any particular characteristic. However, one must also consider that some people have argued that the lack of perfect correlations among family members for intelligence scores indicates that environment is the primary factor in the determination of intelligence. The arguments take several forms, but the most convincing is that bright people tend to provide better environmental conditions for their children. However, data like those provided by Galton which compared the adopted children of the Roman Catholic Popes with the sons of eminent men remain to be explained if the validity of the argument is to be sustained.

STUDIES OF TWINS The evaluation of the contribution of heredity to intelligence has been made more rigorous by the study of twins, some reared together and sharing a common environment, and others separated from birth and thus exposed to divergent environments.

There are two kinds of twins: identical and fraternal. Identical twins come from the same fertilized egg. Through some mischance in cell division, two individuals arise from only one fertilized ovum. Identical twins have identical genetic inheritance, at least in terms of their chromosomes. Fraternal twins come from nearly simultaneous fertilization of two eggs in the mother. They have no more genetic correspondence than brothers and sisters (siblings), since both the sperm and the egg in each fertilization have different assortments of genes just as with siblings. In the past few years it has been possible to determine with greater precision whether twins are identical or fraternal. Identical twins must be of the same sex and have identical physical characteristics (appearance) and blood composition. Identical twins have been found to be very much alike in many other characteristics, including the patterns of electrical activity in the brain, which can be recorded from the scalp by means of the electroencephalogram (EEG). These similarities are present even if the identical twins are brought up in different environments from birth. Identical twins have often been reported to achieve very similar intelligence test scores even if they have been raised in separate environments, but dissimilarities in intelligence have also been reported. The majority of investigations have indicated a close similarity in measured intelligence for identical twins, less similarity in intelligence between fraternal twins, and least between brothers and sisters.

As pointed out earlier, identical twins do not always have identical environmental conditions. The findings of studies that compare fraternal and identical twins generally favor the genetic inheritance of some traits but are difficult to interpret, because the home environments of the identical twins *could* be more alike than that of fraternal twins. Furthermore, the development of identical twins before birth could be more uniformly affected by intrauterine factors than is the development of fraternal twins. But positions in the uterus and other physiological occurrences could also act to make identical twins less alike and fraternal twins more alike than might be expected. Another difficulty is that studies of twins who have been reared apart often do not take sufficient account of the fact that the separated twins (separated by adoption, usually) are not randomly placed into new circumstances, but are commonly placed by social agencies into homes similar to their natural ones.

STUDIES OF FOSTER CHILDREN The intelligence of foster children tends to be fairly closely correlated with the measured intelligence of the foster parents, especially the mother, but the size of the correlation is much less than that of the correlation between the intelligence of mothers and their own children. The most striking resemblance is found between a child's intelligence and his natural mother's intelligence, even when the child has been raised with foster parents.

A summary of 52 studies on the correlations of intelligence found among people of different degrees of relationship has been made and is given in Figure 2-9. The range of the correlations found in these studies is shown by the horizontal lines in the rows and the correlations from each study are given as points on the line. From this presentation we can observe that there are generally much closer relationships between twins from the same fertilized egg than between those from different eggs. In general, the data support a polygenetic inheritance of intellectual *potential* which is not sex-linked.*

GENERALIZATIONS ABOUT INHERITED INTELLIGENCE From Galton's time to the present, the available evidence appears to support the generalization that heredity has an important influence on the intelligence of the individual. One way to understand this effect is to think of the genetic factors as setting limits or ranges for intelligence, the upper boundaries of which can be attained by people under appropriate circumstances. Intelligence test scores can be significantly influenced by differences in the environment, but the upper limit of intelligence, and presumably intelligence test scores, which a person can reach via the most favorable environment is set by genetic mechanisms.

What circumstances are effective in stimulating the development of intelligence? It seems clear that the hereditary mechanism underlying intelligence is polygenic—that is, a great many combinations of genes act to set the upper limits of intelligence test scores. From data obtained from other kinds of genetic experiments we know that environments that are beneficial to an individual with one set of genes may not be conducive to the best development of an individual with another set of genes, even though the phenotypic characteristics produced by the two genotypes are similar. Thus there need not be any one kind of environ-

* It should be noted that correlation coeficients are not directly interpretable in terms of the degree of association between two variables. Correlational techniques are discussed in Appendix B.

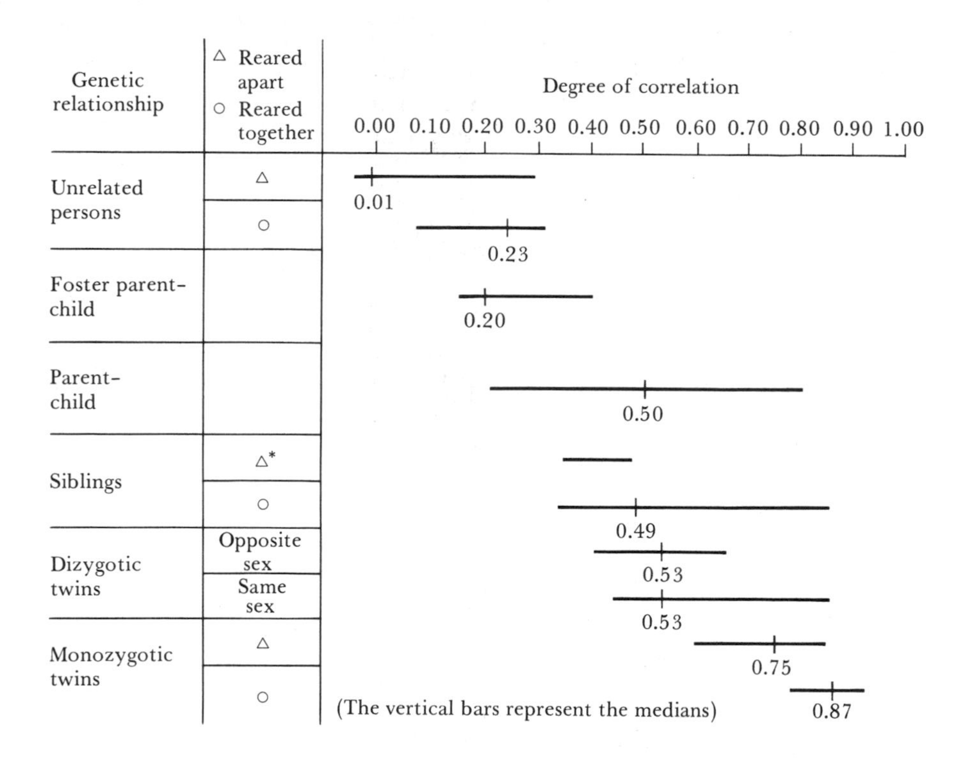

Figure 2-9 *Medians and ranges in correlation coefficients for "intelligence" test scores from 52 studies. Asterisk indicates insufficient studies to obtain a median. (Adapted from Table 1 in L. Erlenmeyer-Kimling and L. F. Jarvik, Genetics and intelligence.* Science, *1963,* 142 *(3595), 1478. Copyright 1963 by the American Association for the Advancement of Science.)*

ment guaranteed to produce maximally beneficial development of intelligence. In terms of numbers, if there were only 10 genotypes for "intelligence" and 10 possible environments, there would be 7×10^{144} possible types of interactions—a sizable number! On the other hand, it is clear that opportunity for development must be present in order for the "intelligence potential" to be fulfilled.

DIFFERENCES AMONG RACES Races are defined biologically as populations that share certain frequencies of occurrence of specific genes and that, as a group, differ from other populations in these gene frequencies. Considerable isolation must have occurred within the population to allow specific combinations of genes to become established and perpetuated within the population. Individuals of a racial group developed similar gene frequencies as a result of sharing the same survival pressures created by their social and geographic environments. Although this definition of "race" is accurate in a biological sense, it is rather difficult to use it in a practical manner. Nevertheless, it does provide a helpful guide toward understanding the meaning of the word.

We should think of genetic effects as acting upon populations and not as specifying absolute characteristics for every individual. Once the effects of the total gene pool upon the expression of any particular single characteristic are recognized, the controversy about heredity's determining the mental abilities of different races is much less significant. In fact, it is often hard to understand why such a controversy still exists. However, disputes continue about the inheritance of "desirable" characteristics by people of different races.

From the earliest periods of recorded history, people of some "in-group" have described outsiders as suffering from devastating character defects. Aspersions are cast on the outsiders' ancestors and race. Of course, the in-group is presumed to be free from such defects and to represent close approximations to ideal individuals. Thus the in-group represents the "chosen people." Naturally, other groups always fall short of the ideal.

Surprisingly, many eminent people have argued for some form of genetic supremacy of one race over others. Galton, for example, stated that the average Negro fell considerably below the average white person on a scale running from Galton's own idol, Aristotle, on the one extreme to an idiot on the other. Recently, in the 1960s, a commission formed by a governor of a southern state reported Negroes to be inferior because of their genetic constitutions, and this inferiority was alleged to be resistant to improvement through education.

When more or less standardized intelligence tests are used, the scores of black people are generally below those of comparison groups of whites. In the northern parts of the United States the differences found between groups of black and non-black people are but a few points on most intelligence tests. Moreover, the longer the black people have lived in the North the smaller the differences become between the performances of comparable black and white populations. Other factors besides "race" affect performance on intelligence tests. Early experiences, home atmosphere, career goals, and aspirations all tend to influence the expression of genotypic endowments, including academic abilities. Naturally, a family's income and community status help to determine these environmental influences.

Of particular importance is the heavy dependence most intelligence tests have upon language abilities. Many tests are language-bound, since a certain vocabulary is necessary for high performance. Even if an extensive vocabulary is not required, language effects (e.g., reading ability) can be expressed through the construction of test items or the instructions themselves. Most tests are also culture-bound, because pictures, drawings, or other materials may be more familiar to one population than another. However, the fact that measured intelligence test scores of black school children improve when they move to the North and continue to improve over the school years makes it clear that the school systems do help to form the expression of intellectual capacities in the formal world of intelligence testing.

The extent to which lack of educational opportunity impairs tested intelligence can be inferred from a study by Kennedy, Van de Riet, and White (1963). Comparing carefully selected populations of white and black children in five southeastern states, they found that the black student averaged more than 20 I.Q. points below the standard for "comparable" white children. Evidence from studies such as this emphasizes the urgent need for improvement in education for black students in this area of the country.

But what if we were to discover that no matter what beneficial treatments were undertaken, the test scores of blacks still remained a few points below those of non-blacks? Most important, we should recognize that an "average value" of population of test scores tells us nothing about any one individual. Black and white populations both have individuals ranging from bright to dull. Each person in each population has inherited a unique gene pool and has interacted with his environment in idiosyncratic ways to arrive at his own set of phenotypic behavior patterns. To think of any racial group in terms of a single stereotype goes against all we know about the mechanisms of genetics.

Since a racial group shares some genes not held by other races we might expect that differences should be found among the races. Unfortunately, differences in characteristics besides intelligence have hardly been studied, yet what little evidence there is indicates that each racial group has some special characteristics. Therefore, it is difficult to know the extent to which there are genetic bases for these special characteristics at the present time.

One final point should be made concerning racial inheritance of intelligence: Since each person has a unique combination of genes, and the expression of any gene-determined trait is modified by the remainder of the genes in the total pool as well as by the particular environment, there may be no one *universally* effective environment that would help toward the realization of a person's potential mental capacities. What may be beneficial for one child may be ineffective for another. No one treatment at preschool, kindergarten, or primary school level will be of equal benefit to all. For example, a heavy school workload might benefit some students while inhibiting others. This means that a careful evaluation should be made of each student's progress in "enhancement programs" designed to help children from environments thought to be damaging to full development, i.e., those called "culturally deprived" or "disadvantaged." Moreover, flexibility to alter programs according to the results obtained with each student should be a prime feature of education.

Inheritance of personality

Attempts to evaluate the extent of genetic influence upon intelligence far surpass all other kinds of research on the genetic foundations of psychological traits. There are several reasons for this. Probably most important is the fact that intelligence scores are relatively stable psychological measures. Intelligence test scores tend to remain rather constant over periods of time and have proven to be reliable and valid predictors of success in college and in certain occupations. Further, there are standardized methods of administration and scoring. No personality measurement technique provides as unequivocal data as does intelligence testing. Stable test scores are necessary in order to determine the lines of inheritance that are used in attempting to trace genetic effects.

Scores on psychological personality tests are far more variable, and their interpretation is far less valid, than are intelligence test scores. In general, scores from different kinds of personality tests have low correlations with each other, and there are many problems in obtaining valid predictions of behavior from such tests. Therefore, it is relatively more difficult to assess traits of personality, and this makes it far more difficult to assess the effects of genetic inheritance on personality. However, personality patterns, like intelligence and other measures of performance, are most certainly the result of polygenic inheritance (in addition to environmental factors). Many genes contribute to the characteristics exhibited in behavior, and their effects of course are modified by the contributions of the total gene pool.

Studies using reliable psychological tests have tended to show the same general pattern of findings as have the intelligence tests. Comparisons of motor skills, such as card-sorting and following a moving target manually, tend to show higher correlations between identical twins than between fraternal twins. Attempts at measuring inheritance patterns of temperament, mood, or other "personality variables" have, however, been less decisive. Some studies have reported positive results and others negative ones. Such experiments evaluate the extent to which personality variables are shared by identical and fraternal twins and by other members of their families. One of the most common suggestions arising from recent studies has been that some personality dimension that can be represented by introversion-extroversion scales may be inherited. This dimension is thought to reflect the extent to which a person is withdrawn and introspective or is outgoing and extroverted. This observation can be tentatively associated with observations of infants in their first 18 months. Some infants were "cuddlers" and others were "noncuddlers." The remainder were "in-between." The cuddlers were children who actively sought contact with family members, whereas the noncuddlers did not. The two extreme types of children did not respond in the same way to the handling provided them. This suggests that a tendency to seek out human contact or to be more withdrawn is genetically specified.

Inheritance of mental disorders

The study of people with acute mental problems allows genetic analysis of human behavior patterns upon which some degree of consensus can be reached. Many kinds of personality disorders can be clinically recognized by therapists, and this makes these disorders relatively easy to use in an investigaton of genetic effects. The mental disorder that has been most carefully studied from the point of view of genetic inheritance is *schizophrenia,* a severe personality disorder.

As a basic consideration, there can be no doubt that the incidence of schizophrenia is higher in families in which at least one member of the family has been previously diagnosed as suffering from the disease. For example, children of a schizophrenic parent have incidence rates of schizophrenia from 5 to 10 percent, whereas the incidence of schizophrenia in the general population is less than one in a thousand. The probability of schizophrenia rises rapidly when more than one sibling or one parent has been diagnosed as schizophrenic and reaches about nine chances in ten for an identical twin of a person diagnosed as schizophrenic when a parent has also been so diagnosed.

Those who do not favor a genetic inheritance hypothesis point out that as the genetic relationship between two individuals becomes closer, the similarity of their environments is also likely to increase.

Generally, the evidence seems to point toward a conclusion that at least some forms of schizophrenia are influenced by genetic factors, but such factors do not entirely account for their occurrence.

Psychopathic and neurotic mental disorders tend to have the same rates of incidence among identical twins as they do among fraternal twins or siblings. Although this result suggests that these two kinds of personality disorganization have less of a genetic contribution than does schizophrenia, it could also mean that less reliable measurements or diagnoses of such disorders were used.

It has been suggested that the genetic inheritance predisposing toward schizophrenia can be thought of as an inheritance of a defect in the "integrative ability" of the brain and the nervous system (Meehl, 1962). A precise definition of this "integrative deficit" is admitted to be beyond science's present knowledge, but this concept can direct us to look for the nature of the genetic defect—namely, a malfunction in the operation of the nervous system—while at the same time suggesting the basic symptom of schizophrenia. This basic and biological deficit is labeled "schizotaxia." On top of this genetic foundation the social environment adds learned reactions specific to the environmental circumstances. The schizotaxic individual has characteristic types of reactions to the environment, but still may not become a schizophrenic as clinically diagnosed:

> If the interpersonal regime is favorable, and the schizotaxic individual person also has the good fortune to inherit a low anxiety readiness, physical vigor, general resistance to stress and the like, he will remain a well-compensated "normal" schizotype, never manifesting symptoms of mental disease (Meehl, 1962, p. 830).

Schizotypes are people with schizotaxic tendencies who do not manifest the full degree of mental disorder resulting when individuals are not so "lucky" as those finding the favorable conditions mentioned in the above quotation. This means that the development of clinically diagnosed schizophrenia depends upon the inheritance of the schizotaxic tendency plus bad luck in having inhospitable environmental conditions, as well as the inheritance of other indirectly related characteristics (such as the inability to resist stress).

One implication of such a view would be that the parents of the schizophrenic may not necessarily have the disease to a debilitating extent. Some parents of schizophrenics have symptoms of "thought disorders," which are not disabling but nonetheless evident. This may mean that the parents were schizotaxic but also more fortunate in circumstances or in inheriting other personality characteristics which mitigated the schizotaxic tendencies.

Even if a tendency for schizophrenia or schizotaxia is inherited, the most significant question remains: How do genetic agents produce their undesirable consequences? Recent evidence obtained from the observation of the sex and bodily defects of children born of schizophrenic mothers bears upon this issue. If a woman experiences a schizophrenic episode within a month before or after conception, the children born will be females (Shearer, Davidson, and Finch, 1967). Apparently any potential males are aborted. If a schizophrenic episode develops later than one month after conception, any male born is likely to suffer from some severe form of damage—e.g., deafness, blindness, or mutism (Taylor, 1969). This suggests that the schizophrenia of the mother is associated with a biochemical change in her blood plasma that can cross the placental barrier and influence the child. This must have extremely lethal or toxic effects upon fetuses with a Y chromosome. In addition, postpartum psychoses (psychoses that occur after the birth of a child) most frequently follow the birth of a male. This can be interpreted as meaning that some chemical factor specific to males (male sex hormone?) arising from the fetus suppresses the mother's schizotaxic tendencies. When the baby is born, the suppressive influence is removed and the schizophrenic episode begins. There is some independent evidence that postpartum reactions can be reduced with administration of male sex hormones.

Observations like these make it easy to jump to the conclusion that schizophrenia is itself a result of biochemical conditions in the blood which affect the fetus. This conclusion, however, is unwarranted. The plasma factor could be a *product* of the schizophrenic condition rather than the cause. Once again, we are faced with a starting point for the study of the biochemistry of schizophrenia, not a solution.

FACTORS INFLUENCING DEVELOPMENT

In a now classic article about unlearned or instinctive behavior, Beach (1955) pointed to the importance of understanding the relationship between environmental and genetic factors. In one experiment, two strains of mice were used; one strain was susceptible to audiogenic seizures (convulsive fits induced by loud, shrill sounds), whereas the other did not have this susceptibility. Crossing the two strains produced an animal intermediate between the two inbred strains; this of course indicated a polygenic determination of the effects. One would expect that the susceptibility to audiogenic seizures came from genetic information which was the cause of the proneness to audiogenic seizures. But, further experiments showed *this need not be the case.* Fertilized eggs were obtained from the uterus or the Fallopian tubes of one strain and implanted in the uterus of the other strain. Sometimes such implants would develop in their new environment, and for those that did it was possible to determine the seizure-proneness of the "transplanted animals." In this study mice were always transplanted from the seizure-prone animals to animals of the strain that was not seizure-prone. The transplanted, seizure-prone mice were intermediate—that is, less seizure-prone than their parental strain and more susceptible than the strain into which they were introduced. One conclusion from this study is that prenatal environment plays an important role in the determination of behavior; and this, as Beach points out, should make us suspicious of attempts to attribute all of the characteristics found in an inbred strain of animals to specific genes for that characteristic. The genes may actually control other characteristics, such as uterine conditions, which may in turn affect the behavioral characteristics.

Hebb (1958) suggests that six factors can be distinguished which affect the developing organism:

1. *Genetic.* This would simply be the gene structure of the egg after fertilization. It should be stressed again that this is the entire extent of the genetic information given to new organisms.

2. *Chemical, prenatal.* All of the nutritive and chemical factors in the uterus as the animal develops would be included in this class. In the study of transplanted eggs of mice discussed above, the uterine environment of the new mother was different from that of the natural mother and this had significance for behavior. Oxygen deficiencies or other deficiencies in the prenatal environment as a rule tend to affect the organ system developing most rapidly during the shortage.

3. *Chemical, postnatal.* In this category would be the effects on development in the chemical or nutritive atmosphere of the neonate (newborn infant). Continued dietary deficiencies are the most likely cause of abnormalities, although other factors could be included in this class.

4. *Sensory, constant.* Within any species of animal, certain kinds of sensory information will almost always be presented to the developing young. To some extent, the sensory environment of one species will be different from that of any other. When one is evaluating the differences in behavior between species, the differences in their sensory world must be kept in mind. The reactions of one species to changes in the environment may be quite different from those of a second species, and it is possible that these differences could result from differences in how the organisms experience their surroundings.

5. *Sensory, variable.* While many kinds of sensory experiences will be the same for members of a given species, there will always be differences for each and every member of the species. No two animals, even identical twins, develop in identical environments. We must take into account the individual experiences during development that play a part in adult behavior.

6. *Trauma, physical.* A traumatic event is harmful to the individual,

sometimes producing the destruction of body cells. The traumatic events Hebb refers to are brief and often outside the normal sensory environment of the members of the species. These intense periods of unusual stimulation can result in changes in the organism that will be influential throughout its entire life. Such occurrences may range from the "trauma" of a harsh delivery, involving the use of forceps that clamp the head of the baby too severely, or they can be accidental events that befall a developing individual. In any case, traumatic events are thought to provide a basis for many unusual modifications of behavior seen in adults.

From this list of classes of factors that influence the development of behavior it is clear that it would be all too easy to mistake the effects of factors 2 through 6 for the genetic effects of factor 1.

The aim of research in the area of the genetic influences is not fulfiled when behavior can be shown to be a result of a certain pattern of genes. Even though genes can determine behavior, we must know how they do so. Do the genes affect the body structure or biochemical activities? Do they change the patterns of activity in the nervous system, the muscular system, or the hormones? Do the genes affect the development of nerve cells in the brain? Do they affect the structure or function of receptor systems?

To describe a pattern of behavior as inherited is a beginning for research rather than an end. Once the genetic influence has been determined, then we are faced with the problem of finding the underlying mechanisms.

In this chapter we present some of the information available today about the effects of genetic inheritance upon behavior; in addition, we stress the possible contribution of genetics to psychology. Modern psychology has been too greatly divorced from the study of genetics because of its historical development. The time for a convergence of the two sciences appears to be at hand and will in all likelihood result in stimulation of new developments in research and theory for both fields.

SUGGESTED READINGS

Hirsch, J. *Behavior genetics*. Dubuque, Iowa: William C. Brown, 1966.

McGuigan F. J. *Biological basis of behavior: A program*. Englewood Cliffs, N.J.: Prentice-Hall, 1963.

McKusick, V. A. *Human genetics*. Englewood Cliffs, N.J.: Prentice-Hall, 1964.

Sussman, M. *Animal growth and development*. Englewood Cliffs, N.J.: Prentice-Hall, 1960.

Watson, J. D. *The double helix*. New York: New American Library, 1969.

3
The origins of behavior

As students of behavior, we are especially interested in those cells that developed to handle the problems of communication among the cells comprising an organism. The cells that in simple organisms transmit information from the outside world (the environment) to other cells of an organism are the early precursors of the nervous system. In animals the nervous system is responsible for the detection of changes in the environment, the transmission of information from the receptor cells to a central station (the brain) for analysis, and the conduction of command messages originating in the brain to the muscles and glands.

The single cell of original life had to perform all of the metabolic and behavioral acts necessary for survival. Later, when single cells grouped together to form larger animals, cells began to specialize their structure and function. Cells began to lose their general, nondifferentiated functions and develop highly specialized ones. Of course, in man, the life of the individual cell depends upon the functions performed by an extremely large number of cells elsewhere in the body. The life of every cell in the body is extinguished when the cells comprising the kidneys, heart, lungs, or parts of the nervous system fail to do their jobs.

By bonding together into more complex animals, the single cells lost a thread of eternal life in the sense that some fragment of one cell would exist in the progeny resulting from the cell divisions that could occur endlessly. On the other hand, complex multicellular organisms developed a new method of continuing life through sexual reproduction and the passing on of genetic materials in the sperm and the egg. From the single cell to the more complicated organisms in the animal world, some similarities among behaviors can be detected. First, we examine some aspects of behavior observed in lower animals and then compare them with man's behavior.

THE BEHAVIOR OF INVERTEBRATES

Behavior is a property common to all life in whatever form it is expressed. In fact, behavior is not even limited to the animal kingdom but can be found in plants too. Certainly a tree does not respond to the chop of an axe as an animal would, but plants do have growth responses to change in the light or other special fluctuations in their environment. For example, rooted plants typically bend toward the source of available light. The relatively rapid reactions to tactile stimulation of plants such as Venus's-flytrap are familiar. In general, seed plants exhibit many of the characteristics of all behaving organisms: sensitivity to certain stimuli, conduction of excitation from one part of the organism to another, and some variety in response patterns. However, the plants have followed different evolutionary paths than have the animals, and our primary interest is in the evolution of animal behavior.

The determination of responses

THE SINGLE CELL—AMOEBA The amoeba has been studied extensively and is of interest to us because many basic principles of behavior can be observed in this relatively simple animal. If we did not know that the animal consists of only one cell, it would be easy to believe that its many responses had to depend upon the presence of many kinds of specialized cells. Consider the following facts about the amoeba.

1. *Its response is dependent upon the nature of the stimulation.* When one side of an amoeba is stimulated, there is an extension of

the organism toward the stimulation (Figure 3-1). If the stimulation becomes more intense, the cell membrane retreats from the stimulated area. Furthermore, the amoeba's surface seems to have areas of greater and lesser sensitivity to stimulation.

2. *Repeated or continued stimulation alters the response to further stimulation of the same kind.* When an amoeba is brought in from the dark and placed under a microscope we observe several changes. Most pronounced among them is a general contraction. After a few minutes the animal adapts to its new environment and resumes its movements. Continued light stimulation does not produce any additional reactions.

While we often refer to an animal or a person adapting to a new or altered environment, modern psychological terminology distinguishes

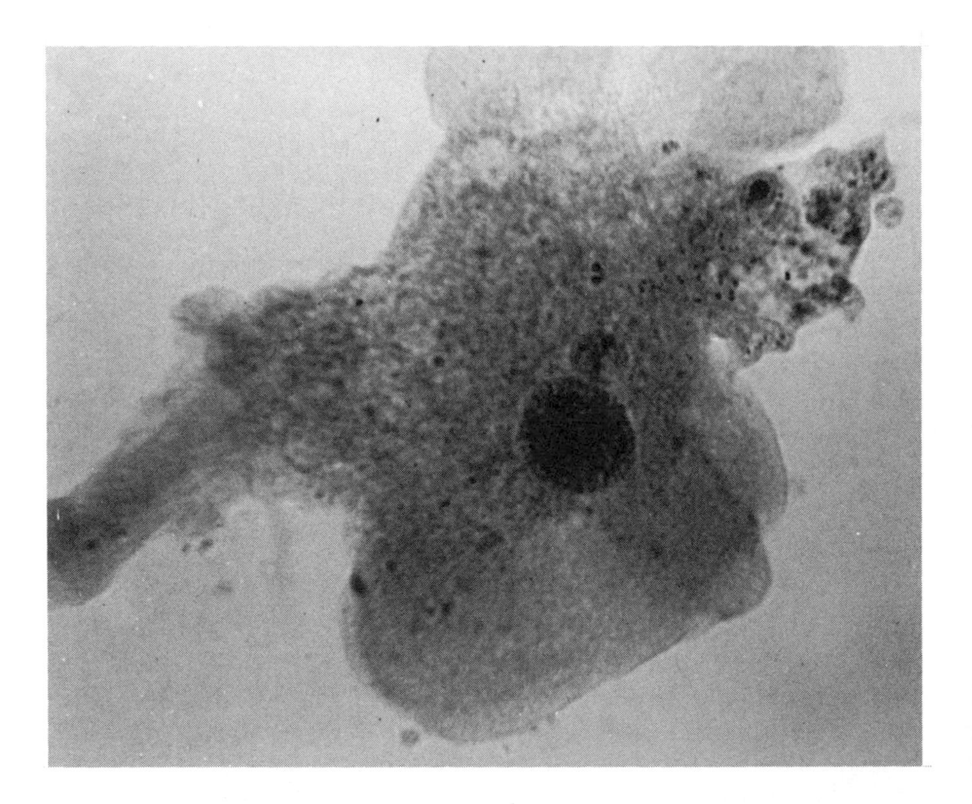

Figure 3-1 *Photomicrograph of an amoeba (enlarged about 130 times). One of the simplest known forms of animal life, the amoeba nourishes itself by enveloping minute organisms and fragments of food. (Courtesy of Chas. Pfizer & Co., Inc.)*

two aspects of an organism's diminished responsiveness to repeated stimulation. If the diminished responses are caused by a reduced reaction in the sensory organs (e.g.) eyes or ears, the term *adaptation* is used. If, however, the reduction in response is produced by the brain or is secondary to changes in attention or fatigue, the term *habituation* is applied. When a response "habituates," it does so despite an unaltered response originating in the sensory organs involved.

3. *Internal states determine responsiveness to stimulation.* The amoeba will normally send a protoplasm probe toward particles near it. However, when it is well fed, more stimulation than usual is needed before such a reaction will take place.

4. *The effects of several stimuli may add together to cause a response that none of the individual stimuli could elicit alone.* One level of stimulation of the surface of the amoeba may be insufficient to produce a response unless other stimulation is added. This additional stimulation may be in an adjacent area (spatial summation) or could closely follow the other stimulation at the same place (temporal summation). The additional stimulation may be less than that normally required to elicit a response by itself. If the two stimuli, neither of which is capable of eliciting a response alone, produce a response when they are coupled in space or in time, then their effects must have *summated.*

COMPARISON WITH HUMAN BEHAVIOR The four principles of behavior expressed in the amoeba are easily seen in man's behavior. At an anecdotal level, for instance, it can be said that some men are responsive to blondes and brunettes, and this would be an example of how responses depend upon stimulus conditions.

The differentiation of the surface of man's body into regions of greater sensitivity is much advanced, of course, with the development of specialized sensory organs, each of which is sensitive to certain types of physical stimulation. With the development of these specialized receptors, the difference between adaptation and habituation becomes more meaningful too, and probably both factors play a part in the ability of younger people to tolerate the intense amplification of modern popular music.

The effects of changes in the internal environment of the body upon behavior are easy to observe. For example, the tendency to buy a hamburger is greatly diminished immediately after a steak dinner. More generally, we find that our internal states, e.g., hunger and thirst, make us differentially receptive to stimuli related to these states.

The ways in which small amounts of stimulation act together to summate their effects can be shown in many ways. One example of this might be when a series of small setbacks causes a person to over-react to the "final straw," whereas the same event on a "good day" would be without effect. Another example, in the form of analogy could be found when advertisers bombard us on commercial television with their ads, time and again, in the hope that the messages will summate their effects and alter our behavior to the manufacturer's advantage and profit.

The behavior of the amoeba has another parallel with that of man. The responses of the amoeba result in the maintance of optimal conditions in its internal chemistry. These optimal conditions are those which best promote the representative metabolic conditions for the organism—in short, those internal conditions which favor the survival of the animal. The *tendency* of animals to maintain suitable internal conditions has been called "homeostasis"; this will be discussed more fully in Chapter 9. It would be a mistake to infer that any animal, the amoeba included, has an "idea" of what these optimal internal conditions might be. However, animals that do not maintain optimal internal conditions perish.

From these elementary considerations it would appear that many of the principles underlying man's behavior can be found in an animal as low on the phylogenetic scale as the amoeba.

However, it must be pointed out that even though the behavior of man and primitive animals shares certain common goals, the mechanisms whereby these goals are reached may be quite different. Our interest, as students of behavior, is to understand both behavior and the mechanisms responsible for it.

Spontaneous activity

Though much of what has been said about the behavior of the amoeba and its relation to human behavior was concerned with responses to stimulation, it should not be concluded that behavior occurs only as a response to external stimuli. Such a view of behavior would represent the organism as a passive machine that responds only when stimulated. Many activities of animals seem to occur spontaneously—that is, without any noticeable external stimulation. In some animals, such as the sea anemone, different muscle systems seem to be endowed with different degrees of spontaneous activity.

Activity is often termed "spontaneous" when its cause is unknown or at least not apparent. Increased activity can arise from stimuli originating in the internal environment, e.g., from the internal organs, or from chemical changes of the body that influence specific brain regions. On the other hand, changes in general activity are often observed that have no known physiological correlate. Many, if not all, psychologists view animals as being spontaneously active and see this activity as being a natural property of all animal life.

If spontaneous activity is accepted as an axiom of all animal life, this means that identical changes in the external or internal world of the animal need not always produce identical reactions, because they would be imposed upon quite different patterns of on-going activities. Moreover, the behavior of animals fluctuates in accordance with different types of rhythms, regulated by both external and internal factors, which influence reactions to stimuli.

Cycles and rhythms

An animal will behave differently at different times as a result of the various rhythms and cycles that affect it. These periodic changes can be associated with alterations in the internal environment or in the external environment. One of the most common cycles is the "day-night" cycle, which is related to available sunlight. Differential activity in response to the light or dark can be observed even among the lowest animals on the scale. Daily activities that are tied to day-night periods are called *circadian rhythms* (*circa* meaning "about," *diem* meaning "day").

Activities such as sleeping, eating, exploration, and the like are all influenced by the time of the day. Some animals, such as rats and cats, are nocturnal and spend most of the day asleep but become active at night. Associated with changes in overall activities such as exploration and sleeping are changes in the ability of an animal to respond to certain stimuli or to learn to do some things. Animals also learn to anticipate the onset of day and night. For example, the sea anemone begins to enlarge itself before nightfall in anticipation of the coming darkness.

Most animals are able to adapt to new day-night cycles if the external environment changes. For example, if animals are placed in an artificial environment in which darkness comes at the time when they have usually experienced daylight, they quickly adjust and behave in accordance with the new conditions.

An interesting experiment showing the significance of internal factors has been shown in the study of sleep phenomena. Subjects who had volunteered to participate in sleep experiments were placed in a room isolated from the normal cues of day and night. No clocks or other means of determining time were available. Subjects could order meals whenever they wished through an intercommunication system connecting the person in the isolation chamber with the experimenters outside. They could turn the lights on or off whenever they felt like it. They could do some small bits of work or listen to music from a tape recorder. In short, they could regulate their schedules as they desired without any clues as to the actual time of day. Within the first few days of isolation, the subjects began to operate on 26-hour days instead of our common 24-

hour days. They added 2 hours to every day, and this effect was cumulative in the sense that their guess as to the time outside the chamber was 2 hours off the first day, 4 hours off the second day, 6 hours off the third day, and so on.

These observations could mean that man has an internal, clocklike mechanism that is at odds with the time schedule based on 24 hours. Fortunately man has the capacity to perform effectively with this shorter schedule.

The behavior of animals is geared into cycles other than the circadian rhythm. Some sea animals' behavior is influenced by the tides of the sea even though they may be removed from the sea and placed in laboratory aquaria. The behavior and moods of many women seems to be closely related to their monthly menstrual cycles. With women we know that the periodic changes of hormones during the monthly cycles are important in influencing behavior. At the same time, we know very little about *how* the hormones themselves come to alter behavior and moods.

To understand behavior we must take into account the changes that are found at different times of the day or at different times in other cyclic periods. Depending upon the nature of the experimental issue under investigation, they may be more or less important, but in no case should they be forgotten or ignored.

Steps toward more complicated behaviors

The amoeba has only one cell and therefore it can have no nervous system, muscle system, or receptor system. Higher on the phylogenetic scale we find animals that are aggregates of single cells, and above them animals that are more than collections of cells—animals that have groups of cells with specialized functions.

The phylum Porifera represents a step toward the complex individual and more complicated behavior. Commonly known as sponges, these organisms are characterized by a group of cells organized into several layers (see Figure 3-2). Shaped like a vase, the adult sponge is fixed to one location. Water containing tiny food particles is drawn in and out of the animal by the beating of specialized cells with flagella, tiny hairlike structures. The water is forced in through one set of holes and out through others. The food particles are extracted from the water by cells on the interior of the sponge.

Each of the cells in the area surrounding the opening at the top is individually irritable. These cells jointly control the size of the opening. Each of the cells surrounding the opening acts as a *receptor* in that it is responsive to the temperature and composition of the water; but in addition, each cell can be affected by the activities of its neighbors. Stimulation of one part of the border around the opening causes the cells in that area

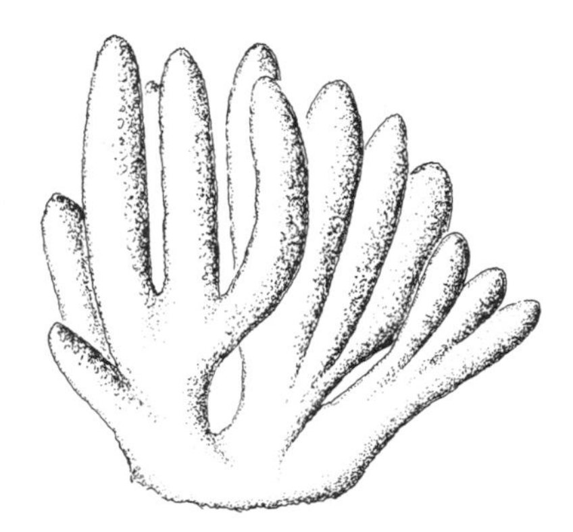

Figure 3-2 *The sponge (phylum Porifera) represents a major step toward the complex individual.*

to contract. This contraction spreads slowly throughout the remainder of the cells. Thus the whole opening closes. This contraction does not depend upon cells specialized for the transmission of excitation. The initial excitation spreads in wavelike fashion from one cell to another. One may observe the beginnings of cells that are differentiated for special purposes, but as a rule each cell functions autonomously.

In the phylum Coelenterata we come upon a more highly developed communication (nervous) system, although it is quite unlike anything found in mammals. One of the representatives of the phylum is the hydra, which is familiar to all students of elementary biology (see Figure 3-3). The tentacles wave about, and the whole animal moves by elongation.

The reactions of the hydra tentacles depend upon the strength of the applied stimulation and the internal environment of the animal, but if an appropriate stimulus is applied to one tentacle, its reactions will quickly be duplicated by the others.

Actually, the activity of the tentacles of the hydra is quite complicated. Four types of specialized cells can be found on the tentacles, they respond to four different types of stimulation. One type of specialized cell is used to attach the hydra to sticks, stones, or plants in the water. Another type seems to be used to prevent the hydra from running into objects or organisms that are not edible. Two types are used to capture prey of different sizes—one for large prey, another for small prey.

In order for the specialized cells on the tentacles to react, two things must occur: First, the cells must be primed by specific chemicals, and second, physical contact must be made with the cells. Thus the receptive systems must be specifically primed for the effective stimulus—which is some type of physical contact.

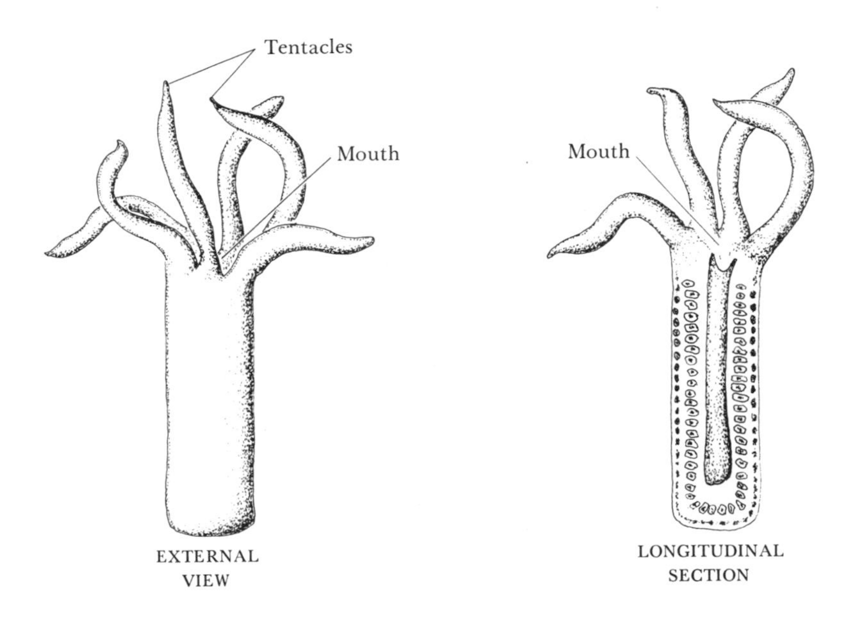

Figure 3-3 *The hydra (phylum Coelenterata).*

The actual feeding response of the hydra (as distinct from tentacle activity) depends on both chemical and physical factors. One specific chemical (glutathione) is essential to the feeding response. This chemical is found abundantly in the body fluids of animals eaten by hydra. It is released into the water when the prey's bodily wall is punctured by the specialized cells on the tentacles. But more is required to elicit the feeding response than the presence of this appropriate chemical. Actual physical contact with objects must be made to elicit feeding.

These rather complex reactions depend upon the specialization of cells for specific purposes and also at least a rudimentary system of communication among cells, that is, a primitive nervous system. This represents a second stage of development of cells toward a nervous system. The first level is represented by cells that are both sensory and contractile, such as those around the opening of the sponge. In the second stage there are specialized sensory cells that have ways to communicate with other cells. A third stage is also found in the phylum Coelenterata and is represented by a *nerve net*. The nerve net is a complex mesh of cells between the receptor cells and muscles. This nerve net is diffusely organized and activates the tentacles in a widespread fashion. When one tentacle is excited, the other tentacles also become excited, because of activity of the neural net.

This illustrates one of the primary roles in behavior of the nervous system. It allows for communication of events among cells and organs separated by relatively great distances. This permits a coordinated response to the stimulus of the entire animal.

Another feature that is prominent in higher behaviors can be observed in Coelenterata. This is *inhibition* of a response. The term inhibition refers to the reduction or elimination of a response through an active suppressive process of some kind. Normally, the specialized, receptive cells on the tentacles used for the hydra's movements are most sensitive to physical contact, but the reactivity of these sensitive cells becomes much less when food stimuli are present. The specialized cells that move the animal from place to place are inhibited by food. This mechanism tends to keep the animal in one place as long as food is available. The inhibition is specific to the movement tentacles, as the specialized cells on the tentacles that protect the animal against nonedible, potentially dangerous objects are not inhibited by food particles.

THE FLATWORM The flatworm, planaria, has been extensively studied by psychologists. This worm is a bilaterally symmetrical animal. The head region is most active physiologically and contains a collection of nerve cells called ganglia. There are two major regions of ganglia, and descending strands of nerve fibers arise from them to run down the two sides of the body (see Figure 3-4). Receptive cells exists in the periphery of the body, and there are light-sensitive cells in the head region that probably are somewhat analogous to eyes.

The planarian has been used extensively in research aimed at understanding the chemical basis of learning and memory. The flatworm is useful because when it is cut in half, both the head and the tail ends will regenerate complete worms. Interesting experimental questions can be asked. For example: If a worm were trained to make a response, would both of the animals that regenerate from the transected planarian retain the response or would the response be found only in animals that regenerate a new tail and not in animals that must regenerate a new head?

The retention of learning by the animal regenerated from the tail animal would suggest that previous learning, at least in the flatworm, was recorded in the organism in a very general fashion. Possibly this general encoding of experiences is chemical in nature.

To investigate these and other possibilities, many studies have been undertaken to assess whether the parent worm's training is retained by those animals which result from regeneration. In some of the experiments, animals were trained to make a response that commonly occurred to one stimulus when another (behaviorally neutral) stimulus was

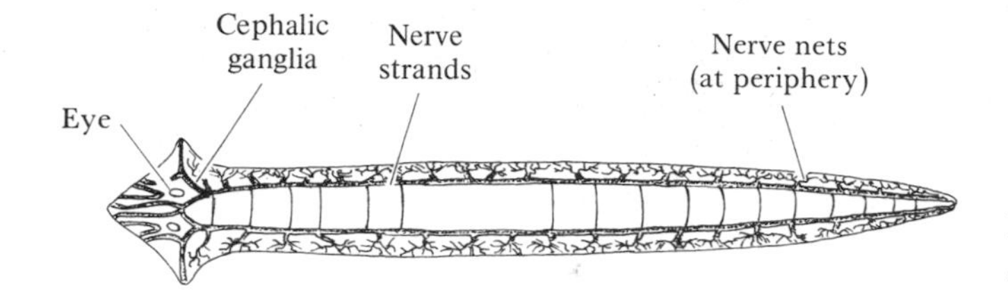

Figure 3-4
Drawing of a planarian.

presented. This is a simple type of learning called "Pavlovian" or "classical" conditioning. The method will be presented in detail in later sections (pp. 246-249), but can be described for the flatworm as follows.

The first step in a classical conditioning experiment is to ascertain that the stimulus used as the stimulus to which the response will be conditioned does not produce the response. Therefore, the worms were exposed to light until the experimenters were convinced no contractile responses were being made to it. Then the conditioned stimulus (*CS*), light, was associated with a stimulus that was effective in producing the response. In many experiments electrical shock to the worm was the unconditioned stimulus (*US*) used to produce the contractile response. The response produced by the *US* is called the unconditioned response or reflex (*UR*). After a number of pairings of the *CS* and the *US* (the light and the shock) the animals come to make a response similar to the *UR* (contraction to shock) to the *CS* (light). This contraction made to the previously ineffective *CS* is called the conditioned response or reflex (*CR*). Generally speaking the *CR* is very much like the *UR*, but conditioning is more than a matter of simple substitution of stimuli. The *CS* does not elicit a response *exactly* like the one elicited by the *US*. The classical conditioning model will be of importance to us throughout this book, and it may be helpful to master the simple steps in this conditioning paradigm early.

It has been found that the planarians are capable of acquiring a conditioned response. Study of the two animals resulting from the single, trained animal revealed that both animals retain something of the original learning. This must be tested by retraining the contraction response after the regeneration process has been completed. Since this requires some amount of time, there would be some "forgetting" of the response even by an intact worm. Therefore, memory for the earlier learning is inferred from the ability of the new worms to relearn the contraction response at a faster rate than exhibited originally by the parent worm or by worms regenerated from cut portions of worms that had no prior training. Both the animals regenerating from the head and the tail regions showed faster learning rates than the other animals with which they were compared. This argues for some transfer of the memories of the training given the parent to the regenerated "offspring." If anything, the animal regenerating from the tail portion seems to relearn the contraction response fastest. This means that the effects of the training are not stored only as changes in the head ganglia in the planarians. The fact that the tail-region animal inherits some knowledge of the avoidance problem suggests that there may be more than one mechanism underlying the learning and memory processes. The point that there may be several mechanisms of memory storage is further supported by research which shows that if the regeneration of new animals from the head and the tail regions takes place in a solution containing a chemical that destroys RNA, then the animal arising from the head region seems to maintain its memory of the training given the parent animal but the animal arising from the tail section does not.

Studies aimed at understanding the chemical basis of learning and memory will be treated later in this book (Chapter 7). At that time we shall examine these studies and their relationship to other kinds of studies on this important problem.

SEGMENTED WORMS The annelids are segmented worms of the type most frequently found in the garden. These animals have not been extensively studied by psychologists recently, but their segmented bodily organization deserves attention because it stands in sharp contrast to the mammalian form and because it is of a type representative of many kinds of insects as well as of segmented worms.

The famous neuroanatomist C. Judson Herrick described the neural organization of the segmented worms and the insects in a way difficult to improve upon:

> The body of a worm may be compared with a loose federation of separate states, each with autonomous self government and responsible to a central power only in its foreign relations. In the insect, to carry out the analogy, the central governing power (head dominance) is stronger, the states (segments) are united in three subsidiary federations (head, thorax, and abdomen), and yet each state retains a measure of autonomy. The machinery of government is almost entirely inflexible, as if it were merely the execution of immutable laws (Herrick, 1924, p. 143).

One interesting, older psychological experiment with earthworms remains of particular interest to students of behavior today. Worms were trained in a maze shaped like the letter "T." After they had learned to go to one of the arms of the T, the anterior five segments of the worm, which included the neural head ganglia as well as some neural centers just below it, were removed. Immediately afterwards the animals' behavior showed that they had retained what had been taught them previously. As the new anterior region regenerated, however, this learning was lost. This implies that the lower segments of the worms had some memory of the previous training, but that the regenerated "head" did not. When it grew back, it came to reestablish its preeminence over the animal's behavior and the learning of the lower regions did not prevail against this "uninformed" new head ganglion.

Both the segmented worms and insects can exist admirably well without their heads and even show definite signs of learning without them. However, some activities that occur in normal animals will not occur if the animals are decapitated, but changes in the external environment can compensate for this loss. For instance, decapitated moths will not lay eggs spontaneously, but will do so with certain special kinds of sensory stimulation. This illustrates the fact that the loose neural confederacy of the segments is not entirely dependent on the central power, the head ganglion. The organization of the nervous system of mammals is entirely dependent on the centralization of the brain.

THE OCTOPUS In the cephalopod popularly known as the octopus we find several improvements in the nervous system and in the range of behavior. The nervous system of the animals contains several head ganglia not dissimilar to those found in the segmented worms, but in addition a specialized receptor for visual stimuli has developed. The octopus has an eye with a movable lens, which can focus light on sensory cells located behind it. The effects of changes in illumination are transmitted by nerve fibers to the ganglionic lobes at some distance from the eye. This primitive visual system is efficient enough so that the octopus can use visual cues to direct attacks on crabs and other food. The nervous system of the octopus is quite rudimentary, and the behavior of the animal is limited in range. For example, it does not seem to be able to overcome barriers placed between it and the food. If it is "aware" of the barrier, it does not seem to be able to coordinate its movements to circumvent the barrier. However, the octopus can learn to inhibit its usual response of catching and eating a crab when one is placed in front of him. By appropriate administration of an electric shock as a punishment when the crab is placed on a given colored card, the octopus learns not to approach the crab, but it will continue to attack the crab when it is on a card of a different color. Surgical interference with one portion of the octopus' brain (the vertical lobe) can produce an astounding change in the animal's reactions. When the animals are tested after surgery, they can still remember not to attack a crab on the "wrong" card if the experimental trials are within five minutes of each other. When the intertrial interval is lengthened to two hours, the animal does not restrain his attack and is punished. In the cephalopod's neural lobes there must be systems for long-term memories that are distinct from those involved with short-term memories. This represents our first contact with two kinds of memory, but it will not be our last. We will come to find that higher forms of life, including man, seem to have several kinds of memory processes.

INSECTS AND SPIDERS With the insect and spiders we reach a peak of complex behavior for the invertebrates. The bees even have what can be described as a language of their own. Ants have a complex social order, but their behavior seems to be governed by relatively inflexible laws. It is important not to confuse flexible or modifiable behavior and complex behavior. We can obtain some insight into some characteristics of the laws that seem to govern the behavior of such animals by inspecting the spider spinning his web. Different species of spiders tend to spin their own distinctive webs. The number of webs they spin is proportional to their food intake. The more abundant the food, the fewer webs spun. Again, as we have seen as far down the phylogenetic scale as the amoeba, the internal environment of the animal, especially as determined by recent food intake, is important for controlling even unlearned reactions.

As with much of the behavior of insects, the spider's behavior is indeed complex. Yet it consists largely of many fixed responses to various stimulus patterns.

> To some extent the spider's motion seems dictated by the growing web, which may be considered as a gradually developing field of force. The varying tensions of long and short segments, the distances between intersections, the lengths of filaments and the angles between them—each furnish stimuli to which the instinctively driven spider is compulsorily obedient (Savory, 1960, p. 118).

This quotation illustrates the complex control that the environment, as interpreted by the animal's sensory system, exerts upon the behavior of the lower animals.

Of an equally complex nature is the communication of bees. Even though many of the details in regard to communication among bees are not completely settled, the work of Karl von Frisch, an Austrian zoologist, stands as a landmark in this research. Von Frisch has spent years studying how bees learn the location of food from other bees. Watching a bee's return to the hive, he found that it communicated its "find" to the other bees in the hive by a dance. The vigor of the dance indicates the amount of nectar left at the source. When the nectar supply is running out, the bees returning to the hive dance slowly or not at all. When the supply is plentiful, the dance is more vigorous. The direction to the food source is given by the angle of inclination from the horizontal. This angle is related to the position of the sun. The intricacies of the sensory determinants of this complicated bee behavior are enormous and not fully investigated. For instance, Von Frisch has found that the bees are capable of relating the direction of the food source to the sun's position even though the sun is itself obscured. (Whether this involves a capacity to respond to the polarization of the light is not known.) While the dance of the bees carries all of this information, there is some doubt as to whether it is used by the bees to which it is directed.

At this level of insect life we find an elaborate communication system. It is a type of communication. In many ways it can be considered as similar to our use of language, since information is transmitted by "dance symbols." Equally fascinating is the capacity of these animals to use the position of the sun in the sky as a reference point in their communication of the position of the food source. Since they can use the sun's position as such a reference point, they must make use of stimuli that people do not normally use (i.e., the polarization of light or the infrared rays). The sensory world of the bee must be one that is quite different from ours.

In addition to the fact that insects communicate symbolically, they also show social behavior. When groups of army ants are placed on a flat surface, free of obstacles, they begin a group march. They march in eccentric circles, controlled by stimuli arising from their own group and a counteracting centrifugal force. In the jungle the army ants run into many obstacles, which more or less randomly alter the group's path. Where there are no obstructions the geometry of the forces is unaltered and results in an almost certain perpetuation of the march until the ants die. The behavior of an individual army ant is completely determined by the group.

In both the bee and the ant we can find caste systems. For example, some bees are workers, some drones, and generally there is a queen. Each bee or ant has a certain role to fulfill in its community and usually follows a certain behavioral pattern commensurate with this role. Animals adopt such roles, however, because of their biological make-up, whereas the caste systems of human society are determined by a social, not a biological, heritage.

Throughout the study of the invertebrates we find many instances of complex behavior and even social organization. Yet invertebrate behavior is rigid. It lacks the flexibility of behavior found in mammals, or even vertebrates generally. The spider builds a type of web whose structure is predictable if we know the species of spider. We turn now to an examination of more general species-typical behavior.

SPECIES-TYPICAL BEHAVIOR

In the past, instinctive behaviors, or simple instincts, were thought to be patterns of behaviors provided an animal by its genetic inheritance. Often, in the past, these behaviors were differentiated from behaviors that are learned throughout the course of development. Many psychologists used to think of behaviors as either learned or innate, that is, instinctive. This partitioning of behavior into two classes was unfortunate, because it led to an "either-or" type of thinking about behavior. Any behavior depends on both the genetic endowment of the organism and its past experiences. To separate behavior artificially into two classes based upon a genetic or a learned component is both false and misleading. As a result, the terms "instinct," "instinctive behavior," and "innate behavior" are inappropriate and should no longer be used.

On the other hand, much of the behavior of the lower animals is stereotyped and common to almost all members of a species. That behavior shared by most, if not all, members of a species can be called species-predictable or species-typical behavior. These terms should not be thought of merely as new words that are being used to replace the old word, instinct. Species-typical behavior is not independent of the environment of the organism or of its past experiences.

A member of any species comes into the world with a species-typical *structure* and quite often shares an environment similar to that shared by other members of the species. Therefore, all members of a species have a great deal of common ground from which future behavior will develop. The species-typical structures we know most about are those portions dealing with the stimuli arising from the environment (the sensory systems) and the response systems with which the animal makes its way through the world. On the sensory side, certain species can detect changes in the environment that are invisible to others—for example, the polarization of light. Differences among species' response capabilities are obvious enough: Some crawl, some swim, some walk, and some fly. It is most likely the case that the brain and/or the nervous systems of species differ in their details too, even though the principles of function of the individual elements of the nervous system are more or less the same throughout the vertebrates.

Given the species-typical structure and environment, species-typical behavior can be thought of as activities that develop in animals exposed to "normal environments"—those which are common to most members of the species. These activities are more or less stereotyped and resistant to modification. In the course of development of an animal, various stages are reached in which these behaviors play different roles, and at each stage certain kinds of environmental support must occur for the behavior to develop. The phenotypic behavior of each member of the species depends upon its entire genetic inheritance (its genotype) and the interaction of this endowment with the environment (as we have learned in the preceding chapter).

Much of what we know about species-typical behaviors has come from studies of rather stereotyped behaviors of lower animals. Some of the work has been based upon stereotyped models of behavior that are too rigid to be adequate representations of the true complexities of animal behavior. However, once the limitations of the model are recognized and kept in mind, they can be profitably studied.

The ethological approach

Much of our knowledge of species-typical behavior comes from the work of European ethologists. Their investigations were quite different from the laboratory-based approach to the study of behavior common in the United States. The naturalists of Europe centered their attention upon stereotyped behavioral reactions of animals observed in their natural environments. The two best-known of the European contributors, Niko Tinbergen and Konrad Lorenz, took somewhat different approaches. Tinbergen began by watching animals in their natural setting, while Lorenz more frequently raised animals under artificial conditions that were close approximations of the completely natural settings. We will consider first the role of the stimulus in the control of species-typical behavior and Tinbergen's work.

Studies of the species-typical behavior of fish and birds suggest that the stimuli that "release" such behavior can be quite restricted. Many people active in animal research use the term "release" to describe the elicitation of a specific behavior pattern by a limited range of stimuli. The ethologist Tinbergen has studied the behavior of the three-spined bony stickleback. This fish displays a number of species-typical behaviors, some connected with the mating cycle. The male stickleback assumes command over a portion of the sandy bottom of his tank or pond. Once in possession of such a territory he will defend it from male intruders. The male stickleback will also show a courtship behavior when a female comes into his area. The courting behavior leads to actions that help to squeeze the eggs from the female and that result in the fertilization of the eggs. The courting behavior, known as the zig-zag dance, is a species-typical behavior. Tinbergen (1951) has investigated the stimulus characteristics that are sufficient to release this courting behavior.

One technique Tinbergen has used is to introduce various shapes into the water near the male stickleback. By altering the character of the stimulus it is possible to determine specific attributes of the pattern that act to release the innate behavior of the zig-zag dance. Only a few characteristics of the female form are responsible for the elicitation of the response. The specific attribute that calls out (i.e., releases) a particular kind of behavior is called the *sign stimulus.* The sign stimulus for the zig-zag dance is a protruding underportion of a figure that need be only vaguely fishlike. The characteristic of a bulging underside of a figure is the important feature of the environmental situation. In Figure 3-5 the various stimuli used to test for the sign stimulus of the courting behavior are presented. The sign stimulus responsible for eliciting the aggressive behavior appropriate to a male intruder seems to be the size and color of the underbelly of a fishlike form.

Tinbergen can manufacture better sign stimuli than those provided in nature, by emphasizing and enlarging the sign-stimulus characteristics of his models. When these special stimuli are presented, they exert more effect upon the animal than any natural stimulus found in the environment. These artificial and exaggerated sign stimuli are called *supranormal sign stimuli.*

If the male fish has been stimulated time and time again to make a courting response, the presentation of yet another protruding female form will not usually elicit another zig-zag dance. In short, we find habituation of the response through repeated occurrences. However, if we present one of the supranormal sign stimuli, this may be potent enough to release the behavior. On the other hand Tinbergen has

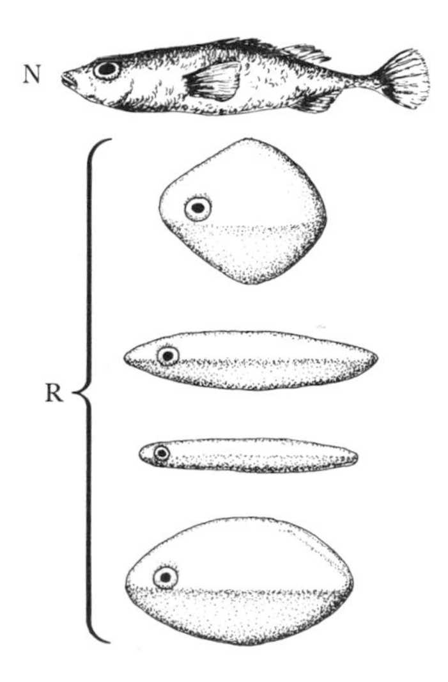

Figure 3-5 *Models of stimuli used by N. Tinbergen in his studies of species-typical behavior in the stickleback. (Fig. 20 in N. Tinbergen,* A study of instinct. *Oxford: Clarendon Press, 1951. By permission of the author and the Oxford University Press.)*

observed that if the response has not occurred for some time in the past, responses often occur even when no sign stimulus is present. It is almost as if energy for a particular response builds up to a certain point, and then the response will occur with a minimal amount of external stimulation. The *energy* of a particular response is specific for the particular response. The effect is not due to general fatigue. The number of recent occurrences of the aggressive responses to other males does not affect the amount of sign stimulation required to release a courting response to a female.

The innate releasing mechanism

The model of species-typical behavior developed from the studies of European ethologists can be described by a model that follows mechanical principles. For each type of behavior there is a specific source of energy available in the organism as well as stimulation of a most specific nature that acts as a releasing device for the energy. The energy when released flows into response systems provided by the species-typical structure and the behavior occurs.

The stimuli that are the appropriate ones for the behavior act as if they open a valve through which the energy may pour, provided that there is sufficient energy for the response available. The more energy available the less external stimulation needed. If the energy supply is low, then a lot of external stimulation is required. The entire system has been termed by Lorenz an *innate releasing mechanism.*

The innate releasing mechanism model is much too simple to be an effective description of behavior. In addition it fails to provide for the necessary contributions of the animal's past experiences and environment to be acceptable as a complete account of species-typical behavior. The worst fault of the model is that it may lead us to believe that the behavior is *understood* when it is only being *described* in terms of the innate releasing mechanism. A description of behavior is only the beginning of research. We must understand the mechanisms of the brain and body that cooperate to produce the behavior and must understand the interactions between the animal and its world that are necessary for the behavior to develop. The understanding of the conditions that must occur during development for certain kinds of behaviors to occur has been furthered by investigations into the phenomenon called *imprinting.*

Imprinting

The sight of a group of goslings following a mother goose is common enough in many rural areas. But in Figure 3-6 we find a group of goslings following

Figure 3-6 *Goslings following Dr. Konrad Lorenz, having been imprinted on Lorenz at an early stage in their development. (By Thomas McAvoy,* Life *Magazine. © 1955 Time, Inc.)*

Dr. Konrad Lorenz just as naturally as they would their mother. Through the work of Lorenz and others we know that most fowl will follow many stimuli presented to them at a "critical time" after hatching. They quickly *learn* to follow the object presented to them. The object, whatever it may be, is *imprinted* into a following-response behavior system. When the imprinted object is presented, the birds follow it. Ducks will imprint sounds and tactile sensations as well as visual objects.

Studies of the imprinting process have led to the suggestion that the manner of presentation of the stimulus to be imprinted is of crucial importance. If newly hatched ducks are kept in the dark for about 15 or 16 hours after hatching, and then placed in a circular runway while an object is moved around the perimeter, the ducks will follow the object around the runway. These conditions proved to be very effective in eliciting durable imprinting. Generally, it has been found that conditions in which the animal is aroused and required to do some work are desirable for imprinting responses. If the young animals are tranquilized with drugs, the following response is poorly imprinted.

Of greatest interest to us is the extraordinary nature of this instinctive reaction. No sterotyped reaction to a specific stimulus is released; rather the animal is prepared to follow and seek contact with any stimulus-object, providing that the overall conditions of stimulation are right.

Even though the range of stimuli that can be imprinted by animals is wide, some objects are more easily imprinted than others. Large, round objects tend to be among the best for the following response of birds. Stimuli can be too strong for imprinting to occur. If the movements of the to-be-imprinted object are too vigorous, the young birds will flee from the object.

Most of the research into imprinting has involved birds that are capable of moving at, or shortly after, birth. How general a phenomenon is imprinting? Do the mechanisms of imprinting extend beyond birds? How many types of behaviors can be imprinted? The answers to these questions are not completely clear. Most research on imprinting has used the "following response" in which the developing bird "follows" some object in its environment but does not follow others. The only other response well studied is that of sexual activity observed later in life. If imprinting were to be defined only in terms of these two responses, then the phenomenon would have to be restricted to birds, in all likelihood. If imprinting is considered more broadly—for example, in terms of a sudden change in reactivity to objects or situations at specific times during development—then the question becomes one that can be studied experimentally, even though it is not answerable at the present time.

There is a definite period of time in which birds are susceptible to imprinting. The precise limits of this period vary from species to species and depend upon the presence or absence of special environmental influences. The fact that there is this special or "critical" period for the development of imprinting calls our attention to the more general idea of critical periods for the development of behaviors.

Critical periods

Birds, as we've mentioned, have a definite period of time after hatching in which imprinting is most likely to occur. The notion of critical periods is a more general idea and describes the finding that animals learn certain tasks more quickly at some developmental periods than at others. If this is so, then the mechanisms responsible for critical periods could be discovered and related to the circumstances that mark the onset and the end of the critical periods.

The beginnings of critical periods seem to be correlated with the maturation and functional use of sensory systems in the young animals. In some birds imprinting will occur to auditory stimuli before it is possible to imprint the animals to visual stimuli. This fact has been explained on the basis of an earlier maturation of the auditory system relative to the visual system. This argument is based upon anatomical and physiological changes in the sensory systems thought to be associated with faster and more efficient neural activity in them. Nevertheless we only know the parallel courses of development of the two types of activities—namely, the beginning of a critical period and maturation of the sensory systems. The onset of the critical periods of young birds is also related to improvements in motor coordination, and this also could be the mechanism related to the beginning of a critical period.

Other scientists believe that the onset of the critical period is determined by maturation of emotional systems of the organism. They point out that the youngest animals do not show many fear and anxiety responses. These reactions develop over the first few days and weeks of life. They also point out that it takes some experience with the environment to allow the animal to learn what is familiar. Since it it usually unexpected or novel stimuli that elicit fear reactions, these reactions would not be expected until the animal had established anticipations as to what the environment holds. The emotion-based argument holds that critical periods in birds begin when the animal can detect changes in the environment and before the maturation of fear responses. The critical period would end when the animal responds with the more mature fear reactions to new or unexpected stimuli.

Unfortunately we cannot decide at this time what marks the onset and the offset of critical periods. We do know that they depend on the maturational state of the animal but are also dependent upon the environment in which the animal is reared. Deprivation of normal environmental stimulation will tend to prolong the usual time of termination of the critical periods, but will not extend it indefinitely.

The concept of critical periods has frequently been applied to the behavior of animals other than birds. It is an appealing idea to consider that many kinds of behavior have special times for development. In one sense the notion of critical periods was one basis of the personality theories which stated that there was a progression of sensitivity from oral to anal to genital regions in the development of children. At the broadest level, it can be said that some degree of maturation of the nervous system, sensory systems, and motors systems must occur for individual types of behavior to occur. This is a far cry, however, from the highly specific behaviors found to be imprinted at certain times in birds.

Critical periods in the development of the mammals seem difficult to establish with any degree of precision. Furthermore, if they do exist, they are not so firmly related to stereotyped behavior as in the submammalian species. What is abundantly clear, however, is that the proper development of behavior depends upon being raised in relatively normal environments. If animals are raised in abnormal conditions, the behavioral patterns observed are likely to be atypical.

Abnormal conditions of development

Even before birth, mammals are being affected by their environment. One should recall that the contribution of heredity to behavior ends with the joining of an egg and a sperm. All subsequent influences are the result of the environment as it interacts with the genetic endowment. Unfortunate positions in the womb as well as unfortunate blood and chemical reactions to the placental blood supply can cause severe neural and behavioral debilities before birth.

If animals are subjected to severe conditions of sensory deprivation after birth, such as being raised in total darkness, degeneration of the light-sensitive portions of the eye will occur. If the deprivation is less severe, as when animals are raised in diffuse and nonpatterned light, then actual tissue damage will be slight but the animals' reactions to visual information will be abnormal. The failure to use patterned visual input early in life results in a permanent debility.

A tragic example of the debilitation arising from lack of use is when a child fails to use both eyes equally early in life. This can arise from a mild or severe cross-eyed condition in which the two eyes fail to operate together and one eye becomes dominant. It can also happen in children whose eyes appear to be well coordinated but in whom one eye comes to be dominant. If this condition goes undetected and uncorrected, the child's nondominant eye will lose the ability to mediate visual activities. This means that if the dominant eye were to become damaged, the older child or adult would be effectively blind. To try to minimize this possibility, pediatricians now check the use of both eyes in children at very early ages and if only one eye is being used, corrective procedures are undertaken. In order for the corrective procedures to be effective, they must be undertaken in the first few years of life.

Many other kinds of behavior can be modified if an animal is raised in an atypical environment. If dogs are raised in small cages which are just large enough for them to grow and move but in which they are deprived of normal interactions with other dogs and people, they develop strange social and emotional reactions. These dogs will be dominated and perhaps even "oppressed" by normal dogs. They will also show confused emotional reactions and be relatively unreactive to painful stimuli. Chimpanzees that were raised with special equipment restricting normal transmission of sensory information from the arms and legs were found to have lost the ability to localize information arising from their skin. Like the dogs just described, they also reacted in a diminished fashion to painful stimuli.

In any study of the effects of isolation or restriction upon behavior, it is necessary to restore the missing experience to the animal at some time. In short, the animal is removed from isolation sooner or later. The transition from isolation to a normal or enriched environment can itself be an important determinant of later behavior. In some studies the behavioral impairments thought to result from deprivation can be reduced by administering tranquilizers to the animal as it is removed from conditions of deprivation. The same alleviation can be produced by gradually introducing the animal to the nonisolation situation. The abnormal reactions induced by the sudden introduction of the animal to its new, more complex world has been termed "emergence stress."

In studies of monkeys reared by artificial mothers (see pp. 298-300), the animals appeared to develop normally but when observed in early adulthood they were incapable of functioning adequately in the sexual sphere. Sexual behavior in adulthood seems to be especially prone to early environmental influences, as seen in the imprinting work with birds and in the effects of early abnormal environments in higher animals.

Many children living in poverty and in the ghettos of the cities experience cultural deprivation. The precise effects of this reduced stimulation relative to cultural factors have not been established, but there is little doubt that this type of privation leads to marked learning deficiencies in school and to reduced performance on the usual tests of intelligence. Various local, state, and federal programs have been undertaken to help alleviate these conditions, but too little data are presently available to determine which will, in general, be the most effective techniques. Moreover, from what we have already learned about the effect of the total genetic endowment upon behavior and the interactions of different genetic compositions with different environments, it may be that no single standard treatment will be effective for all types of children. In addition, children entering remedial programs may be subjected to an "emergence stress," which—because of the likelihood that the deprived child might feel embarrassed or awkward in his new situation—could be even greater in magnitude than that found in animals.

HORMONES AND EARLY DEVELOPMENT

Hormones are chemicals that are released into the blood stream by the ductless (endocrine) glands of the body. Some hormones act only on one or a few portions, systems, or organs of the body while others act more generally. Hormones will be discussed in detail in Chapter 4, but at this point it will be helpful to consider the effects of the sex hormones (those released from the testes in males and the ovaries in females) upon behavior and especially the *development* of behavior.

In overall perspective, hormones affect behavior in one of two ways: They help organize behavioral patterns or they activate previously existing patterns. Hormones help organize behavior early in life, usually prenatally in man but for short periods of time after birth in other animals. After the animal has matured, hormones activate only existing behavior.

The activation of sexual behavior

From work using the guinea pig, it seems that there are substantial differences among animals in the intensity of adult sexual behavior. This is true for both males and females. The sexual vigor of the animals does not depend upon the amount of sex hormone present in the adult, since, if the animals are castrated in adulthood, the administration of sex hormones restores sexual vigor only to precastration levels. However, even though adult hormone levels may not be correlated with sexual behavior, hormones could have important behavioral influences earlier in development. Figure 3-7 shows the effect of castration and hormone supplementation on the sexual behavior of animals and illustrates the return of sexual behavior to precastration levels.

In general once an animal has matured, hormones tend to activate behaviors that have been established. Many patterns of behavior, including sexual behavior, are available to the animal but are more likely to be activated only when appropriate hormone levels are reached. In most animals both male and female patterns of behavior are possible, but in most normal conditions one or the other is clearly predominant. For example, both male and female animals in many species can exhibit "mounting behavior," the male sexual response. The male sex hormone releases this response and the female hormones suppress it. Therefore, if adult animals are castrated, the mounting response be-

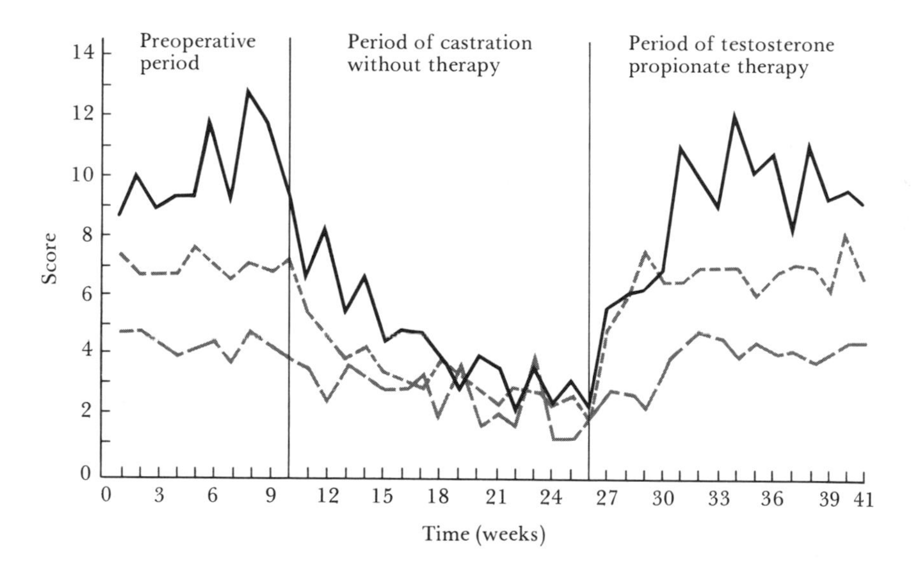

Figure 3-7 *Effect of castration and subsequent replacement treatment with testosterone propionate daily on the mating behavior of high-, intermediate-, and low-score male guinea pigs. (Adaptation of Figs. 1 and 2) in J. A. Grunt and W. C. Young, Consistency of sexual behavior in individual male guinea pigs following castration and androgen therapy.* J. comp. physiol. psychol., *1953,* 46, *138-144.)*

comes less common in males and somewhat more common in females. In general, however, castration of animals below the primate levels eliminates sexual behavior. In animals below the primate levels the elimination of sexual behavior takes longer after castration in males than in females, whose sexual behavior usually is closely tied to periods of estrus. Only in primates does sexual activity occur other than in estrus, and only in women is sexual activity found for extended periods of time after loss of the ovaries.

The sex hormones activate other behavior patterns than those related to sex. The urination behavior exhibited by dogs is quite different for the two sexes. Males tend to stand and lift a rear leg, while females squat. Often young puppies exhibit components of both patterns while they are growing up, but one pattern becomes established during that stage of development when the sex hormones reach near-adult levels. Castration of an adult female dog will often induce attempts at the male pattern of urination, which appear to be a sort of rebound phenomenon against the loss of the female hormone. In the castrated animal of both sexes, the urination pattern of either sex can be established by appropriate hormone administration.

The male sex hormone also is related to aggression. Administration of this substance causes an increase in aggression and a lowered threshold for the elicitation of aggressive reactions in many species. The defense of an animal's territory and its hostile reactions to visitors are enhanced in birds with increased male hormone levels. The administration of female sex hormones produces less clear-cut effects. In some (perhaps in most) species, the female hormones tend to produce a more placid animal but in other species they can enhance aggressiveness. In intact animals, aggressiveness and activity are closely tied to the monthly reproductive cycles.

The organization of behavior

Hormones not only activate existing behavior patterns of an organism, they also play an active role in establishing the patterns themselves. Once again, this effect is probably best observed in sexual behavior.

A freemartin is a cow that is the twin of a bull. The blood circulation of the calf and that of the bull in the mother have some interconnections and because the male hormone systems develop first, the calf will be flooded with male sexual hormone before its own hormones become effective. This results in a failure of the female system to develop; the ovaries never differentiate. The freemartin is permanently sterile. A similar effect can be produced in birds by administering male hormones to female birds; this produces a reversal of sex.

If male sex hormones are given to a pregnant female, the amount of this hormone that reaches the fetal animals can be increased. This influences both the development of the sex glands and the neural substrates of sex behavior in the brain. The prenatal administration of male sex hormones produces masculinization of the female's behavior. Female animals receiving this treatment before birth never come into estrus, "heat," in later life. More significant is the observation that females masculinized by male sexual hormones do not show normal sex behavior if they are castrated in adulthood and then given female hormones in large amounts.

On the other hand, prenatal administration of female hormones can interfere with the production of male hormone and, subsequently, with normal male development. The effect is much like physical castration of the animal early in life. Absence of male hormones in infancy —because of castration or feminization via female hormones—creates an animal with female patterns of sexual receptivity. This animal is capable of exhibiting cyclic behaviors related to the estrus cycle if ovaries are transplanted into it in adulthood. If ovaries are transplanted into animals castrated after infancy, cyclic changes in behavior related to estrus are not observed. This type of observation supports the widely accepted view that it is the male sex hormone that organizes behavior in a male direction and that in its absence development proceeds in a feminine course.

There are critical periods early in life during which the hormones' organizing influences will be effective. After the end of a "critical period," hormone treatments have little, if any, effect upon the organizing of behavior. The critical periods vary from species to species and, to a lesser extent, from animal to animal. In the guinea pig the critical period is over by birth, while in the rat it extends a few days after birth. The guinea pig is born in a much more "finished condition" than is the rat. The critical period for hormone effects upon differentiation of human sexual behavior is not precisely known but it may extend somewhat beyond birth. In adult behavior the effect of sex hormones is to *activate* patterns of behavior that have been established in part by the organizing influences of sex hormones during the earlier, critical periods.

The terms "organization" and "activation" as applied to hormone effects are reasonably accurate descriptions of behaviors, but what is being activated and what is being organized? The time is appropriate for investigations into these questions. In many cases, we know it is the brain—and especially certain regions within it—that is being affected. In other cases, the animal's reactions to the environment have been altered by other means. To understand how hormones alter behavior it is necessary fully to understand how behavior is governed and changed.

Hormones and the environment

The release of the sex hormones, as well as other hormones, is determined in part by the environment of the animal. Here the environment includes not only the physical conditions of temperature, humidity, and so forth but also the social environment of the animal. Our knowledge of the influences of hormones upon behavior and their interaction with environmental influences has been extended by careful investigations of the behavior of the ring dove.

Doves, like other birds, do not have anything that even closely resembles an estrus cycle. The breeding season is determined by a complex of internal and external factors. Part of the reproductive success of the birds is due to the fact that stimuli which arise during the activities of courtship and the building of the nest are effective in governing the control of hormones, which in turn guide the production of eggs.

Visual stimuli associated with birds are necessary for the laying of eggs. Most birds will not lay eggs in isolation, but a pigeon will do so if it is allowed to see another bird of the same species through a glass window (or even if she can see her reflection in a mirror). How the visual and the hormone systems are so finely organized is a mystery, but the extent to which the systems are associated is reflected by the fact that female doves show less female hormone production when they are allowed to see a castrated, noncourting male than when they are allowed to see a normal, courting male.

Peripheral bodily changes

The stimuli produced by nest-building behaviors also serve to accelerate the processes that lead to egg laying. Through the release of a different set of hormones, parental behaviors must be released after the eggs have hatched. Doves feed their young with a milk that is formed by the epithelium of the crop. One female hormone acts upon the dove's crop to make it more sensitive to stimuli produced by the pecking responses of the young birds. In this case, the hormonal effects are upon a peripheral bodily organ. Other examples of the effects of hormones upon peripheral structures can be shown. When an adult male rat is castrated, small sensitive papillae that are normally present on the penis disappear. Administration of male sex hormone can restore the papillae, and their return coincides with the return of mating behaviors. Another peripheral phenomenon that is hormone-induced is the development of a brood patch in birds. A brood patch is a portion of the belly of a bird that loses its feather covering, develops more blood vessels, and also becomes more sensitive to touch. A brood patch develops before the eggs are laid and, in some species, stimulation arising from the brood patch helps to terminate egg laying.

Hormones can also influence behavior by changes in bodily conditions of a general nature. For example, nest building in rodents can be stimulated by any manipulation that tends to create a lowered body temperature. One method is to reduce the environmental temperatures, but other ways are effective also—including removal of the thyroid glands, the gonads, the adrenal glands, and the pituitary. All of these methods share the characteristic of producing a lowered bodily temperature, although they produce wide ranges of other more specific effects as well.

The mechanisms by which hormones influence behavior and its development need not be only by way of altering or influencing the central nervous system. Hormones can act systemically (as in the case of temperature and nest-building behaviors) or they can affect specific peripheral organs. All three types of actions can occur together or in various combinations.

Research into both the peripheral and central changes induced by hormones is currently a very important direction of research, and preliminary investigations indicate that the changes in physiological and anatomical functions caused by the hormone will be subtle in nature. Because of their importance for behavior they must be understood. In the next chapter we shall try to provide some background information into the mechanisms of the body that are responsible for behavior and also consider the roles played by hormones more generally.

SUGGESTED READINGS

Breland, K. and Breland, M. *Animal behavior*. New York: Macmillan, 1966.

Maier, N. R. F. and Schneirla, T. C. *Principles of animal behavior* (Enlarged ed.). New York: Dover, 1964.

Scott, J. P. *Animal behavior*. Garden City, N.Y.: Doubleday, 1963.

Scott, J. P. *Early experience and organization*. Belmont, Calif.: Wadsworth, 1968.

Tavolga, W. N. *Principles of animal behavior*. New York: Harper & Row, 1969.

4

The biological basis of behavior

In *Chapter 3* we considered the origins of behavior. In this chapter we turn our attention to the mechanisms of the body that are responsible for behavior—in particular, the nervous system. The cells of the nervous system are responsible for many functions, among which are (1) recognition of changes occurring both inside and outside the body; (2) transmission of this information to a central processing unit (the brain and the central nervous system); and (3) transmission of signals from this central processing unit to the muscles and glands of the body so that the appropriate activity can take place.

The complexity of the nervous system is overwhelming. The brain alone has been likened to a cellular city with more than 12 billion inhabitants—and the figure of 12 billion is now thought to be probably a gross underestimate of the number of neurons in the brain. The number of interconnections among the cells probably exceeds 300 trillion. Moreover, the interconnection of the cells may not be stable and unchangeable even in the adult animal. Time-lapse photographs of brain nerve cells grown in tissue cultures show these cells to be in constant motion, changing their positions and contacts with each other from moment to moment.

In this chapter we shall begin with a preliminary sketch of a single nerve cell and then progress to consider the gross structural units of the nervous system. Then we will describe the relationship between the nervous system and the chemical messenger system of the body, the endocrine (ductless) glands, before concluding the chapter with a comprehensive look at the neuron and its activities.

THE NEURON: A PRELIMINARY VIEW

The basic units of the nervous system are single cells called *neurons*. The nervous system is a massive collection of billions of neurons. To understand how the nervous system operates we must understand the construction and workings of the units of which it is composed.

There is, of course, a functional resemblance between the single neural cell found in higher animals and all single cells. All cells must have nourishment and means of eliminating their waste products. All cells have membranes, nuclei, other protoplasmic structures, and patterns of reactions to appropriate stimulation. Neurons differ from other cells in the body in that they are specially constructed to transmit excitation swiftly from one portion of the cell to another, even though the distance from the point of excitation to the end of the neuron may be considerable.

Our brains are essential to our existence, and the brain is nothing more than interconnected masses of cells. Our perceptions, experiences, behavior all depend on the brain's activity. Our hopes, dreams, and aspirations, in principle, are products of the activities of the single cells of the brain.

A highly schematic drawing of a neuron is presented in Figure 4-1. The three most important parts of this structure are the dendrites, the cell body, and the axon. The dendrites usually are small filaments that branch out from the cell body in various directions and upon which many other cells make contact. The cell body houses the nucleus, the metabolic machinery, and other mechanisms common to all cells. The axon is a substantial process, which may extend a considerable distance, at least in some cells. It usually has around it a fatty sheath (called myelin), which serves as "electrical insulation."

The basic job of a nerve cell is to transmit information in the form

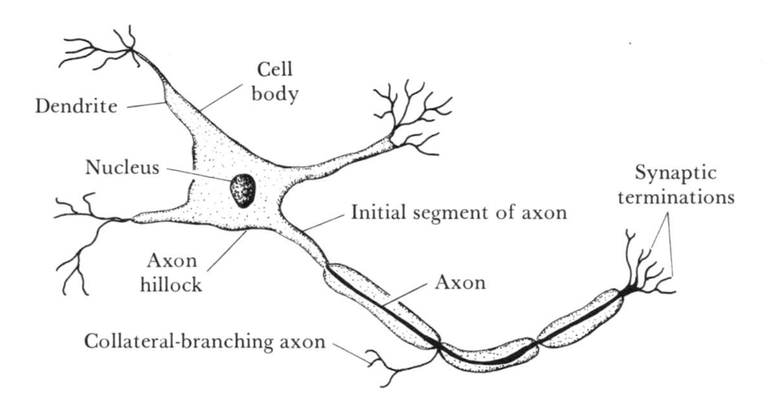

Figure 4-1 *Schematic drawing of a neuron.*

of abrupt electrochemical changes in its membrane. These membrane changes, which will be discussed at greater length later in this chapter, actually constitute the principal activity of nerve cells. The membrane changes move rapidly down the axon to affect other cells; these influences are usually considered as beginning at contact points on the subsequent cell's dendrites. These dendritic changes, in turn, influence the membrane of the cell body, and if the effects are large enough, they will cause a region near the place at which the axon leaves the cell body (the axon hillock) to produce a total membrane discharge, which will proceed down the axon. Therefore, we generally think of excitation as arising in the dendrites, spreading to the cell body, and (under appropriate circumstances) being carried to new locations via the axon. Some axons reaching a cell, however, end up on the cell body rather than the dendrites.

This description is a gross oversimplification of neuronal cellular activity, and we will expand the information later in the chapter. Our first task, however, will be to examine the gross morphological features of the human brain.

THE NERVOUS SYSTEM

In general, the nervous systems of man and mammals can be divided into two major divisions: the peripheral and the central portions. The peripheral nervous system is simply the neurons and their processes (axons and dendrites) that lie outside the bony vertebral column and the skull; those that lie inside these bony protective coverings are called the central nervous system, or CNS. (The spinal cord as well as some large bundles of fibers are inside the vertebral column and the brain, of course, lies within the skull.) Although there are some functional as well as geographic differences between cells in the peripheral and central nervous systems, in general the mechanisms of operation of cells in both divisions are similar.

There are many ways in which the study of the nervous system can be undertaken. One way is to consider how it evolves in the developing animal.

Development of the nervous system

Embryologically, the nervous system of all vertebrates develops from a "neural tube," which is comprised of primitive nerve cells. This longitudinal structure is the forerunner of the spinal cord.

Neither the brain nor the spinal cord ever loses this original tube-like organization. The hollow portion of the tube becomes the ventricular system, which is filled with cerebrospinal fluid and continues as a central core in the spinal cord—although it becomes a complicated and intricate complex of spaces in the brain. However, the entire ventricular system is continuous from one end in the brain to the termination at the posterior end of the spinal cord.

As maturation progresses, the cells of the tube in the region that will become the brain divide and form new cells more frequently than cells in other regions. As a result, certain early prominences and flexions of the tube appear, which are the precursors of later adult brain structures.

Figure 4-2 shows the structure of the anterior portion of the nervous system of the human embryo at 5 or 6 weeks, 11 weeks, and 4 months after conception. In the embryo of 5 weeks of age the initial flexion (bend) of the neural tube has occurred at a place where the diameter of the neural tube has become narrow. This area will become what is called the *midbrain.* Ahead of it is the *diencephalon,* from which structures known as the *thalamus* and *hypothalamus* will soon differentiate. Ahead of this is the beginning of the *forebrain,* from which the higher brain structures will arise.

On the side of the forebrain can be seen the *optic cup.* This portion of the forebrain will grow and migrate away from the neural tube. It will move out to become the retina of the eye, which contains the specialized cells that are capable of detecting light. The cells of the

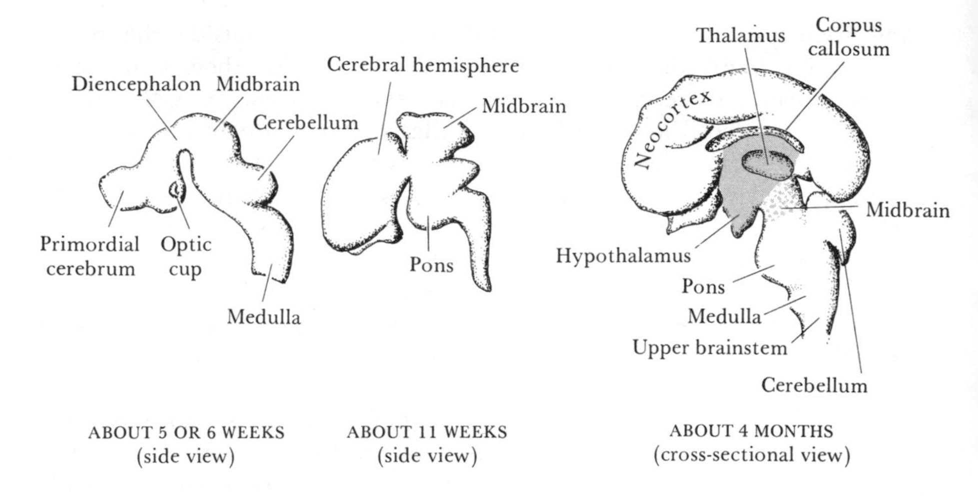

Figure 4-2 *Stages of brain development of human embryo. Shaded area represents the diencephalon (thalamus and hypothalamus), and the dots indicate the midbrain.*

retina are unique in this migration to form a kind of CNS "outpost" away from the protection of the skull. The beginning of the *cerebellum* and *medulla* can also be found at this early stage of development.

About 11 weeks after conception, the embryonic forebrain has expanded considerably. In man this structure consists of cells that will form the neocortex, which covers the surface of the brain. At this stage of development, the midbrain is relatively prominent but its favored position will be short-lived.

The cerebellum develops in close relationship with the pons. The word "pons" means "bridge," and this brain region can be thought of as a bridge between the midbrain and the medulla—that is, a bridge from the higher and lower brain regions to the cerebellum. After birth the cerebellum will be an essential mechanism for the coordination of motor movements and bodily balance; much of the pons houses large bands of nerve fibers going to and from the cerebellum.

By four months after conception, the brain has assumed a shape that approximates its final form at birth. (Since in some ways the outline of the brain resembles a sphere, each side is sometimes termed a hemisphere.) However, much is left to be done. The cerebellum is still in a very primitive condition, but it will not be needed until mechanisms for more coordinated movements have developed some time after birth. The neocortical mantle has been formed in a rudimentary fashion, even though new cells will be added to it continuously until well after birth. The thalamus and hypothalamus have become distinct as portions of the diencephalon, and the midbrain has assumed its adult position. The medulla and upper brainstem (the spinal-cord extension that lies just below the medulla) are nearing completion.

The region of the medulla will contain cells that are concerned with the regulation of many internal organs, including mechanisms governing heart rate and breathing, as well as control of the facial muscles. The cerebellum will become a neural center controlling balance and posture as well as acting as one of the coordinating centers of information from many of the senses. The midbrain is also a region containing cells that participate in the control of internal organs and also cells that help coordinate movements with incoming sensory information. They contain important regions for the control of eye movements, and they probably act to modulate the information arising from other sensory modalities in as yet unknown ways.

The thalamus is generally divided into a dorsal and ventral division. The word "dorsal" refers to a direction meaning "toward the back" and "ventral" means "toward the belly." To understand this use of the terms, man must be thought of as being on all fours with his head looking straight forward in a doglike position. Thus for the present purposes the dorsal thalamus would be the "top" and the ventral the "bottom." This system of naming does not always work, however, and the only way to be correct all of the time is to keep in mind the dorsal-back, ventral-belly dimensions. The dorsal-ventral division of the thalamus is related to a fundamental difference in activities. Cells in the dorsal thalamus receive input from the sensory systems and send axons to higher brain regions, especially regions of the neocortical mantle. Cells in the ventral thalamus assist in modifying motor activities of the organism.

The hypothalamus, located just ventral to (beneath) the thalamus, is the major coordinating region for the internal organs of the body and acts to organize many types of behavior, especially those related to emotion and motivation. As will be seen, this region is important quite disproportionately to its relatively small size.

The forebrain develops into three major sections: (1) the neocortical surface of the brain; (2) the basal ganglia, a set of structures that participate in the modification of motor movements and also to some unknown extent in the regulation of sensory input; and (3) the limbic system, a set of structures surrounding the thalamus and which are thought to be of particular importance to the control of the emotions and motivation.

Although our discussion may have given the impression that the brain is a discrete series of segmental structures, this is not actually the case. All brain regions are intimately related. The brain is continuous and interconnected, part to part. Some brain regions are especially concerned with rather specialized functions, but each part operates in cooperation with many other parts and each cell of each system is influenced, directly or indirectly, by almost every other cell in the brain.

General principles of neural development

Nerve cells are formed by normal cell division (mitosis) from cells along the lining of the ventricles. This process of cell division occurs along the entire length of the ventricular system. The cells that are actively involved in the formation of nerve cells are called *neuroblasts,* but this is a rather general term used to describe neural cells of a primitive form. In principle, some neuroblasts along the lining of the ventricle seem to move slightly off the ventricular surface, where they incorporate chemicals needed for cell division and then drop back toward the ventricular surface before cell division takes place. One of the daughter cells will often start migrating away toward its final location, while the other may return toward the ventricle lining to repeat the process once again.

During development, cells seem to have a rather definite plan of development and migration established for them. To begin with, cells of different regions are formed at different times. The cells of the brainstem, medulla, and midbrain differentiate from their neuroblast parents long before the cells of the neocortex and cerebellum. Once formed, the nerve cells follow quite specific migratory routes, often over long distances, to reach their final positions. In Figure 4-3 groups of cells are shown as they migrate together along the neural tube of the chicken brain before hatching occurs. We do not know what starts this migratory movement or what ends it, nor can we account for the fact that some populations of cells—often involving a large number of cells—will differentiate, migrate, and then disappear before birth.

Not only do cells migrate toward specific locations in the brain and spinal cord, but the cell processes that grow out to muscles from the cell bodies in the spinal cord also show an amazing specificity in seeking certain muscle groups. Equally astounding is the fact that the types of muscles originally reached by a nerve process act to determine the character of the cell in the central nervous system.

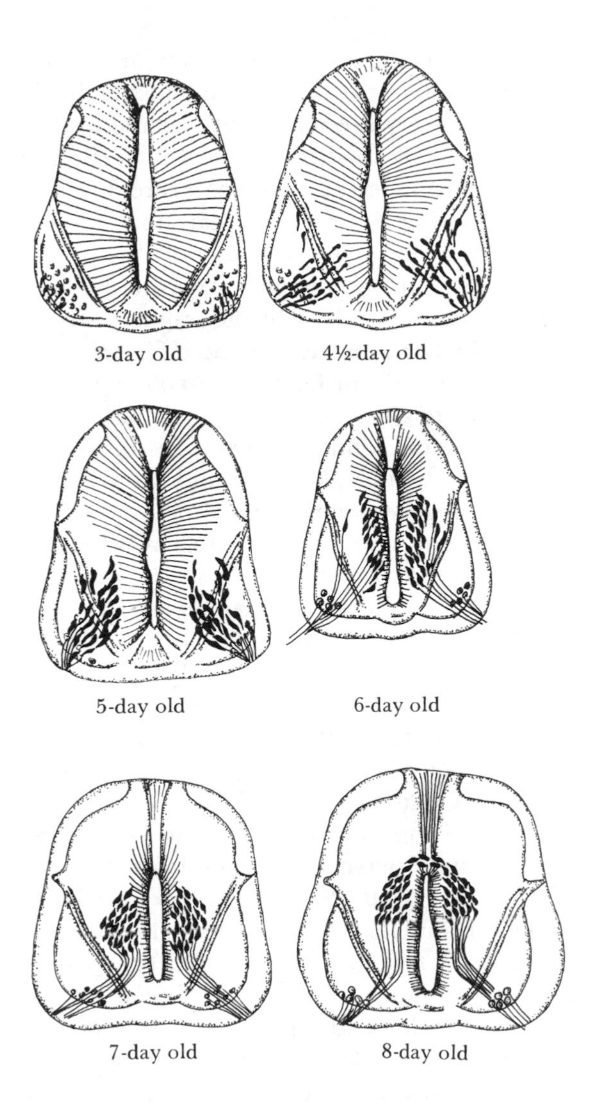

Figure 4-3 *Diagrammatic representation of the segregation and subsequent migration of cells making up the thoracic column in the chick embryo. In the 3-day-old chick embroyo, the somato-motor and the viscero-motor cells form a compact column. Beginning with the 4½-day-old embryo, there is a migration of preganglionic neurons. The remaining four diagrams illustrate the shift of the migrating cells from a ventro-lateral to a medio-dorsal position in embryos on the fifth, sixth, seventh, and eighth days of incubation. (From R. Levi-Montalcini.* J. morph., *1950,* 86, *253-283. Reprinted by permission of the author and the Wistar Press.)*

Nerve-muscle specificity During development, axons of nerve cells grow out into regions of skin and muscles from the primitive neural tissue of the embryonic spinal cord. Some of these processes will become axons, which will run out to the periphery of the body to control muscles, whereas processes of other cells will become dendrites and transmit information from the skin and muscles to the central nervous system. Great specificities of growth and function govern the creation of these systems in the developing organism.

As nerve processes grow out into the periphery of the body to make contact with particular muscles in the area, the muscle confers a new and very specific quality on the nerve cell whose axon has reached it. This new quality produces alterations in the fostering cell and in the central nervous system where the cell body is located, and this modification is more or less unalterable afterwards. Before original muscle contact, the neuron can "accept" contacts with many kinds of muscles, but after original contact the neuron develops a "preference" for muscles like those of the original group.

In higher animals the specification of neuron-muscle interaction occurs very early in fetal life. At later times, if nerve fibers get separated (e.g., through accidental cuts) from their muscles, they often will regenerate and send their processes to the original muscle groups. There is some flexibility, however, and if the original muscles cannot be reached by the regenerating neural process, they can reach other muscle groups or even end up on blood vessels or other nerve processes. Nerve processes that are cut usually regenerate in the periphery of the body but will not do so in the central nervous system.

NERVE-RECEPTOR SPECIFICITY Early in life, cell processes acting as receptive dendrites grow out from clusters of developing cells (neuroblasts) alongside the primitive spinal cord. As they reach the periphery of the body—for example, a skin area—they acquire a special property, a "local sign," of the region they have reached. The term "local sign" refers to the fact that in adult organisms direct electrical stimulation of a given nerve coming in from the periphery always produces the effect that would have resulted from stimuli arising from the peripheral skin or muscle area usually served by the nerve. This is true even though the nerve may have been moved or isolated surgically. It is as if activity in the nerve has come to be recognized as arising from some local, restricted region and this recognition is permanent.

If a strip of skin running from the middle of the back to the middle of the abdomen is removed from a larval frog, turned upside down and replaced on the frog, several remarkable events can be observed—including, first of all, the regrowth of the skin patch. Nerves that would normally supply the upper back now grow into skin that would ordinarily cover the abdomen, and nerves that would normally reach the abdomen grow into skin destined for the back. What happens when stimuli are applied to the back of the frog (which now has abdominal skin on it)? Will it respond as if it had been stimulated on the back (in accordance with the normal nerve supply), or will it respond as if the abdomen had been stimulated?

The answer is that the nerves reaching the rotated skin are modified so that the nerve cell processes reaching back skin tells the frog "back." Thus the frog makes responses that are inappropriate to the site of stimulation, scratching its underside when it is stimulated on the back (abdominal skin) and vice versa.

If the same experiment were performed on animals after a nerve had been normally "specified" by a skin area, (e.g., abdomen or back), then rotating the skin should make little difference in response to stimulation. Stimulation of skin of the back would always elicit responses directed to the back regardless of whether stomach skin had been placed there. This occurs because the nerve sprouts that reach the transplanted skin would be those in the vicinity that had already been "labeled" *back*. Since they had been specified earlier, this specification would remain.

For cells in both sensory and motor systems, then, there is a period, early in development, during which there is little or no specification of the information or movements these cells will serve. However, once original contact is made with a sensory surface or a muscle group, the die is cast and a permanent relationship is established.

The developing nervous system shows a remarkable degree of specificity during growth. Processes growing toward the brain from the retina of the eye, for example, reach predestined points in the visual centers of the midbrain with remarkable accuracy even after attempts have been made to disrupt the process—such as cutting and twisting them. Through all the debris and destruction caused by disruption of the pathway, the centrally growing processes manage to find the places located by similar processes in normal animals. The factors governing this highly specific growth are largely unknown, although chemical influences and levels of metabolic activity are undoubtedly involved.

From studies of the developing nervous system, everything seems to point toward a remarkable degree of specificity in the connections established between central agencies and peripheral mechanisms as well as between different regions of the central nervous system. These highly specific associations are established early in life and remain immutable thereafter. Often we have occasion to wish it were otherwise —as, for example, when a nerve supply to a particular body region is so badly damaged that recovery cannot occur. It would be helpful if another nerve supply could be diverted into the region and be able to take over the functions of the damaged system. But this is not the case. Specificity of function is the ever-present rule of the nervous system after specification has occurred early in life.

GROSS STRUCTURE OF THE NERVOUS SYSTEM

Having discussed the development of the brain and nervous system, we will now turn to a review of the finished product. All our illustrations will involve the nervous system of man but most of the fundamental properties of organization are common to all mammals.

The brain

At the top of the spinal cord, we reach the pinnacle of man's neural development, the brain. We may think of it as beginning at the medulla and continuing upwards through pons and cerebellum, midbrain, hypothalamus and thalamus, limbic system and basal ganglia, before it reaches the cortex (see Figures 4-4 and 4-5). In man the neocortex covers the surface of the brain and is extremely convoluted, as can be seen in Figure 4-6. The major neocortical areas are labeled in the sketch provided in Figure 4-7. The significance of these convolutions can be appreciated when one recognizes that about one-half of all of man's neocortex lies hidden from sight in the valleys (sulci) between the convolutions (gyri). Neocortex ranges in depth from about 1.5 to 4.0 millimeters in different cortical areas in man and from 1.0 to 2.0 millimeters in lower animals.

Cortex and *neocortex* are terms used to refer to cells arranged into more or less easily observed layers. The word *cortex* is the more general term that can be applied to any neural tissue arranged in layers. *Neocortex* refers to cortex that has six layers; other types of cortex have fewer layers. The "neo-" portion of the word reflects the belief that this type of cortex was the most recent phylogenetic acquisition in brain development among animals; however, this concept is a much debated point and the best course to follow is to think of neocortex as the most complex type of cortex, containing at least six recognizable layers.

At the top of the spinal cord is an enlarged region called the medulla (or medulla oblongata) and above it, the pons. All of the fiber tracts carrying information from the body ascend through this region, as do the nerve fibers descending from those higher regions of the brain which control bodily movements. In the pons and medulla, however, there are groups of nerve cells that send axons downstream into some of the most important internal organs. These clusters of cells (nuclei) act as centers for the activities of the heart and lungs, and their integrity is essential to life. Throughout the center of the midbrain and pons there is a network of cells that are believed to exert general and diffuse influences upon the activity of the higher regions of the brain and motor movements of the body. This region is called the brainstem reticular system (see pp. 109-112). Finally, in the pons, there are important interconnections with the cerebellum, the latter structure (as we have indicated) being regarded as important for maintenance of balance and posture as well as refinement and coordination of bodily movements. In addition the cerebellum receives information from all of the sensory systems and, in conjunction with the brainstem reticular formation, acts to regulate and control the activity of higher divisions of the brain.

Above the pons is the midbrain. Ascending and descending fiber tracts also pass through this region, and in it the reticular formation occupies a central position. At the top of the midbrain there are centers for movements related to vision and audition. At the bottom there are groups of cells that participate in coordinating motor movements.

Immediately above the midbrain is the relatively small but most important area called the hypothalamus. The border between the midbrain and hypothalamus is marked by the mammillary bodies, which are part of the hypothalamus. This region contains many groups of nerve cells that function as centers for many kinds of behavior related to maintaining the individual and perpetuating the species.

The hypothalamus extends both ahead and behind the optic chiasm. This is the point at which the optic nerves, one from each eye, come together; and it is at this point that some fibers are exchanged between the two optic nerves before the fibers continue back to reach areas in the dorsal thalamus. From the thalamus, information about visual events is transmitted (by axons of cells located there) to restricted areas of the neocortical surface. In a similar fashion, information arising from other sensory systems is transmitted to other, equally restricted, neocortical regions by other thalamic cell groups (nuclei).

The corpus callosum, a most prominent feature of Figures 4-4 and 4-5, is a collection of a large number of axons that connect areas of one hemisphere with corresponding areas of the other hemisphere.

The thalamus, located above the hypothalamus, has several kinds of cell groups (nuclei). One type contains cells that receive axons from one of the sensory systems and relay this information to the brain's neocortex, probably introducing certain modifications of the information too.

A second type of activity arises from regions of the ventral thalamus that are related to the modification of motor activities. There is yet

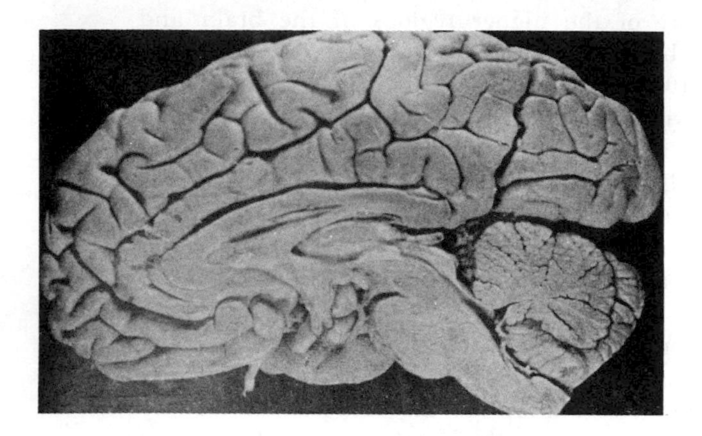

Figure 4-4 *Brain sectioned in the median plane. (From E. Gardner,* Fundamentals of neurology *(4th ed.). Philadelphia: W. B. Saunders Company, 1963.)*

another type that has not been previously discussed. This third type of thalamic area contains cells that project to wide regions of neocortex and other higher brain regions. Since cells in these nuclei diffusely bombard brain regions, their role in behavior is similar to that of the brainstem reticular formation.

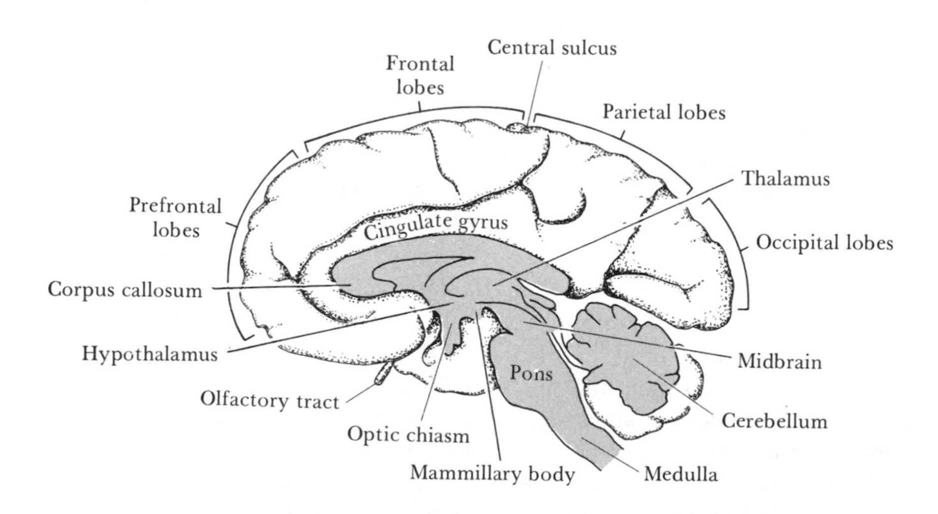

Figure 4-5 *Diagram of medial surface of the brain shown in Figure 4-4. (Adapted from E. Gardner,* Fundamentals of neurology *(4th ed.). Philadelphia: W. B. Saunders Company, 1963.)*

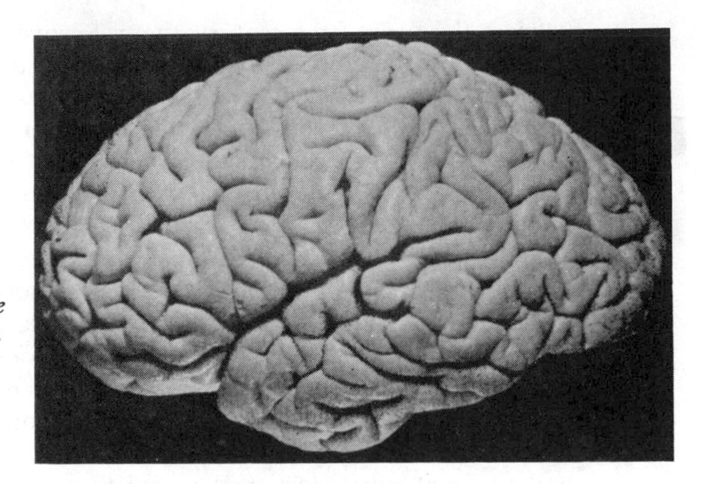

Figure 4-6 *Lateral surface of the human brain. (From E. Gardner,* Fundamentals of neurology *(4th ed.). Philadelphia: W. B. Saunders Company, 1963.)*

The fibers leaving the thalamus from the relay nuclei for vision all go into the visual projection areas in the occipital lobes. The axons of cells in the thalamic relay nuclei for hearing reach cells in special areas of the temporal lobes, and neocortical cells just behind the central sulcus receive impulses originally arising from receptors in the muscles, joints, and skin (the somatosensory system).

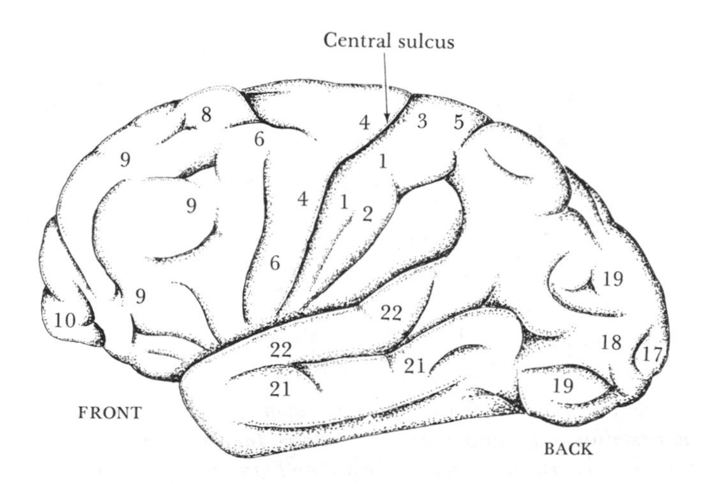

Figure 4-7 *Lateral surface of the human brain showing the numerical designations of cortical areas developed by Brodmann.*

Before the turn of the century, many European anatomists had developed intricate methods of describing the different regions of the neocortex. These methods were sometimes based upon the cellular organization of the regions and sometimes were based upon the interconnections of one region with others. The most widely used system is that proposed by Brodmann, which designates neocortical areas by numbers. The areas shown in Figure 4-7 with the numbers 3, 1, and 2 on them are those that receive most of the input relayed from the dorsal thalamus (which arose from the somatosensory system). Some somatosensory information is projected to the areas just ahead of the central sulcus as well. Area 17 is the neocortical area that receives information from the visual relay nucleus, and areas 18 and 19 are called "visual association areas." The dorsal portion of the temporal lobe is that neocortical region associated with audition. The regions ahead of the central sulcus (designed 4 and 6) are the primary motor areas. The major sensory and motor areas are also illustrated in Figure 4-8.

In Figure 4-8 we may compare the relative amounts of brain surface occupied with the reception of sensory information and with motor activities. As one goes higher and higher in the phylogenetic scale, the amount of brain committed to a given sensory (or motor) responsibility

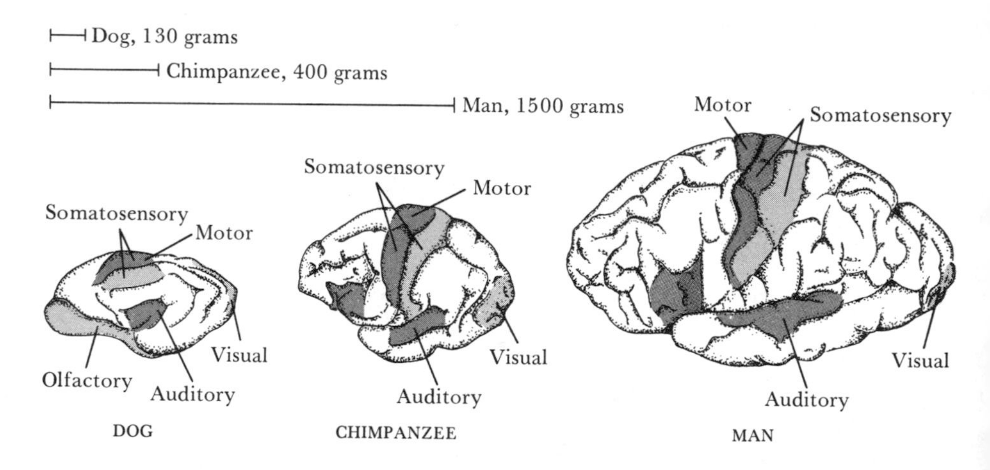

Figure 4-8 *Lateral views of three mammalian brains drawn to scale to show the relative sizes of primary sensory and motor areas of the dog, the chimpanzee, and man. (Adapted from G. W. Bartelmez, Man from the point of view of his development and structure, in* The nature of the world and of man, *by H. H. Newman, by permission of the University of Chicago Press. © 1926 by the University of Chicago. All rights reserved.)*

becomes less and less. Areas of neocortex that have not been identified with specific sensory or motor tasks are called *association areas.* (In passing we should note that it is often assumed, implicitly at least, that the greater the amount of association cortex, the greater will be the behavioral flexibility of the animal. This is speculation, however, since the precise determination of amounts of association cortex and satisfactory definitions of complex behavior have not yet been made.)

The thalamic relay cells of the somatosensory system project to cells behind the central fissure in a rough approximation to the location of the receptors in the body. Today we know that there are many cells other than those located in the primary somatosensory areas that receive fibers coming in from specific body receptors. For example, the primary motor areas also receive a number of afferent fibers from the muscles and skin. Thus, while there is anatomical and functional evidence for describing certain areas as motor and others as sensory, we must recognize that a considerable overlap exists in function throughout the cortex.

The primary motor areas just mentioned lie immediately anterior to the central sulcus (areas 4 and 6 of Figure 4-7). The term *motor cortex* or *motor strips* refers to areas of cortex in which the majority of cells have axons that extend down into the spinal cord and end upon cells whose axons project directly to muscles in the periphery of the body.

The control of muscles

When one considers control of the muscles of the body, one generally includes the muscles themselves, the nerves running to them from the spinal cord, and the mechanisms of the central nervous system—whose cells participate in the control or regulation of the muscle activities. Outside the spinal cord, the peripheral mechanisms of the nervous system related to muscular control are those nerve cells having axons that end not in contact with another nerve cell but rather in muscle. Chemicals released at the termination of the axons produce a contraction of the muscle. At the end of the axons there is a swelling or enlargement known by several names, one of which is the *terminal* (or *end*) *bouton* of the axon. It is in this region of the end bouton that chemicals are stored in minute packets. Probably each packet contains the same number of molecules of this transmitter chemical as the next. When the changes in the axon membrane reach the terminal bouton, some of the tiny packets release their chemicals into a very small space between it and the muscle. This "special region" of a muscle is sensitive to the chemical released, and when the chemical is detected at this special region the muscle contracts. In most muscles of an adult animal these specialized zones of muscles are the only zones responsive to the chemical released by the terminal boutons of the axons. The place where the axon end boutons are just next to the muscle is called the neuromuscular (nerve-muscle) junction. The chemical (acetylcholine) released at the end boutons of axons that reach the muscles responsible for moving the body is the same as that found at the junctions between some, but not all, nerve cells in the brain.

The contractions of all kinds of muscles are governed by nerve fibers: Both the somatic muscle system, which moves the body, and the muscles of the internal organs are controlled by the central nervous system. The nerves that run to somatic muscles are called, collectively, the *somatic motor system*. The nerves that end in the muscles of the internal organs and glands are called the *autonomic nervous system*.

THE SOMATIC MUSCLE SYSTEM The organization of the peripheral somatic muscle system is less complex than the peripheral organization of the autonomic nervous system. Cells in the motor areas of the neocortex and other forebrain regions initiate impulses which arrive at cells in the spinal cord.

In some species these descending axons reach large cells in the ventral aspects of the spinal cord, whose axons in turn leave the cord and project directly to muscles. Such cells are called motoneurons (motor neurons). In other species, the axons descending in the cord end upon small cells (interneurons) near the large motoneurons. Axons from these small cells make direct contact with the motoneurons. The significance of these two arrangements is not known. In any case, it is over the axons of the motor neurons that neural impulses reach the muscles.

If anything happens to damage the nerves that run from the spinal cord to the muscles, the muscles become limp and cannot be contracted by normal means. In other words, a complete flaccid paralysis is produced when the motor nerve supply to the muscles is interrupted. Interestingly enough, muscle activity also depends upon the nerves that run *from* the muscle to the cord and higher centers (the *afferent* nerves). If these afferent nerves are severed the muscles become weak and flaccid, too. Muscle movements depend upon a complex interplay in the cord of afferent (sensory) and efferent (motor) impulses.

Certain simple behavioral acts are organized within the cord. For instance, when the patellar tendon is struck, certain muscles of the leg contract; this sends your foot forward in the knee-jerk reflex often demonstrated in the physician's office. This reflex *can* occur without assistance of the higher areas of the nervous system, but normally it is modulated by higher nervous centers. We should recognize the extent of this modulating effect even in simple reflexes. Even though the physician taps your crossed knee with his rubber hammer, you *can* consciously inhibit the reflex. Excitement or arousal increases the size of the reflex. The basic mechanism is built into the spinal cord, but it is under the direct influence of the brain.

The motor areas of the neocortex are not arranged haphazardly. There is a systematic organization in which adjacent cortical cells influence neighboring muscle cells. One interesting facet of the organization of the motor cortex is the ratio of the number of neural cells to the number of muscle cells in a given body area. In general we observe that those areas of the body which are concerned with fine discriminations and delicate movements have the greatest number of controlling cells in the cortex.

However, the axons that run to the motor neurons in the cord originate in many other places in the cortex than the "classical area" just in front of the central fissure. There are secondary and tertiary motor areas for most muscle groups. Stimulation of any area of the neocortex can produce bodily movements when the animal is unanesthetized and free from physical restraints. There may be a great number of highly organized motor areas of the brain of which we know little, and *all areas* of the cortex may be involved in the production of our normal behavioral acts. There is probably no area of the brain that is entirely motor or entirely sensory in function.

THE AUTONOMIC NERVOUS SYSTEM The autonomic nervous system is "in charge of" the internal organs and glands. It is divided into two basic components: the *sympathetic division* and the *parasympathetic* division. Anatomically, the sympathetic division is defined by two long nerve trunks, running in parallel, which lie outside of the spinal cord along its ventral surface and extend from the base of the skull to near the tail-end of the vertebral column. The nerve fibers that extend outward from these "sympathetic trunks" make contact with the viscera (internal organs) and glands. The action of the sympathetic division is to prepare the body for emergencies and stress by increasing the reactions of the viscera and by altering bodily metabolism.

The parasympathetic division includes the cranial nerves, which supply the internal organs and certain of the facial muscles. A second component of the parasympathetic division leaves the spinal cord near its base and supplies internal organs in the pelvic region. In general the parasympathetic division acts to maintain the essential processes of digestion, food metabolism, and excretion, and maintains an overall high level of efficiency for the vegetative processes.

Some experts on the autonomic nervous system believe that the traditional anatomical subdivisions are inadequate, because the division of labor among the two divisions is not absolute. Some fibers of the sympathetic division tend to produce effects that promote general body maintenance rather than prepare the body for emergencies—that is, in a functional sense they act like fibers of the parasympathetic division. The same kind of "reverse situation" is found with some fibers of the parasympathetic division—that is, they act as if they "should" belong with the sympathetic division. In addition, the status of most, if not all, internal organs reflects a balance between the amounts of sympathetic and parasympathetic activity reaching them. Perhaps a better delineation would be to divide the autonomic nervous system into subgroups on the basis of the neurotransmitters used in the contacts between nerve cells or between the axons and the glands or muscles affected. Another method that might be used to distinguish two or more divisions of the autonomic system would be on the basis of differential reactivity to drugs.

Because there is no complete agreement about the most useful method of defining the divisions of the autonomic nervous system, we will abide by the traditional approach—with the warning that the sympathetic-parasympathetic division may not be entirely accurate. Figure 4-9 shows some of the internal organs and their relationship to the two traditional divisions of the autonomic nervous system.

There are many mysteries remaining to be solved with regard to the autonomic nervous system. One of the most pressing is the relation of the peripheral autonomic nervous system to higher regions of the brain. We have discovered the regions of the neocortex that are most closely associated with the regulation of the somatic muscles, but we know very little about regions of the neocortex that contribute to the regulation of the internal organs. It is clear that the hypothalamus and the limbic system are involved in the regulation of the internal organs and glands, but nothing is known about *how* these areas are tuned and modified by the neocortex.

The internal organs and glands are regulated in part by the higher portions of the nervous system, but there is another controlling and regulating system that merits our attention: the endocrine system.

The endocrine glands

The body's glands can be categorized on the basis of whether they secrete their chemical contents through a duct or not.

Glands that secrete their chemicals through ducts produce their effects upon a highly restricted portion of the body—namely, those regions into which the ducts lead. If they do not secrete through ducts

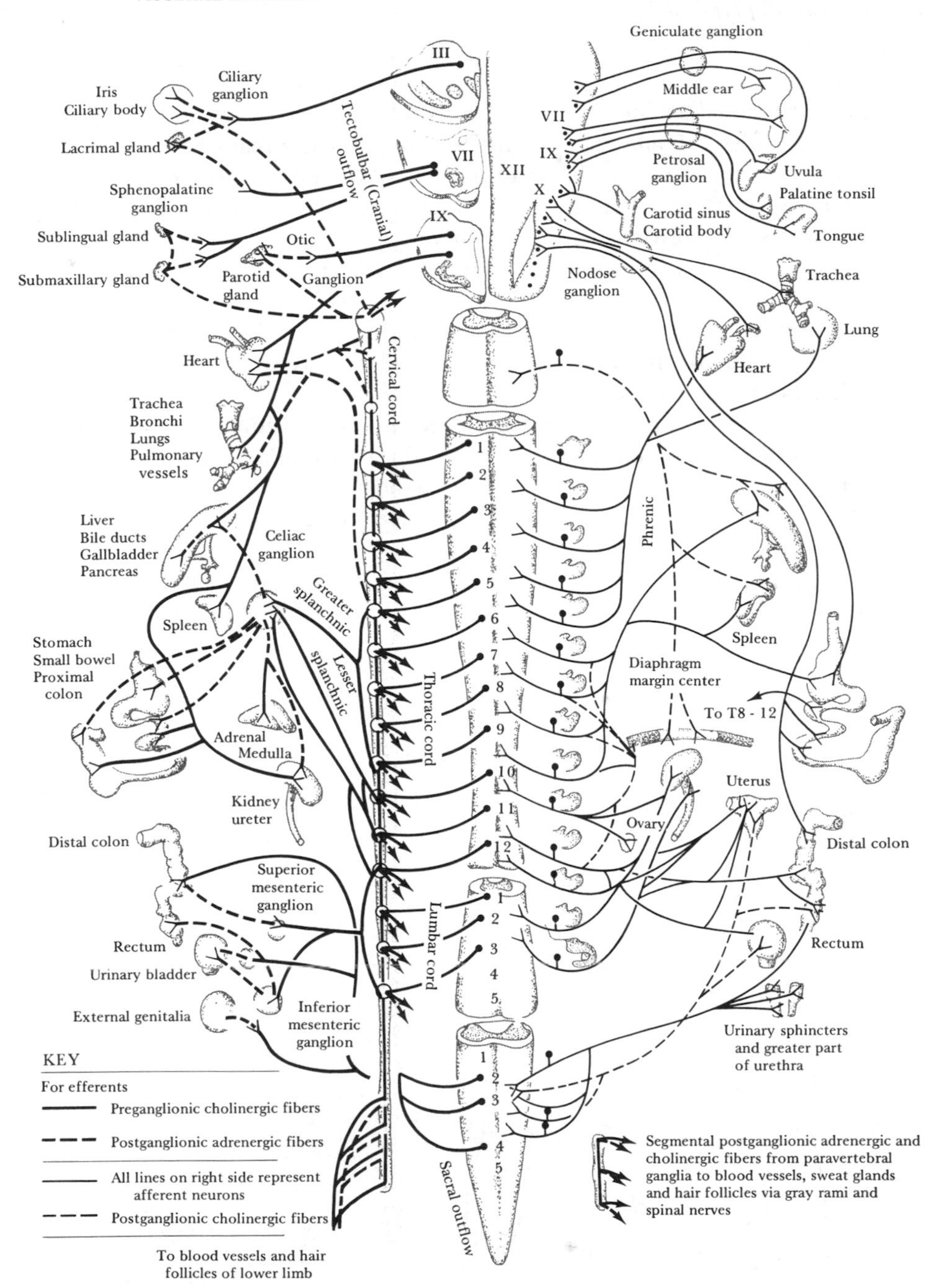

Figure 4-9 *Diagrammatic representation of the autonomic nervous system with emphasis on the efferent and afferent nerve supplies to internal organs. (From T. C. Ruch and J. Fulton,* Medical physiology and biophysics *(18th ed.). Philadelphia: W. B. Saunders Company, 1960.)*

they are called *endocrine* glands. Substances secreted by the endocrine glands, called *hormones,* are sent into the blood stream and, therefore, may cause effects of a widespread nature. Many hormones are of extreme importance in the individual's behavior and development. Figure 4-10 illustrates the positions of the major endocrine glands.

There are many hormones secreted by the *pituitary* gland, which lies below the anterior margin of the hypothalamus. This gland is often called the master gland of the body, for its hormones influence the secretions of many other endocrine glands as well as a number of other bodily activities.

At least nine hormones are secreted by the pituitary gland. These hormones control the growth of the body; stimulate the sex glands; control the secretions of the adrenal glands; stimulate milk production in females; control the development and hormonal secretion of the thyroid gland; stimulate production of the hormone *insulin* by cells in the pancreas; regulate blood pressure; and control the reabsorption of water by the kidneys. Since the endocrine system is like a chemical communication

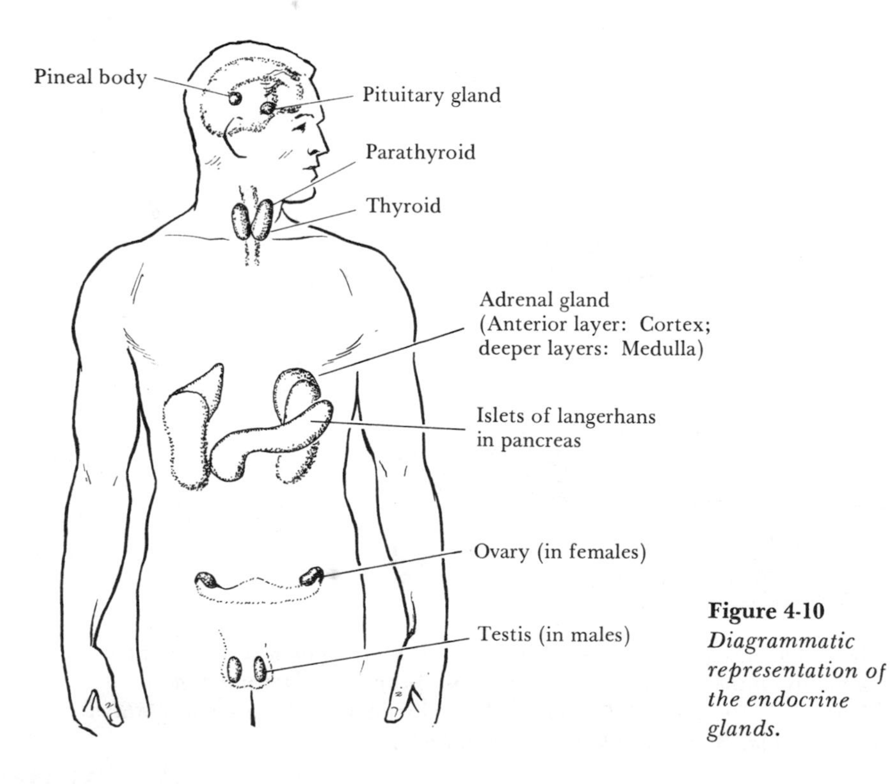

Figure 4-10 *Diagrammatic representation of the endocrine glands.*

system, sending messages throughout the body via the circulatory system, the pituitary gland can be thought of as a central communication center for this system. One type of message that holds special interest is that which regulates and controls growth.

Two types of hormones are involved with growth: the pituitary hormone *somatotrophin,* and the hormone *thyroxine,* which is secreted by the thyroid glands.

Malfunctions of the thyroid gland result in too much secretion or too little hormone secretion. When too little *thyroxine* is secreted everything slows down. In children, this results in arrested physical and behavioral development. Children so affected are described as suffering from *cretinism.* They usually have a severe form of mental retardation. In adults, an underactive thyroid gland will produce a disease known as *myxedema,* in which the skin becomes thick, the hair becomes dry, and weight gains may occur. Mental activities become less vigorous in myxedema.

An overactive thyroid gland will produce the condition known as *hyperthyroidism.* With this condition, people become very nervous, heart rates increase, and the general metabolic functions of the body are disturbed.

Iodine is an important chemical for the proper functioning of the thyroid gland. The thyroid picks up iodine from the blood and combines it with other chemicals to produce *thyroxine.* This chemical is changed into different forms in the body's cells, and these transformed chemicals control the rate at which oxygen and food are metabolized by the cells.

On top of the thyroid glands are the several, very small parathyroid glands; they produce hormones that regulate calcium and phosphorus balances in the body by governing the release of phosphates by the kidneys and by dissolving bone to liberate calcium. If the parathyroids fail to work effectively, the supply of calcium and phosphorus in the blood becomes depleted, and this condition will affect the usual activities of both nerve and muscle. Excessive nervousness and muscle spasms often result.

Insulin is a hormone secreted by the pancreas; it acts upon individual cells to allow blood sugar to enter them. People unfortunate enough to produce too little of this hormone are commonly called *diabetics.* When there is an insufficient amount of insulin, the individual cells cannot absorb and use the available blood sugars and the blood sugar becomes elevated. With the injection of insulin the cells can absorb the sugar, and the blood sugar level drops toward normal. The actual mechanism whereby insulin controls the cell's membrane to allow sugar to enter is still unknown.

The adrenal glands (located on top of the kidneys) secrete hormones from their outer layers (cortex) and their centers (medulla). The medulla of the adrenal glands is under neural control (see Figure 4-9), whereas the cortex is regulated by hormones released by the pituitary. The hormones produced in the adrenal cortices control the carbohydrate and sodium balances of the body, while the adrenal medulla produces epinephrine (adrenalin) and norepinephrine (noradrenalin).

The cortical hormones of the adrenal glands that are best known are *cortisone* and *hydrocortisone*. These substances are most important in assisting the body's reactions to stress and to diseases that tend to produce inflammation. Many inflammatory diseases and allergic reactions are now treated by supplemental administration of these hormones. *Addison's disease* is a term used to describe the symptoms produced by malfunctions of the adrenal cortex. It includes muscle weakness, low blood pressure, and a tendency to tire easily.

The hormones epinephrine and norepinephrine, secreted by the medulla of the adrenal glands, act upon the body in ways that tend to help it mobilize for emergency reactions. Epinephrine stimulates secretion of sugar by the liver, increases the heart rate, and raises the blood pressure by increasing the heart rate. Norepinephrine raises the blood pressure through constriction of the peripheral blood vessels. The hormones of the adrenal gland, especially the medulla, act in a coordinated fashion with the sympathetic division of the autonomic nervous system to produce complete bodily preparedness for emergencies. The combined reactions of the sympathetic division and the adrenal glands are sometimes referred to as sympathetic-adrenal reactions.

The role of the sex hormones in differentiating the brain early in life has already been discussed. Undoubtedly these hormones play an important role in sexual behavior at maturity, as well. In addition, the sex hormones regulate the development of the "secondary sexual characteristics": body hair, beard, breasts, etc. In the male, sex hormones are secreted by the testes, but in the female the hormone system is more complicated. Two of the three types of hormones secreted by the ovaries, the estrogens and progesterone, are important for normal sexual activities and the monthly estrous cycle, as well as for the development of secondary sexual characteristics. The third ovarian hormone relaxes the muscles of the birth canal so that the baby can pass at the appropriate time.

It must be remembered that the reactions of any endocrine gland are controlled by the environment as well as by the activity in other endocrine glands. This was demonstrated in the previous chapter by the example of the ring dove. These birds will lay eggs only when they are allowed to observe a male exhibiting courtship behaviors. This visual stimulation produces changes in the bird's endocrine system that induce egg laying. How the environment influences hormone production is not well understood, but it must involve the sensory systems and also those regions of the brain which influence the master endocrine gland, the pituitary. As the sensory systems will be described in the next chapter, we will next consider those brain mechanisms most closely associated with the regulation of the endocrine glands.

The limbic system

The term "limbic lobe" was first used by Broca in 1878 to designate the cortex that surrounds the upper portions of the brainstem. The limbic system is a common denominator of all mammalian brains. Figure 4-11 shows the

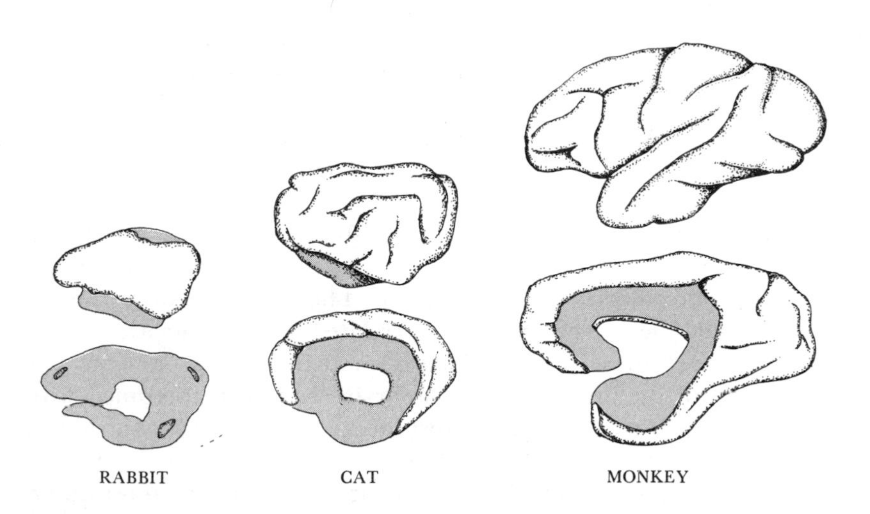

Figure 4-11 *Lateral (above) and medial (below) surfaces of the brains of a rabbit, a cat, and a monkey. The limbic lobe (shaded area) forms a common denominator in the brains of all mammals and seems physiologically to be a common base for a variety of behaviors involved in self-preservation and preservation of the species. Note how the limbic lobe surrounds the thalamus (the word* limbic *means "forming a border around"). (Adapted from P. D. MacLean, Studies on the limbic system ("visceral brain") and their bearing on psychosomatic problems, in E. Wittkower and R. A. Cleghorn Eds.,* Recent developments in psychosomatic medicine. *London: Pitman Medical Publishing Co. Ltd., 1954.)*

areas of the brain that are designated as limbic system in the rabbit, cat, and monkey. As the amount of neocortex increases, the *relative* amount of brain tissue in the limbic system decreases.

The limbic system is comprised of groups of nerve cells existing as cortex (in layers) or in nuclear groups; tracts of fibers interconnect them. The major units are listed below and are illustrated in greater detail in Figure 4-12.

1. The hypothalamus
2. Nuclear masses of the amygdala, septal area, anterior nucleus of the thalamus
3. Cortical areas: hippocampus cingulate cortex, orbito-frontal cortex, temporal pole, etc.
4. Fiber tracts connecting various regions of the limbic system, e.g., the fornix, stria terminalis

Outside of the term *hypothalamus,* which has been mentioned before, the terms used to describe the limbic system (Figure 4-12) must seem strange. They are uncommon and difficult to master. Throughout the remaining chapters we will be returning to study some of them in connection with learning, motivation, and emotion. The diagram presented in Figure 4-12 will be useful at these times. For the present, a brief summary based on evolutionary trends may provide an overview of the system.

In animals below mammals, there is a sharp functional distinction between the forebrain areas that are on the lateral surfaces of the hemispheres and those which are in the middle. The lateral surfaces contain nerve cells and fibers that seem to be related to the somatic muscle system that is used to move the animal around in its environment. The cells and fibers of the middle of the forebrain seem to be occupied with regulation of the internal organs. Most structures of the limbic system are derived from tissues of this middle position. Figure 4-13 shows a highly schematized submammalian brain; arrows designate those interconnections with the hypothalamus of areas thought to be primitive representations of the hippocampus, septal area, and amygdala. These same connections exist in mammalian brains, only in the more highly developed brains the limbic structures have moved and rather long fiber tracts stretch between the structures. For example, in the schematic brain shown in Figure 4-13 the hippocampus lies adjacent to the septal area and the septal area is adjacent to the hypothalamus. In the more advanced brain diagramed in Figure 4-12, the same interconnections are found—but now a long fiber tract called the fornix must be used to maintain them.

Notice that there are two bundles of fibers lying in the hypothalamus

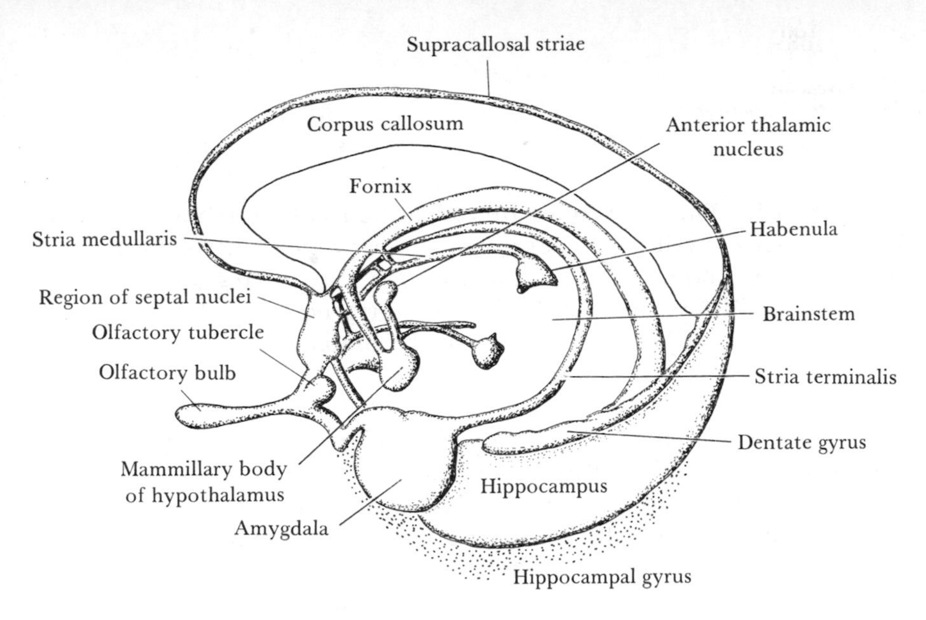

Figure 4-12 *Schematic representation of the relationships among various subcortical structures of rhinencephalon, as if seen through lateral surface of the brain. (Adapted from P. D. MacLean, Psychosomatic disease and the "visceral brain": Recent developments bearing on the Papez theory of emotion.* Psychosom. med., *1949,* 11, *338–353.)*

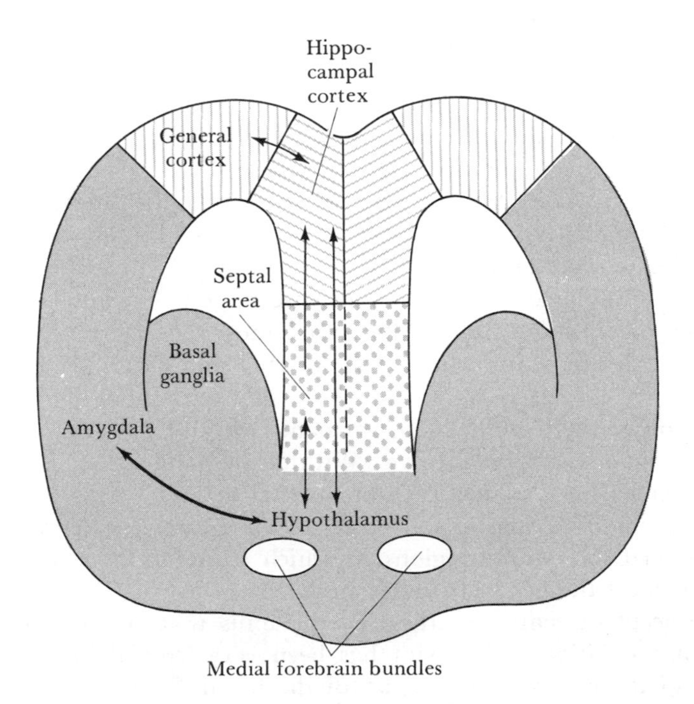

Figure 4-13 *Highly schematized drawing of a primitive, premammalian brain, showing interrelationships of areas thought to be precursors of the limbic systems structures in mammals.*

in Figure 4-13. These structures are called the medial forebrain bundles. In most higher brains they are systems of very small nerve fibers that run along the bottom of the brain from the anterior regions back into the midbrain. They pass through the lateral reaches of the hypothalamus and represent a major system by which the limbic system communicates with lower regions of the brain.

In higher brains the original proximity of the amygdala and the hypothalamus is also lost. The interconnections are maintained through the development of another long fiber tract, the *stria terminalis.* But, however distorted and displaced the limbic system becomes in the complicated brains of higher animals, all of the structures maintain their close association with the hypothalamus.

As mentioned before, the hypothalamus is an area at the base of the brain just anterior to the upper end of the brain stem. About the size of a large marble in adult man, it is an extremely complex structure, which comprises the most ventral part of the diencephalon, lying just below the thalamus. The hypothalamus itself is not a homogeneous structure but is made up of regions with different functions and roles in behavior.

Electrical stimulation of the anterior hypothalamus, through implanted electrodes, produces effects that are typical of those mediated by the parasympathetic division of the autonomic nervous system. Stimulation of the posterior portions of the hypothalamus results in activities of the emergency type served by the sympathetic division (increased heart rate, blood pressure, and respiration). However, the effects of electrical stimulation of the hypothalamus are not restricted to the internal organs. When the anterior portion is stimulated, there is also a general reduction in the tension of the somatic musculature. When the posterior regions are stimulated, there is an increase in somatic muscle tensions. Thus the organization of the hypothalamus reflects a "total body system," which acts to influence both internal and external organs and muscles.

A division of the hypothalamus into anterior and posterior areas is a very gross method of description. Within the anterior and posterior zones are much finer anatomical systems that are related to the control of more specific functions of the body. In some cases the term "center" has been used to indicate regions in which stimulation or lesions can selectively affect the behavior under study.

The concept of centers in the hypothalamus that participate in the control or regulation of behavior has been very fruitful in our understanding of the central organization of the brain. There are regions in the hypothalamus that regulate the sleep-wakefulness patterns of the animal, the initiation and cessation of eating behavior, water-intake, and aggressive behavior. These brain systems will be discussed in appropriate sections of later chapters.

Anatomically, the hypothalamus is organized into many nuclear groups. Certain nuclei have been more or less clearly associated with certain behaviors—for example, eating or drinking—while others have not. It is a mistake to think, however, that systems of behavior must always be associated with specific nuclei. Nuclei are groups of cells that are distinct enough from other surrounding areas to be labeled when they are appropriately stained and viewed under a microscope. Functional systems of behavior may be found in part of one nucleus, or they may extend through several nuclei, or even be widely scattered and not associated with any particular nuclear grouping.

Other subcortical systems

Other than the limbic system, among the neural mechanisms of the brain which lie beneath the neocortical mantle are two that are of special interest to psychologists: the diffusely projecting systems and the basal ganglia.

THE DIFFUSELY PROJECTING SYSTEMS Cells located in several subcortical regions participate in the regulation of the overall activity of the nervous system. These cells project to wide expanses of the central nervous system and act to enhance or inhibit activities in these areas. They are called diffusely projecting systems because their fields of influence are much broader than usually found in the traditional sensory or motor systems.

Three regions of the central nervous system are thought to be the most significant portions of the diffusely projecting systems: (1) the brainstem reticular formation; (2) the posterior hypothalamus; and (3) certain thalamic nuclei.

Throughout the spinal cord and running to the forward margin of the midbrain, there is a central core of nerve cells whose processes intertwine and interconnect so much as to appear as a fine mesh or *net* (reticulum) when appropriately stained and viewed under a microscope. This system of small cells with intermingled processes probably has many similar functions throughout its extent, but the system has been most extensively studied at the level of the midbrain and medulla. In the upper regions of the cord it is referred to as the brainstem reticular formation. Figure 4-14 shows a cross-section of the brainstem with this

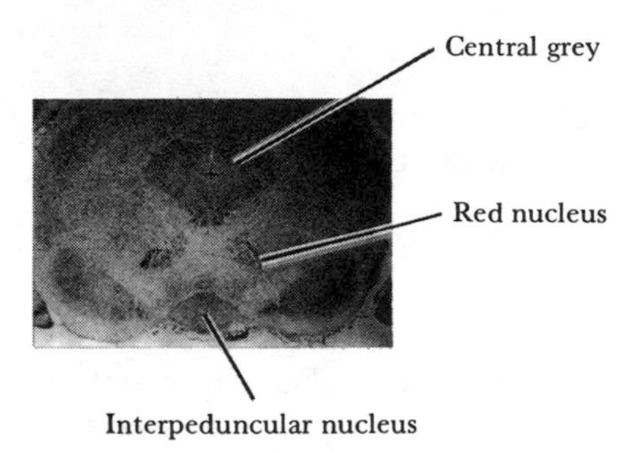

Figure 4-14 *Photomicrograph of the brainstem of a rat. Enclosed areas represent portions of the brainstem reticular formation.*

area outlined. The structure has been described as the neurological basis for learning, motivation, and the general alertness of the body and brain. There is no doubt that it does participate in many activities, but there is also no doubt that its participation is not *essential* to any of these activities.

Cells in the brainstem reticular formation act upon other cells located in upper regions of the brain, providing a diffuse rain of nervous impulses. Whether the bombardment is completely diffuse is an unsettled question. It may be that not all areas of the reticular formation bombard all areas of the brain with an equal intensity. However, some theories in psychology have assumed a complete generality of diffuseness of reticular formation activity, which is an oversimplification of the structure's activity. Assuming a generally diffuse bombardment, these theories then relate this bombardment to an activation or arousal of the brain. Evidence supporting this view has been obtained from studies of the electrical activity that can be recorded from the neocortical surface of the brain.

By electronic amplification, one can record the changing patterns of electrical potentials originating in the brain from electrodes placed on the brain surface or even from the scalp. These patterns originate in the neocortex and reflect the arousal or alertness of the person or animal from whom the records were obtained. Electrical stimulation of the brainstem reticular formation alters both waking and drowsing electroencephalographic (EEG) patterns to ones that are indicative of great arousal. Some of the EEG recordings obtained before, during, and after brainstem reticular formation stimulation are presented in Figure 4-15.

The brainstem reticular formation also can produce facilitation or inhibition of reflex movements of the extremities. The response of a leg to a tap of the patellar tendon reflex (the knee jerk) is easier to obtain and is of greater amplitude when certain areas of the brainstem reticular formation are stimulated. The brainstem reticular formation is a system (or systems) of neurons that modifies both the activity of the higher

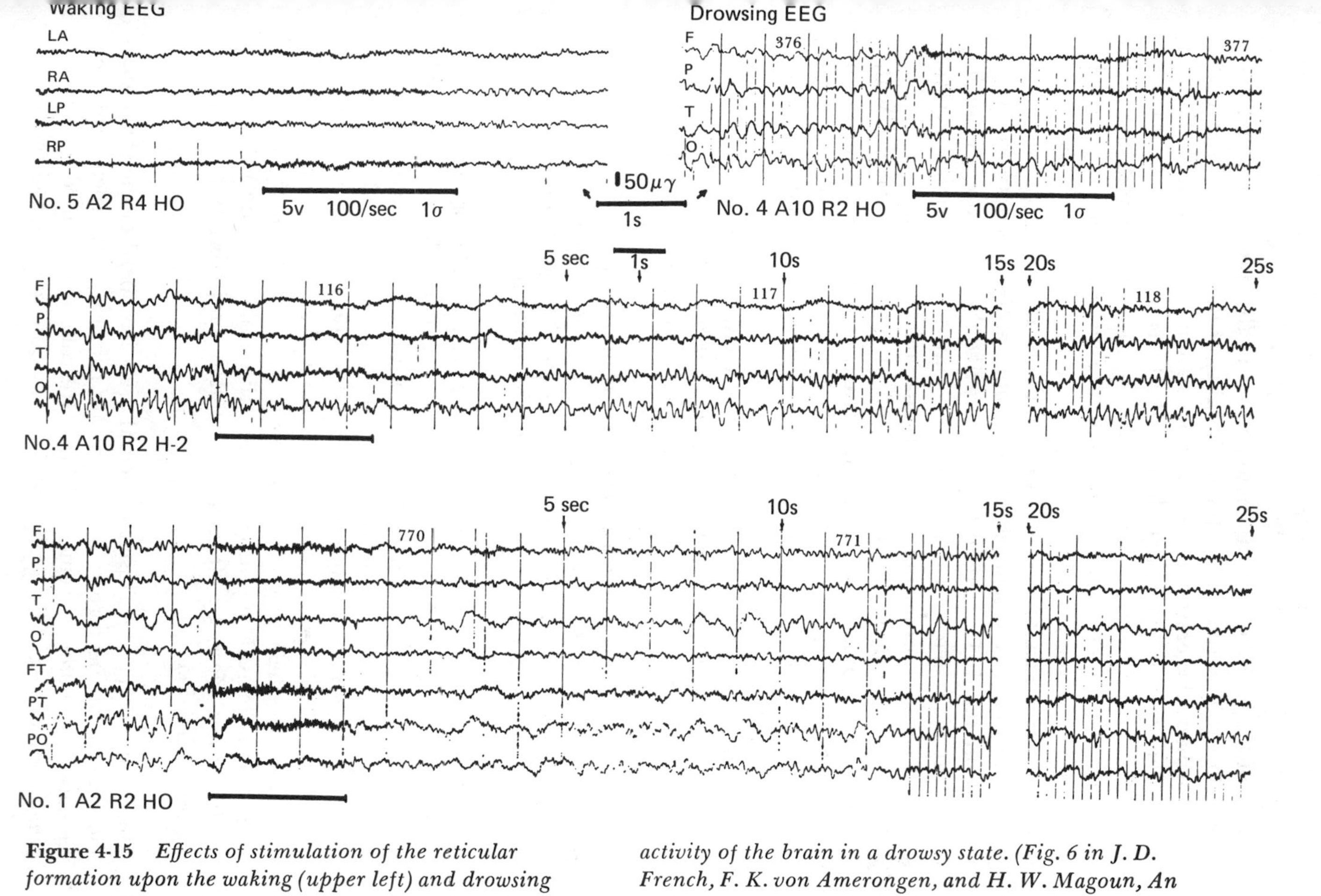

Figure 4-15 *Effects of stimulation of the reticular formation upon the waking (upper left) and drowsing (upper right) electroencephalograms. Two lower tracings illustrate long-lasting effects of such stimulation on the activity of the brain in a drowsy state. (Fig. 6 in J. D. French, F. K. von Amerongen, and H. W. Magoun, An activating system in the brain stem of monkey.* AMA arch. neurol. psychiat., *1952,* 68, *577–590.)*

regions of the brain and of the motoneurons in the spinal cord. Presumably it does this by controlling the excitability of the individual neurons.

Throughout the brainstem reticular formation, there are several subsystems that cannot be distinguished on the basis of microscopic appearance. These subsystems are differentially sensitive to chemicals applied to them. For example, when compounds like acetylcholine are injected into a region of the reticular formation, the brain waves produced are those of a more relaxed, less aroused condition. If norepinephrine is injected into exactly the same location, a more aroused pattern of brain waves is produced. These results and others like them produced throughout the limbic system reveal that two and maybe more chemical subsystems can coexist throughout the same anatomical system.

The forward end of the brainstem reticular formation merges with the posterior hypothalamus. It is from this area that electrical stimulation elicits reactions of the sympathetic branch of the autonomic nervous system and evokes related changes in the somatic musculature. These effects are coupled with general arousing effects throughout the brain. As a result the posterior hypothalamus is considered to be a part of the diffusely projecting systems of the central nervous system.

In the thalamus several nuclear groups produce rather generalized effects in many areas of neocortex. Stimulation of these nuclei tends to produce changed patterns of electrical activity in broad neocortical zones—toward either more or less aroused states. It is possible that the activating and inhibiting projections from the diffusely projecting thalamic nuclei that reach the neocortex produce the rhythmic fluctuations often found there.

The three diffusely projecting systems are responsible for augmenting and reducing activity at higher and lower regions along the central nervous system. Consequently, they influence both motor activities and activities of higher brain regions. All three regions share diffuse projections to wide regions of neural tissue, and they also share loose interweavings of fine dendrites and axons. It is likely that many sleep-inducing drugs produce their effects by influencing one or more of the diffusely projecting systems. Many drugs which activate or excite are thought to produce their effects by altering the diffusely projecting systems in an opposite direction.

THE BASAL GANGLIA A cluster of neural areas lies ahead of the thalamus and beneath the neocortex; these areas are primarily concerned with the regulation of motor movements. These are collectively called the *basal ganglia* and consist of the *globus pallidus, caudate nucleus,* and *putamen.*

For many years, these regions were considered to be servants of the motor regions of the neocortex, but recently their contributions to more complicated behaviors have been investigated. In some animals, disturbances of the caudate nucleus produce the perseverance of on-going behaviors. The basal ganglia also influence the processing of sensory information in poorly understood ways.

THE NEURON

Now that we have discussed the overall organization of the central nervous system, we shall consider the details of the building blocks out of which that system is made: the single nerve cells, or neurons.

No one knows how many neurons could be found in the brain of man or of any other mammal. The figure generally given (about 12 billion) is clearly an underestimate. Of these more than 12 billion cells, there are some 60 or more types of neurons that differ in shape; presumably these differences in shape are related to the cells' activities. No greater mistake could be made than to believe that all neurons resemble the schematic drawings of nerve cells like that shown in Figure 4-1 (p. 84).

When a special stain has been applied to show the cell body and its axon and dendrites, one can see structures such as are shown in Figure 4-16. Two major structural characteristics are found in most neurons: a large, diffusely branching dendritic region; and a large, pipelike process called the axon, which leaves the cell body to make contact with other cells and which has at its end the chemical apparatus required to release transmitter chemicals at point of contact with other cells.

If the cell body of a single, large, motoneuron of the spinal cord—which might really be 50 microns in diameter—were enlarged to the height of a man, its axon would be somewhat more than one foot in diameter and might reach as far as 25 miles on this enlarged scale. Actually, in this highly magnified scale, axons of 2.5 miles in length would be common. The dendritic regions would cover more modest ranges of 150 feet or so. Hopefully, this enhanced scale may help provide perspective on the long, large axon relative to the shorter dendritic processes—even though the actual sizes are 40,000 times smaller than just described. The differences between the dendritic branches and the axon reflect their quite different functional roles. The dendrites and the cell body provide the surfaces that are influenced by the axons of other nerve cells. The axon provides the mechanism of transmitting the special re-

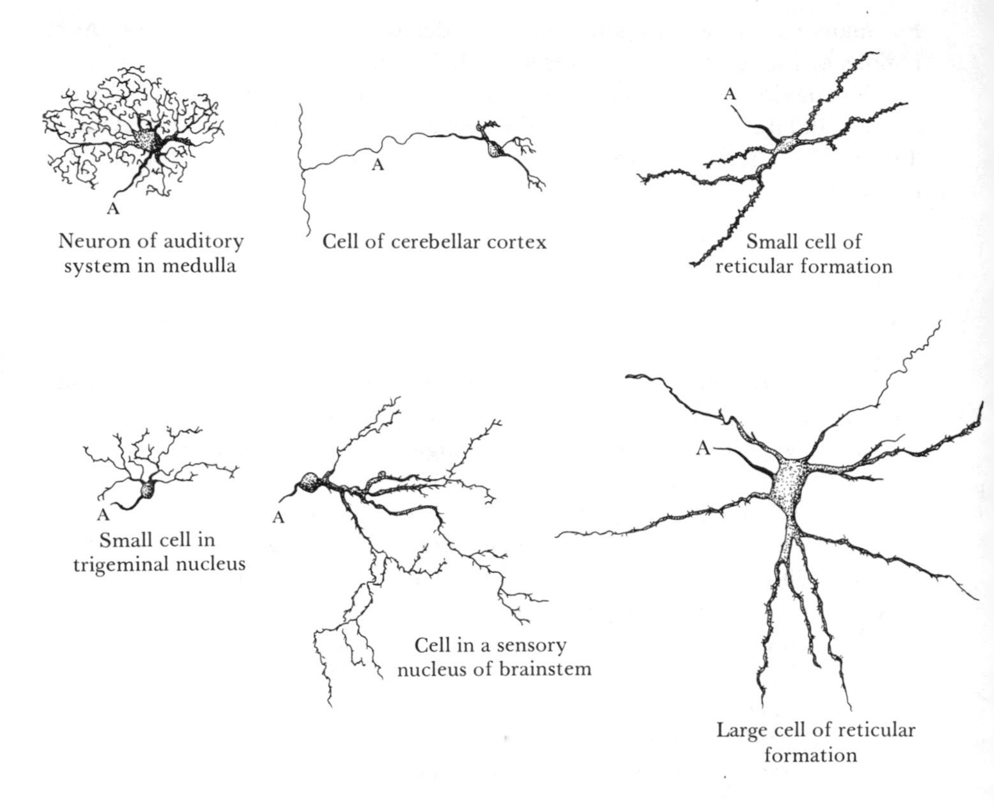

Figure 4-16 *Scaled drawings of some characteristic neurons whose axons and dendrites remain within the central nervous system. (Courtesy of Dr. Clement Fox, Wayne State University.)*

actions of the neuron cell body to other cells a sizable distance away. As many as 10,000 synaptic contacts may be made on the cell body and dendrites of a neuron. The cell's axon makes but a few contacts with other cells.

The cells of the human brain are not different in appearance or physiological reactions from the cells of brains in other mammals. This means that whatever the qualities of behavior that distinguish man from other animals, they, too, must be explained in terms of cellular activities common to all higher animals. It also means that knowledge of the principles concerning the activities of nerve cells can be derived from animal studies and the findings "transferred" to our understanding of the operation of the human brain.

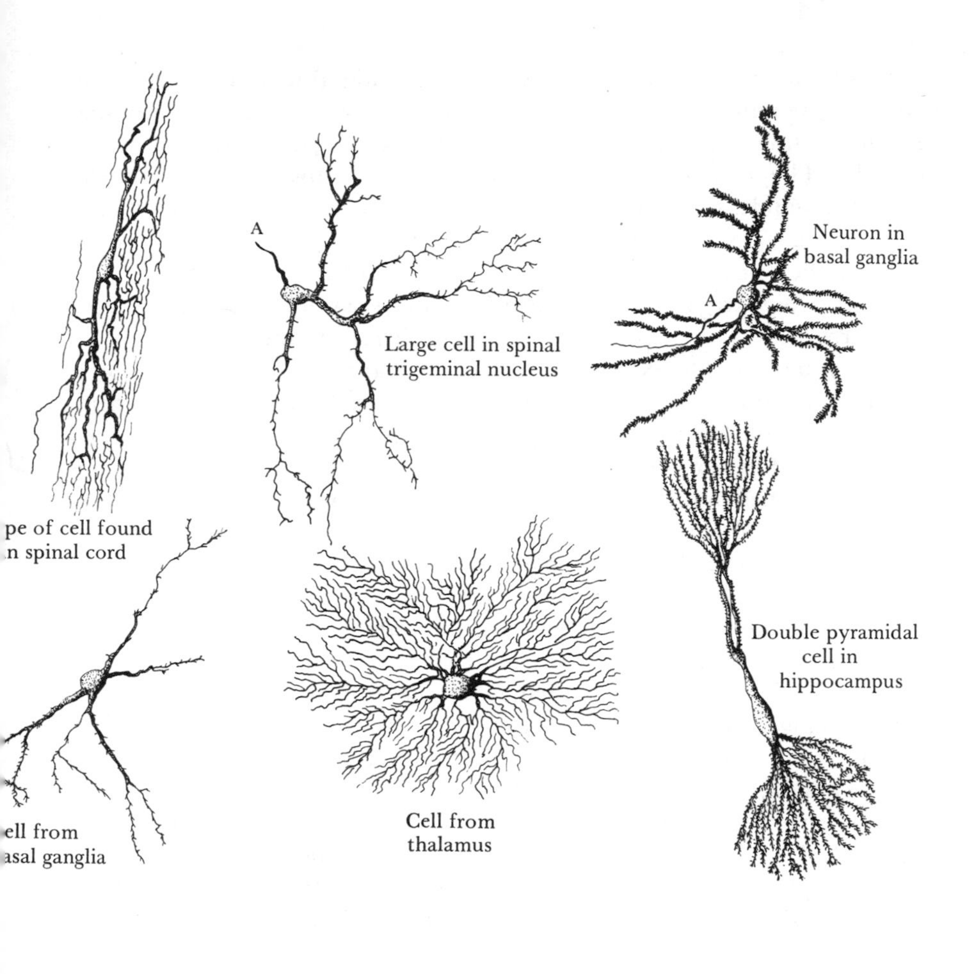

The cell body In its cytoplasm, the cell body of a neuron contains mechanisms responsible for the natural metabolic activities common to all living cells. It has a nucleus containing most of the genetic information in the form of DNA; mitochondria, which produce required energy through the metabolism of glucose; and many sites of protein formation. The neurons are highly active metabolically; correspondingly, they have a great number of mitochondria. In addition, running throughout the cytoplasm of the cell body are many cavities and thin membranes surrounding them. These infolded membrane surfaces wind in and through the cell body in a most intricate fashion.

Nerve and muscle cells both show a considerable difference in the electrical potential on the inside and outside of their cell membranes. In the resting state the inside of the cell is negative relative to the outside. The charge across the membrane is substantial, amounting to 70-thousandths of a volt. This electrical charge arises from differential distribution of ions, particularly sodium (Na^+) and potassium (K^+) on the two sides of the membrane. These positively charged ions are normally segregated to the outside of the membrane. This condition is referred to as the "polarized" state, which is found in the normal, resting situation. The Na^+ ions are actively transported to the outside of the cell membrane. Once outside, they are prevented from returning until the membrane pores through which they could pass are unblocked. This "blockade" of the Na^+ ions can be changed at appropriate times. While the distribution of K^+ is largely responsible for maintaining the electrical potential during the resting state, it is the Na^+ ions that are most significant for the change from the resting state to the "active" or "excited" state.

When the cell membrane becomes activated, the blockade that prevents the return of the Na^+ ions is lifted and these ions can rush into the interior of the cell. The change in the cell's membrane is due to actual changes in the membrane itself. The exact nature of these changes has not been definitely established, but they are related (1) to changes in the alignment of the lipid molecules that make up portions of the cellular membrane or (2) to the removal of calcium ions that have been blocking the pores. In any case, when either or both of these events happen, sodium ions can and do rush into the cell's interior. This reestablishes a condition of near equilibrium for Na^+ ions; thus the active state of a neuron is called a "depolarized' condition.

The rapid change in electrical potential across the cell membrane when it moves from the resting state to the active state produces the large electrical change that is usually described as the action or "spike" potential. A tracing of a cellular action potential is shown in Figure 4-17.

Two types of influences reach every neuron. One type causes a partial reduction in the polarized, resting condition of the membrane. This is an excitatory influence and consists in sodium ions being readmitted to the cells. The second produces effects in the opposite direction. More Na^+ ions are pumped to the outer surface of the cell membrane to produce a situation in which even more Na^+ ions are on the outside than usual. As a result, the cell is "hyperpolarized" and it is more difficult than usual to cause the "depolarized" or active state. The influences that tend to produce a reduction in the segregation of Na^+ ions are

Figure 4-17 *Action potential of a nerve fiber. (Adapted from H. S. Gasser, The classification of nerve fibers.* Ohio j. sci., *1941,* 41, *145–159.)*

termed *excitatory,* while those which produce an enhancement of the segregated condition are called *inhibitory.*

The dendrites Arising within the cell body of most nerve cells are many fine processes that extend around the cell body in several directions. Some dendrites can be fairly long, but as a general rule they are much shorter than the axon. Near the cell body the dendritic fibers contain sites of metabolic and protein-making activities (which the axon does not). These sites also provide an increased area for the axons of other cells to make contact. It is estimated that the dendritic surface of neurons in the cortex provides 15 times more available surface area than that of the cell bodies alone. Arising from the host of dendritic processes are small processes called "spines." These dendritic spines are most likely points of contact with axons arising from other cells.

Excitatory or inhibitory activities beginning in dendrites spread slowly toward the cell body. These events are termed "graded responses" because their effects are maximal at the point where the initiating events first occur, and they become less and less at points farther away from the point of original activity. The action potential generated by the cell membrane is not a graded response; when it occurs the membrane depolarizes to the maximum extent possible (all at once) and then it spreads down the axon to reach other cells. Whether an action potential is generated depends upon the sum total of the depolarizing influences reaching a trigger zone of the cell body—which is usually near the place at which the axon leaves the cell body. All of the excitatory (depolarizing) and inhibitory (hyperpolarizing) influences that reach this portion of the cell body—whether arising from sites on the dendrites or on the cell body itself—*summate* their effects in this one region. If the resultant is sufficiently depolarizing, the trigger region produces a *total* cell body depolarization that spreads down the axon as the *nerve impulse.*

The dendrites receive influences from thousands of other cells. Different types of influences reach different places on the dendrites, and there seems to be a highly systematic distribution of input to the dendrites. For example, the axons arising from cells in the visual relay nucleus of the thalamus will reach one particular portion of the dendrites of cells located in the visual neocortex. Axons from cells in the visual areas of the opposite neocortical area will reach another dendritic region. Axons from cells in still other regions will occupy other places along the dendritic trees. This specialized distribution of terminals along the dendrites is another example of the high degree of specialization found throughout the nervous system. Even within the incredibly complicated and interconnected systems of the brain, there is a vast degree of specialization.

The axon

It is down the axon that the nerve impulse travels in the form of depolarization of the membrane. The action potential generated at the cell body proceeds down the axon to its end at the enlarged endings called "boutons" or "feet." The axon serves as the channel by which one neuron influences others.

The spread of the action potential occurs in an all-or-none fashion. The flooding-in of the Na^+ occurs to the total ionic capacity of the membrane. The reaction is just as vigorous far away from the cell body as it is close to it, that is, there is no decrement in the reaction as it moves along. It is like a long string of gunpowder that has been ignited by a match. The flame will move from the lighted end, and the reaction at any point is determined by the amount of gunpowder at that point.

The rate at which the depolarization moves down the axon depends upon the diameter of the axon. The thicker the axon, the faster the rate of conduction. In the largest axons, the depolarization travels up to 100 meters per second.

Most, if not all, axons are surrounded by supportive cells, which wind their membranes around the axon. The membrane may lap back and forth around the axon many times and the tissue in cross-section looks something like the cross-section of a tree trunk. Fatty material is included in the supportive cell membrane; this acts as an electrical insulator. The membrane with its fatty material is called *myelin.* (An illustration of myelin structure is shown in Figure 4-18.)

The myelin does not surround the axon in one continuous sheet. Rather, it occurs in discrete "lumps" with gaps between the

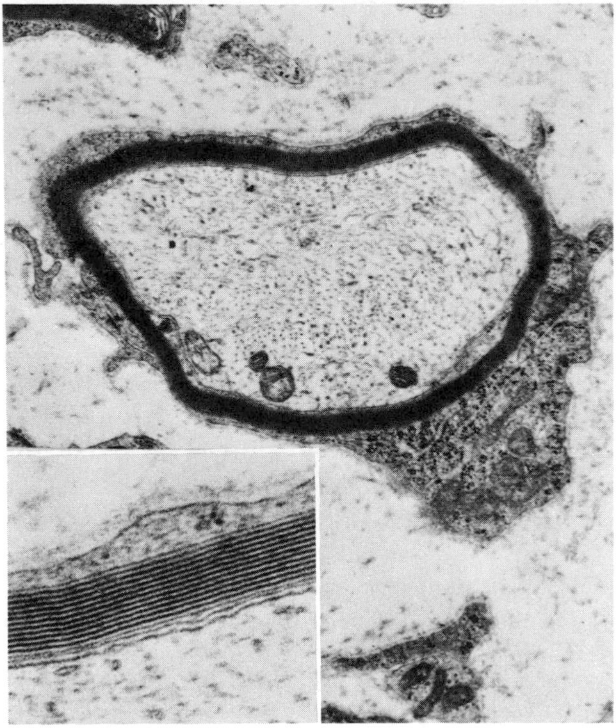

Figure 4-18 *Electron microscope photograph of a cross section of peripheral nerve axon of the rat. The myelin sheath is derived from the Schwann cell (x15,000). Insert in left corner shows fine detail of myelin sheath (x60,000). Note the Schwann cell cytoplasm extending beyond the outer margins of the myelin. (Courtesy of Dr. J. J. Bernstein, University of Florida. Lead citrate, uranyl acetate stain.)*

lumps; these breaks in the myelin are called the nodes of Ranvier. They are not merely bare spots, free of insulation, but are points at which smaller "collateral" axons may leave the main axon and also points at which other cells can affect the transmission of the depolarization down the membrane. Depolarization of the axon occurs only at the nodes of Ranvier and not underneath the myelin-covered areas. Thus very little of the actual surface of the axon ever depolarizes. In this way the myelin acts to conserve the energy of the cell and its axon. Diseases which result in the breakdown of the myelin sheaths around axons disrupt the transmission of the depolarization down the axon, and if severe and progressive, such diseases can lead to awkwardness, sensory difficulties, paralysis, and death.

The synapse

The depolarization, which is the nerve impulse, travels to the far end of the axon at which point there is an enlargement called (as we have said) the end bouton. This causes the release, from small packets, of chemical transmitter substances which then affect the membrane of the next cell. The packets themselves are called synaptic vesicles, and some are shown in Figure 4-19.

The point of contact between the end of an axon and another neuron is called a *synapse*. In a complete synapse there is the enlarged end of an

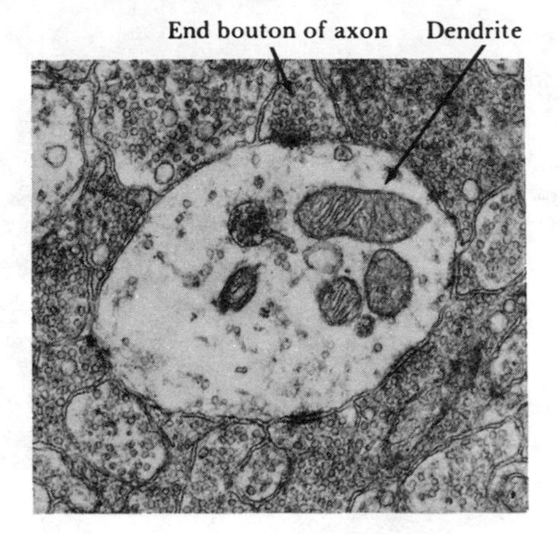

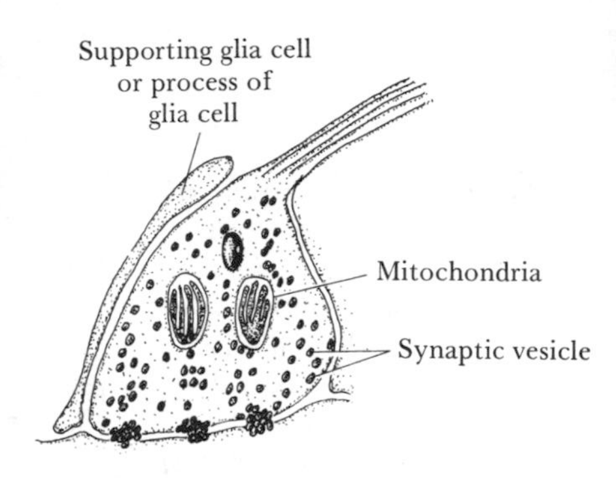

Figure 4-19 *Photograph (left) and schematic drawing (right) of a synaptic ending based on electron microscopy. (Photograph courtesy of Dean E. Hillman, Kenneth A. Siegesmund, and Clement A. Fox; drawing adapted by permission of the Rockefeller Institute Press from E. De Robertis, Submicroscopic changes of synapse after nerve section in the acoustic ganglion of the guinea pig.* J. biophys. biochem. cytol., *1956, 2, 503–512.)*

axon, a small gap called the synaptic cleft, and the membrane of the next cell. The terminal boutons can be in contact with membrane segments of the cell body or the dendrites of the next cell.

The chemical housed in the packets found in the axon terminals is released into the synaptic cleft, where it causes the next cell's membrane to alter its polarized state. The alteration may be to cause a partial depolarization, in which case the chemical influence is called "excitatory." The resistance to sodium ions flowing into the cell is partially broken down, and therefore a partial "depolarization" occurs. Other types of chemicals can produce an increase in the number of sodium ions on the outside of the cell membrane, a "hyperpolarized" state. The hyperpolarizing effect is considered to be "inhibitory," because it makes it more difficult to cause a complete depolarization of the cell.

Whether an axon end bouton produces an inhibitory or an excitatory effect depends upon the chemicals released into the synaptic cleft. At any moment in time the membrane of a neuron is being influenced by hundreds of synapses—some leading to partial depolarizations and others leading to hyperpolarizations. As mentioned before, if the *total* excitatory (excitatory-inhibitory) effects reaching the triggering zone in the cell body are sufficient, the cell will initiate a complete depolarization, which spreads down its own axon and affects other cells with which it is in contact.

We are reasonably sure that there are several types of chemicals that act as transmission agents across the synapses of the brain. Acetylcholine, the chemical found at the neuromuscular junction, is certainly one transmitter agent. It is likely that norephinephrine and serotonin are also neurochemicals active at some synapses.

The presumed neurotransmitters are found in different concentrations in different main regions. The posterior hypothalamus is relatively rich in norephinephrine, and the medial forebrain bundle has relatively high amounts of serotonin, for example. The significance of these differential densities of neurochemicals is not certain, however. An abundance of a neurochemical in specific brain regions does not necessarily imply that that neurochemical is *the* neurotransmitter used in those regions. These regions could be storage sites or be acting as "pipelines" for neurochemicals that will be used by cells at other places.

The tendency for a nerve cell to depolarize is regulated partly by the inhibitory endings on the cell. This is due to the hyperpolarizing influences of chemicals on the membrane. Because the hyperpolarizing influence occurs on the cell on the far side of the synapse, this effect is called postsynaptic inhibition. There is another type of inhibition in the nervous system termed presynaptic inhibition. In this case, the excitatory axon terminals are themselves rendered ineffective by the influences of other axon terminals that touch them. This arrangement is an unusual case of an axo-axonal synapse and is diagramed in Figure 4-20.

Modern techniques of electrical amplification allow the recording of the electrical potentials that are generated by the many synaptic events affecting a single cell. An excitatory influence causes a reduction in the electrical potential across the cellular membrane. This is a partial depolarization of the membrane, which produces a reduction in the segregation of differently charged ions across the membrane. A postsynaptic inhibitory synapse causes an increase in the electrical potential across the membrane. This is a partial hyperpolarization, which results from an increase in the segregation of differently charged ions across the membrane. Presynaptic inhibition fails to influence the electrical potential across the membrane, because the inhibitory effect is produced at the axon bouton of the excitatory neuron.

Neuroglia

There are two types of neural cells in the brain. The first is the neuron, whose most important role is the conducting of a neural impulse over long distances over the axon. The other type of neural cell is the neuroglial cell. Glia cells act to support the activities of neurons (the term "glia" means "glue"). These structures are the glue that lies among and between the neurons. However, they do more than just hold other cells together. They provide metabolic support to neurons and are constantly exchanging chemicals with the neurons. In fact, the association of glia cells with neurons is so intimate that some investigators believe the "unit" of neural activity is a neuron-glia unit.

There are two main types of glia cells in the brain: astrocytes and oligodendrocytes. Astrocytes are the cells which have many short processes that swarm around neurons and sometimes form a bridge between the tiny blood vessels which go through the brain and the neuron. It is likely that these astrocytes explain why many chemicals and drugs injected into the body fail to reach the neurons of the brain. The intimate relationship of astrocytes with neurons is illustrated in Figure 4-21.

In the central nervous system, oligodendrocytes are usually thought to be the cells whose processes wind around the axons of cells to form the myelin sheaths. In the periphery of the body, the myelin sheath is formed by another type of cell (the Schwann cell).

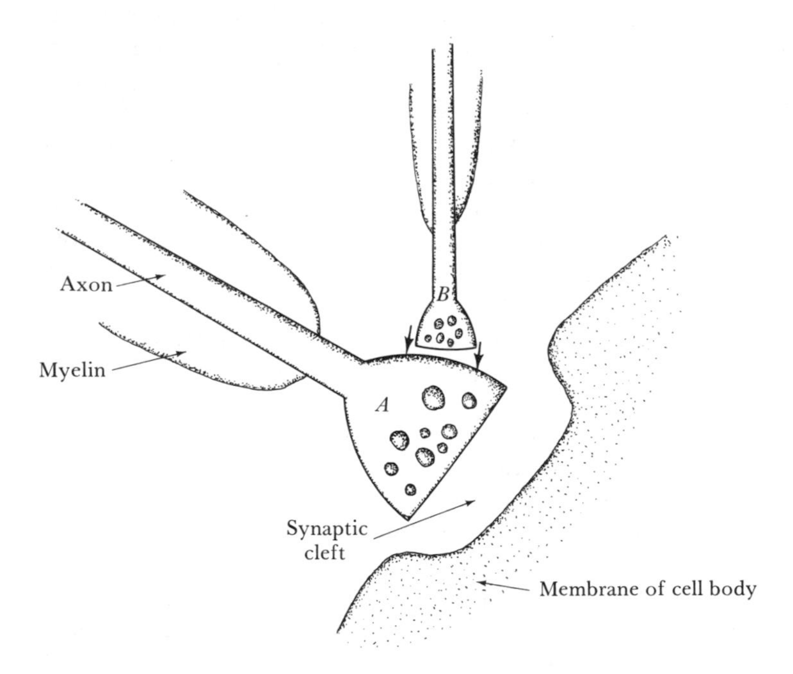

Figure 4-20 *A diagrammatic representation of presynaptic inhibition. The excitatory axon terminal A is prevented from discharging its transmitter substances into the synaptic cleft by nerve impulses arriving at axon terminal B.*

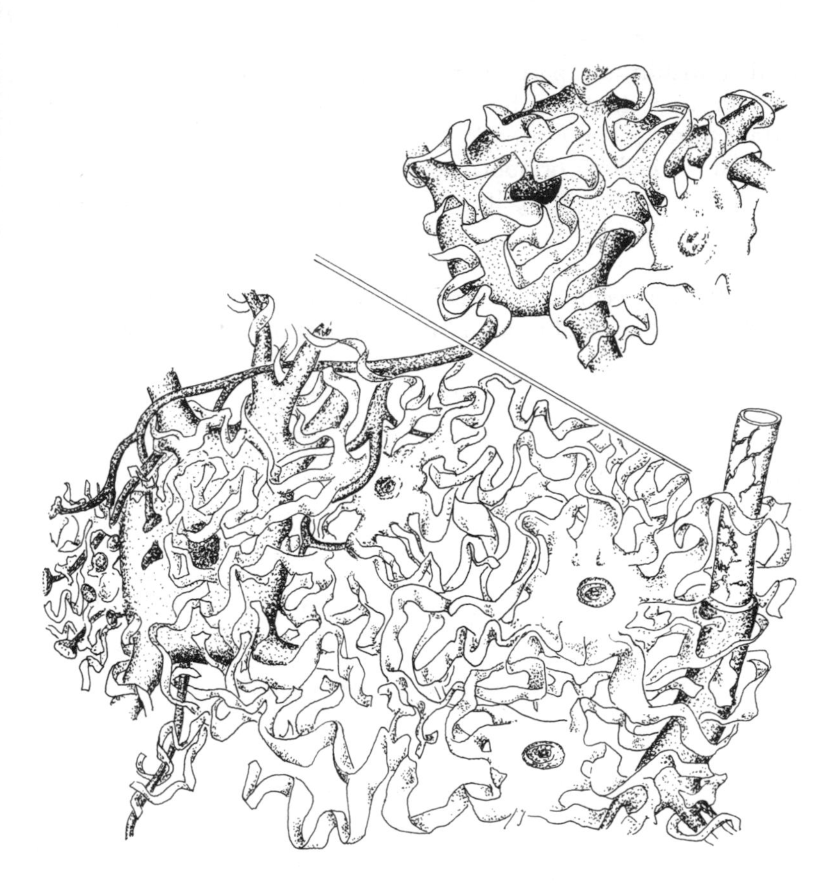

Figure 4-21 *Drawing showing relationship between the neuron and surrounding glia cells. The large cells on the left are nerve cells. On the right is a capillary; both neuron and capillary are covered by thin glial membranes. (Fig. 1, p. 181, in Holger Hydén, Ed., The neuron. Elsevier, Amsterdam, 1967.)*

Trends in research

Many of the directions of research made possible by advanced technology will be discussed in later chapters. In the next chapter, for example, we will show how recordings of single cell activities have helped explain the function of neocortical areas that first receive visual information. In later chapters we will find recordings from single cells to be valuable indices of learning and motivational mechanisms.

The use of microchemical techniques has been important in establishing the fact that within any particular anatomical system there may be several subsystems in each of which the common element is the use of the same neurotransmitters. The evaluation of chemical subsystems has been especially fruitful in research on motivation. The chemical microanalysis of proteins in neurons and glia cells will be described in later chapters on learning and memory.

The development of new technical skills and methods is, in itself, not science. But each new technical advance does allow us to learn more and different things about the brain and its relationship to behavior.

SUGGESTED READINGS

Butler, C. M. *Neuropsychology: The study of brain and behavior.* Belmont, Calif.: Brooks-Cole, 1968.

Eyzaquirre, C. *Physiology of the nervous system.* Chicago: Year Book Medical Publishers, 1969.

Isaacson, R. L. (Ed.) *Basic readings in neuropsychology.* New York: Harper & Row, 1964.

Whalen, R. E. *Hormones and behavior.* New York: Van Nostrand, 1967.

5
Sensory mechanisms

W*e live* in a world of people and things—books, trees, sunshine, snow, friends, loved ones, strangers. We take our perceptions of them for granted; we take for granted that they are the way they seem to be. But is this book, for example, really the thing we perceive it to be? If this book is placed in a position at which the light strikes it from a different angle, the color of the cover may seem different. Has the color of the book changed? No, you will say, it is an *illusion* caused by the angle of incidence of the light. But how can we decide which appearance is the illusion? Plato proposed that all of our *real* objects are only illusions.

The philosophical question of the ultimate truth or falsity (the veridicality) of perceptions lies outside the domain of scientific psychology. Such questions may lead to interesting hours of discussion, but as behavioral scientists we want to understand the mechanisms whereby we perceive the world. Assuming that we live surrounded by a world of objects that we know through our senses, how do these sensory mechanisms work? Perceptions of the world of objects begin with the detection of changes in the physical energies impinging upon specialized receptive organs. In the case of visual perception these energies are described as light waves or quanta of light. In hearing, the energy is in the form of waves of increasing and decreasing compressions of the atmosphere. For touch, the skin must be compressed. Before any kind of perception can occur, some energy change must be detected by the individual.

In the body there are many kinds of specialized organs, collections of cells that are especially sensitive to certain kinds of changes in physical energies. We might be inclined to think of these organs, called receptors, as similar to television cameras on the outer edges of the body that tune in on events taking place in the environment. This is an especially appealing analogy in the case of vision. With a little imagination the analogy could be extended to all the senses. In fact, the myth that the sensory mechanisms do work in such a fashion seems to be perpetuated by magazine articles and some "scientific" books intended for the layman. Let us examine the analogy. The eye is the television camera. The receiver is somewhere in the brain. Electrical signals (pictures) are relayed to the receiver in the brain. But what then? What good would such an electrical picture be in the midst of millions of neurons? Our problem is not solved by the television analogy, for we must also postulate "someone" in the brain to watch the pictures transmitted to this organ. We would have to start all over again investigating this new "being" watching the TV set. Our problem is much more difficult than understanding a biological TV transmission scheme.

We must try to understand how the changes in energy at the receptors are transformed into changes in the rates of discharge of millions of neurons and then how these neural changes are incorporated into ongoing brain activities that are reflected in behavior. The activities of receptor cells become encoded as neural impulses, which are transmitted considerable distances over many axons. The neural code, however, differs from codes used (for example) for private communication between a country and its secret agents. Such codes are used in the transmission of messages; they begin with a plain, understandable text at the transmitting end, and this identical message is reconstructed at the receiving end. In sensory codes, the original receptor message is never reconstructed in the nervous system. It is worked into the activity of the millions of neurons of the brain in a systematic way.

The assumption of a little man in the head is the easy way out; it is too bad we cannot take it. Rather, we must learn the brain's various codes and rules of integration. We are not yet very close to this goal. However, in the first sections of this chapter we shall present some of the available information about sensory systems in general. Then we shall consider each system in terms of receptors, pathways to the brain, and the brain itself.

TOWARD A DEFINITION OF PERCEPTION

Let us examine the problems that bear on a definition of perception. First, let us bear in mind that all we *know* about the world or other people comes to us via our own receptor systems. Our receptor systems and the subsequent processing of the information that originates in them are responsible for two aspects of perception: (1) our own unique mental states and (2) the coordination of our behavior with perceived events in the outside world.

The investigation of the conscious events that are so much a property of what is considered to be "perception" have tended to be ignored by psychology, because so little is known about consciousness itself. It is easier to study observable behaviors of others than to study the hidden mental events that occur within the "mind." Proponents of the behavioristic movement in psychology denied that the study of conscious states was of any particular value for the understanding of behavior. This, however, merely overlooks the problem of conscious experiences. Furthermore, the scientist's interest in the examination of mental states is a legitimate one, but an *experimental* approach to perception first depends upon investigations into the anatomical and physiological systems involved in the reception and processing of information arising outside the body and from the careful observation of "perceptual behaviors."

The task of psychology is to build theories that accurately predict behavior. As we shall see in subsequent chapters on learning, there are psychologists who do not believe we need to say anything about perception to account for behavior. Other scientists say we must have theories that take the conscious or unconscious effects of environmental stimulation or both into account. Psychologists work in many different ways, each following his own orientation about the best way to understand behavior. The various sensory systems of the body together lay the ground work for perception of the world as this phenomenon is generated by the brain in response to stimuli arising from within and without the body.

GENERAL PROPERTIES OF SENSORY SYSTEMS

We may think of ourselves as involved in two worlds: an external physical world around us and an inner world beneath the skin. The physical world is composed of things and people. Physics and chemistry tell us that these are really complicated collections of atoms, molecules, and energy. The inner world beneath the skin is a world of atoms and molecules too, but patterned so as to constitute the person. People are made of many systems that usually work harmoniously to maintain the larger system of the individual. At this point the systems of primary importance to us are the sensory systems. These systems generally are located close to the skin, which is the membrane separating the inner from the outer world. The perception of environmental changes begins at the receptor organs. We perceive changes in the outer world because of changes in our receptors and their associated sensory systems.

Sensory systems have three levels of components: (1) the receptors themselves; (2) the transmission pathways in the central nervous system; and (3) the mechanisms of the brain, especially the neocortex. These regions receive the neural impulses as they arrive over the transmission lines.

Understanding the sensory mechanisms requires learning how information is processed at all three levels. Where appropriate we will present illustrations of the types of transformations of information occurring at these levels when discussing specific sensory systems.

Overall organization

In higher animals, the receptor organs have become highly specialized. For example, our eyes do not respond to smells or sounds. Each receptor organ has developed so that it transmits information to the brain only in response to certain kinds of stimulation. In addition, receptors are sensitive only to a narrow portion of the total energies that reach them. We do not hear all possible sounds or see all possible lights. The ear is responsive to sound waves of frequencies between 20 and 20,000 Hz.[1] Changes in air pressure of higher or lower frequencies are not detected by normal auditory apparatus. We should bear in mind that other species need not have these same limitations. Dogs can detect frequencies much greater than 20,000 Hz, and as a result dog whistles (which people do not hear) can be used to call them. Some insects seem to be able to detect the plane of polarization of light waves.

All sensory systems have some common attributes. First of all, there are specialized receptor cells grouped into a receptor organ. These cells act to translate activity in the physical outer world into alterations in the firing of afferent neurons going to the central nervous system and the brain. *The receptor cell is sensitive to specific physical and chemical*

[1] Herz (Hz) is a measure of frequency and means cycles-per-second. Thus a 1000 Hz tone is a tone with a frequency of 1000 cycles-per-second. This tone could also be called one kilo (thousand) Herz. A twenty-thousand-cycle-per-second tone would be a 20-kiloHerz tone. This can also be written as 20 kHz.

changes in its immediate environment and in turn effects changes in neurons to which it is connected.

The neurons connected with the receptor cells have processes that reach to higher levels of the central nervous system by two routes. The first is a fast, direct projection system made up of large cells and large axons. This system provides a mechanism of fast transmission of neural impulses from the receptor to the higher brain regions. A second system carries the sensory information over small, short axons in a relatively slow manner. Axons in the fast conducting system usually project to the thalamus, where they end on cell bodies in specialized nuclei. The thalamic cells then send axons to cells in the sensory areas of neocortex as well as to other higher brain regions.

The smaller nerve fibers of the slower systems reach other thalamic nuclei, which project to wider regions of neocortex than do cells in the thalamic areas reached by the cells of the faster conducting systems. In addition the cells of the short-axon, slowly conducting systems project diffusely into the brainstem reticular formation. The brainstem reticular formation and certain thalamic nuclei have cells that relay sensory activity to very wide areas of neocortex. These sensory systems are diagramed in Figure 5-1.

Sensory systems are not one-way systems that always proceed upward to the neocortex. Most, if not all, sensory systems have efferent ("down-

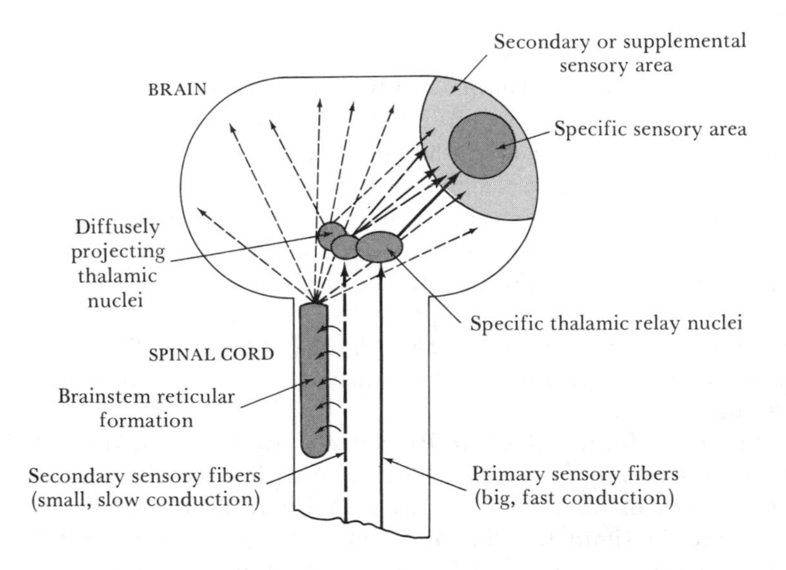

Figure 5-1 *Primary (unbroken lines) and secondary (broken lines) afferent fibers in somatosensory system.*

stream") pathways, probably beginning in the primary sensory receiving areas in the neocortex, which act on receptor cells or on cells near them in the chain of transmission to the brain. These efferent tracts can suppress or alter the information sent toward the brain. Thus the central nervous system itself can regulate the information coming to it from the peripheral receptors.

Receptor properties

Receptor activity that is caused by the changes in the physical world must be rewritten into a neural code. The receptor cells must in some way alter the activity of neurons connected with them. This means that the single neuron's resting state of membrane polarization must be broken down, and the resulting depolarization of the neuron must be sufficient to trigger the total cell body and axon depolarization so that it spreads as the *spike potential* (or firing) of the nerve cell. The means by which changes in the external environment are translated into changes in neural activity are highly individualized for each receptor system. While all of the cells in each sensory organ operate according to the same principles, each of the sensory organs has a different mechanism to affect the neurons that will carry their information to the brain.

VISUAL RECEPTORS

Man can discriminate only a small portion of the spectrum of electromagnetic radiation. While the nature of electromagnetic waves is not completely understood, the radiation can be easily measured (in terms of wavelengths). The common techniques for measuring electromagnetic radiation provide a spectrum running from the small peak-to-peak wavelengths of gamma rays to the long peak-to-peak wavelengths of the waves used to transmit radio signals. The electromagnetic spectrum is illustrated in Figure 5-2. The small portion of this spectrum to which man can respond lies between the wavelengths of 450 to 750 millimicrons. As mentioned before, other animals have somewhat different capacities of wavelength discrimination.

We have been careful to talk of *electromagnetic waves,* not *light waves,* a term which refers only to the wavelengths to which man is sensitive. The same problem of terminology exists with color. Within the visual spectrum we can discriminate different wavelengths. Most often we indicate our wavelength discriminations in words (*red, green*) or by behavioral responses that indicate a discrimination has been made—for example, stopping at a red traffic light. Our discrimination between wavelengths

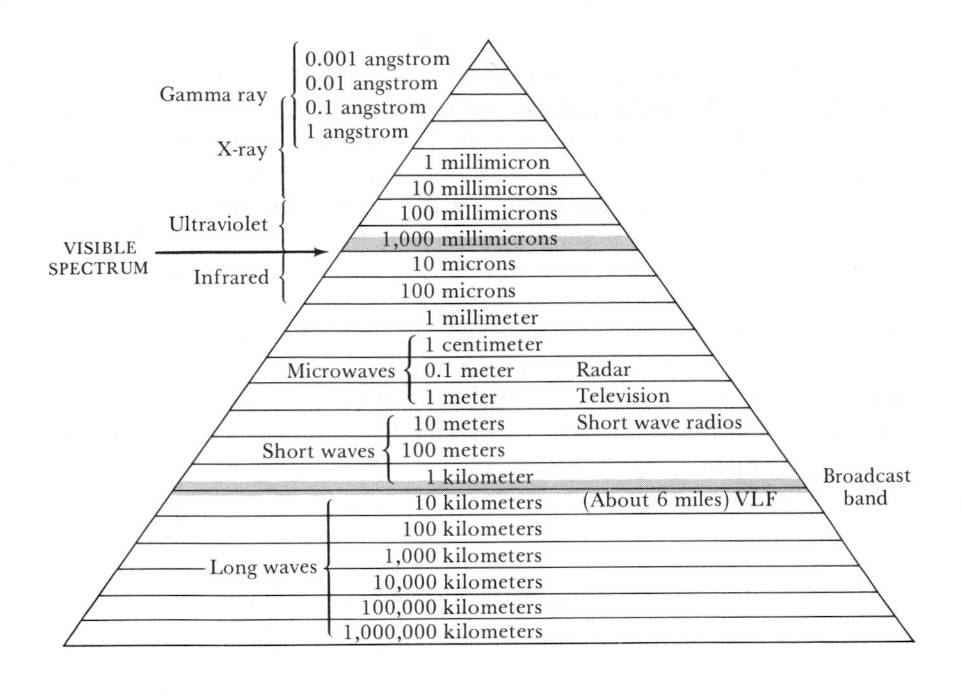

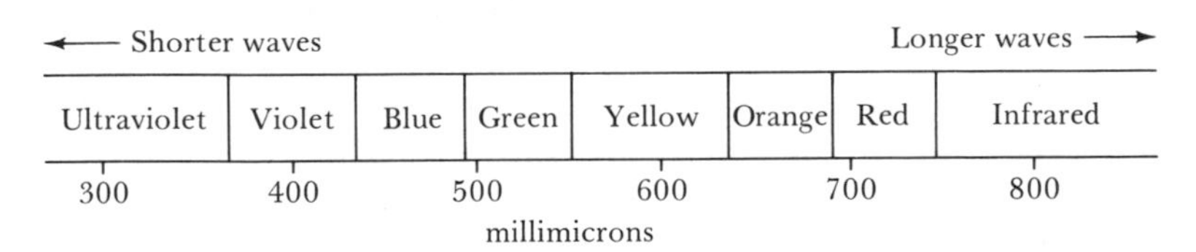

Figure 5-2 *Diagram suggestive of the electromagnetic spectrum, with closeup of segment of visible light (below). The entire spectrum encompasses so wide a span of wavelengths that they cannot be expressed in a single unit of measurement. (Adapted from John L. Chapman, The expanding spectrum.* Harper's Magazine, *July, 1964, pp. 70–78. © 1964, by Harper & Row, Publishers, Incorporated. Reprinted from Harper's Magazine by the artist's permission.)*

is the basic operation. The perception of a color as such is due to the organization and structure of our nervous system and the wavelengths of electromagnetic energies reaching the eye.

Structure of the eye

The eye is a finely constructed device that acts to focus the images of objects from the outer world upon the receptive cells that are located on the back inner layer of the eye, the retina (see Figure 5-3). The receptive cells in the retina are called rods and cones, terms originally used to describe their shapes, although they are best distinguished on the basis of the chemicals in them.

The electromagnetic waves come in through the cornea, the aqueous humor, the lens, and vitreous humor. The lens and cornea focus them on the retina to provide a clear image. In this process the image is inverted so that an upward-pointing arrow is actually pointing downward on the retina. The image upon the retina excites, in various ways, the receptors. The activities induced by the light reaching the rods and cones cause changes to occur in these structures; these changes in turn affect the neural cells whose axons leave the retina and project back into the central nervous system. These neurons are called the *ganglion cells,* and it is their axons that reach the specific thalamic relay nucleus for vision: the lateral geniculate nucleus. Other of their axons also extend into the hypothalamus and midbrain.

Distribution of rods and cones

The rods and cones are distributed over the back of the eyeball, in the retina. In the central portions of the retina there is a great preponderance of cones relative to the number of rods. At the approximate center of the retina there is a depression called the *fovea* (or *fovea centralis*), which contains only cones. In and around the fovea there is the greatest density of cones, but the ratio of cones to rods becomes less and less toward the periphery of the retina until the only receptor cells are rods.

The retina is a very complicated structure, containing much more than the rods and cones and the ganglion cells whose axons project into the brain. It also contains a host of other types of cells. Some appreciation for the organization of the retina can be gained from examining Figures 5-4 and 5-5. One curious point of organization is that the other cells and the ganglion cell fibers are all piled up on top of the rods and cones. In order for light to reach them it must pass through layers numbered 10 through 4 in these figures. This would seem to be

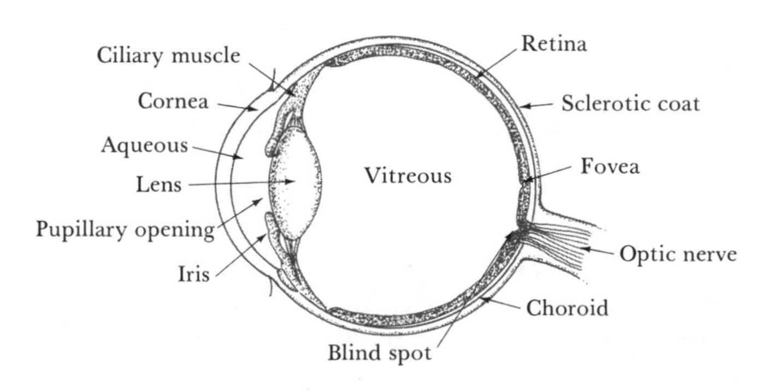

Figure 5-3 *Simplified representation of the human eye.*

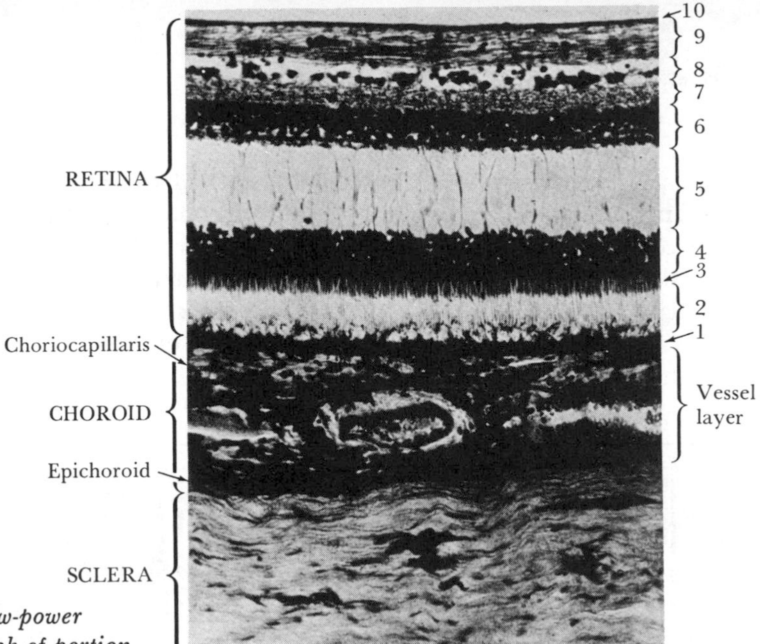

Figure 5-4 *Low-power photomicrograph of portion of retina, choroid, and some of the sclera of the human eye. Numbers correspond to layers of the retina shown in Figure 5-5. (Adapted from A. W. Ham and T. S. Leeson,* Histology *(4th ed.). Philadelphia: J. B. Lippincott Company, 1961.)*

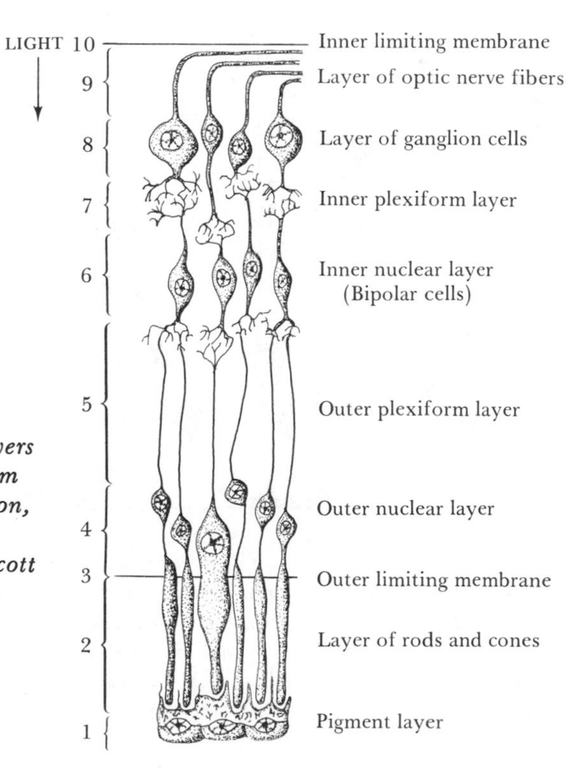

Figure 5-5 *Diagram of layers of the retina. (Adapted from A. W. Ham and T. S. Leeson,* Histology *(4th ed.). Philadelphia: J. B. Lippincott Company, 1961.)*

an inefficient design, but the cell bodies and their processes lying between the retina receptors and the lens are almost transparent. We cannot complain of the results of this system, for calculations made on the basis of optical properties of the eye indicate that as little as one quantum of light per receptor element may be sufficient to cause perceptible activity. Figure 5-6 shows the retinal structure in even more detail.

The depression of the fovea results from the fact that in this one area

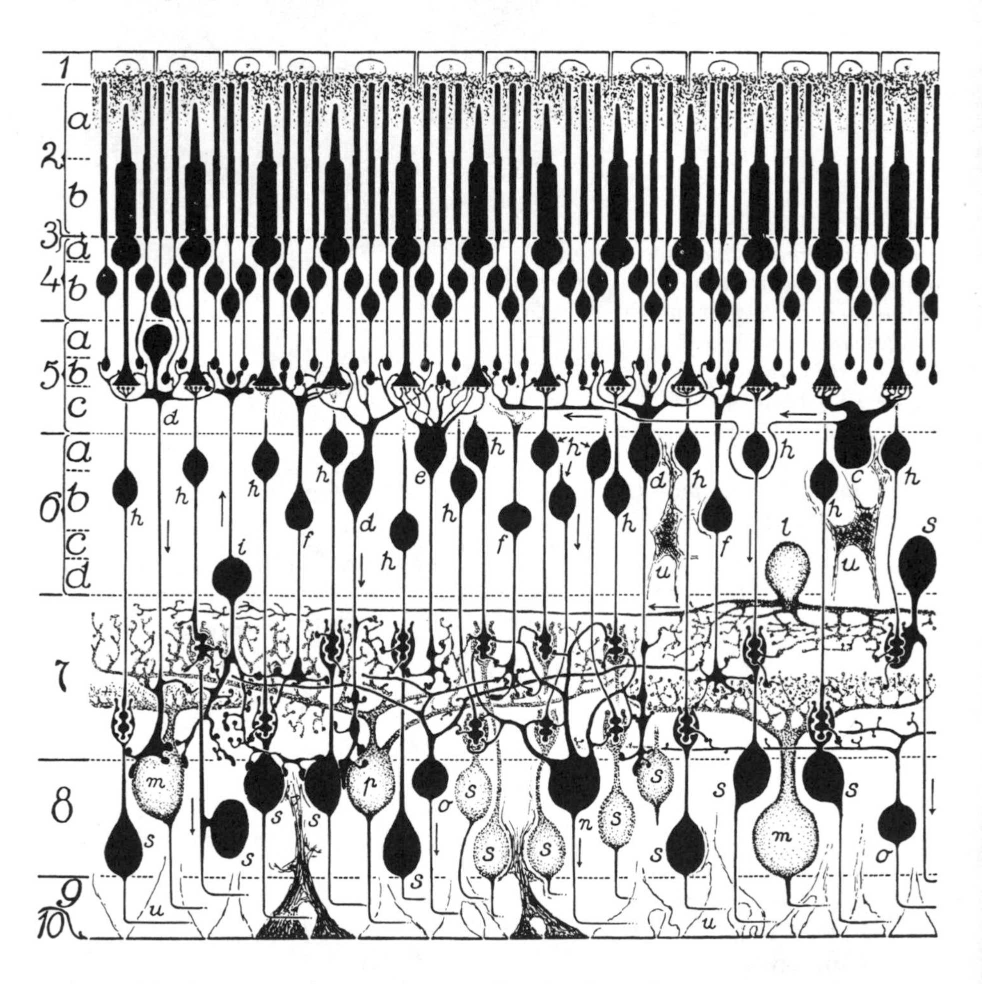

Figure 5-6 *Reconstruction of primate retina showing primary neuron types and their synaptic relations. The letters on the drawing identify these cells: c—horizontal cells; d,e,f—diffuse or polysynaptic bipolar cells; h—individual cone (midget) bipolar cells; i,l—amacrine cells; m,n,o,p,r,s—ganglion cells. (Reprinted from* The retina *by S. L. Polyak by permission of the University of Chicago Press. © 1941 by the University of Chicago. All rights reserved.)*

of the retina the ganglion and bipolar cells are not piled on top of the receptors but are pushed off to one side.

One other structural feature of the eye is of some importance to our understanding of perception. At the place where the axons of the ganglion cells leave the eye as the optic nerve, there are no receptors at all. This region is called the optic disc, and we are blind in this area. Ordinarily, however, we do not notice any gap in our visual experience unless conditions are specially arranged for us to do so. Somehow the brain "fills in" this deficit in sensory information.

Photopigments

In each rod and cone there are outer segments filled with chemicals collectively called the *photopigments.* Corresponding to the rod-cone division there are two classes of photopigments: rhodopsin and iodopsin. Rhodopsin is found only in the rods, and iodopsin only in the cones. Examination of the ultrastructure of the rods and cones reveals that the photopigments are "packaged" in what appear to be layer upon layer of translucent discs, which look something like poker chips. A photograph of this packaging system is shown in Figure 5-7.

When light strikes these photochemicals, a bleaching process begins, which alters the energy state of the photopigment. This alteration is the process that changes the polarization of the cell membrane. This change in cell membrane polarization initiates the neural impulse used to signal a change in the electromagnetic input to the receptor cell.

The study of visual pigments has a long history and a promising future. Today we know a great deal about the synthesis of rhodopsin and are rapidly learning about iodopsin. A summary of the rhodopsin cycle is presented in Figure 5-8.

RHODOPSIN AND NIGHT VISION Rods contain the photopigment, rhodopsin. This chemical is bleached by the incoming light and this releases energy, triggering the cell's response. After a rod's rhodopsin has been bleached, a considerable amount of time is required (in the dark) for the resynthesis of rhodopsin. This must take place before the cell can be excited again. During normal daytime vision the rods remain bleached and therefore relatively unresponsive. But after we have been in the dark for some time, rhodopsin regenerates and the rods recover their sensitivity. This process is called *dark-adaptation.*

There is a period of time after entering a dark motion picture theater during which we can see only very poorly. *The recovery of visual perception in the dark follows just about the same time course as the regeneration of rhodopsin.*

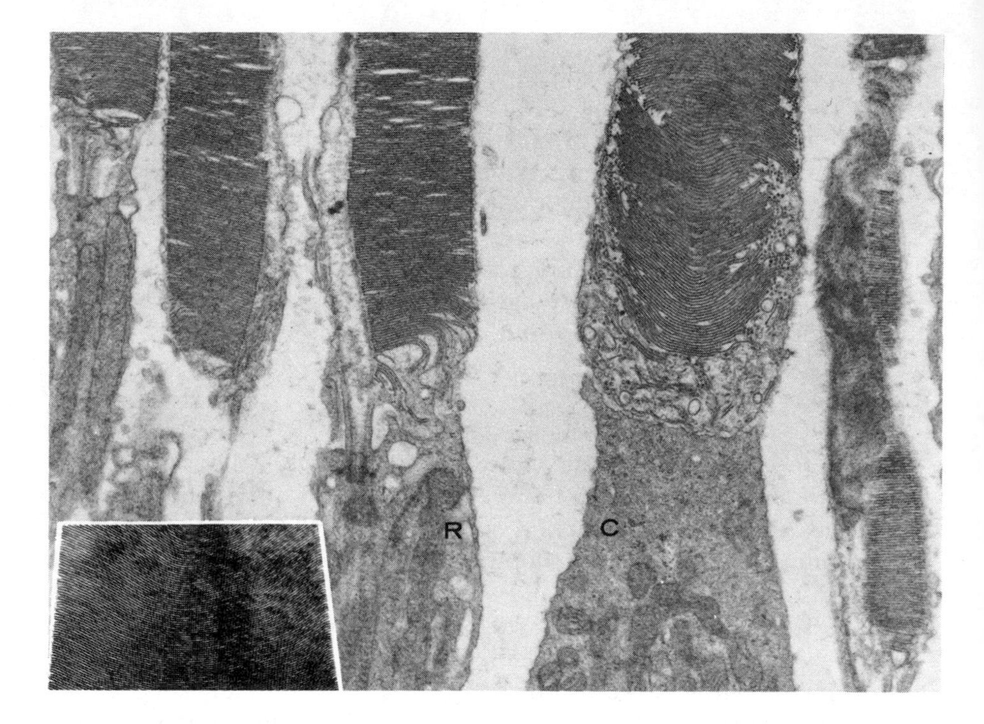

Figure 5-7 *Electron micrograph of the rod and cone of retina of the Rhesus monkey showing the junction of the outer segments with the inner segments (x10,400). (Courtesy Dr. A. I. Cohen, Washington University.) Insert in left corner shows disc-like microstructure of a portion of an outer segment of cone visual receptor in the goldfish (x23,400). (Courtesy Dr. J. J. Bernstein, University of Florida. Lead citrate, uranyl acetate stain.)*

The cones, which contain iodopsin, are less sensitive to the bleaching effects of light than the rods. The rods are the most sensitive to small amounts of light when they have been able to regenerate their supply of rhodopsin in the dark. Figure 5-9 shows that the longer an animal stays in the dark, the more sensitive his eye becomes to test flashes of light. Curve A shows the quick drop in threshold that can be attributed to the dark adaptation of the "daytime" (cone) receptor system. Curve B reflects the slower but more extensive adaption due to regeneration of rhodopsin in the "night" (rod) system. Since the rods are found in greatest concentration at the periphery of the eye, night vision is best at the edges of the retina. Our chances of detecting small sources of light at night are much better if we do not look directly at the spot where

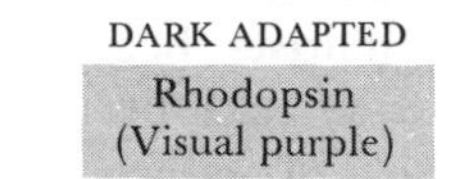

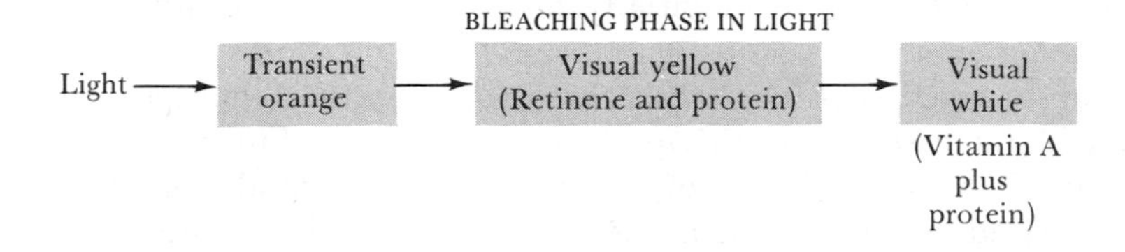

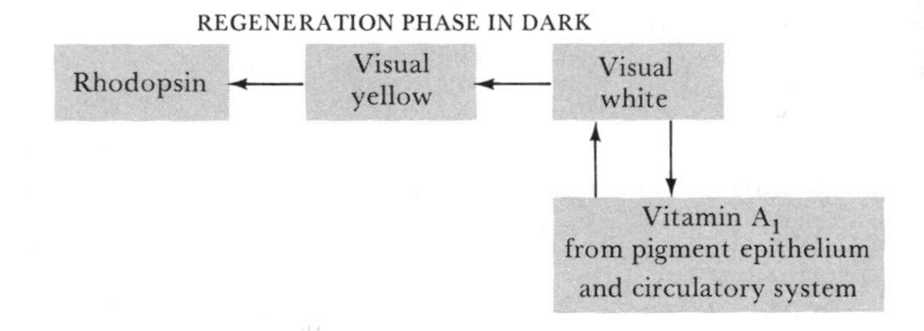

Figure 5-8 *Diagrammatic representation of light effects on photopigment rhodopsin, and its subsequent regeneration in the dark.*

we expect the light to be. If we look to the side of the light source, the light will fall on the periphery of the retina, which is the area of greatest rod population. Lookouts scanning the horizon for lights of ships are therefore directed not to look directly at the suspected target.

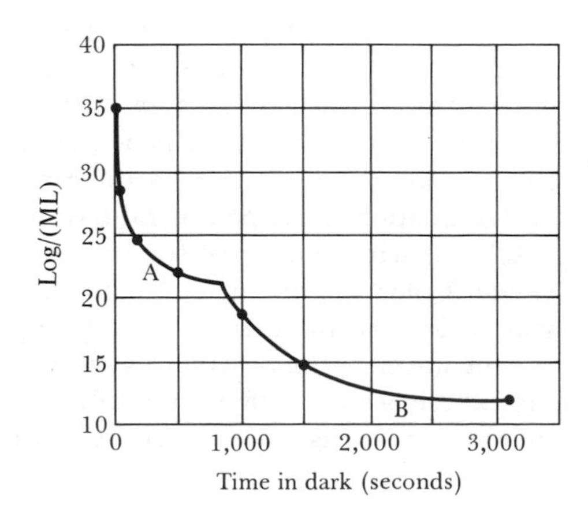

Figure 5-9 *Dark-adaptation curve of frog, based on response indicated on electroretinogram. (Adaptation of Fig. 6 in L. Riggs, Dark adaptation in the frog eye determined by the electrical response of the retina.* J. cell. comp. physiol., *1937, 9, 501.)*

CONES AND IODOPSIN Much less is known about the cone system of the retina. Only recently have scientists been able to identify iodopsin chemically, although its presence had been predicted long before its discovery. The regenerative cycle of iodopsin is similar to that of rhodopsin, and the principle by which the iodopsin acts to initiate the activity of a single neural element is essentially the same; but there are some important differences.

The iodopsin reaction is faster than that of rhodopsin. Time spent in the dark will increase the sensitivity of cones to light, but the cones do not achieve the same degree of sensitivity to light as do the rods following dark-adaption. Although the cone system is less sensitive to light than the rod system is, it provides us with the highest visual acuity in the fovea and with color vision.

The mechanisms for color

Color perception refers to discriminations the human and some animals can make within the range of the visible spectrum. In order to be described as color discriminations, these discriminations must be based not on brightness or other features of the stimulation but on a special sensitivity to specific wavelengths of the electromagnetic spectrum.

It is not likely that the rods are capable of providing a neural basis for discriminations among wavelengths. There may be more than one kind of rod in the eyes of higher animals, but the general belief is that these structures could only provide a limited discrimination between portions of the short wavelengths (blues) and the remainder of the spectrum. There is little doubt that the cone system is responsible for most color discriminations.

Let us accept the proposition that the cone system mediates color discriminations. Does this mean that there must be more than one kind of iodopsin? In order for us to live in the world of multiple colors—which we do—we must have receptors built to discriminate among many different wavelengths. This in turn means that we must have cones containing pigments that will be bleached more effectively by one wavelength than by another. This differential bleaching due to wavelength of illumination is the peripheral basis of color discrimination.

Like all sensory experiences, color exists as a response within the individual. Color is not found in the nervous system. All neurons are the same color, as are their electrical responses. Differential sensitivity to certain wavelengths provides us with the peripheral basis for color, but the experience of color results from the processing of this fundamental information at higher levels of the central nervous system.

Traditional color theories

Probably the importance of vision and the beauty of the perceived world of color account for the early and continued attempts to explain color. Theories of color vision were among the very first psychological theories. Modifications of old theories and the creation of new theories proceeds to the present. No one theory is perfectly satisfactory, and each contains something of special merit.

THE YOUNG-HELMHOLTZ THEORY In 1801, Thomas Young suggested that there were three types of nerve fibers running from eye to brain. He thought that these fibers corresponded to the three primary colors. Some fifty years later, Helmholtz extended Young's theory, which had not received a great deal of attention. Through Helmholtz's successful efforts to relate this theory to the laws of "color mixture," the modified theory became widely accepted. It is probably the most well known of all theories of color perception.

The Young-Helmholtz theory assumes three varieties of cones having different photopigments. Each photopigment is presumably most sensitive to one portion of the visual spectrum. One type is specially sensitive to short wavelengths (blue cones), another is specially sensitive in the middle range (green cones), and the last type is specially sensitive in the long wavelength area (red cones). While each type of cone has a region of greatest sensitivity, all have *some* sensitivity to other wavelengths. Color is determined, according to the Young-Helmholtz theory, by the brain on the basis of the relative amounts of excitation coming from the three different cone systems.

When we perceive a colored object we make a discrimination of its wavelength. This reaction is referred to as hue discrimination. We say "that is aqua," "that is chartreuse," "that is magenta," and so on. We have learned to make color discriminations, and, also, we have learned to label the discriminations in accordance with the rules accepted by the majority of people in our culture.

Two stimuli can be of the same hue but differ in other qualities. A color can be more or less *saturated*. The saturation of a particular hue refers to the amount of white or gray mixed with it. The less of these neutral components mixed with a given hue the more saturated it is. Brightness is another quality that is different from both hue and saturation, and it is related to the intensity of the light reaching the eye.

With the Young-Helmholtz theory it is possible to explain saturation and brightness in terms of the responses observed in the three cone systems. The perceived hue is determined by the *relative* amounts of activity in the three cone systems. Brightness is determined by the absolute level of activity in all three systems. How can the Young-Helmholtz theory explain the quality of saturation, or the degree to which the hue is diluted with white or gray? White light—for example, sunlight—had been known for a long time to be a mixture of many hues. When a prism is held appropriately, a ray of white light can be changed into a full spectrum of all the visible wavelengths. The Young-Helmholtz theory proposed that we see all of the spectral hues through three basic color receptors, red, green, and blue cones. White was believed to be a combination of activity in all three cone types. Saturation, as a quality of color perception, was explained by the balance existing among the activities in the red, green, and blue cone systems.

HERING'S THEORY A second major color-vision theory was developed by a scientist named Hering; it stemmed from the introspective analysis of color sensations. Many people who have tried to analyze impressions into components have felt that the experience of yellow is somehow a "primary experience"—one not susceptible to further analysis. Today, this sort of introspective evidence is considered to be far less impressive than it was historically. Nevertheless, Hering developed a theory that included yellow as one of the irreducible color mechanisms at the peripheral level. Hering's theory assumes the existence of three cone systems, but posits that the responses of each cone system can produce two kinds of reactions. These cone systems contain one of each of the following chemicals: (1) a white-black pigment, (2) a yellow-blue pigment, and (3) a red-green pigment.

This theory assumes a breakdown of the photopigments to produce white, yellow, and red experiences, whereas the reconstitution of the pigments was assumed to elicit black, blue, and green experiences. The basic objection to the Hering theory came from the necessary assumption that a given neural fiber had to carry two kinds of sensory information, e.g., black *and* white or blue *and* yellow. This contradicted one of the basic notions of nerve physiology at the time: the *doctrine of specific nerve energies*. According to this doctrine a nerve fiber could carry only one quality of sensation, and certainly the doctrine of specific nerve energies seems widely applicable in the nervous system. However, some single cells in the visual relay nucleus of the thalamus do in fact act as if they were doing just what the Hering theory proposed. Some cells respond vigorously to yellow, and their response rate falls below "spontaneous" rates of discharge when responding to blue. Cells in the thalamus are quite removed from the receptors in the retina, however, and their activity need not reflect the activities of the rods and cones. Studies in which microelectrodes were used to penetrate the retina of fish have shown some cells that respond to both red and green, but in a different manner to each. To one color (e.g., red) there is a change toward greater hyperpolarization of the cell and to another color (e.g., green) the cell might reflect a partially depolarized condition. No one is entirely sure from which type of retinal cell the recordings are coming. Unfortunately, attempts to relate these bidirectional changes of membrane potentials to the activity in ganglion-cell axons leaving the retina have been unsuccessful. This means that the cells of the retina that respond in the biphasic direction are not closely tied to the information that reaches the brain.

Electrical activities of the retina

As with electrical studies of all regions of the nervous system, electrical potential generated in the eye can be evaluated at many different levels. Recordings can be made at the level of the single units—i.e., receptor cells, ganglion cells, or other retinal cells—or activity of a larger population of cells. The latter method often includes measuring electrical potentials across the entire eye.

Two terms are often used with reference to the electrical potentials recorded at the receptor organs in all receptor systems. These are *receptor potential* and *generator potential.* Receptor potentials include all the electrical activities that arise from the receptor when it is stimulated. Generator potentials, on the other hand, are electrical activities that play a definite role in the translation of receptor activity into neural discharges in cells projecting toward the central nervous system.

An example may clarify this distinction. Suppose some imaginary animal such as a unicorn had receptor cells sensitive to cosmic rays. Recordings from these receptor cells might show a change in electrical potentials when a cosmic ray struck the receptor. This would mean that the electrical response was a "receptor potential," but would it mean that it was also a "generator potential?"

Let us consider the diagram in Figure 5-10. In A, a cosmic ray strikes the receptor from the left and causes a reaction. This produces a release of chemicals at *S*, which trigger activities in the dendrites that lead to a cellular response of the neuron *N*. Underneath the receptor, the electrical reaction recorded at the receptor is shown. Underneath the neuron several action potentials are shown to represent its response. In this case neuron *N* is affected by the release of chemicals and not by the electrical potential generated by the receptor. The electrical response of the receptor is incidental to the arousal of the neuron. In this case we would term the electrical reaction of the receptor a *receptor potential.*

In B, however, the electrical potential produced by the receptor

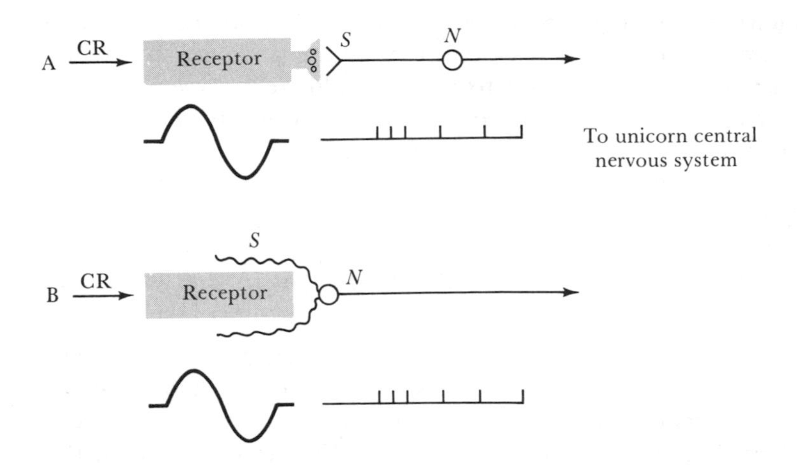

Figure 5-10 *Schematic diagram of hypothetical cosmic ray receptors in unicorns illustrates difference between receptor and generator potentials. In* A *above, a cosmic ray at the receptor could initiate a change in electrical potential (shown below it) and also cause a chemical to be released onto dendrite of next cell. This would cause discharges in second cell that move toward the central nervous system. In* B, *the receptor produces the same electrical response, but in this cause the electrical response itself causes a depolarization of the second cell's dendrites. In this way the electrical potential* generates *the response in the second cell, and it should be termed a generator potential.*

directly excites the dendrites surrounding it. It is the electrical potential that causes the neuron to respond. In this case the receptor's electrical activity would be called a generator potential.

Several large potentials can be recorded from the eye. One is a steady potential difference that exists across the eyeball under most normal circumstances. Of greater importance are the changes in electrical potential generated across the retina in response to light. This response is called the electroretinogram or ERG. Most investigators believe that both the steady potential and the ERG are receptor potentials. They can be extensively modified by drugs or other means without altering the effectiveness of the visual mechanism. An illustration of an ERG is shown in Figure 5-11.

A possible generator potential has been found to occur early in the ERG, perhaps at the area marked X in the figure. The portions of the curve marked *b* and *c* represent the combined results of the activities of different types of cells, but they are not essential to the initiation

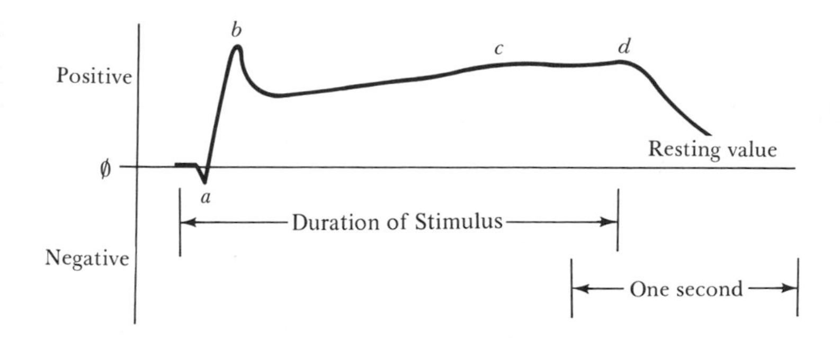

Figure 5-11 *Schematic diagram of a "typical" ERG.*

of action potentials in the optic nerve. Even so, abnormalities in the ERG traces of man can be used as a reliable index of certain kinds of retinal disease.

The shape of the ERG depends upon the type of animal and the conditions under which the recordings are made. Some animals have retinas containing only rods; the retinas of others contain only cones. Some have mixed populations as does man.

In the mid-1920s, techniques of recording from single nerve fibers were first developed in the physiological laboratories of Lord Adrian in England. The first successful recording from single axons of the optic nerve were made in the horseshoe crab, but the technique was soon extended to single fibers of the optic nerve of the frog and subsequently to optic nerves in mammals. Information from both crabs and frogs has been valuable to our understanding of the visual system.

Three types of cell responses were found in the axons of the ganglion cells in the frog eye. There are "on" cells, "on-off" cells, and "off" cells, as illustrated in Figure 5-12. An "on" cell responds with a burst of action potentials when light strikes the retina; it continues to discharge, although at a reduced rate, all the time the light is on. "On-off" cells respond vigorously at the onset and offset of the light but are otherwise mostly silent. "Off" cells are inhibited by the light, but they fire with a burst when the light is turned off. These types of response occur with increases and decreases in illumination, not just with the transition from absolute darkness to light. Moreover, these types of discharges (discovered first in the frog retina) have been found in the optic nerves of most vertebrates, although the relative distribution of cell types changes greatly among animals.

The axons arising from ganglion cells in the retina of the frog eye

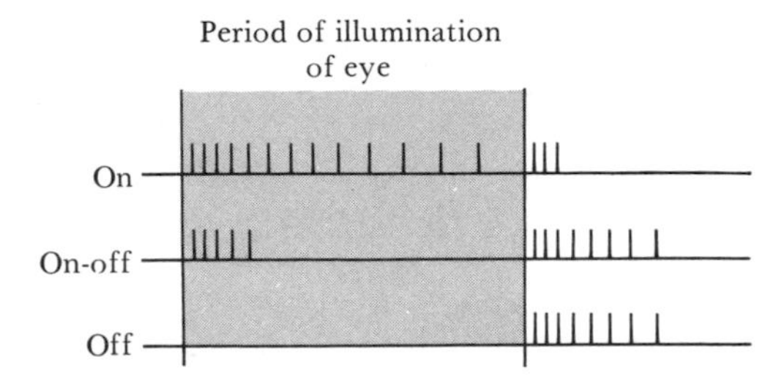

Figure 5-12 *The three types of discharges found in single fibers of the optic nerve of the frog by Hartline. The "on fibers" discharge shortly after the eye is illuminated and show an elevated discharge rate while the eye is stimulated. The "on-off" fibers discharge both at the onset and the offset of the light. The "off fibers" discharge only at the offset of the stimulation applied to the eye. (Adaptation of Fig. 1 from H. K. Hartline, The response of single optic nerve fibers of the vertebrate eye to illumination of the retina.* Amer. j. physiol., *1938,* 121, *400–415.)*

were found to respond when light stimulation reached receptors in a retinal area roughly a square with 1 millimeter sides. This area of the retina is called the receptive field of the ganglion cell, because it contains receptor cells whose activity influences a single ganglion cell. Receptive fields can be defined for single cells at any level of any sensory system. In vision, receptive fields are defined as the area of the retina that, when stimulated, will produce alterations in the rate of discharge of a single ganglion cell, a cell in the lateral geniculate nucleus, or a cell in the visual cortex. In all sensory modalities, "receptive field" indicates the peripheral area that influences cells at higher levels in the system. The receptive fields defined at one level may not be like those found at another level. In general the receptive fields mapped for cells in the visual cortex will be different from those mapped for cells in the thalamus, and the "thalamic" receptive fields will be different from those mapped from ganglion cells in the retina.

The size of a receptive field depends upon the intensity of light used to stimulate the retina. The stronger the light, the larger will be the receptive field (Figure 5-13). Receptive fields have two components: an excitatory region and an inhibitory region. Probably the most common type found from mapping the ganglion cells in the retina are those with excitatory centers and an inhibitory ring around the center. If light strikes the center, the rate of discharge of the ganglion cell is increased; if the light strikes only the surrounding region, the ganglion

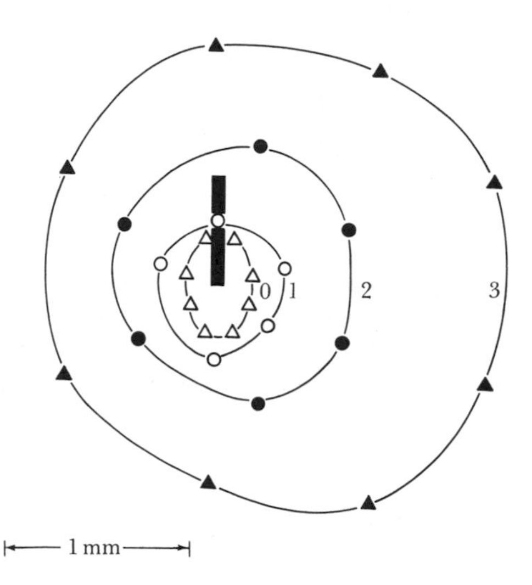

Figure 5-13 *Receptive field of optic nerve fiber in the bullfrog. Four intensities of illumination of the eye were used, represented by the numbers (logarithms). Note that as the intensity of light is increased, the area on the retina that produces responses in the fiber increases. (From H. C. Wagner and M. L. Wolbarsht, Receptive field of bullfrog.* Amer. j. ophthal., *1958,* 46, *46–59.)*

cell is inhibited. Not all receptive fields have an excitatory center and an inhibitory ring. Moreover, receptive fields overlap to a considerable extent. This means that the activity of any particular receptor cell can contribute to several receptive fields.

From the beginning of such studies it was noted that many ganglion cells did not respond when the retina was totally illuminated but responded to movements of small stimuli in a given direction. This was explained on the basis of receptive fields. For example, total retinal illumination would activate both the excitatory and inhibitory portions of the receptive field, and these effects would cancel each other out. A smaller light moving across the retina could selectively strike the excitatory or inhibitory regions. In Figure 5-14, a schematic receptive field is shown that would allow the ganglion cell to respond when a small target is moved in one direction but not in the opposite direction. This model derives from the fact that stimulation of the inhibitory zone before stimulation of the excitatory zone will prevent a response of the ganglion cell, whereas initial stimulation of the excitatory zone will produce a response.

The interaction of excitatory and inhibitory zones provides a simple mechanism whereby a considerable amount of sensory coding can be accomplished in the retina long before the information is transmitted to higher regions of the central nervous system.

The selectivity of ganglion cell discharge to certain kinds of movements and patterns has been known for some time, but as research

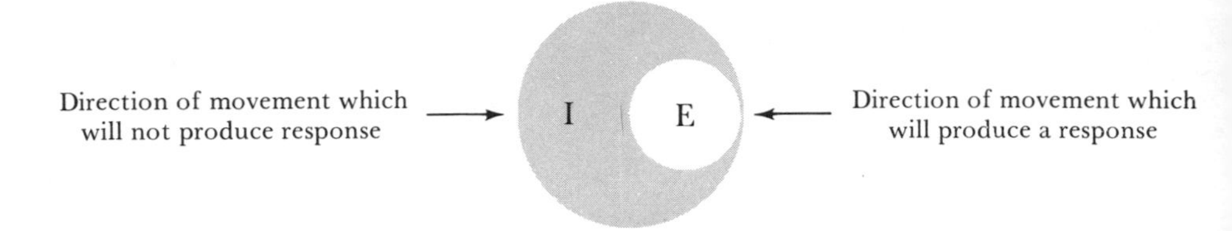

Figure 5-14 *Schematic distribution of excitatory and inhibitory fields of the retina which allow cells of sensory system to respond only when light is moved across it from right to left. Movement of light in opposite direction would stimulate inhibitory field first, inhibiting reaction when light reached excitatory field. Simultaneous stimulation of both fields would elicit no response.*

progresses we are continually surprised as to the degree of specificity shown. In frogs some receptive fields respond only to small, moving, buglike patterns of stimulation. The following types of optic nerve fibers have been found in the frog:

1. *Edge detectors.* These units respond to a lighter or darker edge moved into the receptive field. They continue to fire as long as the edge remains in field.
2. *Bug detectors.* These units respond to small, moving targets that have sharp edges.
3. *Changing contrast detectors.* These units respond to light or dark edges moving in particular directions.
4. *Dimming detectors.* These units respond when illumination is reduced. Their responses are like those of "off" fibers.
5. *Dark detectors.* These units fire more vigorously the darker the illumination (Maturana *et al.,* 1960).

In general, it is likely that every type of animal has receptive fields aligned in specific ways that are of adaptive importance to the animal. These highly organized receptive fields found at the retinal level represent a packaging of the visual information into useful terms *before* advanced processing occurs in the central nervous system. Thus the brain receives from the eye information that has already been subjected to some distillation and analysis. The type of distillation and analysis performed depends upon the species. Some investigators believe that lower vertebrates, such as the frog, exhibit more organization of visual information at the retinal level than is found in the primates. They believe that the packaging and processing of visual information goes on at the neocortical level in the primates and man. This may be true, but it is also possible that we have merely failed to discover the appropriate prepackaged receptive field units in the more advanced animals.

AUDITORY RECEPTORS

The auditory system acts to transduce changes in air pressure into altered patterns of neural discharges, which we recognize as sounds. The human auditory mechanism works effectively for air pressure changes occurring between 10–20 and 16,000–20,000 Hz at the low and high ends, respectively. Changes of lower or faster rates are not detected, although other animals can detect changes that are beyond the range of human hearing. We have already mentioned the use of dog whistles; bats can detect frequencies up to 100,000 Hz. The fact that we can respond only to a limited range of air pressure changes—our auditory range—is similar to the case with vision, wherein our eyes are responsive only to a small portion of the electromagnetic wave spectrum.

There are several types of transformations of energy between the changes in air pressure in the environment and the changes in nerve impulses. These can be appreciated from the structure of the receptor apparatus.

Structure of the ear

The external, shell-like structure of the ear (the pinna) probably is useful in funneling changes in atmospheric pressure into the auditory receptors of the lower animals, but in man these external features of the ear serve little function. Just inside the pinna, through a short passage (the external meatus), is the eardrum (tympanic membrane), which moves in and out in response to changes in air pressure. This vibration of the eardrum is transmitted by a *mechanical linkage* of three bones (malleus, incus, and stapes) of the middle ear to the inner ear. The inner ear is filled with fluids. The mechanical vibrations of the bones of the middle ear are translated into moving waves in these fluids by the in-and-out movements of the oval window. The motion of the inner-ear fluids is translated into neural changes by receptor cells located on the basilar membrane. Figure 5-15 presents a schematic diagram of the human ear.

In Figure 5-15 the basilar membrane has been drawn as a straight,

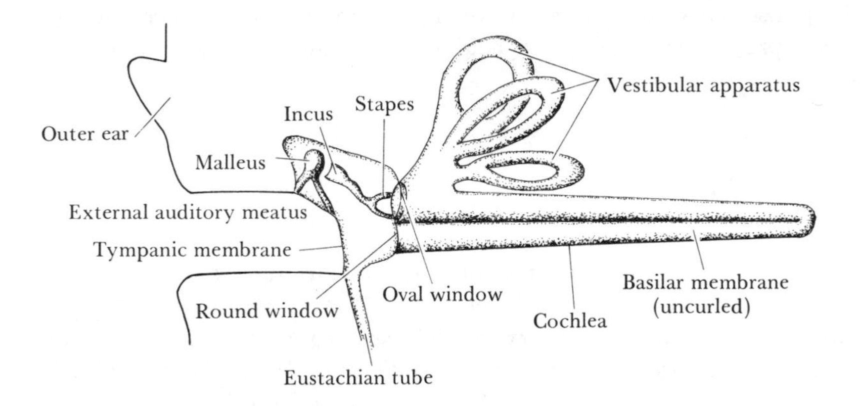

Figure 5-15 *Diagram of the peripheral mechanisms of audition. The cochlea, straightened here, is naturally twisted about three and a half times—rather like a sea shell.*

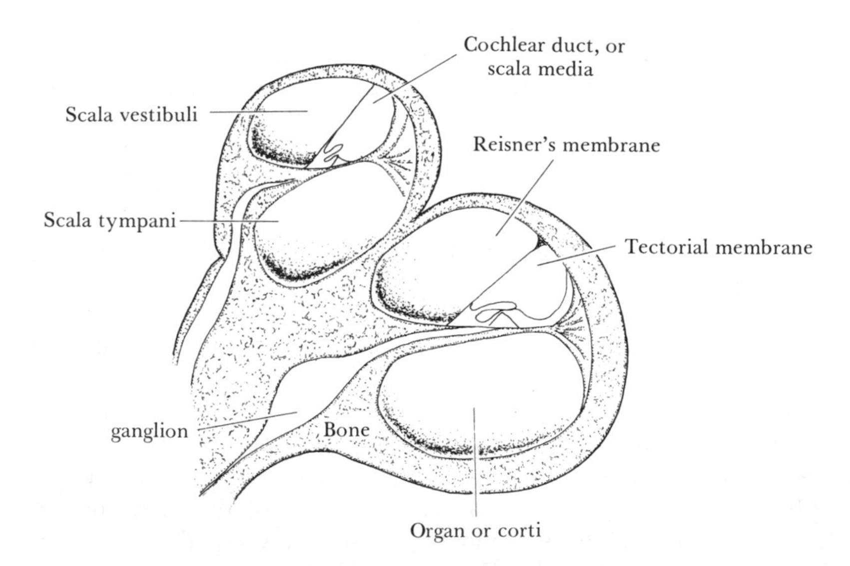

Figure 5-16 *Schematic cross-section through the cochlea showing two turns, each containing auditory apparatus. The organ of Corti contains the auditory hair cells and lies on the basilar membrane; the location of the ganglion which contains the cell bodies of the nerve cells whose processes reach the hair cells of the organ of Corti is marked on the cross section.*

flat surface. Actually, it is curled up inside a bony structure that resembles a snail's shell—which accounts for the name *cochlea.* The basilar membrane extends throughout the length of the cochlea. Waves in the fluid medium produce up-and-down movements of the membrane. The place of greatest oscillation of the basilar membrane is determined by the frequency of the vibration of the oval window. The actual receptor cells, the *hair cells,* are located on the basilar membrane. As the basilar membrane moves up and down, the hair cells are distorted and this causes them to become "activated."

A cross-section through the cochlea is shown in Figure 5-16. As can be seen in this illustration, the hair cells on the basilar membrane are surrounded by dendritic processes of cells located in a ganglion (the spiral ganglion) in the bony portion of the cochlea. The relationship of the hair cells to the dendritic fibers surrounding them is shown in Figure 5-17. The question of how the distorted hair cells cause a neural impulse to be initiated in the dendritic fibers is not yet resolved. For many years it was believed that the activated hair cells produced a local generator potential, which caused a depolarization of the fiber wrapped around the hair cell. There is some evidence, however, that there may be chemical transmission between the hair cells and the surrounding fibers, so that the synapse between the cell and the fiber could be electrical, chemical, or both.

The neurons whose cell bodies are in the spiral ganglion and whose dendrites wrap around the hair cells send axons into the central nervous system.

There are three fundamental properties of hearing that need to be considered: discrimination of frequency, perception of intensity, and the localization of sound in space.

The first property, frequency discrimination, can be explained on the basis of the response of the basilar membrane to different frequencies. For very low frequencies, the entire basilar membrane vibrates at the imposed frequency. For other frequencies "traveling waves" are established in the fluid-filled cochlea and produce maximal displacement of the basilar membrane at different places. Because of the construction of the cochlea and basilar membrane, higher frequencies cause the greatest distortion of the basilar membrane near the oval window—with lower tones displacing the basilar membrane farther out, away from the oval window. For most tones, then, frequency is signaled by the location on the basilar membrane that is most displaced by the cochlea vibrations.

The perceived intensity (loudness) of the auditory signals is a different matter. If the ear is stimulated equally intensely by sounds of different

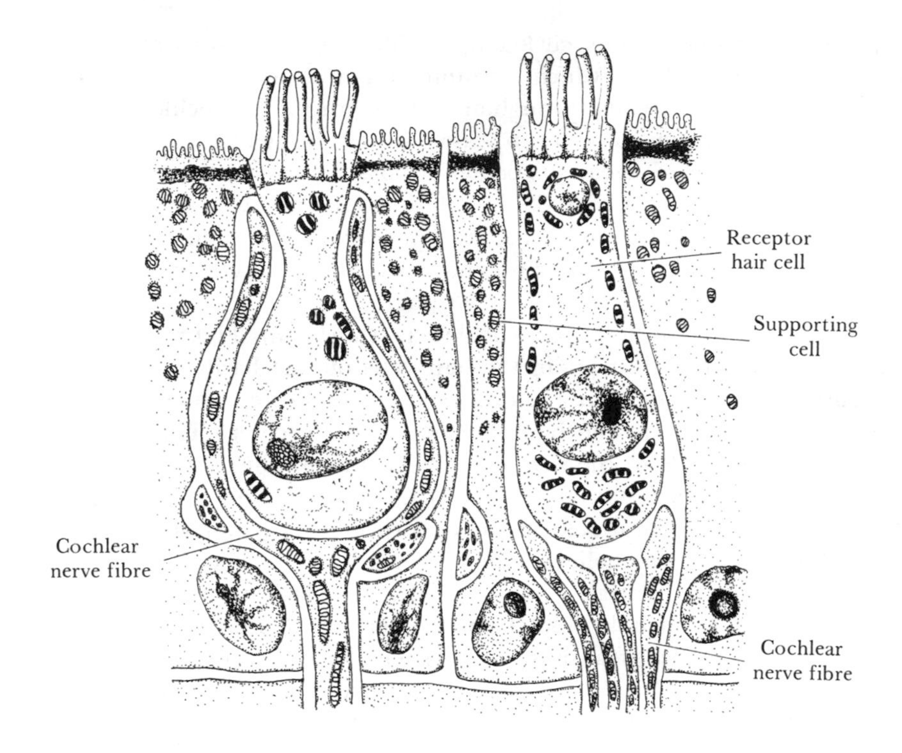

Figure 5-17 *Illustration of how dendrites of cells located in the spiral ganglion approach and wind around the base of hair cells in the cochlea. (Fig. 4.7, p. 53, in G. M. Wyburn, R. W. Pickford, and R. J. Hirst,* Human senses and perception. *Toronto: University of Toronto Press, 1964. Reprinted by permission of the publisher and Oliver and Boyd, Edinburgh.)*

frequencies, they do not seem to be equally loud. The auditory apparatus is most efficient in the range of 1000 to 4000 Hz. This is primarily because of the ways in which the ear canal, middle ear bones, tympanic membrane, and oval window work together. Thus sounds in the range of 1000 to 4000 Hz are perceived as being louder than sounds of other frequencies presented at the same intensity. Sounds in this favored frequency range will be those most readily detected at low intensities.

The neural mechanisms that account for the perception of loudness are not completely known. To be sure, more neurons will be activated by strong tones than by weak tones, but—more importantly—the pattern of discharge of individual neurons sending impulses into the central nervous system is different at different intensities.

The localization of sounds in space will be discussed later in this chapter when the processing of auditory impulses at higher nervous system levels is considered.

Electrical activities of the ear

There are several electrical potentials that can be recorded from the cochlea. Different regions of the cochlea are maintained with different electrical charges, and therefore in the resting state considerable electrical potentials can be recorded between many regions. When movements of the fluids that fill the cochlea occur, they impose changes in these standing electrical potentials.

THE COCHLEAR MICROPHONIC The best-known electrical potential that is recorded from the cochlea is called the cochlear microphonic. It is a large electrical potential that can be recorded even from electrodes placed on the auditory nerve as it leaves the cochlea. In fact, when first discovered, the cochlear microphonic was recorded from the auditory nerve and was interpreted as being the summation of nerve discharges leading to the brain. This, in turn, led to the overly simple view that the cochlear mechanisms merely acted as a telephone that sent along to the brain the exact frequencies received at the oval window.

It was soon discovered that the cochlear microphonic follows frequencies up to 70,000 Hz. Not only is this a far higher frequency than any one can "hear," but it is also much faster than any neuron can discharge. (The maximum discharge rate of some specialized neurons is about 2,000 Hz, and most nerve cells cannot fire more than 800 Hz.)

The cochlear microphonic is produced at least in part by some of the hair cells on the basilar membrane. It does not, however, represent discharges of nerve cells. Furthermore, it is a complex potential made up of many components from different structures of the cochlea. We still do not know whether it should be regarded as a "generator potential"—that is, whether it represents an electrical change that actually causes the neural fibers surrounding the hair cells to become activated.

The cochlear microphonic does give us information about the state of the hair cells. Changes in the cochlear microphonic can be used as a diagnostic tool to evaluate the causes of certain kinds of hearing disturbances.

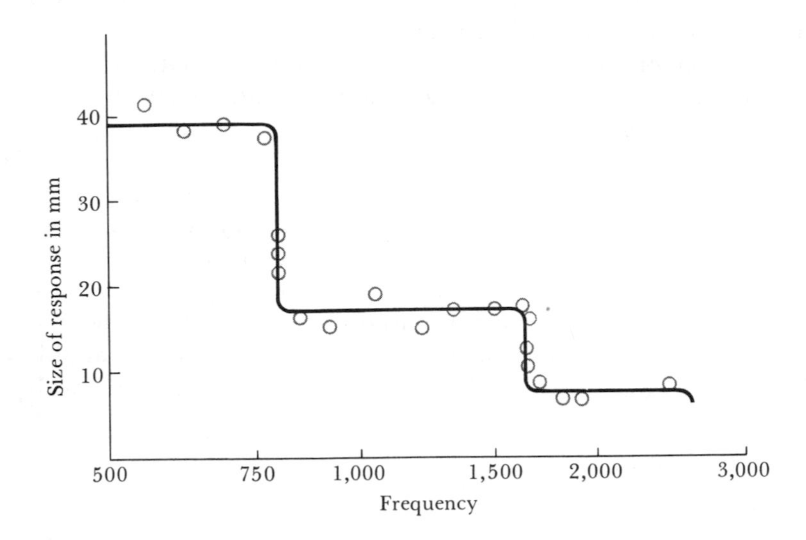

Figure 5-18 *The reduction of the size of the action potential in the auditory nerve of the cat as frequency is increased. (Fig. 152, p. 395, in S. S. Stevens and H. Davis,* Hearing. *Wiley, 1938.)*

Auditory nerve responses

The individual nerve fibers that make up the auditory nerve can be recorded in a gross manner to give a picture of the total activity found in the nerve. The striking result obtained from such recordings is that there is a "following" of frequencies in the auditory nerve for frequencies up to about 3000 Hz. This means that many fibers respond at the same time to each cycle of the tone at frequencies of these lower ranges. This presents a problem, of course, since individual nerve cells cannot fire this rapidly. An explanation of these results is suggested by consideration of the size of the response found in the auditory nerve at different frequencies.

Figure 5-18 shows the amplitude of the auditory nerve response recorded at different frequencies. There are considerable reductions in amplitude around 800 Hz and at 1600 Hz. This suggests that at frequencies below 800 Hz neurons can follow the response precisely but that when a tone's frequency is over 800 Hz, neurons begin responding to alternate vibrations; over 1600 Hz neurons respond to every third vibration. Although the neurons are responding to sets of three vibrations, not all neurons respond to the same set of three vibrations. Thus the total nerve response beyond 1600 Hz is only one-third as large as the magnitude of response found at frequencies below 800 Hz.

At frequencies beyond 3000 Hz, frequency is signaled by the discharge of neurons at different places along the basilar membrane in accordance with the traveling waves created in the cochlear fluids.

Single-cell responses

The activities of single nerve cells of the spinal ganglion and their axons in the auditory nerve can best be described as a "best-frequency" response pattern. This idea can best be shown by reference to an illustration. Figure 5-19 shows in schematic form the response patterns of three cells; these resemble the responses of cells actually found in several experimental studies. The responses of the cells to different frequency tones are plotted for a wide range of intensities. The shaded areas represent the areas of intensity and frequency in which a neuron responds. Note

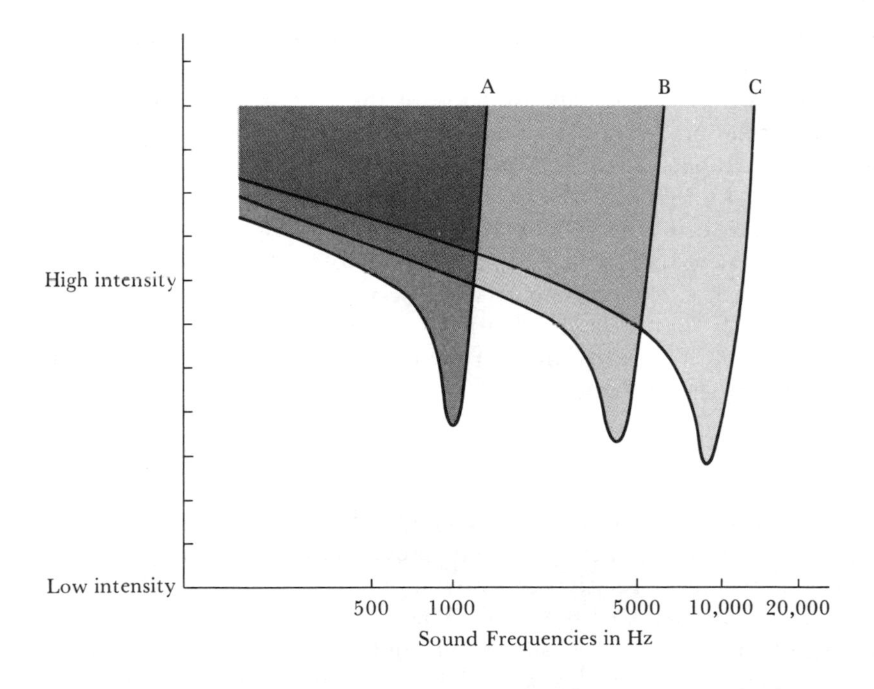

Figure 5-19 *Hypothetical response patterns for three single nerve fibers in auditory nerve. Cell* A *has a "best frequency" around 1000 Hz. Cell* B *has a "best frequency" around 4000 Hz, and Cell* C *has a "best frequency" around 8000 Hz.*

that fibers of all cells respond in the lower frequency ranges, although fiber A is rather more sensitive—that is, it will respond to low frequency tones presented at lower intensities—than the other two fibers. As the frequency scale is ascended, cell A drops out at about 1000 Hz and does not respond at any higher frequencies. Since it responds to the smallest intensity at a frequency of about 1000 Hz, this can be considered its "best frequency."

Similarly, the frequencies at which the smallest intensities are required to produce a response are 4000 Hz and 8000 Hz, respectively, for cells B and C. These would be the "best frequencies" for these cells. The pattern of response for all cells is quite similar: a gradual sloping of the frequency-intensity curve toward the "best frequency," at which point there is a more abrupt change toward greater sensitivity. After this "best frequency," there is an abrupt cut-off of response for all frequencies.

These response patterns are likely the result of activities initiated in the dendritic distributions of these cells to hair cells on the basilar membrane. Since most of the basilar membrane vibrates to low tones, all regions would be affected and this could account for the response of all of the cells to the low tones. The sharp upper cut-off, however, is surprising, as it is likely that distortion of the basilar membrane at the region of maximum vibration to adjacent regions is not this sharp. This sharp upper cut-off may mean there are mechanisms among the hair-cell receptors that inhibit the cells beyond some higher cut-off region.

If the response of any cell in Figure 5-19 at a low intensity is compared with that at a high intensity, it is easy to see that a cell responds to a narrower frequency range at the low intensities than at the high intensities. This influence of intensity on a cell's response range represents one means by which intensity can be encoded for transmission to the central nervous system.

The vestibular apparatus

Connected with the cochlea and embedded in a continuous bony structure is another sensory mechanism, the vestibular system. It provides information about the position of the head relative to gravitational pull and also about the accelerative movements of the head. The relationship of the cochlea to the vestibular apparatus is shown in Figure 5-20. The entire bony structure that is the cochlea and the vestibular apparatus is encased in the bone of the skull. The components of the vestibular apparatus include (1) the three semicircular canals and (2) the regions of the utricle and saccule. A general, schematic representation of the vestibular and auditory systems is provided in Figure 5-21.

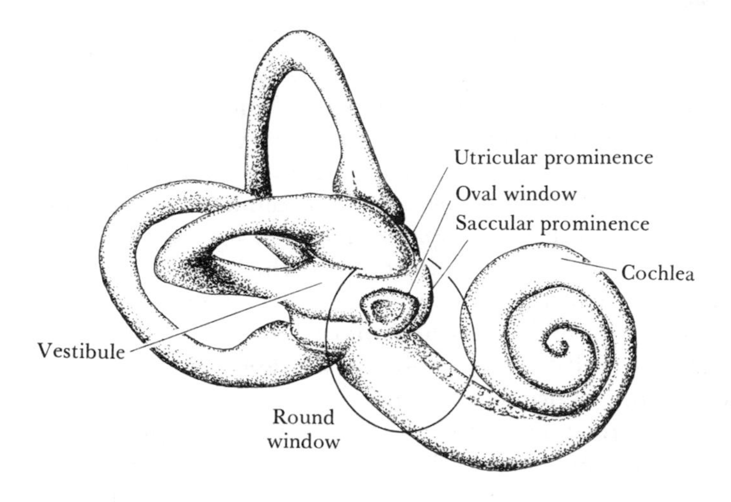

Figure 5-20 *Drawing of the gross anatomical appearance of the vestibular apparatus (semicircular canals, saccule, and utricle) and the cochlea.*

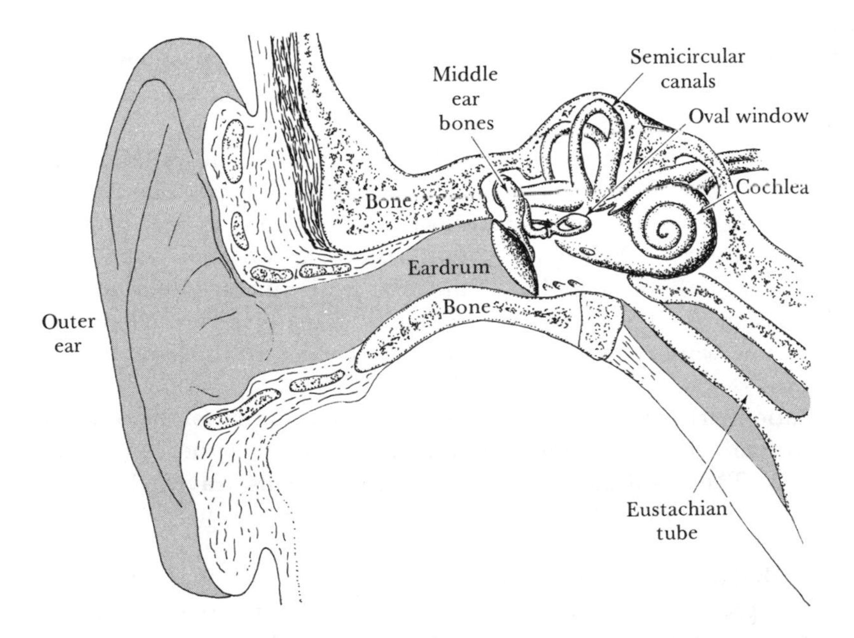

Figure 5-21 *General representation of cochlea and vestibular systems.*

The three semicircular canals and the utricle and saccule are all filled with fluid. The three semicircular canals are at right angles to each other. Within the semicircular canals there are hair cells, as on the basilar membrane, which are embedded in ampullae, tissues that extend into the fluid-filled inner space. They swing, more or less freely, when the head moves in the direction in which the semicircular canal is oriented. The hairlike processes of the ampulla end in another soft tissue mass, so that when the head is moved a sheering movement occurs across the hair cells. This motion is the appropriate stimulus for the hair cells of the semicircular canals.

A different kind of receptor system exists in the utricle and saccule. In these regions, the tissue in which the receptors are embedded is covered by a material with a jellylike consistency, which contains tiny granules of calcium carbonate. These small, hard, and heavy particles are suspended in a sacklike arrangement that will stimulate nearby hair cells when the animal's orientation is changed relative to the earth's gravitational pull. In crabs, the hard particles used in the small sacks are lost periodically and the animals insert grains of sand to make up for the loss.

In an overall view, the three semicircular canals provide a mechanism whereby angular rotation and accelerations of the head can be detected. The utricle and saccule provide a mechanism for the detection of the head's position relative to gravity, but this mechanism is of less use in man than in some lower animals. Man uses vertical-orientation information arising from the visual system to a greater extent than most lower animals.

The vestibular apparatus quickly adapts to stimulation. After adaptation occurs, no signals are sent from this sensory system. Thus, if an animal is subjected to a constant velocity of rotation, it will quickly adapt to the rotation. When the rotation stops, new signals representing the change will be sent, but adaptation will quickly occur to the new circumstances. The vestibular system represents an excellent example of how sensory systems respond to change in the stimulating conditions.

Information arising from the vestibular system reaches the central nervous system over the vestibular branch of the auditory nerve (cranial nerve VIII). The vestibular and auditory components travel along together, but they follow divergent routes once they get to the central nervous system.

The vestibular system operates in close cooperation with the cerebellum to allow appropriate balance and coordination of motor movements in the light of information arising from all of the sensory modalities. Infections of the inner ear can affect both the labyrinth and cochlea, since there is fluid communication between them. Thus abnormalities of hearing and of motor balance can result from such diseases.

THE SOMATOSENSORY SYSTEM

The term somatosensory system refers to all of the sensory mechanisms that convey information to the central nervous system from the skin, muscles, and tendons.

Sensory mechanisms of the skin

Many different sensations can arise from stimulation of the skin. These include touch, pressure, temperature, and pain. At the same time there are many types of sensory receptors in the skin. Some of them are shown in Figure 5-22, along with their relative distribution at various depths in the skin of the finger. For some time it was believed that each type of receptor produced specific types of sensations—for example, cold sensations from Krause's endbulbs, warmth by Ruffini's corpuscles. However, while there is some special sensitivity of each type of receptor to a particular type of skin sensation, the simplest of all the receptors—the free nerve endings—can mediate all forms of skin sensations. This was discovered by study of the cornea of the eye. which has *only* free nerve endings.

The specialization of the other receptor types can be illustrated by the Pacinian corpuscles. These receptor units are very sensitive to pressure on the skin but insensitive to changes in skin temperature. Various other receptors respond to one, two, or three types of stimulation but are insensitive to others.

We still are not sure exactly how activity in the receptor unit causes a change in discharge over the sensory nerve fiber. In the case of the Pacinian corpuscle, a generator potential arises in the corpuscle in response to pressure. This generator potential causes a shift toward depolarization of the nerve fiber, which enters directly into the middle of the corpuscle. However, the free nerve endings do not end in any receptive unit that can produce a generator potential. Furthermore, the nerve endings around a hair follicle are probably stimulated by the mechanical distortion produced by the bending of the hairs.

Each single neuron involved in the transmission of information about touch is activated by stimuli over a small region of the skin.

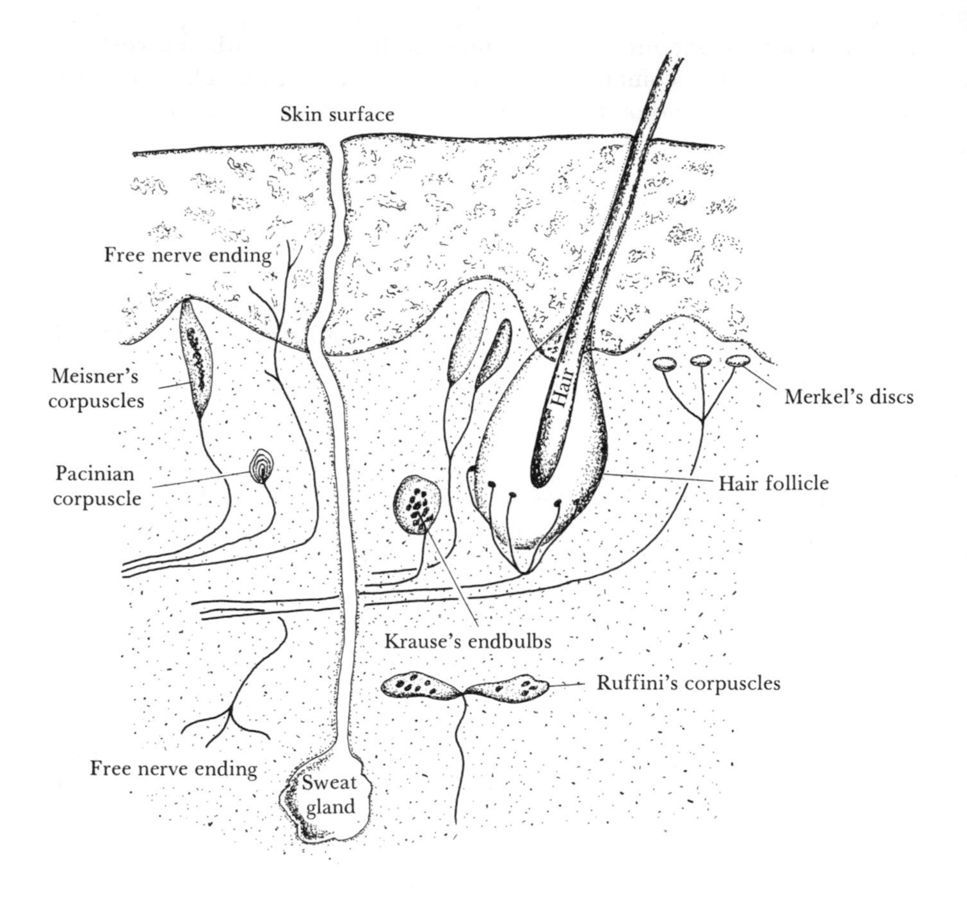

Figure 5-22 *Schematic representation of different skin receptors.*

This region in which stimuli will initiate activity in the nerve fiber is called the receptive field of that fiber. The fibers whose terminal processes end around hair follicles also respond to stimuli arising over a number of such hair follicles. The receptive fields of nerve fibers collecting information from hair cells is usually larger than that of fibers serving other types of touch receptors.

The touch receptors are not distributed equally or uniformly throughout the skin surface. There are regions of great tactile sensitivity—such as the tips of the fingers, the tip of the tongue, the lips, and the palm of the hand. The skin of the back is one of the least sensitive skin regions.

It may well be that skin regions change in sensitivity over the course of development. For example, early in life a rabbit's ears are quite sensitive relative to other skin regions (see Figure 5-23), and this ear sensitivity seems to decline over the first few weeks of life. These observations, however, may be due to the fact that there are large numbers of blood vessels in the animal's ears which are very near the skin surface at birth. The linings of blood vessels are richly endowed with free nerve endings, which can mediate many types of sensations, including pain.

There are probably no receptors specifically designed to initiate pain sensations, although the free nerve endings have historically been associated with pain. Actually, peripheral pain is a very complicated sensation. Often two or more "waves" of pain arise from a single wound in the skin. If the skin is pricked with a pin, there is a quick, sharp pain followed by a slower, more fiery sensation, which is often the most discomforting. The slower, longer-lasting pain may result from the activation of receptors by chemicals released by cells at the damaged site. The first response is probaby the direct response of the receptors to the insult.

Pain can seem to arise from regions other than that actually damaged. There are several well-known examples, including the pain that seems to arise from the left arm and shoulder during a heart attack and the ear pain sometimes associated with some types of ulcers. Pain that seems to arise from one part of the body when, in fact, it arises from another, is called "referred pain." This error in reference is thought

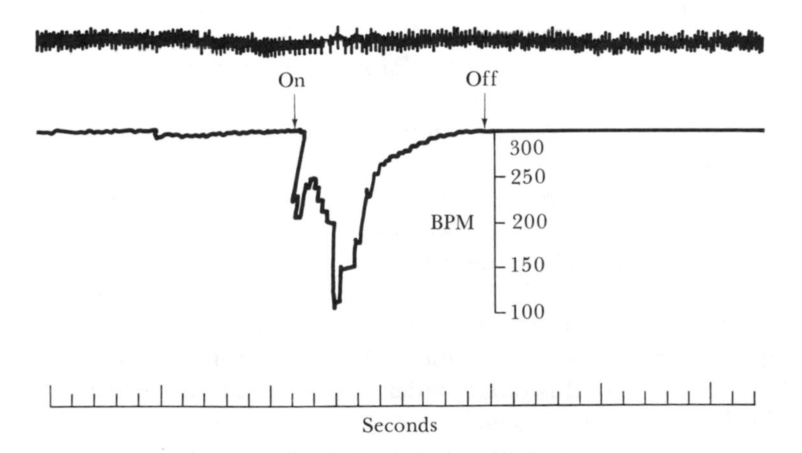

Figure 5-23 *Heart-rate response of seven-day-old-rabbit to ear-stroking. (From A. J. Nonneman and R. L. Isaacson—unpublished observations.)*

to arise from "cross-talk" between neurons of different systems that lie close to each other in the brain or brain stem. No perfectly adequate explanation is available for the phenomenon.

Sensations of temperature arise from the skin when it is appropriately stimulated so as to produce heat loss or gain. While some specialized structures in the skin have been associated with cold or with warmth detection, free nerve endings can also mediate the awareness of temperature changes. Whatever the peripheral receptors, small regions of the skin surface seem more or less exclusively responsive to heat or to cold. Thus, any small area of skin is responsive to heat or to cold but not both. Probably the temperature responses of a skin area change over time with the growth and change of peripheral nerves in the area.

Information arising from muscles and tendons

Working in a coordinated fashion with the receptors of the skin are the receptors in the muscles and tendons. While muscles are supplied with several types of receptor systems (such as free nerve endings and Pacinian corpuscles), major emphasis has been placed upon the two receptor systems that signal the degree to which the muscle is being stretched. These are the Golgi tendon organs and the spindles in *intrafusal* muscle fibers. Most muscles have both types of sensory systems.

Tendons connect muscles to the bones or connective tissue at their two ends. Muscle tissue is specialized so that it can shorten itself during contraction. As a muscle contracts, strain is placed on the tendons and this exerts a pull on the bones of the skeleton to which the muscle is attached. If the muscle is not contracting, it can be passively stretched by the contractions of other muscles. Normal movements involved in walking, writing, and other motor acts involve the coordinated contractions of first one set and then another set of muscles. The status of the muscles is signaled to the central nervous system by the receptors in the muscles, spindles, and tendons. The contractive force of the muscles is signaled by the tendon organs, and the degree to which the muscle is itself passively being stretched by other muscles is signaled by the muscle spindles.

This general arrangement is illustrated in Figure 5-24. In this figure the general arrangement is shown under A; what happens when the muscle fibers contract is illustrated under B; the condition when the muscle is passively stretched is shown under C.

Another factor has been introduced in this figure. This is the gamma (γ) efferent system. These fibers are small-diameter motor fibers that leave the spinal cord along with the large-diameter motor fibers to

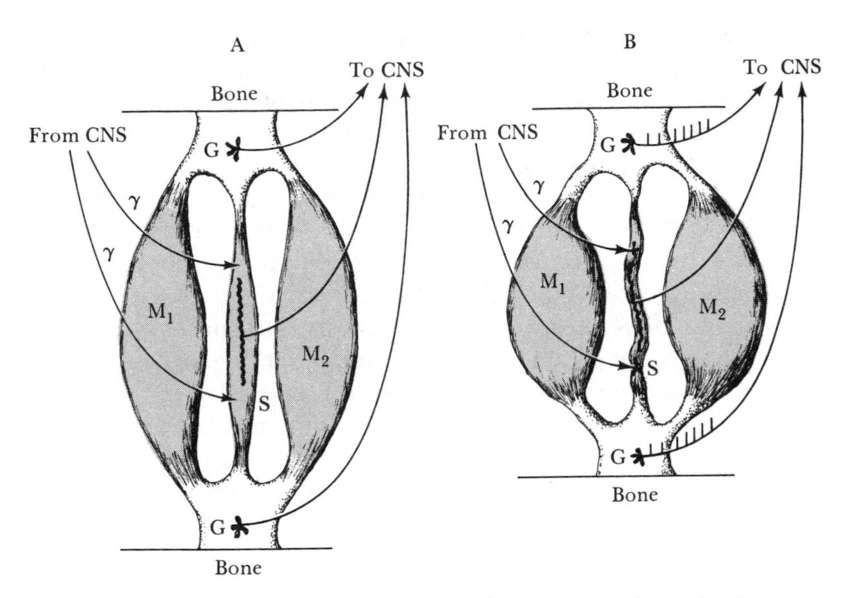

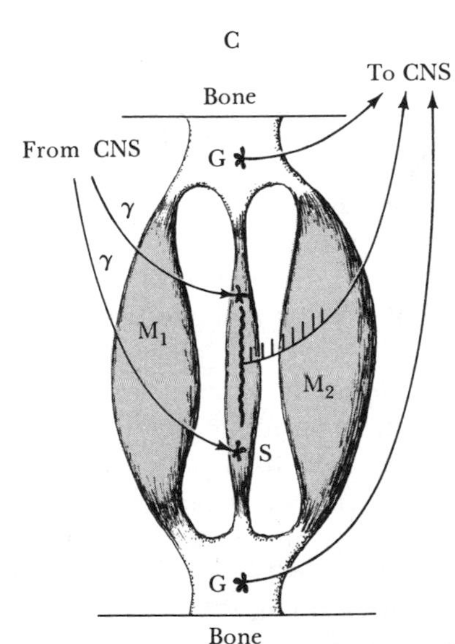

Figure 5-24 *Schematic diagram of tendon and muscle receptor systems.* M_1 *and* M_2 *are large contractive muscle fibers.* S *is the spindle in intrafusal muscle fiber which lies parallel to regular muscle fibers.* G *in the Gogli tendon organ. The* γ *denotes gamma efferents. Note that as* M_1 *and* M_2 *contract, as represented in* B, *there will be tension applied to tendons but the spindle actually receives less stretch than before in* A. *The short vertical strokes, on top of the lines indicating the neural fibers leading to the central nervous system, represent the discharges arising from the Golgi tendon organs at this time. In* C *we see the effects of the muscle being passively stretched when there are increased discharges from the muscle spindle.*

reach the major muscle fibers themselves (not illustrated in Figure 5-24). These smaller motor fibers do not reach the larger muscles but reach the ends of the intrafusal muscle fibers. These regions of the intrafusal fibers are contractile, and when the gamma efferents are active the spindle is stretched in a way that is indistinguishable from what happens when the muscle is passively stretched. Activity over the gamma efferent system thus increases afferent activity arising from the muscle spindles. In principle it is a way for the brain and central nervous system to regulate sensory activity at the muscle receptor level. This efferent system is thought by some investigators to be a model of central nervous system control applicable to all sensory systems. But, efferent (motor) fibers do not reach the receptors in all sensory systems. Nevertheless, in other sensory systems the control of sensory events by the brain could be exerted at higher levels along the lines of transmission from receptors to the brain rather than at the receptors themselves. In short, the brain can regulate information reaching it from the peripheral receptors, and at least in the muscle-spindle system this regulation is found right at the receptor level.

THE CHEMICAL SENSES

The senses that act to detect and evaluate odors and tastes can be considered the chemical senses. The receptors in these two systems are responsive to chemicals that find their way into the nose or the mouth. The olfactory sensory system works closely with the taste system, as we have all recognized when we have difficulty in tasting food when our noses are "stuffy" during a bout with a common cold. The intake of food usually stimulates both the olfactory and the taste receptors.

The olfactory receptor mechanisms are located deep within the nose in what is called the olfactory epithelium. Protruding from the olfactory epithelium are millions of tiny hairs, which are thought to be the surfaces upon which odors produce membrane changes. The primary olfactory receptive cells are supported by large cells that look like columns with little more than the small, hairlike processes sticking beyond the supporting cells, as illustrated in Figure 5-25.

The axons of the primary receptive cells project back into the olfactory bulb where contact is made with other neurons. The olfactory nerve arises from these second-order neurons of the olfactory bulb and projects to the brain. The olfactory nerve is the first cranial nerve (Cranial Nerve I).

The degree of specialization of the hair cells in the olfactory epithelium is unknown. The neural activity is initiated by chemical

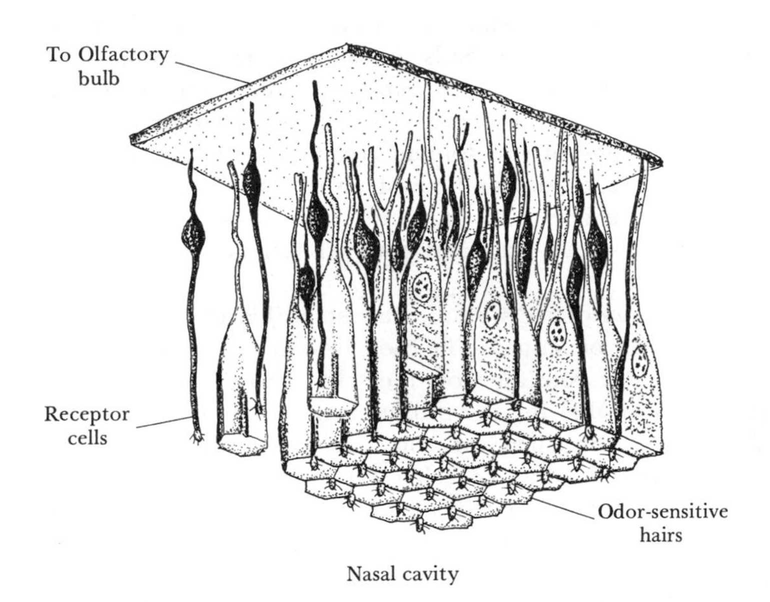

Figure 5-25 *Diagram of olfactory epithelium including the olfactory receptors in black and supporting cells. Note that the hairlike processes protrude into the nasal cavities. (Fig. 172, p. 338 from W. S. Krieg,* Functional neuroanatomy *(2nd ed.). New York: Blakiston, 1953.)*

absorption, but whether certain hair cells are responsive only to one type of odor or to many is debatable. It seems likely, however, that the shape of the chemical molecule is important in determining whether it will affect the hair cell.

The receptive cells for taste also have tiny hairlike processes that reach outside of a budlike structure. These taste buds are located along the top of the tongue, and to a lesser extent some can be found on the back of the mouth. The taste buds are located near the top of the small mounds ("papillae") that lie along the tongue's surface. There may be one, ten, or hundreds of taste buds in each papilla, depending upon the animal species being studied. Some animals, such as the rat, have only one taste bud to a papilla. Inside the taste bud there may be several taste cells arranged like orange slices. Each taste cell has a fine hairlike process which extends out into the fluid-covered surface of the tongue through a pore in the top of the taste bud.

Traditionally, it has been thought that there are four primary tastes: sour, salt, bitter, and sweet. Minute stimulation of a single papilla indicates that each is responsive to only one of these four basic tastes. Since there are many taste buds in each papilla, one would have to conclude that all the buds in a papilla mediate only one sensation. There is also another factor operating in the distribution of taste receptors: certain regions of the tongue contain papillae that are especially responsive to a particular type of taste. The front part of the tongue is especially sensitive to sweet, while the back is especially sensitive to bitter. Responses to salty and sour stimuli are located at the middle of the tongue.

Certain characteristics of the stimuli are responsible for the initiation of the different types of tastes. The positive-valent metallic ions of salts are apparently responsible for the salty taste, while the free hydrogen ion is responsible for the initiation of a sour taste. It should be remembered that the chemical solutions taken into the mouth become dissolved in the saliva covering the tongue, and the ions of salts and acids become dissociated to some extent as this happens. Saliva also exerts a buffering effect on acids applied to the tongue, reducing the acidity (pH) of the solution before it reaches the papillae. Very little is known about the molecular or ionic characteristics of the solutions that evoke sweet and bitter tastes.

Microelectrode recordings made of the activity of taste buds have shown that chemical stimuli cause slow and more or less regular activities to be produced in them. These potentials are probably not generator potentials, because they take a long time to be initiated in the taste buds. The afferent nerve discharges occur before these slow potentials develop.

Information reaches the central nervous system from the tongue over the branches of three separate cranial nerves, as shown in Figure 5-26. The back of the tongue is served by fibers of the glossopharyngeal nerve (Cranial Nerve IX), while the anterior portions are served by a branch (called the chorda tympani) of the facial nerve (Cranial Nerve VII). Some few fibers of the vagus nerve (Cranial Nerve X) reach taste receptors in the throat, larynx, and pharynx. General sensations of touch and pressure originating on the tongue reach the central nervous system over the trigeminal nerve (Cranial Nerve V), but no taste sensations are carried over this nerve.

Chemical receptors are also found associated with blood vessels just above the heart in what are called the carotid and aortic bodies. These receptors are sensitive to the amount of oxygen and carbon dioxide levels in the blood and the acidity (pH) of the blood. These receptors are the first link in reflexes which control respiration. These chemical receptors differ from the chemical receptors subserving taste

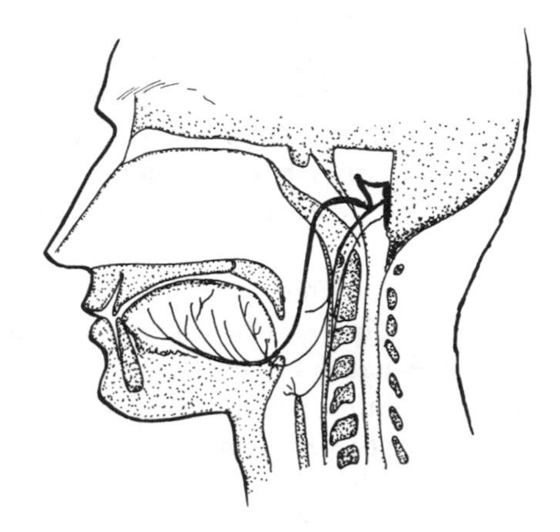

Figure 5-26 *Diagram of cranial nerves serving taste receptors of the tongue and throat.*

and olfaction in that their activities do not produce sensations, so far as is known.

Activities of the receptors will be of little value to the organism if their influences are not transmitted in a reasonably efficient fashion to higher neural regions. It is this aspect of the sensory systems we will consider next.

SENSORY SYSTEMS: LINES OF TRANSMISSION

Information arising from the receptors must get to the central nervous system for further processing. The information is encoded in the form of changes in the firing rate of neurons regardless of how the change is initiated at the receptor. The understanding of how the receptor-induced activities affect behavior involves understanding how the information reaches the central nervous system.

The lines of transmission from periphery to the brain are complicated, and unfortunately there are few universal rules that are applicable to all sensory systems. In general each sensory system has its own way of sending information. Moreover, each has its own complexities and idiosyncrasies.

One mistake should be avoided in thinking of the transmission of sensory information to and within the central nervous system. This is the assumption that the lines of transmission are just that—ways in which earlier neural activity gets transported, *as is,* to a higher region.

The pathways from receptor to brain are not passive but *active,* and the form and probably the content of the information passing along in them are altered at each synapse along the way.

As one general principle, we can say that all of the sensory systems have several synapses between neurons imposed on the path from the periphery to the neocortex. Just how many synapses intervene depends upon the particular sensory system. It is at these synapses that the messages can be altered.

Another principle with general application is that at least some portion of the pathways leading to the brain cross over from the side at which they enter the spinal cord to the opposite side of the spinal cord or brain. Thus information ascending to the brain goes along two lines, one on each side of the body. For example, information arising from the right arm or hand will proceed upward in the spinal cord on both the right and left sides. All of the nerve fibers enter on the right side of the cord, but some will cross over to the left almost as soon as they enter the cord. This does not mean that the two pathways are carrying equivalent information. Usually the pathways that cross over from right to left (or left to right) are the larger, faster-conducting fibers that bear more significance for behavior. This fact is related to another aspect of sensory conduction, namely: there usually are several pathways or routes over which information may move. In some systems there are routes made predominantly out of small fibers with little myelin covering and with many synapses, as well as routes made up of large fibers with heavy myelin covering and few synapses along the route. In such cases the large-fiber system is thought to be a more recent phylogenetic development that carries the information to the thalamus and neocortex, which allows the finest discriminations to be made. The smaller fiber systems are thought to be more primitive, allowing only more gross evaluations of the environment. These assumptions are probably less than completely accurate, but they serve at least as guides about which our thinking can be organized.

One final overall principle is that all transmission of sensory information to the neocortex involves a connection through the nuclei of the dorsal thalamus. The one prominent exception is olfaction. The dorsal thalamus and the neocortex evolved together, and the fact that sensory systems "relay" at this point in their progression to the neocortex is not surprising.

With these words of introduction, we shall next turn to a consideration of how the neural activity initiated at the receptors reaches the brain.

The olfactory system

The transmission of olfactory information to the brain is *not* representative of the other major sensory systems. Information proceeds from the olfactory bulb to the brain via the first cranial nerve. Upon reaching the brain it separates into two or three bundles called tracts. Most higher species only have two: a lateral olfactory tract and an intermediate olfactory tract. Some animals that follow odor trails have a medial olfactory tract, but this third tract is seldom found in higher animals.

Fibers of the intermediate olfactory tract project into many regions of the structures of the limbic system located toward the middle of the brain, where they mix with the fibers of the *medial forebrain bundle,* which runs along the base of the brain. The fibers of the lateral olfactory tract also contact the limbic system structures located in the more lateral aspects of the brain—for example, the amygdala. Because of the close association of the olfactory system with structures of the limbic system, the latter has sometimes been termed the *nose brain* (rhinencephalon). This name provides a mistaken impression of the limbic system, however. It is little concerned with the sense of smell.

The olfactory system has little if any projection to the neocortical surface. Its fibers reach more primitive cortical regions along the sides of the brain near its ventral surface and those regions of the limbic system which were mentioned above. These relationships place it in marked contrast to the other sensory systems.

The visual pathways

The optic nerves are made up of the axons of ganglion cells in the retina. These axons proceed from each eye back along the base of the brain to a meeting point below the anterior hypothalamus, where they then turn up and into the brain. The point at which they come together is called the optic chiasm (or optic chiasma). In primates, at least, most of the fibers proceed from the optic chiasm to the dorsal lateral geniculate nucleus. From there, the majority of cells project to restricted portions of the neocortex. These neocortical areas are termed the *visual neocortex.*

These are the simple facts of the visual pathways, but there are modifications and qualifications that must be considered. As an initial step toward understanding the more complex aspects of the visual projections, consider Figure 5-27.

In this figure we can see that at the optic chiasm some fibers from each eye cross to the other side of the brain while others remain on

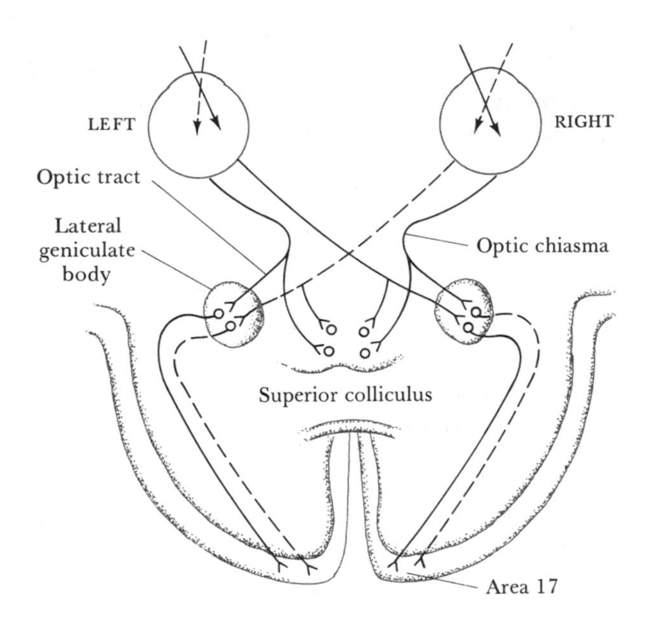

Figure 5-27 *Visual pathways. Light from objects in right visual field reaches left half of retina; light from left visual field reaches right half. Note that information from right or left of retina is transmitted to same right or left hemisphere. Collaterals from optic tracts reach visual reflex centers in the midbrain. Determine visual effects of damage to visual pathways made before and after optic chiasma.*

the side where they originate. The arrangement is not haphazard. The axons of ganglion cells located on the outer (temporal) halves of each retina remain on their sides of origin while the axons of ganglion cells located in the nasal halves cross to the opposite side of the brain. In turn this means that each lateral geniculate and each cortical hemisphere receives information only about one-half of the visual world. The left lateral geniculate nucleus and the left visual neocortex receive direction information only from the right half of the visual field. The right lateral geniculate nucleus and right neocortex receive information directly only from the left half of the visual field. In the present context, the term visual field would mean all of what can be seen when one looks straight ahead at a far-off point.

In man about 50 percent of the fibers from each eye cross over to the other side at the optic chiasm. The actual percentages of crossed and uncrossed fibers varies from species to species. Animals whose eyes are set farther apart on the head have fewer optic nerve fibers that stay on the same side, and in lower vertebrates all optic nerve fibers cross to the opposite side of the brain at the chiasm.

The division of the axons of ganglion cells of the retina into nasal and temporal halves is probably not absolute. There probably is a region near the midline of each retina that projects to both lateral geniculate nuclei. Although this assumption has not been established beyond all doubt, such a condition would explain a number of observations otherwise difficult to explain—for example: Why does the center of the visual field often remain useful after damage to one visual neocortical area that should produce an absence of vision in exactly one-half of the visual field?

ORGANIZATION OF THE LATERAL GENICULATE NUCLEUS In the primates the common pattern of the cellular construction of the lateral geniculate nucleus is one of multiple layers of cells. Each layer receives input from only one eye. In man, who has six layers of cells, three layers receive fibers from one eye and the three other layers receive fibers from the other eye. An illustration of the lateral geniculate nucleus of a monkey is shown in Figure 5-28.

Across each layer of cells in the lateral geniculate nucleus, there is a systematic projection from the retina. If a portion of the retina is damaged, cells in specific segments of the three layers of cells that receive input from that eye will degenerate. Distribution of the lateral geniculate cells' axons to the neocortex is also highly regular. This regularity

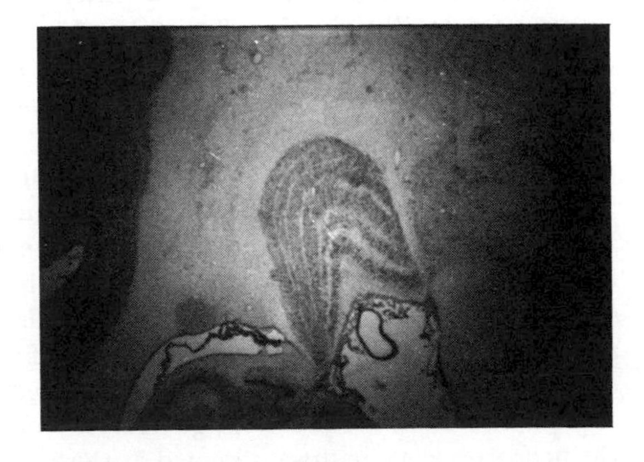

Figure 5-28 *The lateral geniculate nucleus of a monkey. The dark regions are densely packed cells, which are organized into six layers.*

is demonstrated by the fact that neighboring neocortical regions receive input from neighboring geniculate regions, which receive input from neighboring retinal regions.

Investigations into the activities of single cells of the lateral geniculate nucleus have been numerous. Microelectrodes are lowered into the immediate vicinity of a cell in one of the layers, and the animal's eyes are stimulated by lights and patterns of different colors, intensities, and directions of movement.

One result arising from this type of research has been the discovery that pairs of cell layers (i.e., adjacent layers, one receiving information from each eye) contain cells that have common response characteristics. Most or all of the cells of a layer respond in similar ways to illumination of the eye with pure lights of a particular wavelength. The cells in the top two layers of the monkey's lateral geniculate nucleus respond to narrow bands of wavelengths. This means they are very selective to particular colors. Cells in the middle two layers are color-sensitive, but they respond in quite a different way to colors. Each cell responds with an increased discharge rate to one wavelength and with a decreased rate to that color's complementary. Colored lights are complementary to each other when they produce a neutral (white or gray) experience if blended together. Reds and green are complements to each other, as are blues and yellows. Thus a cell in the middle two layers of the geniculate nucleus may increase its rate of firing to red but decrease its rate of firing to green. Another opponent cell might increase its discharge to yellow and be inhibited by blue. An illustration of this opponent-cell type of discharge is presented in Figure 5-29.

Cells in the bottom two layers of the lateral geniculate nucleus seem to be less sensitive to color. They frequently reduce their rate of discharge in response to illumination. In some ways they seem to have response characteristics that resemble the activities of rods in the retina. Rods are not very selective in responding to colors, and they respond to a change in total illumination.

The responses of the lateral geniculate nucleus have been modified from the responses of the retina receptors and the activities of the ganglion cells whose axons reach the geniculate nuclei. This results from interaction among the axons as they reach the geniculate cells and from synaptic bombardment upon geniculate cells (some of which probably arises from cells in the neocortex). Other influences upon the geniculate cells probably originate in the diffusely projecting systems of the brain.

From the cells in the lateral geniculate nucleus, axons project toward the neocortex over pathways known as the visual "radiations." The name radiation is used to describe the way in which the fibers "fan out" on

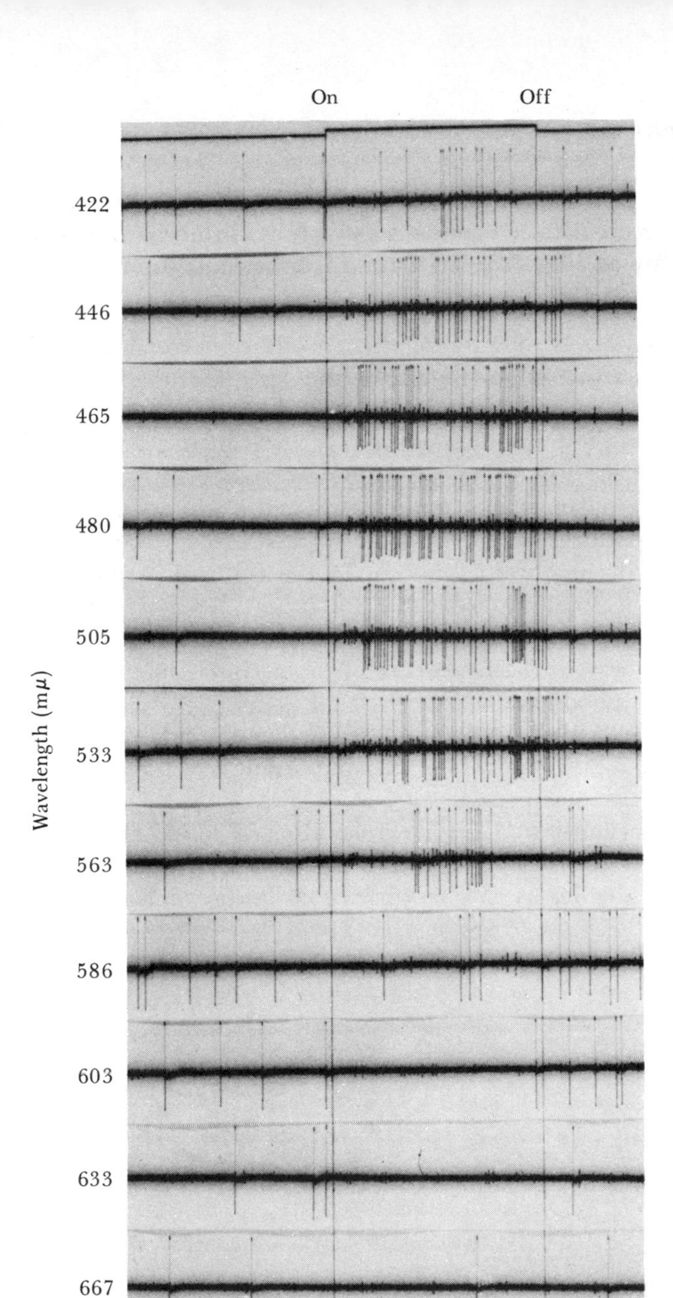

Figure 5-29 *An example of a cell in the monkey lateral geniculate nucleus that acts in an "opponent-process" fashion. This cell responds to increased activity to wavelengths from 465 μ (blue-green) to 533 μ (orange-red). Its activity is suppressed in the range of 600 μ. (Courtesy of R. L. DeValois, University of California at Berkeley.)*

their way. Each geniculate cell contacts many cells of the visual neocortex, probably as many as 5000. We shall return to consideration of the role of the neocortex shortly.

OTHER VISUAL PATHWAYS Figure 5-30 shows additional pathways of the visual system. Some fibers do not go to the lateral geniculate nucleus but, instead, reach the superior colliculi in the midbrain. Others follow the same general route but end ahead of the colliculi in what are called the pretectal nuclei. Still other fibers follow routes into the general region of the hypothalamus, and some may actually end upon cells there. Most of these hypothalamic fibers probably pass through the hypothalamus and end in the midbrain, but not in the colliculi. Some of them probably reach the midbrain reticular formation. As shown in Figure 5-30 there is a possibility that some fibers may diverge from the visual radiations on the way to the neocortex of the occipital lobe to arrive at portions of the temporal lobe.

The fibers of the visual system that reach the superior colliculi have been thought, in higher animals, to be important for moving the eyes so as to obtain the best retinal pattern. However, they probably are involved in processing visual information also. In lower animals, such as amphibians, the colliculi are the only visual mechanisms of the forebrain that are available. As the neocortex and dorsal thalamus evolved,

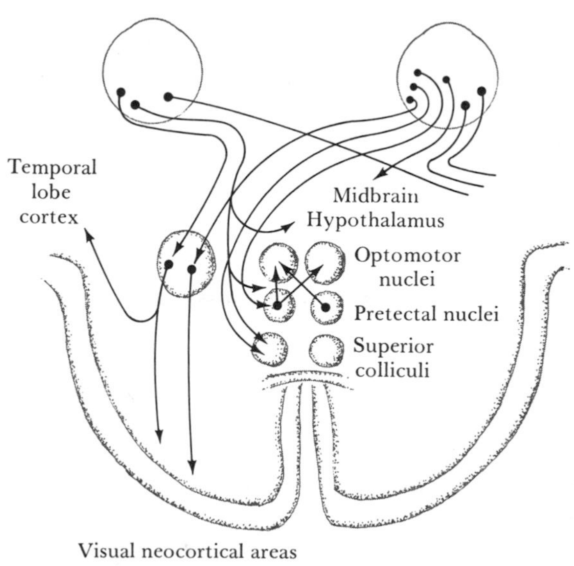

Figure 5-30 *Schematic drawing of visual pathways, including some whose functions are not well established.*

they supplanted and overrode the collicular system, and we do not know how many residual abilities remain in the collicular systems.

Recordings made from single cells in the hypothalamus and in the temporal lobe neocortex have indicated that there are some cells in these regions which are responsive to visual stimulation. The role of such cells in behavior has not been established, but there is good evidence that the temporal-lobe neocortex makes the processing of information in the visual cortex more efficient.

The routing of visual information from the eye to the brain follows many different pathways, although the geniculate-neocortex system is probably the most important for the higher animals. Yet, our comprehension of the visual system and its operation will come about only when we understand the significance and capabilities of the other pathways, too.

The auditory and vestibular pathways

These two systems arrive at the central nervous system over two branches of the auditory nerve (Cranial Nerve VIII). Afterwards, each component travels forward in different ways. Their sharing of the auditory nerve arises from their common origin in the cochlea—although this occurs in functionally separate regions.

The auditory projections to the neocortex are shown in Figure 5-31.

As can be seen in this figure, almost as soon as they enter the brainstem, the auditory fibers divide into two groups: those which cross over and those which do not cross over to the other side. The axons of subsequent cells in the pathways continue toward the higher reaches of the central nervous system in parallel fashion. However, interaction between the two parallel systems occurs all the way along the line. This arrangement is of special interest in the auditory system, because one of the important functions of this sensory modality is to localize the origins of sounds in space. In part this is done by the differences in the time of arrival of sounds at the two ears. The higher auditory mechanisms must make these comparisons. Note that at the level of the trapezoid body and the inferior colliculi, auditory fibers make connections both with cells on the same side of the brain *and* with cells on the opposite side of the brain. Note also that the areas receiving the two inputs are interconnected with each other. We shall return to this aspect of the auditory pathways later.

Recording from single nerve fibers in the auditory system reveals changes in response patterns at each stage along the transmission lines. This may have been expected because a similar situation was found in the visual system; this reflects the fact that information is processed along all of the ascending sensory pathways at every synapse.

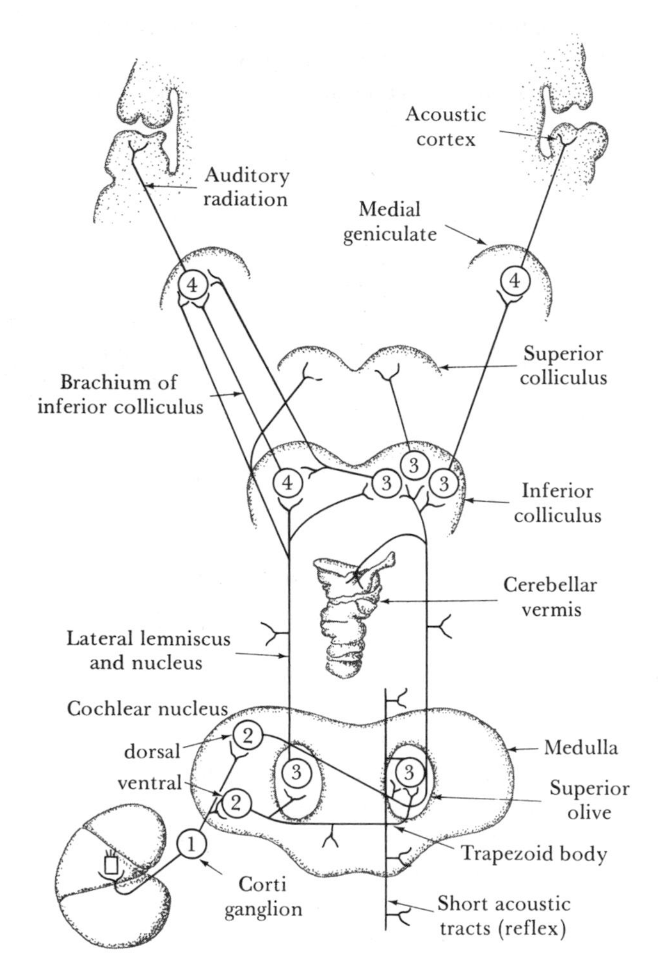

Figure 5-31 *Afferent acoustic pathways. Numbers in circles represent first, second, third and fourth neuron of chain. (Fig. 4 from H. Davis, Psychophysics of learning and deafness, in S. S. Stevens, Ed.,* Handbook of experimental psychology. *Wiley, 1951.)*

The auditory system translates differences in the frequencies of sounds into differences in spatial locations in the central nervous system. This is begun at the basilar membrane in the cochlea. Particular regions of the basilar membrane are activated by particular frequencies. Thereafter, within the auditory system, a regular distribution of nerve cells is found at every auditory station. Similar tones excite neighboring neural regions. This means that a tone of 1100 Hz will affect cells near those affected by a tone of 1000 Hz. A 3000-Hz tone will affect cells located farther away. It is as if the tissue were laid out with one end containing cells affected by low frequency tones and the other containing cells affected by high frequency tones, with an orderly progression of excitable cells in between.

The direction of sounds is determined by two factors: differences in the *intensity* of sounds and differences in the *arrival* of sounds at the two ears. The auditory system is built so as to allow comparisons of these two factors. A mechanism for comparing the times of arrival of sounds at the two ears has been discovered at the level of the superior olive (see Figure 5-31). Cells in this region have long dendrites, which extend in two opposite directions. One of the dendrites receives information from one ear and the other receives information from the other ear. If one dendrite is activated by its dendritic contacts just before the activation of the cell's other dendrite, its normal response is inhibited. This simple mechanism provides one means whereby the differences in the time of arrival of sounds at the two ears can be signaled to the brain as a distinct event.

In the auditory system more intense sounds are transmitted along the auditory pathways faster than less intense sounds. This means that if one ear is nearer a sound source than the other, the impulses arising from the "closer ear" will move toward higher centers than those from the "farther ear." This illustrates how intensity of stimulation can be transformed into the "time of arrival" of impulses at higher auditory centers.

The medial geniculate nucleus of the dorsal thalamus, which is associated with audition, differs in many ways from the lateral geniculate nucleus, which subserves vision. One important difference is that the cells of the medial geniculate nucleus receive input from sensory systems other than the auditory. In the lateral geniculate nucleus most cells are exclusively responsive to visual input. The significance of the greater mixing of sensory information at the medial geniculate nucleus is not known, but it may be related to differences in the behavioral effects produced by blindness and deafness, especially early in life.

The fibers arising from the vestibular apparatus enter the midbrain and then project to a series of special nuclei located just below the cerebellum. Some fibers probably reach the cerebellum directly. In any case, the main interconnections of the vestibular system are with the cerebellum and secondarily with the motor neurons throughout the entire extent of the spinal cord.

The somatic pathways

Probably nothing rivals the somatic sensory system for sheer complexity of conductive pathways to higher centers of the nervous system. A schematic overview of the systems involved has been attempted in Figure 5-32. Certain fundamental principles of this system's operation can be understood from studying this figure in conjunction with the text description.

Along the left-hand side of Figure 5-32, the several types of receptors in-

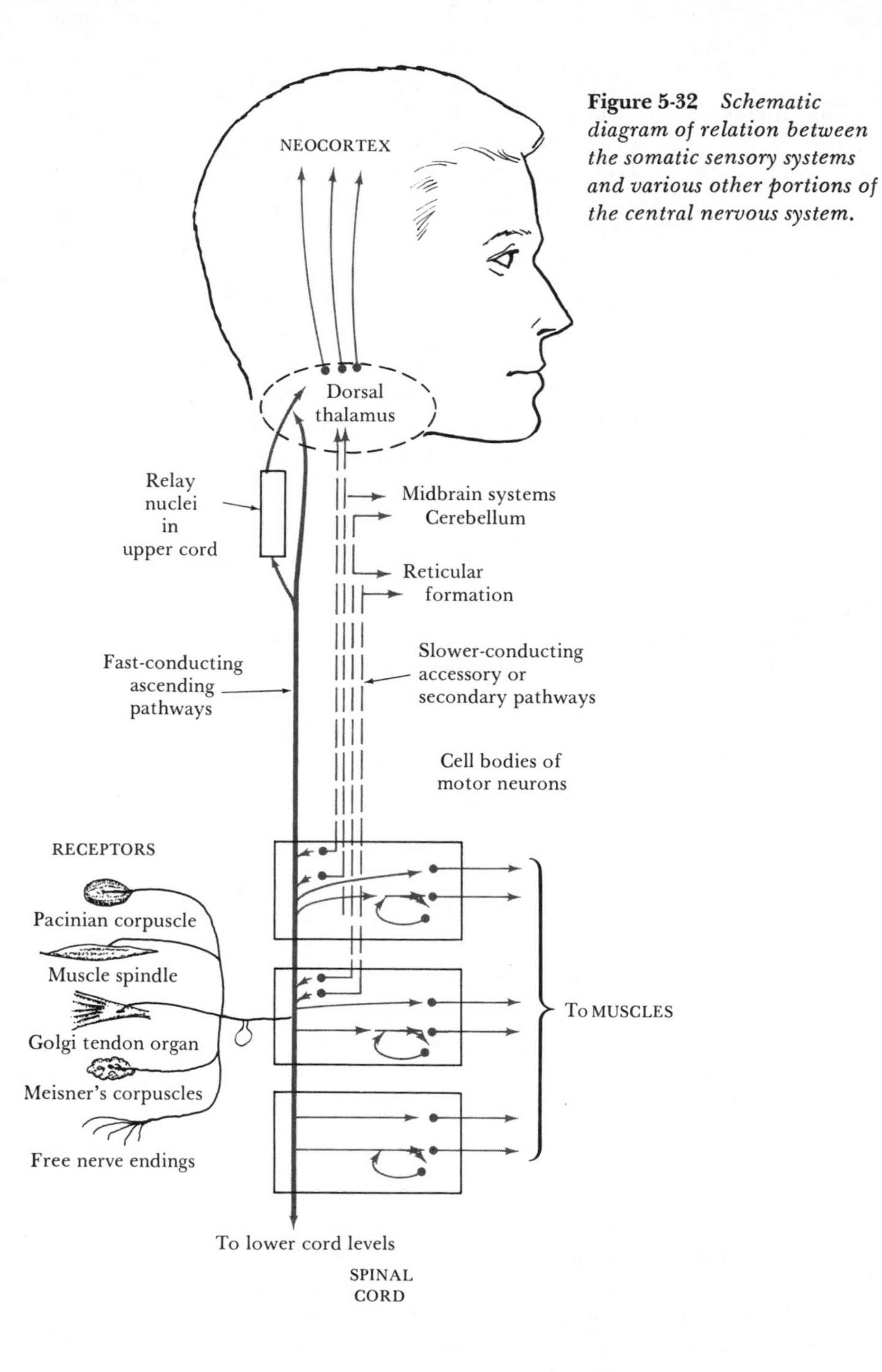

Figure 5-32 *Schematic diagram of relation between the somatic sensory systems and various other portions of the central nervous system.*

volved in somatic sensations are portrayed. All of the neurons that come in contact with these receptors have nuclei that lie in pairs just outside the back of the spinal cord. One member of each pair serves the right side of the body and the other member the left. These paired ganglia are called the *dorsal root ganglia.* There is a pair of dorsal root ganglia for every spinal nerve along the extent of the spinal cord. These cells are of a very special type. They have one long process which reaches from the receptor to (and past) its own cell body in the dorsal root ganglion and then proceeds into the spinal cord. The process that goes toward the receptor acts like a dendrite as an impulse is generated in it through the action of the receptor cells. On the other hand, it is also like an axon in that it conducts the impulse as an "action potential" and is myelinated. (Probably neither analogy is particularly useful in describing this cell, which is unique among neurons.)

Once the process of the dorsal root cells goes inside the spinal cord a number of arrangements are found. Synapses are made with cells on the same side and the opposite side of the spinal cord. Some of the synaptic contacts are with motor cells, while others are made upon neurons whose axons remain within the central nervous system.

For these latter cells, three general projection systems are possible. Some cells have long axons which project considerable distances (1) to the thalamus, or (2) to nuclei in the upper spinal cord, whose cells subsequently project to the dorsal thalamus. These long fibers can run toward the thalamus in the large-fiber, fast-conducting pathways, or in the "accessory systems," which also carry information to the reticular formation, cerebellum, and certain midbrain regions related to the regulation of body movements. Other cells have axons that project for shorter distances within the cord, going to cord segments above or below the place at which the original fibers enter the cord. These fibers participate in systems coordinating bodily movements. A third type of cell has axons that are short and feed into loops of neurons that can perpetuate activity for some period of time after the arrival of the original stimuli.

The spinal cord is filled with many ascending and descending tracts related to the spread of information from the periphery of the body to many areas of the spinal cord, the brain stem, and the forebrain. The study of these pathways can be a subject for thorough investigation in itself, and any simple portrait of the cord's functions can only be misleading. Furthermore, we still do not know all of its principles of operation despite years of intensive research.

At the level of the dorsal thalamus, most of the somatosensory information arrives at nuclei that collectively are called the ventrobasal complex.

These nuclei contain cells whose axons project to restricted neocortical regions. In some of the nuclei the cells are responsive only to stimuli arising from the receptors of muscle and skin, while in others the cells may respond to stimuli arriving over many modalities.

In those thalamic nuclei which are more or less the exclusive recipients of somatic information the cells that receive information from nearby bodily regions are grouped together. This results in a "somatotopic map" of the body being represented in the nuclei. The cells in these thalamic regions also project to the neocortex in a consistent fashion so that the "bodily maps" are found at the neocortical surface.

One interesting aspect of these cellular maps of the body is that the number of cells related to a region of the body is related to the sensitivity and fine-motor movements available at that region rather than by the total body size of the region. For example, the hand has a much larger representation in the map than does the back—even though the latter has the greater mass and skin area.

The central projections of cells concerned with the sense of taste go to the ventrobasal nuclear groups of the thalamus. Cells responsive to taste activities are found in the most inward regions of the ventrobasal complex, but yet nearby the cells are responsive to mechanical stimulation of the tongue. It is apparently the case that these "taste cells" in the thalamus project to neocortical regions in somewhat the same way as cells that are responsive to tactual stimuli. In most species the thalamic "taste cells" are exclusively responsive to taste. The rat is one exception in that its thalamic taste cells are also responsive to tactual stimulation.

NEOCORTICAL CONTRIBUTIONS TO SENSORY PROCESSES

The areas of the brain's neocortical mantle that receive the projections from the specific sensory nuclei of the dorsal thalamus are often considered to be most important regions for the perception of sensory events in higher animals. In mammals and primates the lower sensory pathways and centers are still available, but they are thought to be permanently bypassed and even actively suppressed by the development of the dorsal thalamus and neocortical systems in more advanced animals.

Certain general features of the neocortical sensory regions can be described. First, all sensory systems, except the olfactory, have relatively discrete areas of neocortical surface at which fibers of the dorsal thalamus arrive.

The olfactory system activities arrive at cortical areas along the lower (ventral) sides of the brain. These cortical areas are more primitive than neocortex in that these areas have fewer than six layers of cells. This type of organization is thought to be representative of cortical tissue found early in the evolution of such tissue.

For the other sensory systems, the fibers that arrive in a given region spread their influences over a substantial number of cells. One example, mentioned earlier, is the visual system, in which one fiber arriving in the visual neocortical area may make synaptic contact with as many as 5000 other cells. Primarily the cells receiving axons from cells in the dorsal thalamus are located in middle layers of the neocortex, and these cells have only short axons; they project to larger cells that lie nearby, above and below them.

The neocortex itself seems to be organized in terms of "columns" of cells. The columnar appearance derives from the fact that a separation exists between lines of cells due to the arrival of bundles of fibers from the dorsal thalamus (and other sites). Recent work (which will be described below) on the activity of cells within a column in the visual cortex shows that the cells in a column share certain types of activities and may do different things than are done by cells in neighboring columns. This is true even though cells in many columns may receive axons from one particular cell in the dorsal thalamus and that a cell in the middle layers of one column may project to cells in several columns.

Cells in any cortical region receive input from different sources. For example, in the visual neocortical region, there is a direct input from the lateral geniculate nucleus. This, however, is not the only input to this region. Fibers carrying information from all of the diffusely projecting systems arrive there—as do fibers carrying information originally provided from other sensory systems. The activity of a cell in the visual cortex can be modified by sounds as well as by visual stimuli. Another source of information to any sensory region of neocortex in one hemisphere is the corresponding region of the other hemisphere. Thus cells in the right visual neocortex are modified by activity coming from cells in or near the same visual neocortical area of the left visual area. The communication between the sensory areas of the two hemispheres is by way of the broad band of fibers (the corpus collosum) connecting the two sides of the brain.

We have noted before that projections of the sensory systems maintain a system of spatial localization as they move toward higher brain regions. Adjacent retinal regions tend to be represented at adjacent thalamic regions, and this is maintained in the visual neocortex as well. Adjacent regions of the basilar membrane of the cochlea are represented in adjacent regions of the auditory neocortex. Adjacent regions of the body surface project to adjacent regions of the thalamus and the somatosensory visual cortex. To be sure, there are distortions of the spatial pattern found in the periphery relative to the neocortex. Examples of the consistent projections of the auditory and somatosensory systems to the neocortex are shown in Figure 5-33. The greater representation of bodily regions with great sensitivity or greater fine-motor control is of special interest. This can be seen in Figure 5-33 by noting the specially large amount of neocortex denoted to the hands and fingers.

The above outlines some of the general principles concerning the neocortical areas that receive fibers from the sensory nuclei of the dorsal thalamus; each of the sensory regions has some special characteristics, which will be discussed next.

Single-cell studies of the visual neocortical area

By introducing a microelectrode into the visual neocortex, it is possible to record the activities of single neurons to flashes of light and to both stable and moving patterns. By moving small lights in various directions receptive fields for the visual system can be mapped at the neocortex in a way that is analogous to mapping receptive fields by recording from ganglion cells in the retina. Receptive fields found at the neocortical level are generally *smaller* than those found at the periphery or at the lateral geniculate, despite the fact that each cell in the lateral geniculate projects to many neocortical cells.

This finding suggests that the neocortical mechanisms actually sharpen the patterns of excitation arising from the retina. This is accomplished by means of complicated interactions between excitatory and inhibitory systems of neurons in the neocortex.

The receptive fields of cells found within a column range in a systematic fashion from simple to complex fields. Cells near the top of a column tend to have simpler fields than those near the bottom, and many cells

Figure 5-33 A: *Localization patterns found in the motor-sensory region of the human cortex. (Fig. 115 from W. Penfield and T. Rasmussen,* The cerebral cortex of man. *Macmillian, 1950.)* B: *The middle ectosylvian (auditory) region of dog neocortex. The lines running diagonally across the area indicate regions of maximum response for a particular frequency. The numbers indicate the "best frequency" for the line underneath. The arrows are used to indicate the general direction of movement of the zone of maximal response as intensity of the imposed frequency is increased (in ear contralateral to hemisphere being examined). (Adaptation of Fig. 2 from Archie R. Tunturi, A difference in the representation of auditory signals for the left and right ears in the isofrequency contours of the right middle ectosylvian cortex of the dog.* Amer. j. physiol., *1952,* 168, *712–727.)*

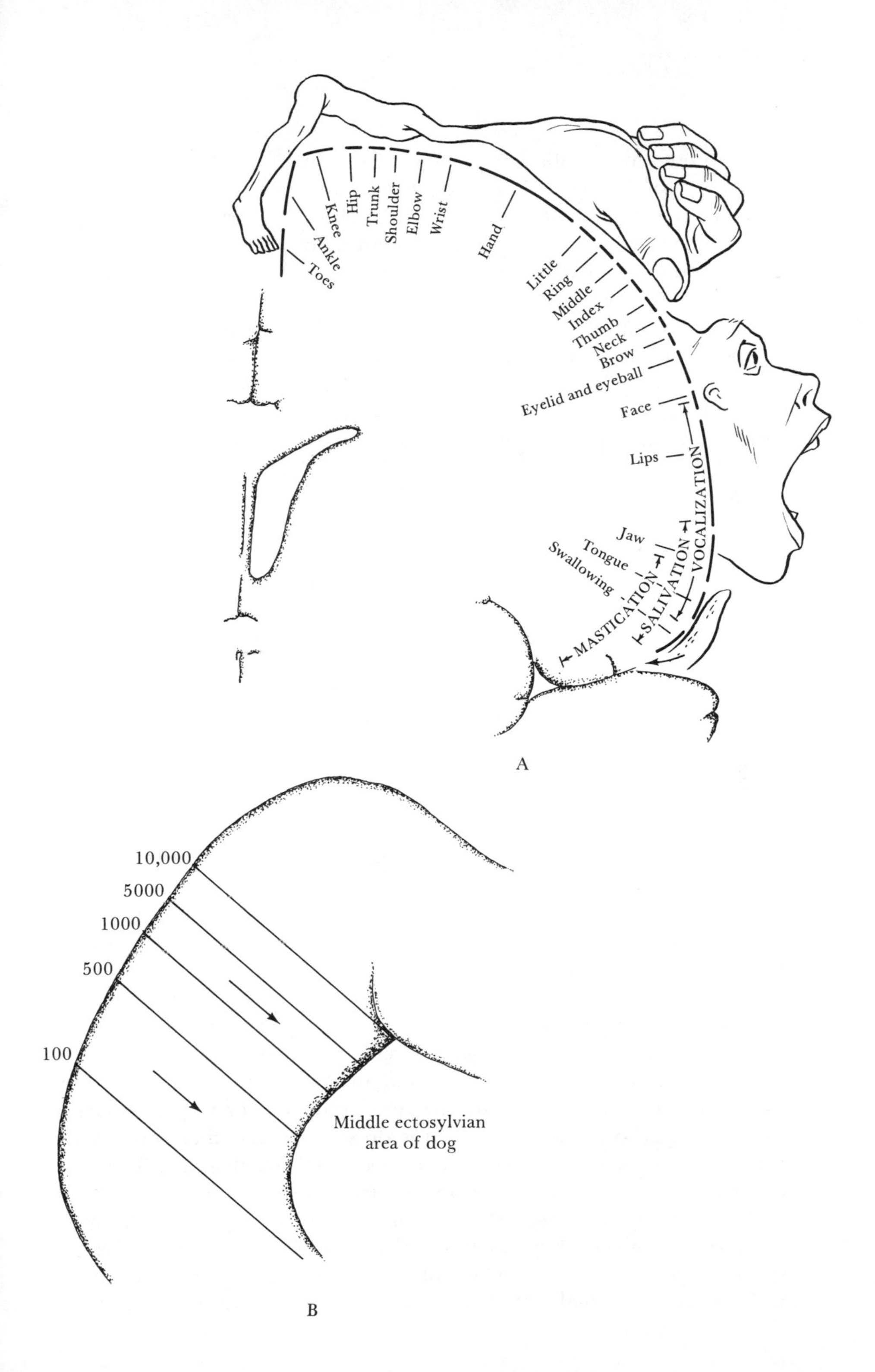
Toes
Ankle
Knee
Hip
Trunk
Shoulder
Elbow
Wrist
Hand
Little
Ring
Middle
Index
Thumb
Neck
Brow
Eyelid and eyeball
Face
Lips
Jaw
Tongue
Swallowing
MASTICATION
SALIVATION
VOCALIZATION
A
10,000
5000
1000
500
100
Middle ectosylvian
area of dog
B

respond only to complicated patterns of stimulation and fail to respond to gross visual stimulation (such as diffuse light flashes). In higher animals, as many as half of the cells in the visual neocortex fail to respond even to very bright flashes—such as from a strobe light—but most will respond to some smaller, restricted patterns moving at a particular rate in a particular direction.

The complicated visual receptive fields at the neocortex must be compounded out of simpler fields found at the retina and at the dorsal thalamus. In this sense, the neocortical surface represents the most elaborate mechanism for resolution of visual information, and this mechanism may provide us with a clue as to the possible behavioral contribution of the sensory neocortical areas. These regions may allow greater resolution and refinement of sensory information than would be possible without them.

The cells of the visual sensory areas are subject to many modifying influences and respond to signals arriving over several sensory systems. Typically, the pattern of a cell's response may be different for impulses arriving over the different systems. These differences can be shown if a "poststimulus histogram" is constructed. This is a way of describing the rate of firing of a single cell after some initial event. Thus in Figure 5-34 the cell responds with one pattern to visual stimuli and with another to a shock applied to the leg. The height of the bar represents the rate of discharge of the cell. The vertical lines imposed upon the horizontal lines indicate the actual discharge of the cell; these are accumulated into a poststimulus histogram. The third trace shows what happens when light and stimulation of the leg are combined. The bottom trace shows that the combining of the visual and the leg stimulation produces a prolonged (but not permanent) change in the response pattern of the cell to light alone. Some cells (about 10 to 12 percent) in the cat neocortex are modifiable in this fashion whereas most are not, even though they may respond to more than one sensory modality. These results show that there are both flexible and inflexible cells in the neocortical portions of the visual system, and there are reasons to believe that similar results will be found in the other sensory systems as well. These results also indicate that even though cells respond to more than one type of sensory input, this does not mean that information concerning the sensory modality is lost—the cell's responses still indicate the route by which the information reached the cell.

The interaction between the cells of the two hemispheres serving the same sensory system is a source of new information about the sensory systems. From studies of single cells in the two hemispheres in animals with decreased visual input to one hemisphere, we learn that the

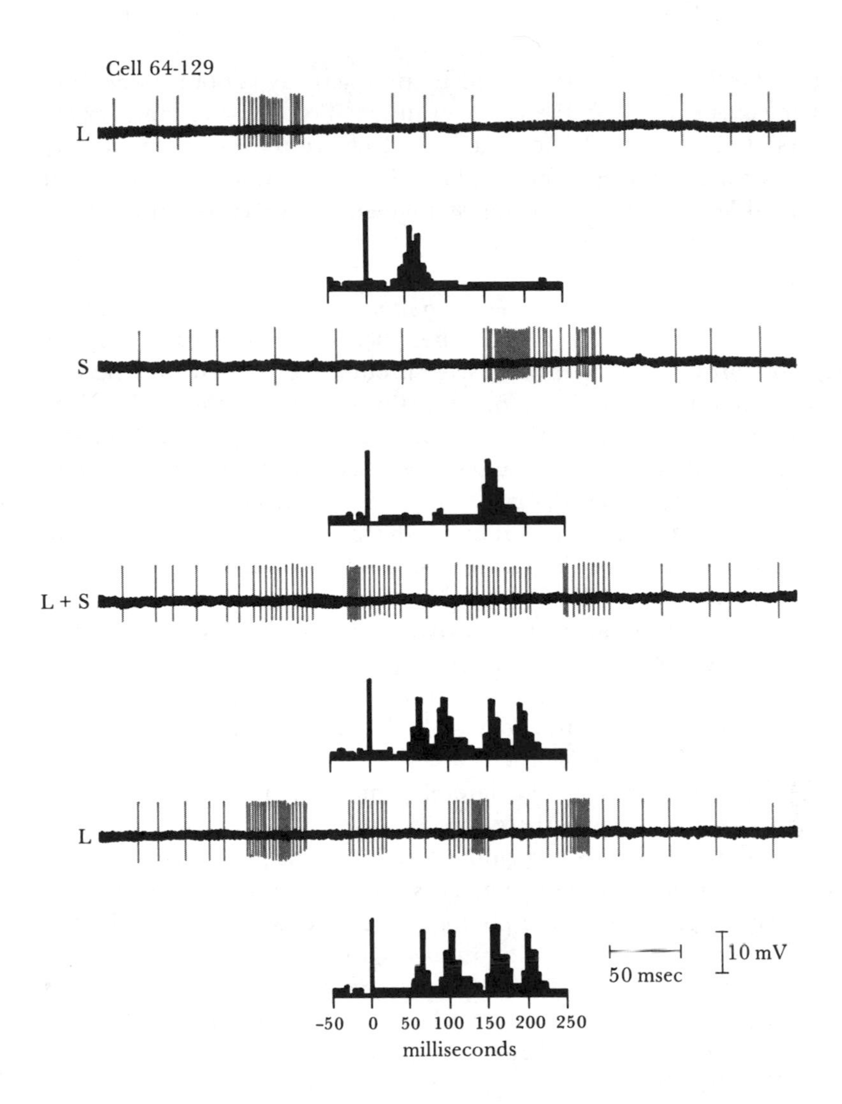

Figure 5-34 *The modification of the response pattern of a single cell in the visual neocortex as shown in the discharges of the neuron and by the poststimulus histogram described in the text. This cell responded to a dark bar in visual field with the pattern designated* L *at the top of the figure. It responded to an electrical shock to the hind limb, as shown to right of* S. *Combining shock and light produced the pattern shown to right of* L + S. *When the dark bar was presented, after the pairing of light and shock, a new pattern of response appeared temporarily, which is shown to the right of* L *at the bottom of the figure. (Fig. 10 from F. Morrell, Electrical signs of sensory coding, in G. C. Quarton et al., Eds.,* The neurosciences. *The Rockefeller University Press, 1967.)*

hemisphere receiving the normal information actively suppresses activity in the hemisphere receiving the reduced input. This suppression is probably reversible if the imbalance is corrected before too long, but it may be permanent if allowed to persist. This evidence obtained from research at the animal level may explain the permanent loss of vision in children who use only one eye during development.

The effects of neocortical destruction

The destruction of the sensory neocortical regions through accident or disease produces profound and permanent disruptions of information processing through the damaged modality. It is important to recognize that a complete loss of sensory function does not follow destruction of a sensory neocortical region, although the deficits observed after damage to a sensory neocortical area are greater in animals higher than lower in the phylogenetic scale. In nonhuman primates, complete destruction of the visual neocortex (area 17) still allows the animal to discriminate some patterns and to locate some small stimuli presented against a relatively homogeneous background. Animals below the primates are able to do more visual tasks without visual neocortex, but in lower animals it is more difficult to establish the precise limits of the neocortex to which the lateral geniculate nucleus projects. In cats, for example, there are at least two neocortical regions that receive projections from the lateral geniculate nucleus. In the rat, fibers from the lateral geniculate project over most of the posterior neocortex and there are wide regions of overlap with the auditory neocortical areas. In general the primary sensory receiving areas become more and more segregated as the phylogenetic scale is ascended, although cells in all neocortical areas may be influenced by activity that is arriving over all sensory modalities. Direct projections from a sensory nucleus of the dorsal thalamus are not essential for information from several modalities to reach neocortical cells; the information can also arrive by means of the diffusely projecting systems of the brain.

Destruction of the auditory neocortical areas does not produce changes in the ability to detect changes in frequency or the intensity of signals. Discrimination of auditory patterns is impaired, but only if the patterns to be discriminated are made up of identical individual tones. If the auditory patterns are made up of different tones, then the discrimination among them can still be made.

In the cat, a very extensive lesion of the auditory regions in the temporal lobes must be made to produce any noticeable effect in auditory discrimination. At least four different neocortical regions must be destroyed on both sides of the brain. If the lesion is only made on one side or if any of the four areas remains intact on either side, then auditory behaviors are not disturbed.

Destruction of the neocortical areas receiving somatosensory input probably produces some reduction in the ability to make fine tactual discriminations, but even this has not been completely established. Recovery from destruction of somatosensory neocortical tissue is often quite good.

Quite a few fibers leaving the ventrobasal nuclei of the dorsal thalamus project to the primary *motor* regions of the brain. This motor area lies just ahead of the somatosensory areas. It is called the motor area because many cells in the region have long axons that project into the spinal cord and help regulate motor movements. Throughout the neocortex, cells like this are found, but they are more dense in the motor region than in other places. Damage that involves both the motor and somatosensory regions produces greater deficits than in either one alone. Rats with large anterior neocortical lesions, involving both motor and somatosensory areas, lose the ability to make fine, delicate grasping movements with the "fingers" of their forepaws. This deficit can be detected only by special tasks requiring such movements. Under most laboratory conditions this defect would never be noticed.

THE NEOCORTEX: GENERAL CONSIDERATIONS

What special contributions are made to sensory activities by the neocortical mantle? This is an important question and one not easily answered.

The neocortical system is superimposed upon more fundamental systems, which seem to work very effectively in lower animals. Some lower animals without benefit of much, if any, neocortex are capable of remarkable discriminative accomplishments. Therefore, while it is the case that the neocortex does seem to provide enhanced powers of sensory acuity in higher animals, the neocortical systems are not the only biological mechanisms available for such tasks.

One role of the neocortical systems may be to provide different types of inhibitory control upon lower components of the nervous system. Several striking observations indicate how complicated this inhibitory control may be. The destruction of a sensory region of the neocortex often leads to an inability to withhold responses to a stimulus in a laboratory training situation. For example, if rats are trained to run down a straight alley for food and are rewarded on trials when a black stimulus is at the end but not when a white one is there, normal animals will soon run the alley only when the black stimulus is there. If the posterior neocortical regions are destroyed, however, the rats will run when either stimulus is at the end of the maze. It can be shown in other experiments that these impaired animals can discriminate the two stimuli—but it is difficult for them to withhold (inhibit) responding to the nonrewarded stimulus. In experiments with cats whose auditory neocortical areas have been destroyed, a complete analysis of their behavioral deficits shows that the failure to discriminate between two auditory patterns stems, in part, from an inability to withhold responses to the pattern to which they should not respond.

The neocortical region on one side of the brain tends to regulate and control the activities of the corresponding region on the other hemisphere. Observations in a human patient and experiments on monkeys show that electrical stimulation of the visual area of one hemisphere does not produce any sign of a sensory experience in the subject unless the fibers connecting the stimulated side with the normal side of the brain have been severed. If this was done, the patient reported seeing a visual, fluttering, event—resembling a butterfly out in his visual world—and the monkeys reached out to grab at some illusory object. Apparently, in the normal situation, the output of the normal hemisphere corrected the abnormal output of the stimulated hemisphere and aborted any abnormal sensory reaction. When this control was abolished, the electrical stimulation of one hemisphere was sufficient to initiate a perceptual event.

In another type of experiment, cats which were rendered incapable of performing a visual problem following surgical destruction of the visual neocortical areas were found to be capable of doing so after lesions of the area just ahead of the colliculi. This experiment revealed a remarkable release of visual capacities that had been lying dormant because of inhibitory input from other regions. Perhaps this suppressive influence is one that is normally produced by neocortical regions.

These few experiments reveal a few of the complicated inhibitory functions in which the neocortex may be engaged. Along with other data, they also suggest in a tentative fashion that the neocortex may tend to inhibit more primitive behavioral reactions that would result from activity of lower components in the sensory systems. In this sense the neocortex frees the animal from domination by either innate reactions to stimuli or simple learned reactions. It would allow for behavior based upon the anticipated events of the future that might hinge upon the response.

SUGGESTED READINGS

Alpern, M., Lawrence, M., & Wolsk, D. *Sensory processes*. Belmont, Calif.: Brooks-Cole, 1968.

Case, J. *Sensory mechanisms*. New York: Macmillan, 1966.

Hebb, D. O. *The organization of behavior*. New York: Wiley, 1966.

McCleary, R. A. (Ed.) *Genetic and Experimental factors in perception*. Glenview, Ill:. Scott, Foresman, 1970.

Vernon, M. D. *The psychology of perception*. Baltimore: Penguin, 1962.

Wyburn, C. M., Pickford, R. W., & Hirst, R. J. *Human senses and perception*. London and Edinburgh: Oliver and Boyd, 1964.

6

Perception: behavior and theory

The word *perception* is used to describe mental experiences and to designate an area of behavioral research. Today research in perception has become as rigorous and well controlled as that found in any area of psychology. On the other hand, perception as a mental experience remains a private phenomenon, known only to the person experiencing it. One of the fascinating aspects of the study of perception is how it came to be susceptible to scientific investigations.

This problem intrigued the 19th-century physiologist Karl Gustav Fechner, who set out to provide a scientific basis for his own religious beliefs. As might be anticipated, he failed to accomplish his own private goal but did found the area of study known as *psychophysics*. Today this term refers to the investigation of the relationships between sensory stimulation applied to some receptor system and some special behavioral response. Most often these responses are indicators of perceptual responses. Sometimes they are as simple as verbal reports that state, "Yes, I see it," or, "No, I can't see it." In many cases the responses required are more elaborate in order to represent more precisely or adequately the perceptual event presumed to be involved—as, for example, when a subject is required to select one of four time intervals in which a signal was presented.

In the first section of this chapter we shall discuss some modern aspects of psychophysics. The aim of psychophysics is to understand man—in this case man as an observer. We shall discuss both early and modern techniques that have been used in this attempt to coordinate our internal reactions with the physical world about us.

Next we shall examine the reasons why some psychologists began to assert that we must study the total "form" rather than the "elements" of perception. At the same time we shall consider some explanations that have been offered for the perception of forms and the relevance of psychological research in which perceptual illusions are used.

In the later sections of the chapter we shall discuss the influence of bodily activity, values, motives, and personality variables on perception. The fact that psychologists discuss the possibility that variables of this kind can affect perception reflects a relatively recent change in emphasis in psychological research.

PSYCHOPHYSICS

The name psychophysics suggests a marriage of psychology and physics. If we think of the setting in which the marriage took place in the middle of the 19th century in Germany, this is a reasonable union. In those days physics and psychology were very different from what they are today. Physics was fairly well established in its Newtonian tradition, with a strong emphasis on measurement. In fact, many philosophers of science held that it was because of this emphasis on measurement that physics advanced so rapidly. Psychology was primarily the study of mental experience. Considering the era's emphasis on research in many areas, what would be more natural than for a scientist with biological, physical, and psychological interests to want to study and measure *sensation*? Psychophysical research did just this: it studied the changes in perception that occur when changes are made in the physical stimuli. While many psychologists still believe that the methods of psychophysics do measure mental experiences, modern psychologists confine themselves to speaking of the relationship between physical stimuli and responses. It will be most useful to consider perception as a "theoretical variable" which is inferred from certain kinds of responses. We cannot know by inference the mental states of any other person, but we can know and study his behavior.

Weber's ratio and Fechner's law

One of the earliest psychophysical observations made was that, in general, the amount of change in sensory stimulation required to allow the observer to report that he perceives a change is proportional to the amount of the sensory stimulation. This is Weber's ratio. Another way of stating this, with symbols, is

$$\frac{\Delta I}{I} = K$$

where

ΔI = increase or decrease in stimulation
I = amount of original stimulation
K = a constant that depends on the particular sensory modality and other variables.

A simple illustration of Weber's ratio is the following:

Q. If a theater sign had a dense grouping of 1000 bulbs, and if the Weber ratio for the particular situation was 0.10, how many bulbs would have to burn out before they were noticed?

A. $\frac{\Delta I}{I} = K.$

$$\text{If } K = .1$$
$$I = 1000$$
$$\Delta I = X$$
$$\frac{X}{1000} = .1,$$
$$X = 100 \text{ bulbs}$$

Therefore, we can predict that if fewer than 100 bulbs were burned out (randomly), observers would not report any change in stimulation. This problem, however, is greatly oversimplified. The Weber ratio could not really be applied to the case of a theater sign, because the grouping of the stimulus elements is important. In our illustration a cluster of burned-out bulbs would be noticed more rapidly than burned-out bulbs that were evenly dispersed.

Fechner simply integrated the basic Weber equation to obtain a general statement about the relation between physical stimulation and mental sensations.

$$\frac{\Delta I}{I} = K \qquad \text{(Weber's ratio)}$$

$$\int \frac{\Delta I}{I} = k \log I$$

This result is often interpreted to read

$$\text{Sensation} = k \log \text{stimulation} \qquad \text{(Fechner's law)}$$

This equation states that sensation varies in a logarithmic relation to stimulation. In effect this means that small changes in the lower ranges of the physical-stimulus scale will produce greater changes in sensation than the same amounts of physical-stimulus changes superimposed upon stimuli of greater magnitude. We have displayed the "sensation = k log stimulation" relationship graphically in Figure 6-1. From it we observe

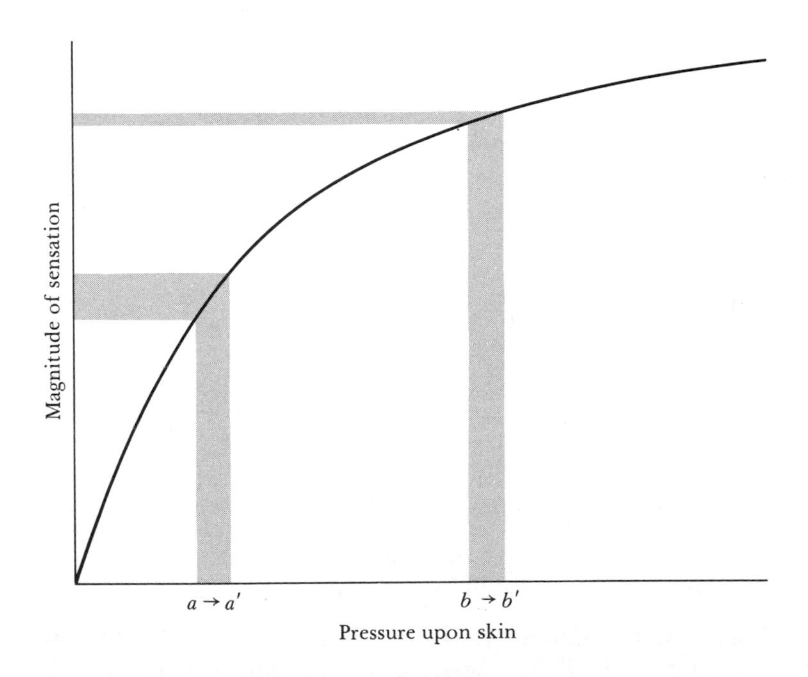

Figure 6-1 *Logarithmic relation between stimulation and sensation. The vertical axis presumably reflects the magnitude of the observer's perception of skin pressure. The same increase in physical pressure on the skin (the distance from a to a′ and from b to b′) creates a greater difference in perception at lower end of stimulus scale than at higher end.*

that a small change in skin pressure (*a* to *a′*) will produce a greater change in sensation when it is imposed on a slight previous pressure than on a great previous pressure (*b* to *b′*). If the initial pressure is high enough, an increment of 2 ounces per square inch may not be reported as any change at all. This would be the case if the ratio of a 2-ounce increment to the original pressure is less than the particular Weber's constant for this type of stimulation.

Power functions of stimulus-magnitude estimates

As research progressed in the evaluation of the relationship between physical stimulation and sensation, discrepancies were discovered between what would be expected on the basis of the Weber-Fechner equations (namely, that the sensation was proportional to the logarithm of the stimulation) and what was obtained in experiments. In many types of psychophysical experiments, it is clear that another type of relation fits the data better. This is especially true in experiments in which the subject estimates the magnitude of a stimulus. Magnitudes can be estimated in many ways, but, whatever the technique, the response is one that represents the magnitude of the sensation experienced. The relationship of the sensation to the stimulus is a "power function." This means that the sensation produced by a stimulus is proportional to the strength of the physical stimulus raised to some power (an exponent). The power to which the stimulus is raised depends upon the sensory system being studied (among other factors).

The simplest formula for this relationship is

$$\psi = K \phi^n$$

where

ψ = magnitude of sensation

ϕ = strength of physical stimulus

n = exponent giving *power* to which ϕ is raised

K = constant that depends upon physical and psychological measurement units being used

An even better description of most psychophysical data is obtained when the absolute threshold for the sensory experience (under the particular experimental conditions being used) is included in the formula. This expanded formula is

$$\psi = K (\phi - \phi_0)^n$$

where ϕ_0 is the effective absolute threshold for the sensation.

In this equation the difference between the physical stimulus applied and the effective threshold is raised to a power determined by the exponent n.

All types of stimulation produce sensations that can be evaluated in terms of magnitude or amount. Sensations of magnitude grow at different rates as stimulation is increased in different sensory modalities. Electrical shocks applied to the skin seem to become more intense very rapidly as the intensity of shock is increased. Size estimates of length of lines become larger more slowly as the actual length of the lines is increased. Visual brightness estimates increase very slowly as the intensity of the visual stimuli is increased. These differences are indicated by different values of n in the equation given above. In the case of electric shock, the value of n is about 3.5; the n for apparent length of lines is about 1.1, and the n for brightness sensations is about 0.5. Curves representing how these exponents reflect the growth of sensations are shown in Figure 6-2. The slopes of these lines reflect the differential increases of sensations as the physical energies applied are increased.

The experimental procedures used to measure magnitudes are most interesting. For example, a subject might be shown a light and told to adjust another light so that it is half as bright, twice as bright, or one-third dimmer (and so forth) as the standard. The intensity settings used by the subject will be predictable on the basis of the power relationship. Also predictable will be the physical settings of the light when the standard light is termed "10" and the subject is told to make the comparison light 5, 7, 12, or whatever. Evidently, there are magnitude scales that we use in a consistent fashion when we react to external stimulation.

Since the power relationship between the magnitude of sensation and physical stimulation can be calculated for many sensory modalities, it is possible to use this information to calculate "cross-over effects" between given magnitude estimates in one sensory modality and those in another. For example, if two gray stimuli of different intensities are shown to a subject, he can be asked to adjust a tone to exhibit the same magnitude relationship to a standard tone as the one he perceives between the grays.

The subject is asked to make a *ratio* between the two auditory stimuli that is similar to the ratio of the differences between the intensities of two gray stimuli. One can think of this as adjusting stimulus A so that the relationship $A:B$ matches that of $C:D$ where C and D are the two gray stimuli and B is the standard tone. In general the results of experiments like the hypothetical one just described have revealed excellent predictability between the two modalities being studied. This means that the equations describing the relationship between sensation and perception are powerful predictors of the magnitude of subjective experience. It would be an interesting exercise to devise experiments of cross-modality matching, including those in which more complicated stimuli are used.

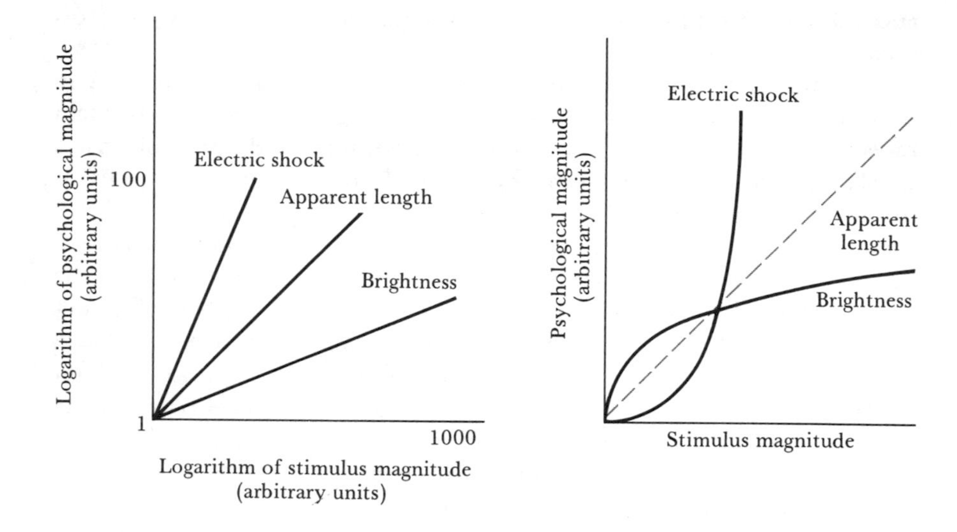

Figure 6-2 *Scales of apparent magnitude of electric shock, apparent length of lines, and brightness plotted in arbitrary units on a logarithmic scale (left) and on a linear scale (right). With the linear coordinate system, the curves can be concave upward or downward depending on whether the power-function exponent is greater or less than 1.0. (Adaptation of Figs. 3 and 4 from S. S. Stevens,* The psychophysics of sensory function, *reprinted from Sensory communication by W. A. Rosenblith, Ed., by permission of the M. I. T. Press, Cambridge, Massachusetts. Copyright © 1961 by the M.I.T. Press.)*

Just noticeable differences and thresholds

Weber's fraction ($\Delta I/I$) was based on the concept of a *just noticeable difference* (JND). It assumes that changes in stimulus conditions are either large enough to cause a perceptual difference or they are not. If they are not large enough, then the observer will perceive no change whatever in the stimulus. A JND is defined to the smallest change in a stimulus that can be detected by the observer. This concept rests in turn upon the concept of a threshold. The threshold is a theoretical concept that indicates an all-or-none boundary condition. If one applies increasing amounts of pressure on a balloon—say, by squeezing it—at some point the balloon will burst. The amount of pressure needed to break the balloon can be thought of as a threshold condition. Any pressure less than the boundary pressure will not break the balloon; any pressure greater than the boundary pressure will. Changes in any sensory stimulation that fall below a threshold will not cause any perceptual change in the observer. Changes in sensory stimulation above this threshold amount of stimulation will produce changes in the observer's perceptions.

We can talk about two kinds of thresholds: a *difference threshold* and an *absolute threshold*. In fact they are very similar concepts, both based on change from prior conditions. The term *absolute threshold* refers to the smallest amount of stimulation that can be detected by an observer.

In measuring an absolute threshold we begin with no stimulation at all and add energy until the observer reports a perceptual experience. If we want to measure the absolute threshold for a spot of white light, we could present this spot to subjects looking at a dark target area in a blackened room (after sufficient time for dark-adaptation to occur). We would present the spot at different intensities and instruct the subjects to respond in a certain way when they saw the white spot.

If we want to measure difference thresholds, we must present an increment or decrement of illumination in the spot and ask the subject to report when this difference is noticed. When measuring absolute thresholds the experimenter wants the subjects to report the presence of a stimulus; in measuring difference thresholds the experimenter wants the subjects to report a change in stimulating conditions.

Measurement of thresholds

Psychophysical methods are techniques used to measure absolute and difference thresholds.

Measurements of thresholds can be done in several ways. The first methods were reported by Fechner in 1860; three are still widely used today.

1. The first method is often called the *method of constant stimuli* (despite the fact that the stimuli presented to the observer are not constant). With this technique, stimuli are presented to the observer one at a time in varying order. If the method is being used to determine an absolute visual threshold, the observer is asked to report if he sees the stimulus. After each stimulus has been presented many times, and the observer has made his reports, it is possible to calculate the number of times the subject reports observing the stimulus at each intensity level. The number of "I-see-it" reports given at each stimulus level reflects how often the subject said the signal was detected at each intensity level. A hypothetical curve, connecting the points and giving the frequency of detection for five stimuli, is presented in Figure 6-3. As the stimuli increase in intensity, the greater the frequency with which they are reported as perceived. Furthermore, as is typical in psychophysical experiments, the frequency of reports of perceptual changes increases most

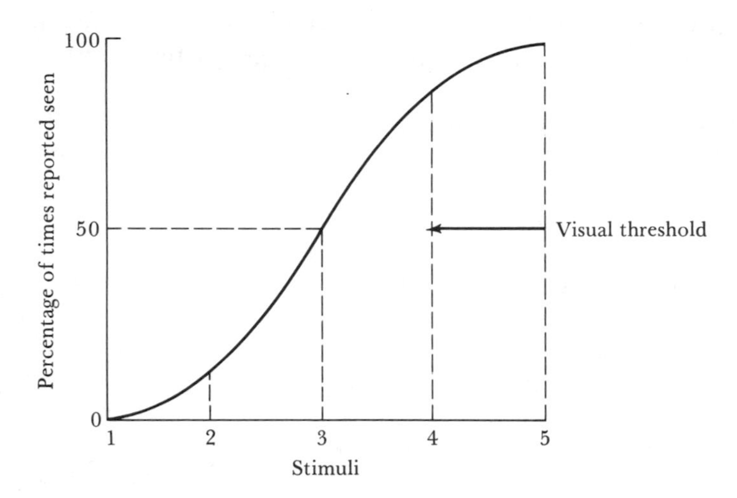

Figure 6-3 *Hypothetical relationship between the proportion of times a stimulus is presented and reported seen and the intensity of the stimulus. Stimulus 1 is the least intense, 5 the most intense.*

rapidly in the middle range of the stimulus-intensity scale. This is reflected in the shape of the curve, which resembles a slanted S. With the method of constant stimuli, a threshold is usually defined as that stimulus intensity which is reported as perceived half the number of times it is presented. This definition is arbitrary and other definitions could serve as well. For example, a stimulus whose intensity is perceived 60 percent of the time might be an equally good threshold.

2. When an experimenter uses the *method of limits,* he presents the subject with a graduated series of stimulus intensities either from the smallest intensities to the greatest intensities or from the greatest to the smallest. The experimenter begins by presenting the subject with one of the stimuli from either end of the continuum. Then he asks the subject if he sees the stimulus. Usually the extreme intensities are selected so that there is no doubt that the subject will report that he sees it if the greatest intensity stimulus is presented and will not report seeing it if the minimal stimulus is presented.

Each stimulus in the series is presented, and the subject again reports whether it is perceived. The series of stimuli is presented in order through the entire range of stimuli or until the subject changes his report from "seeing" to "not seeing" or the other way around, depending on whether an ascending or descending series is being presented.

3. In the third method, the *method of average error,* the subject adjusts a stimulus until it matches some given standard. The subject has control of a knob or dial by which he can increase or decrease the stimulus intensity. The basic operation of matching is repeated many times. The difference between this method and others is that the subject is required to make a judgment of equality between the stimulus under his control and the standard. Thresholds are determined by the mean (average) stimulus intensity set by the subject. This presumably is the point at which the sensation reaches a region of intensity that is indistinguishable from the standard.

The threshold assumption

Each of the three methods described above produces a number, expressed in physical units of measurement, which is called a threshold. These numbers are often considered as more or less reliable estimates of some "real threshold," which cannot be measured directly. The real threshold would be a boundary between sensation and no sensation or between a change in sensation and no change in sensation, depending on whether we were speaking of absolute or difference thresholds. The threshold concept can be illustrated by the steplike jump in the graph of Figure 6-4. Along the abscissa, we have represented a physical-energy scale. It could be a scale of light intensity, for example. On the ordinate we have represented essentially two conditions: stimulus perceived and stimulus not

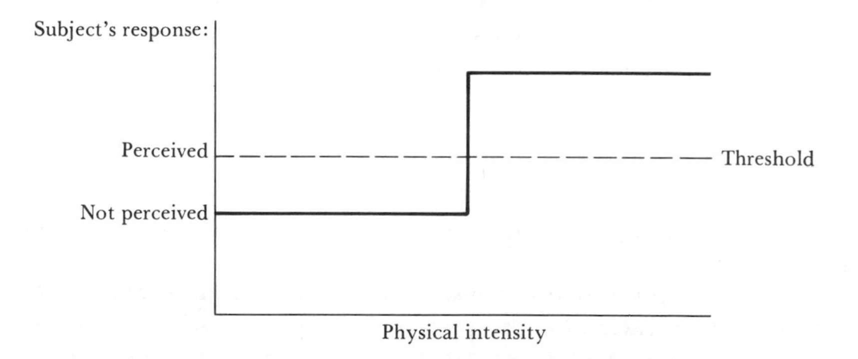

Figure 6-4 *Graphic presentation of the threshold assumption. As the physical stimulus increases, some point is reached when the excitation is sufficient to cause a perceptual response to it. Crossing the threshold is an all-or-none event on any presentation of stimulus.*

perceived. As the intensity of the stimulus is increased, some point is reached at which perception takes place. As we already know, this point is called the threshold. Yet, curves like this are never found when data from psychophysical experiments are analyzed.

Usually a slowly rising curve is obtained as was represented earlier in Figure 6-3. This, plus the fact that different psychophysical methods often yield different estimates of the threshold point, raises doubts as to the usefulness of the concept of a sensory threshold. But there are still other problems for the concept of thresholds.

SIGNAL-DETECTION THEORY

If one considers the task of the subject in a psychophysical experiment, it becomes evident that both his expectancies about the experimental situation and the reward system set up by the experimenter must have a profound influence on behavior. Even though the subject tries to report his experiences honestly, the *sequence* of stimuli presented by the experimenter and the payoffs to the subject affect the observer's reports.

As an illustration, let us think of a radar operator watching the face of his scope. The radar operator may be functioning in an early warning system, and he knows that any blip appearing on his scope face could be an enemy missile on its way. Detection of the missile is important for the initiation of countermeasures.

Radar screens tend to have some degree of background activity, or *noise*. The blip is really an intense point of light superimposed on a background of less intense and constantly varying light. If the radar operator has been observing the screen for months without a signal (blip) occurring, and nothing has been said to make him think there is any change in the world situation, he will tend to believe it unlikely that a blip will occur.

The fact that an enemy missile has never appeared on the screen can thus lower the radar operator's estimate of the likelihood of one's appearing at all. It is in this way that the sequence of stimuli presented to subjects affects their responses, that is, by biasing the estimates of the likelihood of future occurrences. However, the payoffs for his possible responses are also interesting.

The radar operator, at any moment, can report the activity on his scope as "missile" or "no missile." At any moment a missile could be present or not. Two kinds of mistakes can be made. If a missile is on its way, a mistake in not reporting it might have terrible consequences. The other type of mistake, reporting a missile when there is none, would waste some interceptor missiles. This would be expensive and represent the cost of this type of error. It would be less expensive, however, than the damage inflicted by an enemy missile. Therefore, it is likely that the radar operator would tend to make the second kind of error in preference to the first. Thus both the observer's past history, as it influences his expectations of the occurrence of a blip, and the payoffs for the various kinds of correct and incorrect responses influence perceptual reports. These factors have been incorporated into a theoretical model of how the human observer detects stimulus change, a model based upon principles derived from more general theories of electronic signal detection.

The decision-analysis model

It has been proposed that our detection of sensory signals can be compared to the performance of electronic devices designed to detect signals against a background of *noise,* which is an unpredictable pattern of activity. This comparison allows us a fresh look at the basic perceptual mechanisms. In the example of the hypothetical radar observer, the detection task faced by the human is one in which signals must be detected against more or less intense backgrounds of noise. Signals of interest must be sorted from noisy backgrounds. Noise can be external, as in a radar screen or a poor radio, or internal, caused perhaps by the spontaneous activity of the nervous system. In any case the problem posed for signal detection is: How do we reach a decision regarding whether we are observing signal and noise or noise alone? Because the theory explicitly provides a model for how this decision is reached, it is called the *decision-analysis model.*

NOISE AND SIGNALS In the decision-analysis model every problem of sensory detection is viewed as one in which a signal is added to a noise background. Noise is postulated as a basic feature of the model and the organism. There may be more or less noise at any moment. Noise can occur in every sensory modality. Although it is possible to think of various sources of noise both in the external world and in the person, *for our purposes let us merely assume that there always is some noise as part of the background for all sensory observations.*

By definition, noise refers to a pattern of activity that is unpredictable. Auditory noise usually refers to an unsystematic sampling of auditory frequencies that change rapidly. Noise in the visual system could refer to an unsystematic pattern of visual wavelengths that also change moment to moment. The intensity of the background noise can also change from moment to moment. While the precise characteristics of the noise at any instant would be impossible to predict, it is possible to make assumptions about the average values of the noise when observed over a period of time. For example, if your radio is tuned so that you get only static, you cannot know how loud that static will be at any one instant. But by turning the gain (volume or loudness) of the radio you can arrange to have the average value of the static greater or less. When the radio is loud, the average value of the static has been increased. Turning the radio down would decrease the average value of the static. Thus it is possible to talk about average values of noise, and, even more, to talk about the *distribution* of noise patterns. By distribution we mean the way in which the unsystematic noise ranges about an average value. In the decision-analysis theory, distributions are similar at all intensities.

The important parts of the decision-analysis model are (1) a background noise is postulated to always be present; (2) the average value and distribution of the noise can be specified to some degree; and given these conditions, (3) *the effect of a signal is to displace the average value of the noise distribution.*

Let us assume in a case of auditory detection that there is a background noise level with an average intensity of X. Subjects attempt to detect a signal presented against this noise background. The signal is assumed to have a *constant intensity* Y (not varying moment to moment like the noise). Mathematically, it can be shown that the distribution of the signal-plus-noise distribution will be the same as the distribution of the noise alone, although it is displaced along the intensity scale. Figure 6-5 shows a hypothetical noise distribution and the effect of adding a signal to this background distribution.

Moment to moment the noise distribution fluctuates about the average value of X, and the signal-plus-noise distribution fluctuates about the average value of $X + Y$.

In the normal course of events an observer in real life or in the reduced laboratory situation can never observe the entire range of either distribution. We must make decisions with less than complete information. If we must decide whether a signal is being presented, we decide on the basis of a *sample,* which can come from either of the two distributions.

Sampling from the distributions In the decision-analysis model the observer is thought to be given a sample from one or the other of the distributions. This observer's job is to decide whether the sample comes from the noise or the signal-plus-noise distributions.

In effect we can interpret this to mean that the observer is given one value from the intensity scale of Figure 6-5. This is a restricted sample, of course, but can serve as the prototype for samples of larger size. Suppose we were to give our observer this sample: an intensity value below the white-hatched area in Figure 6-5. Clearly, this sample must be from the noise alone. The signal-plus-noise distribution can never produce such a small intensity. By the same reasoning, intensity samples greater than the hatched area can occur only when the signal is added to the noise. However, values in the hatched area can occur from either the noise or the signal-plus-noise distribution. To make decisions in this area of uncertainty, the observer must set up a *criterion,* a value on the intensity scale somewhere in the shaded area, and report any value greater than this criterion as most likely to have come from the signal-plus-noise distribution and any value below the criterion point as most likely to have arisen from noise distribution alone. What determines the point where this criterion is placed by the observer?

SETTING THE CRITERION The decision-analysis model proposes that the location of the criterion point is determined by (1) the payoffs to the subject from the possible outcomes of his responses and (2) the observer's estimates that the signal-plus-noise or the noise alone was presented.

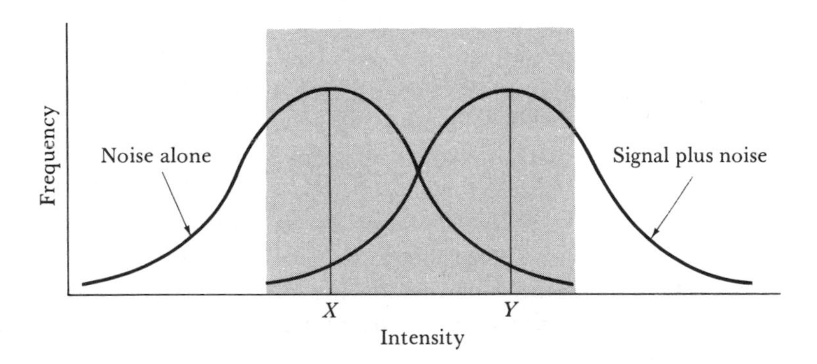

Figure 6-5 *Effect of adding a sensory signal to a noise distribution as proposed in the Tanner-Swets theory. Ordinate represents frequency with which a given intensity is obtained; abscissa represents a hypothetical intensity scale. Mean of noise distribution is located at X; mean of signal plus noise is located at X+Y. Generally, effect of adding stimulus is to intensify noise distribution. Distributions of noise and signal plus noise are assumed to be identical.*

Table 6-1. **PAYOFFS FOR OUTCOME IN MISSILE EXAMPLE**

	Outcome of observer's responses	
Actual event	*"Signal" (Missile)*	*"No signal" (No missile)*
	Outcome of observer's responses	
Missile coming	Save area from destruction	Destruction of area
No missile	Waste of expensive interceptor	Continued tranquility

The payoffs to an observer can vary for each possible outcome of his response. If the subject can say only, "Yes, the signal was presented," or, "No, the signal was not presented, noise alone was there," then a payoff table can be constructed. Table 6-1 presents a possible payoff table for our radar operator in the earlier example, and Table 6-2 presents a possible payoff table for an observer in an experiment. Tables like these represent both the rewards and penalties for correct and incorrect responses. Too often, in many real-life situations it is impossible to calculate the payoff for certain entries in the table. In the laboratory, however, a payoff system can be exactly specified and explained to the observers. Table 6-2 represents a balanced payoff in which both kinds of correct and both kinds of incorrect responses are rewarded and penalized equally. It is easy to create payoff tables that are not balanced. The payoff for correct identification of the signal as a signal can be heavily rewarded, and the penalty for saying "signal" when noise alone is presented can be made minimal. Such a payoff table would bias the observer toward reporting signals at the expense of his "noise" responses. In the formulation the effect of this biased table would be to set the criterion lower, more toward the bottom of the shaded area than the top in Figure 6-5.

The observer's estimates of the likelihood of the two events, a signal plus noise or noise alone, will also alter the position of the criterion. The effect of increasing the probability of one or the other of these is to move the criterion away from the favored distribution. If the observer

Table 6-2. **PAYOFFS FOR OUTCOMES IN EXPERIMENT**

	Outcome of observer's responses	
Actual event	*"Signal"*	*"No signal"*
Signal + noise	+10¢	−10¢
Noise alone	−10¢	+10¢

expects that noise alone is more likely to be presented to him, the criterion will be placed near the top of the shaded area. If he believes the signal plus noise is more likely to occur, then the criterion is moved lower. Figure 6-6 shows the effect of rewards and penalties and the effects of the observer's expectancies on the location of the criterion. If the payoffs are biased and the noise-alone and signal-plus-noise presentations are not subjectively equal, then the effects of each manipulation combine to produce a joint effect. The location of the criterion can be calculated by use of a "maximum likelihood ratio," which takes into consideration both rewards and penalties and the probabilities of occurrence of the two stimulus conditions.

SIGNIFICANCE OF THE DECISION-ANALYSIS MODEL First, we might ask what has happened to the familiar concept of the threshold in the decision-analysis model? We began by assuming a noise-alone distribution, which provides a background for all signals. Then, we assume certain effects of signals on this background noise. Next, we learned that a criterion was established to decide whether the sample should be assigned to the signal-plus-noise or the noise-alone categories. The word *threshold* did not once occur. One of the most interesting features of considering sensory detection in light of the decision-analysis model is that the threshold concept need not be used. Perhaps this concept is not needed to understand perceptual phenomena.

We know, of course, that intense signals are easier to detect against a

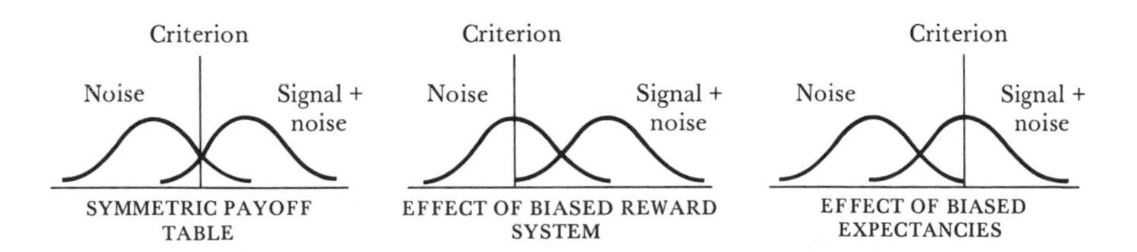

Figure 6-6 *Effects of payoff and observer's expectances of outcomes on criterion placement according to the decision-analysis model. Left, placement of observer's criterion for discrimination when reward for correct identification (signal plus noise) is balanced by some degree of penalty for incorrect identification, and observer's expectancies have not been biased; middle, observer shifts criterion when reward for correct identification is greater than penalty for error; right, criterion is shifted to accommodate observer's expectancies when he has been led to expect noise more than the signal, although reward and penalty are balanced.*

noise background than are weak signals. The decision-analysis model explains this by assuming that weak signals add a smaller constant to the noise distribution than do intense signals. Very strong signals could displace the average value of the signal-plus-noise distribution so far along the intensity scale that there could be little or no overlap of the two distributions and thus little or no range in which decisions would be uncertain. Weak signals might only displace the signal-plus-noise distribution a short distance on the intensity scale and result in making practically the entire distribution a zone of uncertainty.

One advantage of viewing sensory detection in terms of signal-detection theory is that rewards and expectancies can be incorporated into the perceptual decision. Thresholds, on the other hand, are usually believed to be some inherent property of the individual and insensitive to changes in expectancies or rewards. When we think of a threshold for the detection of light, for example, we think that there is some intensity of light that is just sufficient to produce a perceptual response. But how do we then incorporate the fact that rewards and expectancies can alter this inherent property, the visual threshold?

PERCEPTION OF COLOR

Let us use our knowledge of psychophysics to consider how people perceive color. First of all we must understand the different effects produced by mixing lights of different wavelengths and those produced by mixing paints.

Artists mix paints, and when an artist uses a pigment that appears to be yellow, he is using material that reflects only electromagnetic wavelengths in the region of the spectrum called "yellow." All other wavelengths are absorbed.

When two pigments are mixed together the colors reflected from them are those reflected by *both* of them. For example, when we mix blue paint and yellow paint, the resultant color is green. This is because neither the yellow nor the blue is a pure spectral color. They both reflect some wavelengths in the green range. The pigments that reflect yellow in the yellow paint are absorbed by the blue paint. Conversely, the blue-reflecting pigments are absorbed by the yellow paint. What is left is what is common to both, namely, the green pigments each paint has within it.

On the other hand, mixing yellow and blue lights produces a whitish achromatic result. When lights are mixed, the wavelengths combine to form a new appearance. With colored lights the effects of one wavelength *add* to the effects of other wavelengths. For this reason the laws describing the addition of colored lights are called *additive laws.* Since the mixing of pigments *reduces* the number of wavelengths *that reach the eye,* the laws of the mixing of pigments are called *subtractive laws.*

Complementary colors

When mixing colored lights, we find that certain hues combine with other hues at appropriate intensities in such a way that their joint effect on us can best be described as neutral in hue—achromatic (colorless). The pairs of colors that will add together to form a neutral experience are complementary colors. Mixtures of hues that are not complementaries produce a hue somewhere in between them. In theory every color has a complementary, although in fact some complementaries are practically unobtainable.

Determination of primary colors

The term "primary colors" is often used, but few people understand just what the term means. In essence it means those colors from which all others can be created. This answer may become clearer when we consider some simple psychophysical experiments.

Suppose a subject is seated in front of a screen upon which two patches of light could be projected from independent light sources. One patch is always a relatively pure, narrow-wavelength spectral color. The other patch is controlled by the subject looking at the lights. The subject has control of the intensity of two pure spectral lights that are directed upon the screen. These two lights converge on a target zone, which is identical in size to the experimenter-controlled patch of color. The subject may be provided with two knobs or other controlling mechanisms. One knob would control the intensity of one color, the other would control the intensity of the other color. The subject is asked to make the patch of light that he controls look just like the one presented on the first patch by the experimenter.

By increasing and decreasing his two lights, the subject can make his patch indistinguishable from the spectral color on the first patch, *provided he has control of just the right two colored lights.* Results from experiments like this have found that all spectral hues can be matched by using two of three colored lights. The three colors must be selected so as to have a red, a green, and a blue. These three essential colors are the primary colors. To match any particular spectral hue, only two colors are needed, but which two primary colors are required varies depending on what color is to be matched. The results of one experiment are shown in Figure 6-7, in which three primaries—a red, a green, and a blue—were used by subjects, two at a time, to match spectral hues.

The exact wavelengths identified as primaries have tended to vary somewhat from one experimenter to another; but the important fact is that observers are able to match the hue of test patches with combinations of two of three primary colors.

What would happen if colored paints were used in this kind of experiment? A pure blue pigment would absorb all wavelengths except the blue reflected. A pure yellow pigment would absorb all but the wavelength in the yellow range. If the two were mixed together, the reflected yellow would be absorbed by the blue and vice versa and no light would be reflected. This would produce a black surface, since all wavelengths would be absorbed by the mixed pigments.

However, even though the match made by the two primary colored lights may be perfect for hue, the combination of our primary colors would not always be sufficiently "saturated" (saturation refers to the amount of neutral, gray or "white" light with which the spectral hue is diluted). In order to have a perfect match for hue *and* saturation, sometimes we must add some of our third primary color to the patch presented to the subject. This reduces the saturation of the *test patch.*

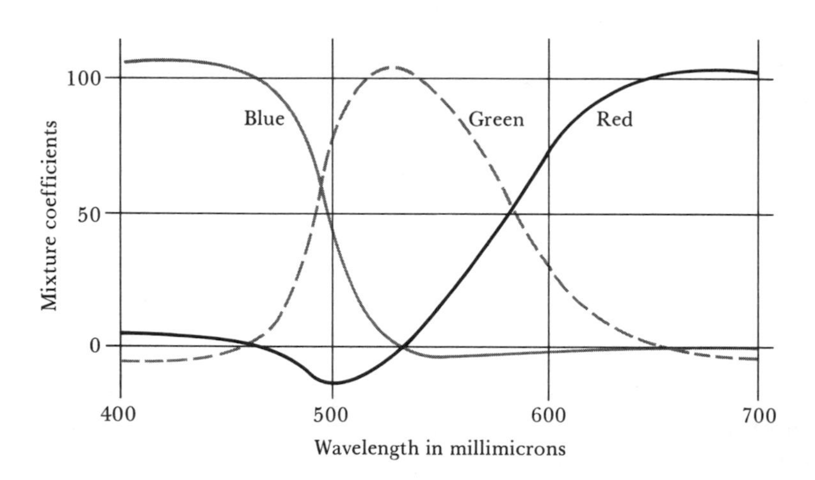

Figure 6-7 *Color-mixing data. Curves represent proportions of each of the three primaries required to match each region of the spectrum. (Adapted from S. Hecht, The development of Thomas Young's theory of color vision.* J. opt. soc amer., *1930,* 20, *23.)*

There is no other way to obtain a perfect match for saturation and hue for all test colors. Figure 6-7 shows the proportions of three primaries used to obtain perfect matches of test patches from each spectral region. Where a color primary curve dips below the horizontal line marked "0," that color must be added to the *test patch* to allow a perfect match.

One should note that "primary colors" are really based upon psychophysical judgments which in turn are founded upon JNDs between the "test patch" and the patch that is controlled by the subject. He reduces the difference between the two patches to the point where his report, whether verbal or expressed in some other way, is that they are indistinguishable. Any number of procedures could be used. The subject could be presented with patches premixed with two possible primaries and asked if they were "the same" as a test patch. The patches could be presented in an orderly ascending or descending series or randomly. A number of patches could be presented, and the subject could select the ones most like the test patch. Two points need to be emphasized: (1) The determination of primaries is based on the use of some psychophysical method, and (2) only certain wavelengths can be used as "primaries."

PERCEPTION OF COMPLEX PATTERNS

Hermann von Helmholtz, the great physicist and physiologist who was concerned with understanding the sensory systems, held that a belief in a mechanism of "unconscious inference" was needed to explain normal perception of figures. He held that we perceive those figures or objects which are most likely to have produced the sensory information reported to the nervous system from the receptors. This inference of *the most likely object* is based on our past experiences with objects and the stimuli arising from them—things we had learned about the world around us.

The concept of unconscious inference in perception has been attacked, especially by Gestalt psychologists. *Gestalt* is a German word meaning *configuration* or *form*. The basic arguments against unconscious inference have been that interference is a conscious phenomenon and that it does not occur instantly, although perception itself does seem to occur at once. Yet people do not report "feeling" that they make inferences, nor do they seem to require time to make them when perceiving objects.

Despite the fact that the battle between unconscious inference and Gestalt psychologists began before the turn of the century, no clear-cut victory has ever been won by either side. There is no doubt, however, that the work of Gestalt psychologists has resulted in the gathering of many important and interesting observations of perceptual phenomena.

The Gestalt movement

In the latter part of the 19th century a controversy existed between two groups of people concerned with perceptual phenomena and their origins. This controversy divided interested parties into two groups:

1. Those who believed perceptual phenomena were innate parts of our physiological apparatus, and
2. Those who believed that past experiences were crucial in determining how we see the world around us.

Helmholtz belonged to this latter group, for his "unconscious inferences" depended upon the person's past experiences with objects. Gestalt psychologists identify with the former group. The philosopher Immanuel Kant had espoused the *innate* viewpoint, whereas the British Associationists stressed the *acquired* characteristics of perception (see pp. 244-245). It was within this controversy that Gestalt psychology arose as a movement in psychological theory. In essence, Gestalt psychologists believe that perception is determined jointly by the nature of the stimuli falling upon the receptors and the innate organization of the nervous system. They hold that the proper study of perception involves examination of mental experiences, i.e., phenomenology. Because of their interests, they were drawn to consideration of erroneous perceptions, or illusions.

What is an illusion? Probably no experience exactly copies reality. All our perceptions are illusory to some extent. Because of this we cannot usefully employ the term *veridical perception. No perception is an entirely faithful representation of objects or qualities found in our environment.* Philosophers have struggled with many different approaches to the nature of truth and what a true perception might be. Despite the lack of a philosophic solution to the general problems of truth and falsity, we must recognize the fact that there exist a number of prominent examples of stimulus patterns that initiate perceptual activities which deviate from what we accept as appropriate perceptions.

VISUAL ILLUSION The well-known Müller-Lyer illusion is reproduced in Figure 6-8. The two horizontal lines are the same length, although the one with the arrows pointing inward clearly seems to be longer. What is it about the two forms that causes the difference in the perception of length? Gestalt psychologists have pointed out, most forcefully, that

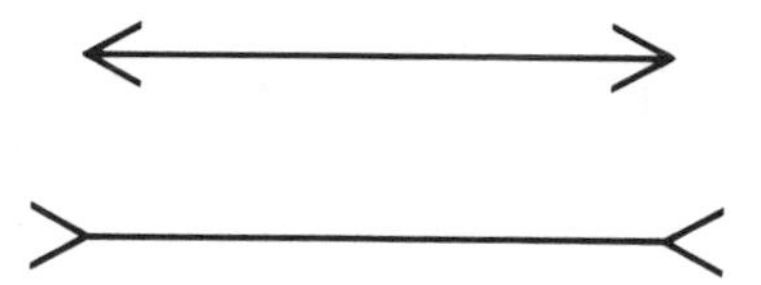

Figure 6-8 *The Müller-Lyer illusion.*

our perceptions are a great deal more than any retinal figure could be. For example, we can perceive three-dimensional figures even though the retinal image is only two dimensional.

One of the illusions presented in Figure 6-9 is more aptly described as an ambiguous figure. This is the famous vase-profile form, and it is possible to see either two faces opposing one another or a vase. What determines which figure will be seen? The perception is divided into two categories: figure and ground. The drawing will appear as a vase when the center portion acts as figure and two faces when the sides are figural. Generally speaking, ground serves as the "backdrop" for figures.

The figure in a figure-ground relationship always seems to have the quality of a unitary perception. This ability to separate the sensory world into figure and ground does not seem to depend upon past experience. Such figure-and-ground perception is found both in rats reared in darkness and in human patients following the removal of cataracts. In other words it seems to be primitive and independent of early experiences both in man and the rat. *In general, Gestalt psychologists believe that the illusory experiences occurring when the geometrical designs of Figures 6-9 and 6-10 are observed are the result of the innate structure of the nervous system.* It is on this point that controversy exists. Other psychologists believe that most perceptions depend upon early sensory experiences and learning.

It is perhaps too easy to identify the Gestalt movement with the study

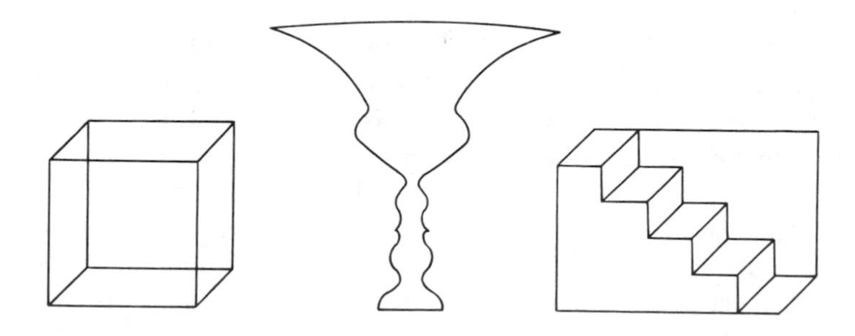

Figure 6-9 *Examples of reversible illusion.*

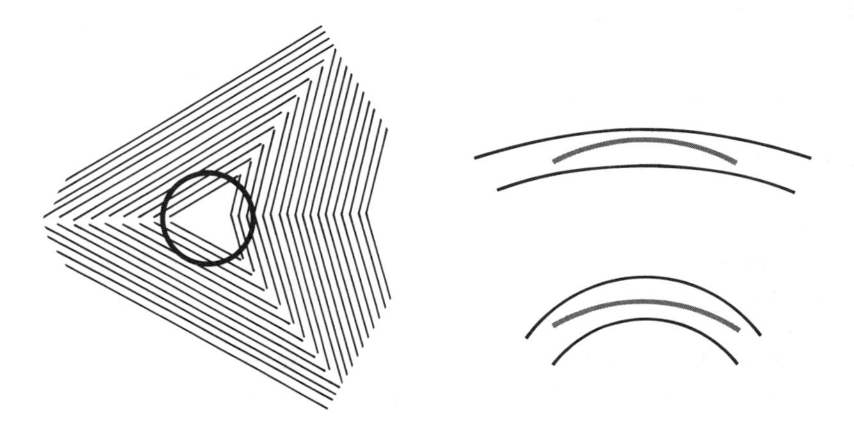

Figure 6-10 *Examples of apparent distortion of figures by their surroundings.*

of optical illusions. Gestalt psychologists are active experimentalists and, as is often profitable in research, have moved the study of illusions into the laboratory. Through laboratory experiments the scientist is often able to isolate relationships between the variables under study. Some Gestalt psychologists use geometric patterns to isolate the characteristics of stimulus patterns that affect our perceptions. It must be remembered that Gestalt psychologists are interested in explaining normal adult perception, and they use the study of illusory or abnormal perceptions as one approach to that end.

Two products emerge from the Gestalt studies of perception: (1) a set of laws that describe the perceptual experiences occurring as a result of specified stimulus conditions and (2) an explanation of the ways in which perception occurred.

LAWS OF PERCEPTION As many as 114 laws were formulated by Gestalt psychologists from their studies of perception, although this list has been abbreviated by some authors, and there are many different interpretations of the many laws. Probably the most comprehensive is the law of *Prägnanz.* This principle is simply that perceptual figures tend toward the "best figure" possible. This is a law of "good form." According to one of the leading exponents of Gestalt psychology, Kurt Koffka, the law of *Prägnanz* "can briefly be formulated like this: psychological organization will always be as 'good' as the prevailing conditions allow. In this definition the term 'good' is undefined. It embraces such properties as regularity, symmetry, simplicity and others" (Koffka, 1935, p. 110).

This law, of course, hinges upon the definition of good form. Koffka leads us to believe that the more regular, symmetrical, and simple the form is, the better it is. If this is understandable, we can now subsume a number of other Gestalt laws under it. For example, the principle of closure—one of the more widely accepted Gestalt laws—states that if a figure is presented which has an open area or gap in its boundary, the observer will tend to perceive the figure with a closed boundary, *other forces permitting.* In other words, if we present a triangle with a portion of one side missing, and if the exposure is brief enough so that the forces aroused by the missing portion are not too great, then the observer will tend to see a complete triangle. By presenting the stimulus only briefly we do not allow the observer to make the gap figural, or, in Koffka's terms, *to arouse other forces.* Another way to exhibit the closure would be to arrange the experiment so that the gap in the boundary of the triangle falls on the blind spot of the eye. As we have learned in a preceding chapter, no receptor cells exist in the blind spot of the eye, so that information reaching the brain would provide information about all of the triangle *except the area of the gap.* No information at all would be sent to the brain about the area of the gap. Under these conditions, perception should be in accord with the closure principle and the precept should be that of a closed triangular figure.

As with many of the Gestalt laws, the principle of closure is often used in contexts somewhat removed from direct sensory or perceptual realms. For example, some might say that the reason a mystery story holds our attention is that we have been given parts of a *verbal figure,* but the parts have not been assembled into a *good figure* until the end. Thus forces are directed toward closure (or good form), and these remain active until the author closes the figure for us.

Gestalt theory was appealing because it could be applied to many diverse phenomena. Such terms as *closure* and *Gestalt* are useful descriptive terms, but they are also vague and too general. There is no doubt that the phenomena described by the Gestalt psychologists are observable and that the perceptual behaviors they describe do happen. However, the existence of the perceptions and related behaviors does not mean that the Gestalt explanations of them must be accepted. The laws developed by Gestalt psychologists may best be considered as labels for descriptions of these perceptual and response tendencies in man. They do not explain *why* these tendencies are exhibited.

Having stressed the more general view of Gestalt psychology—that our perceptions are unlearned reactions which depend upon the innate organization of the sensory and nervous systems and the sensory patterns presented to the observer—we shall discuss the innate properties of the nervous system that are assumed by Gestalt psychologists to account for our perceptions.

THE PRINCIPLE OF ISOMORPHISM Gestalt psychologists seek explanations of perceptual experience in terms of physiological activities in the central nervous system. Their basic principle is that for every perception there is a corresponding physiological activity in the brain that is *isomorphic* to the mental experience. (The mathematical relation of isomorphism is that two figures are isomorphic if the points of which they are comprised are connected in the same way. If we were to draw a figure of a triangle on a piece of elastic material, like rubber, then no matter how we distort the rubber surface, the connections between the adjacent portions of the figure are always the same. Each new figure created by distorting the rubber surface is isomorphic to the original triangle and to other figures produced by distortion of the figure.) This principle asserts that when we perceive a triangle, there exists in the brain a physiological representation of a triangle that maintains certain aspects of triangularity. What kind of triangularity could exist in the brain, where the neocortex is a highly convoluted mass of cells? Almost every single portion of its surface area is curved. A perception of a flat triangle could not depend on the existence of a flat triangular form on the surface of the brain. Nonetheless, the Gestalt principle of isomorphism asserts that in the brain there must be a form of physiological excitation that maintains "triangularity" in order for the related perception to occur.

In effect, the Gestalt view holds that when a pattern of excitation on the retina is transmitted to the brain, a form is produced in the visual projection area of the brain that is isomorphic to the retinal image. Our visual perception of any geometric form is based upon the presence of a form of physiological activities in the visual projection areas of the brain.

In Gestalt theory, the form existing in the brain is in part determined by the form of activity transmitted to the brain from the receptors, but it is also determined by the structure of the brain itself. The "form" existing in the brain is a pattern of excitation in the electrical fields provided by the brain tissue. This brain form is influenced by electrical forces existing in adjacent brain areas. For example, in the Müller-Lyer illusion (Figure 6-8) the fact that one horizontal line appears longer than the other is explained on the basis that the forms of excitation in the visual area of the brain that correspond to the horizontal lines *are,* in fact, of different lengths. The form corresponding to the line perceived as longer is longer than the form corresponding to the line perceived as shorter. The field effects produced by the different types of lines at the ends of the two longer lines influence the electrical brain fields of the two forms in different ways. The arrowlike endings act to shorten the figure in the brain fields, whereas the inverted arrow endings act to stretch out the electrical fields. Thus the ends of the stimulus patterns have actually altered the *physiological forms*. The explanation is based upon electrical phenomena that would occur in any similarly constituted electrical field. As can be seen, Gestalt theory explains perception on the basis of physical characteristics of forms found in electrical fields in the brain. Our perceptions correspond to the final electrical form in the brain, according to this view.

If we were to accept the principle of isomorphism and the corresponding belief that perception is in some way related to the electrical form existing in the visual areas of the brain, would this be sufficient to explain perception? One thing we must avoid is a theory that provides us only with a display in the visual area, which then must be observed by a "little man in the head." Gestalt psychology would have us assume that figures in the world are transmitted to the visual areas, and sometimes the transmitted figure is distorted because of the nature of the material in the brain and activity in other areas. But, what then? We must have some theory to explain how these physiological forms are capable of instigating behavior, and some theory by which these brain forms are translated into awareness to account for the mental experiences of perception. One of the serious problems that exist for the Gestalt theories of psychology is that these next links in the theoretical chain leading to behavior have not been forged. Whatever else, we must have a theory that gets us further than the existence of a television-like projection of images to the brain's visual cortex.

There are other bases for doubt about the usefulness of the principle of isomorphism. These center on the results of studies of the nervous system. First, the size of the visual projection area that receives fibers from the foveal area of the retina greatly exceeds the size of the visual projection area receiving fibers from the rest of the retina. Should this not produce a considerable amount of perceptual distortion? Our visual experiences do not seem to be distorted in this way. We do not see portions of figures in the center of our visual fields larger than other portions falling more on the periphery of the retina.

A second type of observation that casts doubt upon the isomorphism principle comes from studies in which electrical or physiological disturbances of the brain tissue were created in the visual projection areas. It has been pointed out that tumors and accidents of brain pathology in the visual areas do not produce the expected disturbances of perception. In one study, gold foil, an excellent electrical conductor, when placed across the visual projection areas of a chimpanzee trained in a visual discrimination problem, did not interfere with the animal's behavior in a visual task. The gold foil was placed so as to disturb any *forms* that might exist in the electrical fields of the visual brain areas. Gold pins inserted in the visual projection area of another animal did not interfere with the animal's responses in the same task. These examples make it difficult to assume that the integrity of a form of electrical activity in a sensory projection area is essential to perception.

Hebb's theory of perception

In 1949, D. O. Hebb, of McGill University, published some ideas that have had a great influence upon certain areas of psychology. For some time, Hebb had studied the development of perception, and his findings led him to formulate a general theory of behavior based in large part on perceptual phenomena. In Hebb's theory, sensory information *becomes* perception. This concept is not the kind of associationistic theory against which Gestalt psychology reacted. Adherents of Gestalt psychology objected to theories that accounted for behavior through principles of association, which came directly from a school of philosophers called the British Associationists, mentioned earlier (see also pp. 244-245). According to their view, small "microsensations" became bonded together to form complete perceptual experiences, according to highly specified rules, through simultaneous occurrence of the microsensations in the past. Gestalt psychologists argued that the form of the electrical activity in the brain was responsible for perception. In their view, past associations did not affect perception directly, although they could influence our *interpretation* of a perception. Perception *per se* was not influenced by experience.

Hebb's proposals represented one of the most thought-provoking contributions yet made to behavioral theory, including explanations for phenomena in the areas of learning, perception, emotion, motivation, and even abnormal psychology. The most essential of all the assumptions made by Hebb is one concerning growth processes occurring at the synapse between two neurons. This assumption, in turn, is intimately related to certain postulates about the anatomical organization of the nervous system.

REVERBERATORY LOOPS In Hebb's theory the nervous system is considered to be a collection of individual nerve cells, whose basic physiological properties we have discussed before (Chapter 3). Their arrangement is such that loops of several cells can be traced. These loops would allow excitation to travel around and around through them. Within the neural loop the firing of cell A would excite cell B, and it in turn would excite cell C. Cell C then would activate cell A once again. A highly schematic loop arrangement of neurons is presented in Figure 6-11. These loops of cells could hold recurrent activities, although they would not continue their firing forever. These circular arrangements, which would permit impulses to go around in them for some time after the stimulation originating the activity has ceased, are called *reverberatory circuits* or *holding mechanisms.*

If a loop arrangement like this were activated by a specific type of sensory input, then the reverberatory activity in the loop could represent a kind of memory for the input that originally started the activity. However, it is likely that activity in such closed loops would be disrupted after a short time. It was thought that these loops could provide a neural basis for relatively recent memories but not for permanent memories. The actual reverberations of the holding mechanisms might only last for a matter of minutes, even under the most ideal conditions. Yet, Hebb maintains that these reverberating systems might be the basis for developing other changes that represent the physiological underpinnings of more permanent memories.

THE GROWTH PRINCIPLE Given the assumption of the holding mechanisms, we now state the major assumption of the theory: "When an axon of cell A is near enough to excite cell B and repeatedly or per-

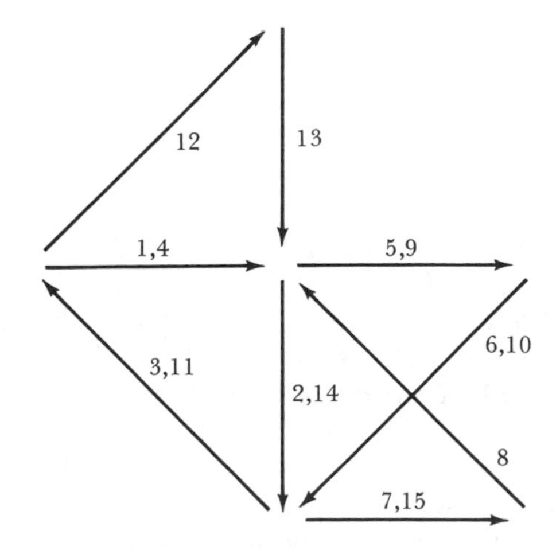

Figure 6-11 *Hypothetical arrangement of neurons which would underlie prolonged reverberatory activity. Neurons would fire in numerical sequence; i.e., neuron (1,4) fires first and again in fourth position. This multiple-path arrangement would "hold" activity for longer periods than simple closed loops of neurons would. (Adapted from D. O. Hebb,* The organization of behavior. *New York: John Wiley & Sons, Inc., 1949.)*

sistently takes part in firing it, some growth process or metabolic change takes place in one or both cells such that A's efficiency, as one of the cells firing B, is increased" (Hebb, 1949, p. 62).

There are many ways in which a growth process like this could take place. For instance, the axon of A might physically grow closer to the cell body of B. The end feet on the axon of cell A could enlarge and cover more of B's surface, and there is the possibility that the release of the chemical transmitter substances from the end feet of A might become more efficient. There must be some permanent changes in the nervous system that correspond to long-term, or permanent, memories. Hebb did not say that these must be the mechanisms involved. He only said that as a function of reverberation, cell A has greater control of the firing of cell B.

THE CELL ASSEMBLY As we have already learned, neurons of the brain and central nervous system have a remarkable number of interconnections with other cells. Each neuron is probably connected with hundreds, if not thousands, of cells. Any input that fires a given cell in the visual neocortex must affect the firing of many other cells in many other brain regions.

Any group of cells indirectly excited by any particular pattern of excitation arising in visual neocortical areas could form a loop capable of maintaining reverberatory activity over a period of time. The types of cells in the loops would vary. Some would be cells that receive information from other sensory systems; some, neurons that interconnect with other cortical or subcortical cells; others, cells whose axons descend to motor cells in the spinal cord. The inclusion of motor cells in these reverberatory loops is important, because it provides a basis for the incorporation of motor activities in perceptual learning.

As a loop of cells is activated repeatedly by identical patterns of visual input, the neurons comprising the loop will become bonded together. This follows from application of our growth principle. After repeated arousal of the same patterns, the whole group of neurons in the loop may be so completely tied together that it functions as a unit. If any portion of the loop is activated, activity in every cell of the loop will follow. These reverberatory loops are thought to be the units of perception. Each loop must be activated many many times before the growth occurring between the neurons bonds them together permanently. When the connections between neurons of a reverberatory loop have become established to the extent that activity in one portion of the loop is sure to trigger reactions throughout the loop, we can consider that the loop of neurons constitutes what Hebb calls a *cell assembly,* the basic building block of all perception.

EARLY AND LATE PERCEPTUAL LEARNING In Hebb's theory the development of perception has been categorized into early and late stages. Normal infants are in the "early learning" stage. They have adequate visual mechanisms, but the neural impulses arising from the visual receptors must be integrated into meaningful units before perception can occur.

What sort of stimulus patterns would first be incorporated into these cell assemblies? Hebb assumes that most of our early perceptual learning involves the development of cell assemblies that represent "lines and corners." There must be a special cell assembly developed for each of the many types of corners and lines. The number of perceptual units, or cell assemblies, needed to build the adult perceptual world must be staggering. Just how many types of different cell assemblies must be formed is beyond estimate, but however many there are, they represent the irreducible units of all perception.

THE PHASE SEQUENCE According to Hebb's position, a form like a triangle *is a complex perceptual entity,* which becomes recognizable only after cell assemblies for the respective angles and lines, as well as the relations between them, have been formed.

Phase sequences are defined as particular orders of cell assemblies and eye movements. Consider the triangle *ABC* in Figure 6-12. When a person centers his visual attention at *A*, cell assembly *a* is presumed to be activated in the brain. Then this point of fixation of the eyes is altered and the eyes move to the line *AB,* and a corresponding cell assembly *ab* is activated. The points of fixation progress from corner to line; line to corner, etc., around the triangle. Each point of fixation elicits firing of the cell assembly that has developed from past experiences with similar corners and lines. The eye movements that bring about a change in visual fixations are important, too, for the sensory feedback from them may act in neural units as the development of the neural counterpart of the perceived triangle progresses.

In Hebb's theory, the figures of our perceptual world are built from cell assemblies, and are represented by their order and interconnecting eye movements. Thus the triangle in Figure 6-12 would be encoded as an order of cell assemblies and eye movements, which might be: corner *A*, eye movement_1, line *AB*, movement_2, corner *B*, movement_3, line *BC,* movement_4, corner *C,* movement_5, line *AC*. This sequence represents the *phase sequence* or perception of the figure triangle. Perception of a triangle differs from perception of a square in both the types of cell assemblies and interconnecting eye movements. Triangles of all sorts would be similar in some types of corner cell assemblies and in some types of eye movements. Categories of perception, e.g., "triangle,"

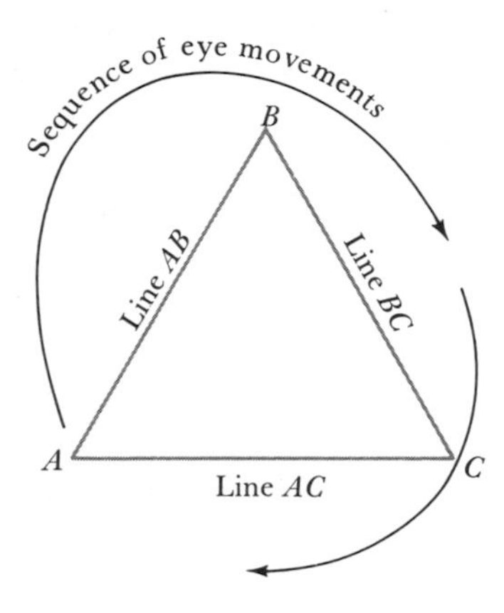

Figure 6-12 *Triangle (ABC) and the sequence of eye movements which might be produced by observer viewing it. Eyes first fixate angle at A, then progress along the line AB to angle C, and so on.*

"square," are created by the occurrence of similar perceptual elements.

In summary: A phase sequence is the collection of cell assemblies and related eye movements that, through experience, have developed a mutual interfacilitation. Sensory information that initiates activity in any part of a phase sequence results in the facilitation of the subsequent arousal of all of its parts. The perception of a figure as an entity first depends upon the firing of all the neuronal elements of the phase sequence by the appropriate sensory stimulation. After further perceptual learning, however, it may be possible for a part of the phase sequence to exert strong enough facilitating effects to trigger the other units. This represents a functional short-circuiting of the phase sequence. Even beyond this, however, it is possible to postulate a neural counterpart to what we think of as *perceptual classes* of stimuli.

DIFFICULTIES WITH HEBB'S THEORY: COMMENTS In the years since Hebb's theory was proposed, a number of observations have been made that make qualifications of it necessary. One of these observations has been the discovery that the receptive fields of cells in a newborn animal's visual neocortex are about the same as those found in the neocortex of adult animals. Evidently experience does *not* alter the receptive fields of the single nerve cells in the visual areas of the brain. The animal apparently comes into the world with a cellular organization that is much as it will be in the adult. A period of early perceptual learning is *not* essential to the development of adult visual fields.

This does not imply that the activities of single cells in the sensory systems are incapable of being altered. If the normal visual input to a sensory system is lacking, then aberrations of cellular responses can be observed. For example, if the normal sensory input to one eye is diminished early in life, then the cells of the neocortex come to respond almost exclusively to the eye that receives the normal input. There has been an active suppression of the activities of cells that normally are responsive to both eyes. That is, the eye which received normal input becomes dominant over the eye which received the reduced input, even when the eyes are stimulated in the same manner. This alteration in responsiveness lasts long after normal visual stimulation is restored, and the change may be permanent.

To alter the activity patterns of cells in the visual areas of the neocortex there must be more than a total diminution of input to both eyes. There must be a selective diminution of input to one eye while the other remains normal.

There is also some question about the effects of early visual deprivation on perception. Much of Hebb's argument about early versus later perceptual learning stemmed from older observations made on patients with congenital cataracts who had these cataracts removed later in life. Recent observations made on similar patients indicate that the development of perception is much more rapid than the earlier reports suggested. In short, the reports of patients summarized previously and used by Hebb in developing his theory have not been substantiated by more recent findings. All of these observations indicate that more of the organization of the visual system has been accomplished at or before birth than had been previously thought.

Because of the failure of attempts to find the anticipated changes in the organization of cellular activities during development, and for several other reasons as well, we must reject certain aspects of Hebb's theory of perceptual development. We conclude (1), that the mechanisms responsible for this development are established genetically and do not stem from early experiences for their completion; (2), that reverberation of neural activities through closed loops of neurons is not required to create perceptual entities in later life; and (3), that early perceptual development involves the coordination of perceptual experiences with the movements of the organism, not with a period of construction of perception *per se*.

Hebb's theory was based upon a neural growth principle, and it is likely that structural changes *can* be found in the brain that are associated with perceptual experiences. These include increases in spike-like outgrowths from dendrites (dendritic spines), which are thought to increase the synaptic contact area between the dendrite and axons.

When animals are deprived of vision, dendritic spikes on neurons in the visual areas are decreased. When these areas are photically stimulated, dendritic spines increase on these same cells.

The tips of axons may also grow to make better contact with other neurons. One current theory holds that as a neuron is especially active, the glia cells surrounding it and surrounding its axon actually shrink in size. This allows the tip of the axon to grow into the extracellular space vacated by the receding glia cells and to allow closer, more effective contact to the cell across the synapse.

We are just beginning to understand the possible structural changes that develop in the organism as a function of experience and training. Most present theories associate structural changes with increased or altered neural activities, but not necessarily with reverberatory activities of closed groups of neurons—as proposed by Hebb. Hebb's theory is of interest both from an historical point of view and because he called our attention to the importance of both early and later growth mechanisms within the brain.

Early sensory deprivation

If animals are placed in rooms with no light whatsoever for prolonged periods, these animals will have pronounced and permanent visual deficits. The complete absence of light produces behavioral deficits, which probably result from degenerative changes that occur in the retina of the eyes. If the retinas of animals reared in darkness are examined through a microscope, extensive degeneration of the cells can be found. This means that some amount of visual input is necessary to maintain a normal, healthy retina that is capable of reacting to visual signals.

If animals are maintained in darkness for long periods in early life, brief periods of exposure to light—a half hour or so each day—will permit maintenance of a normal anatomical structure of the retina. If this exposure to visual stimuli is of the usual kind—e.g., just allowing the animal to wander around its cage or an exercise area—then visual development will be normal. On the other hand, should the animal be exposed only to unpatterned, diffuse illumination, the animals will develop a visual deficit. This visual deprivation is reflected in the recognition of patterns. Animals can be fitted with goggles with translucent glass, have their eyelids sutured closed, be permitted to experience light only while their heads are in white sacks, or treated by other means to allow only a formless visual world. The ideal condition to be produced for pattern-vision deprivation is the one that would be experienced when one is in a very dense fog.

Animals subjected to pattern-vision deprivation are not blind, but they often fail to detect differences among patterned stimuli. However, it is often difficult to determine the visual capabilities of the animals by normal testing procedures. The deficits produced are ones that made it difficult for the pattern-deprived animals to use the visual information when they are moving about. Normally, visual inputs and motor movements are coordinated and interwoven so as to produce a unified visual world. The pattern-deprived animals have difficulty putting the visual input together with their own bodily movements. On the other hand, if the deprived animals are tested so that they are not moving when observing the patterns and making their responses, adequate pattern recognition can be demonstrated.

To train pattern-deprived animals to move through a single maze to approach one visual pattern in preference to others would be difficult if not impossible. Yet if the animals are restrained and conditioned to make discrete responses that do not involve total bodily movements to each of several patterns, their visual capabilities would seem normal. Thus it is not the neural mechanisms for pattern detection or recognition that have been altered. Rather, it is some more advanced mechanism of the brain that integrates the patterns with movements of the animal through space. This result leads to more general consideration of how a constant visual world is achieved under normal circumstances.

The constancy of the world

What allows us to perceive a stable world despite total bodily movements and despite the considerable movements of the eyes, which occur almost all of the time? How does the world appear the same when eye movements, both large and small, occur so frequently? Why doesn't the visual world appear to jump with each movement?

Although we don't know all of the mechanisms involved in the creation of a "stable world" in the face of constant movements, one principle can be called the "feedforward" systems.

FEEDFORWARD MECHANISMS Feedback and feedforward are terms adapted from engineering; they have achieved popularity in describing certain activities of the nervous system. *Feedback* refers to the "sensory return" from a movement or an activity that is used in further regulating the activity. A thermostat used to control a furnace initiates heat production when the temperature becomes too low. As a consequence of its initiation of furnace activity, the temperature is raised. This is the feedback portion of the system. When the temperature reaches the desired level the furnace is turned off. The feedback (increased temperature) turns off the furnace. In a biological system, sensory information arising from moving an arm to pick up a pencil from the desk acts as feedback that helps control adjustments of the movement to reach the pencil efficiently and to inform the nervous system when the pencil has been reached.

Feedforward is a term used to describe anticipatory events that occur before movements are initiated and that prepare the organism for the actions. To continue the simple example of reaching for a pencil: Before any motor movements are actually started, there are changes involving the somatosensory systems and the autonomic nervous system. These are preparatory changes for the movement. As the movement is initiated, activity over the gamma efferent system establishes a bias on the muscle spindle receptors appropriate for the intended effort. It is as if the muscle receptors are "preset" for a given amount of effort in the motor response. At the same time, there are anticipatory changes in the blood vessels of the arm and hand that are also geared to the anticipated degree of effort. As the neural discharges from the motor regions of the brain are begun that affect the motoneurons of the spinal cord and are responsible for the arm movements, neural activities are directed into the spinal cord sensory tracts and nuclei, which presumably act to ready these systems for the feedback from the response. All of these events are instances of how the nervous system prepares itself for future activities through what can be called feedforward systems.

In visual perception, and also in the other sensory systems, feedforward and feedback mechanisms play a critical role. Disruptions of either cause vast distortions of the perceptual world. When the body or the eyes move, preceding neural impulses have been directed to the eye muscles to accomplish these movements and to other regions of the brain, providing a presetting of these regions to receive the new sensory information. Normal perception depends upon the appropriate matching of the expected feedback with the obtained feedback. In some way, the feedforward mechanisms provide a model of what the new feedback will be like. Normal perceptual experience probably reflects the matching of the expected with the obtained rather than either one alone.

Even though these mechanisms are still somewhat speculative, it is likely that the stability of our perceptual world arises from the usual good degree of matching the expected sensory input with the actual sensory input. The mechanisms—whatever they are like and wherever they might be in the brain—must operate swiftly and without reaching awareness. An important point would be that perception of the environment depends not only upon the environment itself but also upon the functions of the brain prior to and during examination of the environment.

Hologramic representations

A hologram is a type of a photograph. It is made, usually, through the use of laser beams. To discuss the production of holograms and their uses in photography and engineering would take us far afield from the study of perception, but certain facts concerning them have provided the basis for some new hypotheses about how information may be stored in the sensory regions of the neocortical mantle.

The process of making a hologram involves the production of interference patterns. If two stones are dropped side-by-side into a pool of water, each makes a series of waves that expand in a circular pattern from the point at which they hit the surface of the water. When two expanding circular patterns meet, they produce a complex pattern of waves, as each interferes with the other. This pattern of interference could be used to reconstruct the disturbances caused by the stones as they hit the water. Holograms are made from interference patterns formed from light waves arriving from two sources. The arrival of one set interferes with the other much as the ripples from one stone interfere with ripples from another. In the case of holograms, the resulting interference pattern is stored on film.

If a hologramic negative is examined by being held up to the light, no image is seen. The film contains only patterns of swirls and rings. But if a monochromatic light is projected through the film, an image is seen which shows the photographed objects.

Moreover, if the light source is smaller than the film, small portions of the hologram can be viewed. The surprising observation is that all portions of the film contain exactly the same images; no matter what portion of the film is viewed, the same complete images will be observed. This means that all of the information about the objects whose "picture" is taken is stored in a similar way over the entire surface of the film. Any portion of the film contains as much information as any other.

Perhaps the brain works on hologramic principles. In the areas of neocortex that receive sensory information from the thalamus, interference patterns could be established between input from different cells in the receptor systems, between the arriving sensory information and ongoing brain activities, between information arriving from the two eyes, or between sensory information from different modalities. The opportunity for interference is abundant; moreover, the interference need not be between the activities of single cells but could be between the large electrical fields arising in the dendritic network found in the neocortex and other brain regions.

If information is stored by a hologramic interference system in the neocortex, it should be stored equally in all portions of the sensory neocortical area. In turn this would suggest that less than total lesions made in these areas should not disturb the information storage (because it is stored everywhere). This is found to be true. Surgical destruction of the neocortical sensory region does not eliminate previously established responses based on information arising from that sensory system. Location of the information within the system is unimportant. Some generalized memory-storage system must be available to the brain, and one such system is the hologram. Hebb's theory also was developed in part to account for the fact of generalized memory storage, but it was based on the establishment of diffuse nets of neurons. The hologramic principle accounts for generalized information storage, too; but it involves different principles of operation.

One fundamental fact is that the memories of sensory activities used in behavior *are* stored in a generalized fashion. They exist throughout the neocortical regions that receive the primary sensory information directly from the thalamus, and possibly in other brain regions as well. The holograph may provide a clue as to how this is accomplished. Perhaps yet another model may be more useful. The application of new models of neural activities always initiate new and informative research on brain function, even if the models themselves turn out to be inadequate.

The hologram is a passive model of potential value in describing how information might be stored. Other models for behavior based on engineering and computer sciences are constantly being applied to the problems of behavior. Of recent interest are active models in which a computer program is written so that incoming signals are scanned for "patterns" and then these patterns are stored for later use with new signals. In this case, the computer program acts upon the incoming signals *before* the storage of information occurs. Perceptual information is stored by the brain in an organized manner and not haphazardly as on a video tape used in television. Adequate understanding of how sensory information is stored must be based upon how the information is processed before storage.

PERCEPTUAL READINESS, OR SET

One of the most common observations made about perceptual experiences is that we tend to see what we expect to see. This phenomenon is often ascribed to the effect of *set*.

The word "set" can be used almost interchangeably with words like "expectancy" or "readiness"; it refers to a disposition to perceive certain things in given situations. It is, of course, closely related to the feed-forward systems described above. Outside of a perceptual framework the word "set" can be used to describe a disposition to respond in a particular way. For example, when a sprinter on a track team is given a ready signal ahead of the starting gun, he expects to hear a gunshot and is able to leave his position faster than if he were not given this preparatory signal. Often it is possible to observe the physical and physiological aspects of motor sets, but it is more difficult to observe preparatory sets for perceptual events. Nonetheless, there is little doubt that such sets do exist and are influential in determining our perceptual experiences.

Perceptual sets may be established by the context of a situation or by past experience associated with it, by instructions for the perceptual task, and by general strategies for dealing with perceptual tasks.

Situational effects

As an example of how the situation itself can operate to affect perception, consider the not improbable situation of being alone in a house at night. You pick a book to read, a ghost story. You get along into the book and become absorbed in the narrative. All of a sudden you see a figure on a wall or in the next room. A ghost! Whatever the stimulus might be in reality—for instance, the light from a passing car—you are set by the story and the circumstances to perceive a ghost. Walking at night through a cemetery while taking a shortcut home is another very good way to establish a preparatory perceptual set.

The environment can prepare us for sensory experiences in subtle ways. In one experiment students were engaged in what they thought was merely an attempt to determine their thresholds for a tone of 1000 cycles per second. The method of constant stimuli was used. A tone of a given frequency was presented at different intensities in time intervals marked off by flashing lights. Some of the tone intensities were so small that none of the subjects reported hearing them, while others were so great that all subjects indicated their presence perfectly. Most of the tone intensities presented fell between these extremes. The subjects were told to report *any sound at all,* and were warned that tones that are just barely audible often seem to be of different frequencies. During the course of the experiment, the experimenters occasionally substituted tones of different frequencies for the standard (the test tone). Very few subjects reported the latter tones although these tones were presented at usually audible intensities. Even after the experiment, the subjects had a difficult time hearing the other relatively loud tones. For example, at the conclusion of the experiment, the experimenters would turn on one of the loud tones of a different frequency from the standard which had been intruded into the series and ask the subjects if they heard anything. About half the subjects heard it immediately, but the other half would not hear it at all until the experimenter explicitly called their attention to the tone by humming at a frequency near standard tone and then "sliding" the hum to frequencies near the tone being presented. When the subjects finally heard it, it appeared suddenly. Some subjects often would claim that the experimenters had just turned it on because it sounded so loud they could not understand why they had not heard it before.

This experiment can be interpreted in terms of a set that was established by the sequence of test intensities given at one frequency. When tones that were divergent from this target frequency were presented, the subjects detected them only poorly.

We can look at the phenomena of perceptual set as a preparation for certain categories of stimulation. With our ghost story example we might say that the reader was prepared for the appearance of ghostlike stimuli, weird and bizarre figures. When a set was established on the basis of a sequence of tones, subjects were prepared for auditory stimuli occurring in a narrow frequency range.

Many methods can be used to make one or another perceptual event most likely in any situation. Information that limits the perceptual possibilities which are likely to occur aids in perception. The important question is, however, just how information about likely-to-occur perceptions acts to make perception easier.

Perception and classification

We can be aware of sensory experiences at many levels. Perhaps the simplest would be whether sensory experience changed or not. Subjects in psychophysical experiments are often asked to report *any* change in the visual experiences occurring at a specific time. The experimenter wants to know if they have detected this change in the stimulating conditions. This simple approach can be extended so as to ask the subject to report what kind of change was made. Did the tone get louder, softer, higher, lower? Still more advanced would be to ask the subject to identify stimuli presented. If a subject were in a darkened room with pictures flashed for a moment or two on a screen in front of him, he might be requested to report not only whether he detected the picture but also what the picture was. In this case a judgment must be made about the briefly exposed picture based in part upon the stimulus presented but also upon more complicated processes—including the memories of, and experiences with, the objects presented in the briefly exposed picture.

Some psychologists actively concerned with understanding perceptual processes propose that we consider perception as the organization of stimuli into *classes*. The basic process of discrimination must be elaborated in the central nervous system to place these activities into classes or categories.

What do we mean when we say we perceive an apple? We usually mean that we have assigned certain sensory signals transmitting information about forms, colors, sizes, textures, and so on, to a class of objects labeled "apples." The establishment of such classes is usually accomplished relatively early in life, but not without difficulties. Confusion among such classes as oranges, balls, and wax apples probably takes a number of years to resolve.

The basis for the establishment of perceptual classes is the effect of this classification upon the internal and external environment. We learn the perceptual classes used by our parents, friends, and playmates, because of rewards, social approval, and the ability to respond adaptively to our environment. If the effects of our perceptual classifications are not satisfactory, then reclassifications can be made, and our perceptual categories are shaped by their effects. The most fruitful ones in terms of their practical benefits and their ability to anticipate the results of dealing with objects in the class (reducing surprises) are retained.

Every perception is simultaneously assigned to a large number of classes. Stimuli are assigned to *object* classes, e.g., apples, chairs, John Jones. This assignment we can call identification or labeling. However, stimuli are also categorized as good-bad, light-heavy, hard-soft and so forth, referring to attributes of the object or object class. Perception depends upon a classification of the stimulus input and the related judgments of the attributes of the object class: goodness, heaviness, uses, etc.

Psychologists who hold to the view that perception can be represented by a process of categorization of stimuli are saying that perception is the result of decisions about the categories to which a stimulus should be assigned. For them, perception is an act of judgment, and they follow in the footsteps of Helmholtz and his "unconscious" inference. As you will recall, the original statement of this principle was attacked on the grounds that perception was instantaneous and did not require an interval of time for a series of logical inferences to occur. However,

Hebb's theory of perception provided a hypothetical mechanism whereby the classification (inference) could be almost instantaneous. Moreover, the principle of the hologram as a means of information storage could easily be extended so as to encompass the simultaneous creation of holographic images of stimuli—each associated with many different, previously stored items of information. Furthermore, Helmholtz' critics were not familiar with the swiftness of modern, high-speed computers. A large series of "inferences" can be calculated by such machines in a matter of microseconds. Although the brain may not work like a computer in terms of its processing of information, those of us living in a "computer generation" have come to accept, if not expect, lightning-fast calculations, thus making Helmholtz' assumption of a series of logical inferences more plausible.

Considering our earlier discussion of the effects of set upon perception, we can now rephrase the matter by use of the general concepts of perceptual classification. We could speak of set as a disposition on the part of the person to expect certain classes of input. In a grocery store we are prepared to use our perceptual category for "apple." The grocery store environment facilitates the perception of all grocery products. When we enter a toy store, we are prepared for classifications such as "ball." After reading a ghost story, we are prepared for classification of stimuli into categories of a more terrifying nature.

This way of talking about set allows us to say that the individual and situational variables that determine perceptual sets do so by preselecting categories of classification. If the stimuli that are presented actually fit into the preselected perceptual categories, then perceptual recognition will be more rapid than if preselection were not made. On the other hand, the preselection of categories will hinder proper recognition of an external stimulus if it does *not* appropriately belong to the present categories. That is, in a grocery store a small, red object will be perceived easily and quickly as an apple. However, if a boy's red ball becomes mixed up with the apples in the store we may not recognize the discrepancy between apple and ball until differences in weight or texture make the distinction clear. Generally speaking, our selection of prior categories as those likely to be useful in a given situation will be reflected in the greater facility with which we make responses suitable to the preselected categories.

Perception under uncertain stimulus conditions

In a normal adult given sufficient time and opportunity, a ball and an apple are correctly placed into different perceptual categories. Confusion between balls and apples will occur only when we are disposed toward the perception of one or the other and when the sensory information is less than complete—for example, when we only glance at the object for a moment. Greater attention to the stimulus input resolves the confusion. Yet, some of the most fruitful techniques found in the study of perception use stimulus conditions in which it is *impossible* to determine the exact nature of the physical stimulus. Several techniques are used by psychologists in situations purposely designed to introduce uncertainty in perception, i.e., to prevent absolute identification (classification) of the stimulus.

In our earlier discussion of illusions we discussed the famous figure that can be interpreted as two faces or a vase (Figure 6-9). This is typical of ambiguous figures: there is no single response that is certain to occur (See Figure 6-13).

Sets to perceive one or another aspect of an ambiguous figure can be established in different ways. Words certainly are frequently effective in establishing perceptual sets, but many kinds of ambiguous stimuli exist. They range from pictures that can be interpreted by observers in many different ways to the ink-blot designs used in some "projective" personality tests.

It is possible to reduce the clarity or details of a stimulus to the extent that responses to it become variable. Stimulus objects can be placed behind cloudy glass to give the object a hazy and indefinite appearance, they can be poorly illuminated, or they can be placed at a great distance from the subject. Probably the most commonly used technique involves the presentation of the stimulus to the observer for only a very brief time. Instruments that present stimuli for short durations at specified degrees of illumination are called *tachistoscopes*. With a tachistoscope the duration

Figure 6-13 *An ambiguous figure, which can be seen as a pretty woman or an ugly one. The observer's "set" helps determine which profile will be seen. (From the modification of W. E. Hill's figure made by E. G. Boring in A new ambiguous figure.* Amer. j. psych., *1930,* 40, *444.)*

of exposure can be systematically varied so that a threshold (expressed in the length of time the stimulus is presented for viewing) can be determined by the use of traditional psychophysical methods.

The effect of uncertain stimuli upon the perceiver is that the stimuli lose properties that usually allow the perceiver precise categorization of them. Therefore, these techniques can be used to force a subject to make judgments that reflect his preselected categories of perception. These preselected categories may reveal interesting qualities of the person making the observations. They could reveal information about the frequencies with which such categories are used by the person and information about his interests, attitudes, values, and motives. Looking at the problem another way, we might say that values and motives affect the perceptual categories used by the observer. Whether values and motives directly affect perception is still a hotly debated issue in psychology. No one questions that attitudes, values, and motives may affect the responses made to stimuli or the interpretations given perceptual phenomena. The central issue is whether we should assume that the *mental experience of the perception* can be influenced by nonperceptual variables such as attitudes and motives.

The core-context argument

Many psychologists believe that the mental experiences of perception are determined solely by sensory information. It has been argued that we should distinguish between a *visual field* and a *visual world.*

The visual field would be the composite of sensory impressions occurring at any moment, whereas the visual world would be the world of objects and things. The visual world would be created with the help of the experiences of the person, whereas the visual field would be independent of these influences. Others who support a similar distinction have argued that we should distinguish between pure stimulus processes initiated by receptor activity and the result of these pure stimulus processes interacting with memory traces of earlier perceptions, which would create something like a visual world.

Pure sensory processes, or visual fields, represent the sensory core upon which all perception is built. This core is determined only by receptor activities and the structure of the nervous system. The context, or visual world, surrounding the sensory core refers to the meaning we have attached to the components of the core. The accretions to the sensory bases of perception which we call meaning are the learned reactions deriving from our individual experiences. But in the core-context theories these processes influence only the outer context of perception. The central sensory core of perception remains fundamental.

In contrast, other psychologists suggest that our perceptions are, from the beginning, the product of almost instantaneous classifications. They reject the primitive and unassailable sensory core. The principle of a sensory core to all perception is rejected because of these psychologists' belief that the nervous system is built to receive "organized stimuli" from the environment and not patches of blue, green, or other pure sensations. They also believe that the classification mechanisms of the brain direct and control both retinal and brain mechanisms so that the perception of pure sensations is impossible from the start. All incoming information arrives in a system that is "waiting" for events of a specific nature, and all information is evaluated against this pre-established context. This line of reasoning has gained support by the discovery of efferent neural fibers proceeding to the retina of the eye from the central nervous system; this would allow for direct modification of the retinal processing of visual information near its origins at the receptor cells.

This issue is lively and not likely to be resolved for some period of time. The question is, which will be the most fruitful approach?

GENERAL FACTORS INFLUENCING PERCEPTION

Psychologists often tend to talk of visual perception, auditory perception, tactual perception, and so forth, as if they existed independently of one another. This fractionation of the study of perception is founded on the belief that it is possible to advance our understanding of perception fastest by the isolated study of various components of perception in the laboratory. Yet in everyday life our visual perceptions occur against an active background of auditory, tactual, and other perceptual activities, as well as our motor activities. Furthermore, since perception can be influenced by the perceptual set or readiness of the individual, we must consider the total expectations of the organism when we are studying the isolated, single system. If attitudes, values, motives, and language can influence perception, then these too must be studied. In this section we shall discuss such general influences upon perception.

Intermodality perception

It sometimes happens that when a person receives certain auditory stimulation he has a perception that is best described as "visual." This is known as a form of *synesthesia.* For example, when a musical note is sounded, some people "see" colors. It has been reported that one subject had relatively consistent color responses when tested over a period of several years. This subject reported that the note C generally produced a red color, whereas F-sharp tended to produce blue-green. Only a few people demonstrate a great amount of this "color hearing." However, most of us tend to think of certain kinds of visual images when auditory stimuli are presented, and we often associate certain colors with sounds. A soft brown color is more likely to be associated with soft auditory stimuli. Our language reflects an intermodality association of perceptual qualities allowing us to use adjectives such as *soft* to describe visual, auditory, and tactual sensations. Many words in our language produce perceptual responses that are similar in some way to the thing or object labeled. Many words in our language probably stem from phonetic similarity to the object portrayed, for example, *babbling* brook, *chirping* bird.

Motor influences

The effects of background sensory information can be rather subtle. The problem of just why the moon looks larger at the horizon than when it is above us in the sky has troubled many competent philosophers and scientists. According to one researcher it depends upon the eye muscles, which are used differently depending on the moon's position. If a person rests on an inclined board to watch the zenith moon and does not have to rotate his eyes upward, then this moon appears as large as do moons on the horizon. This then is an example of how motor activities (and quite likely the sensory reports of tensions in the various eye muscles) alter visual perception without producing noticeable effects appropriate to their own sensory modality. The illusion of the moon's being larger at the horizon than when directly above has been shown to be caused also by cues related to distance and size (e.g., trees and buildings) that are usually present as the moon is viewed near the horizon. The importance of such cues can be easily observed. On a clear night make a fist so that you can see through a small hole and look at the moon when it is near the horizon. You will observe the moon's apparent size shrink. Bending down and looking through your legs at the moon will reduce its size, but not so much as will looking through the small hole of your fist, which acts to eliminate other stimuli from around the moon.

In many studies the effects of other muscles and sensory systems upon visual perception have been demonstrated. For instance, a person's perception of a vertical line can be displaced by applying an electric shock to one side of the subject's neck or by inclining the subject to one side. These results could be due to activities aroused in motor systems of the central nervous system controlling the muscles or due to the sensory feedback to the central nervous system from the muscles and tendons. Evidence can be cited for either view, although it is most frequently assumed that the sensory-feedback aspect is of major importance. Since the effects of muscle tone can play such a significant role in perception, we must keep in mind that all normal perception occurs against a background of specific muscular positions and activity. Study of the motor contributions to our perceptual activities has been somewhat neglected in the last half-century. Certainly it is true that the end-product of successful perception is measured in the practical usefulness of action, behavior, and effective motor responses.

Values and attitudes

We have already discussed some effects of sets on behavior and perception. Social context, one's own past experiences, and other factors can prepare us for perceptual events. This readiness for certain perceptions, or sets, prepares us for stimuli of certain categories. Now we shall find that sets may be established by still other factors.

In one experiment, men were provided with impoverished visual stimuli, such as those presented by tachistoscope, and asked to write stories about what they thought they saw in the stimuli. Hungry men mentioned food-related objects more often than did men who were not hungry. Even though the stimuli were supposed to be the basis for the stories, this experiment only provides evidence of what the subjects wrote in their imaginative stories. The occurrence of food-related objects could be explained by the fact that the subjects were thinking about food and incorporated these thoughts into their stories. While the hungry subjects wrote about more food-related objects than nonhungry subjects, the stories of the hungry men did *not* include more direct references to food than did the stories of the nonhungry men. This could have occurred because the subjects were in a situation in which going without food could have been interpreted as a patriotic duty. This might have tended to suppress any direct conscious expression of ideas about food.

The relation between a person's values and his recognition threshold for words related to these values was also studied. Subjects were given a written test that measured the relative interest a subject had in six value areas. The experimenters predicted that people with considerable interest in one value area would have a lower threshold for words related to that area than subjects with different values. In general the predictions were upheld. A person who obtained a rather high score in the area of economic value tended to have a low threshold for words like *income,* for instance.

One basic criticism of studies dealing with relation between motives and perception is simply that people who are motivated in a particular way or hold particular values are merely more familiar with words related to these motives or values than other people. Familiarity with words, by itself, can produce lower thresholds in tachistoscopic experiments. This criticism was answered in an unusual way in one experiment. The subjects in this study were selected on the basis of the amount of motivation toward affiliation with other people. The subjects were instructed to indicate the clearest and most apparent picture out of a group of four that were presented briefly by tachistoscope. In every group of four pictures, one contained people and three contained only inanimate objects. Subjects who were high in the motive toward affiliation with others selected the picture containing people as clearest more than did subjects low in the affiliation motive. It is difficult to explain these results by recourse to differential verbal familiarities or on the basis of a greater familiarity with faces by the group high in the affiliation motive. The problem of how an affiliation motive could enable the subjects to see a picture of a person more clearly has yet to be solved. Perhaps subjects high in the affiliation motive have a readiness to classify stimuli into categories associated with people.

Reward and punishment

Motives may operate to establish sets—that is, a perceptual readiness for certain kinds of stimuli. These then affect our perceptions of the world about us. Can we establish changes in perception through application of rewards or punishment?

In one study, pairs of figures were presented to subjects after a training period in which one of each pair of training figures was arbitrarily chosen to elicit a reward when named by the subject and the other to elicit a punishment by the awarding or taking away of pennies (see Figure 6-14). After this training, the test figures were presented and subjects were asked which figure they saw. They could respond by naming the figure for which they were either previously rewarded or previously punished. No rewards or punishments were given when the compound figure, which contained both the reward and punishment figures, was presented. The experimenters believed that the effects of the rewards and punishments would be to make the reward figure clearer and more readily perceived than the punishment figure in this compound drawing. The reward figures tended to be perceptually selected by the subjects.

Before interpreting this experiment as a demonstration of the effects of rewards and punishments upon perception, we must recognize that the subjects' verbal responses were rewarded and that we have no information concerning whether their perceptions were altered. The results could

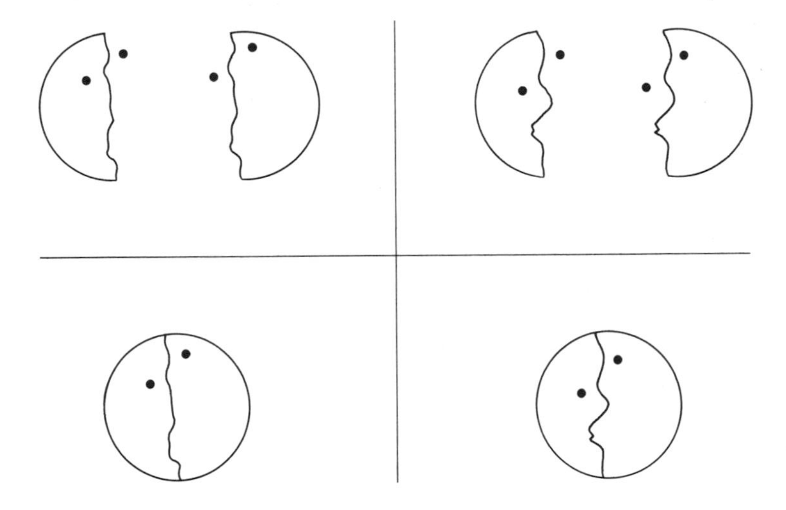

Figure 6-14 *The figures used in an experiment by Schafer and Murphy on the effects of rewards or punishment on perception. Perception of each pair on the top was rewarded or punished; test figures appear on the bottom. (Adapted from R. Schafer and G. Murphy, The role of autism in a visual figure-ground relationship.* J. exp. psychol., *1943* 32, *335–343.)*

be explained simply on the basis that one name could have become more frequently reported than another. Thus the experiment could be interpreted solely in terms of reinforcement and punishment of a verbal response and not as a change in perception. Extreme care must be exercised in determining the effects of other types of variables upon performance when one attempts to measure perceptual changes. However, other experiments have demonstrated that stimuli associated with rewards do tend to be seen more frequently and more clearly than those not associated with rewards.

The effect of associating a figure with punishment is less clear-cut. Small amounts of punishment tend to have little if any effect upon figure selection. When the punishment is stronger, say an electric shock of moderate unpleasantness, the figure associated with the shock is seen less well than figures not associated with punishment. However, when a figure has been associated with a very unpleasant shock, there is some evidence to suggest that the figure becomes *better selected* by subjects, at least under conditions that allow them to "get away from" the unpleasant stimulation. The names *perceptual defense* and *perceptual vigilance* are used to refer to behavior that indicates poorer recognition of some figures and better recognition of others due to degrees of pleasantness or unpleasantness. Often the pleasantness or the unpleasantness is inferred from information about the subject's personality. In a moment we shall return to this topic, which is a much-debated issue in perception today.

Value of objects and perceived size

People who believe in a central sensory core in perception find it difficult to imagine that rewards or punishment can directly affect the perception of figures, although the evidence continues to mount in this direction. Can such an obvious and straightforward perceptual quality as object size be affected by the value of the stimulus to the observer?

In one experiment designed to answer this question, two groups of children were asked to estimate the size of coins both when the coins were present and when they were not physically present. Two experimental groups were established on the basis of their social backgrounds. One group came from relatively poor and the other from relatively wealthy families. The subjects turned a knob to regulate the size of a circular patch of light projected on a screen in front of them. It was expected that the children from the poorer backgrounds would value the coins more than the wealthier children. If value affects perception—in this case perception of the size of coins—then the group of children from the poorer family conditions should overestimate the size of the coins. The experimental results confirm this prediction when size judgments were made with the coins present in front of the subjects. In addition, the amount of overestimation increased with the monetary value of the coin up to the half dollar. When the size of the coins was estimated only on the basis of memory (actual coins not present), the degree of overestimation of size by children from the poorer families was less. The children from wealthier backgrounds overestimated only the quarter and half dollar. Earlier, we discussed the necessity of controlling for the effects of familiarity in studies relating motivational variables to perception. Can the results of this experiment be explained on the basis of familiarity with coins? To do so, we would have to assume that the wealthier children had more experience with coins and their greater familiarity led them to be more accurate than the children of poorer circumstances.

While this is a possible explanation, it does not appear to account for the results of more recent experiments. In one instance, subjects under hypnosis were given false biographical information to accept as their own. A subject was instructed to believe he was from a poor home at one time and from a wealthy home at another time. When provided with poor backgrounds, subjects overestimated coin sizes; with rich backgrounds they underestimated the sizes. Since every person was both rich at one time and poor at another, the experiment controls for degree of experience or general familiarity with coins.

From the evidence available, we must recognize the influence of attitudes and motives upon perception. Accepting this conclusion, however, still leaves us with the exciting challenge of determining *how* these influences are manifested. A similar problem is found when one attempts to evaluate the effects of culture upon perception.

Culture and perception

From the early research that began just after the turn of this century, the argument has been repeatedly advanced that people living in the more primitive cultures tend to perceive objects more as they are physically than as they appear in perspective. That is, they tend to exhibit greater shape and size constancy than do people from more highly developed societies. The drawings of people in primitive cultures are "flat" and free from the perspective found in drawings and paintings common to European and American art. However, we must be careful to distinguish artistic art forms and the perception of objects by individuals in the cultures. Art *may* reflect perception, but it need not. Artistic expression is largely determined through the expectations of the culture as to what art should be like. In addition, art forms and methods of art production tend to be faddish and consequently changeable. As a result, psychologists have turned to examining, through experimental techniques, the perception of people in primitive cultures so as to contrast this perception with that of people who live in more highly developed societies.

One type of research has been to examine the depth perception of students in South Africa. As with other facets of the South African government, the schools are totally segregated under the policy of apartheid. In a picture of animals and a hunter in which the cues of depth were provided by differences in the foreground and background, the white pupils were much more likely to see depth differences than were the black pupils. All of the children became more skillful at recognizing depth cues as they progressed through the school systems, but the white children always remained superior in detecting and using the depth cues to infer the three-dimensional representation. We do not know the reasons for greater perception of three dimensions as a function of the amount of education that the children had received. It is interesting that illiterates tend to have much more difficulty in perceiving perspectives and dimensions in photographs and in art forms than do literate students. When illiterates are shown drawings of animals made from a perspective above and to the side of the animals, they tend to report seeing a picture of a dead animal because the legs are so short relative to the size of the body. In their experience animals with short legs are dead.

It is now fairly well established that illiterate people living in Africa are unable (or find it extremely difficult) to interpret drawings or photographs as representations of three-dimensional objects. They also have great difficulty in manipulating spatial relationships, and there is evidence that they have difficulty in finding embedded figures (such as finding a star hidden in a design of straight or curved lines). Even so, it is *not* likely that there is a racial contribution to this inability to perceive three-dimensional properties from pictures. Studies of white adults who have lived in isolation show that these people are unable to respond in a three-dimensional way to two-dimensional representation. The cause of the inability to use flat illustrations in a three-dimensional way can probably be found in the early life experiences of children. Early experience with books and pictures in the home is probably an essential circumstance for the use of pictures and the interpretation of the depth cues found in them. Schooling does have an effect upon the appreciation of depth in pictures, but in many instances it probably comes too late to the isolated or deprived child and is inadequate to compensate. Probably a continuous exposure to pictures from an early age onward is necessary for the appreciation of depth from two-dimensional representations.

One might ask whether a deficiency in being aware of depth perspectives in illustrations is an important loss. A few moments' reflection on the considerable use of illustrations in science, medicine, and the technological trades makes us realize that understanding what is portrayed in illustrations is very important. When students come from impoverished backgrounds relative to pictorial representations, new ways may have to be developed to communicate such material. Specific research must be undertaken to explore new possibilities for educational and vocational training to picture-deprived individuals. The use of colors, motion pictures, and stereoscopic materials may be of tremendous benefit. Investigations into the effects of early deprivation of pictorial representations should also point out to psychologists that conclusions based upon European or American subjects may not be appropriate for people in other cultures with different techniques and histories and even art forms.

Language and perception

Three separate aspects of the relation between language and perception need to be stressed. First, we can stress again that we can never directly be aware of the mental experiences of another person. All we can know are verbal reports, written or spoken, or indicator responses of some kind. These reports constitute the basic materials of perceptual study. We talk to each other about the view from our windows, our perceptions of others, the colors in a painting, but the only thing available to us that can be used to understand perception in others is verbal behavior. Verbal behavior is a subject unto itself, and we must be careful to recognize that it can introduce error into our experiments and into discussions of perceptual phenomena. We might fall into the conceptual mistake of assuming that every descriptive word must refer to some perceptual activity. Or we might make the opposite error of assuming the absence of a perceptual event because it is not labeled with a word. The problem exists even though we restrict the subject to "yes" or "no" responses to signal the occurrence of perceptual events.

Second, we must recognize the dramatic yet utterly common fact that verbal messages from others are the most common means used for the establishment of sets. If a ghost story prepares us for special classes of stimuli, it must do so by means of the information encoded in verbal materials. We must admit, however, to having practically no knowledge of just how words act to perform these perceptual miracles.

Third, we must recognize the possibility that language itself can act to shape our perceptions. It has been suggested that language influences (or alters) the nature of the perceptual processes themselves rather than merely the verbal responses and the reporting of perception. One of the most common illustrations in support of this theory is that people in some cultures do not have separate words for the green and the blue portions of the visual spectrum and that they may actually see green and blue as more alike than would speakers of languages that make verbal distinctions between them. However, their ability to match color patches correctly suggests that they do see such distinctions. The question of the effects of language is open, but it represents a fascinating, although difficult area of research.

The perceptual activities of man are one exciting facet of his life, but they are far from being the only aspects of behavior that we must consider. Our next step in understanding the fundamentals of behavior takes us into studies of how we learn. Although the study of learning developed from philosophical interpretations of perception, the two areas have developed rather independently.

Perception without awareness

The concept of threshold is a pervasive one in perception. *If* we assume a threshold to exist as a boundary between awareness and a lack of awareness, then it becomes meaningful to ask questions such as, "Is it possible to have perceptual discrimination below the threshold for awareness?" Certain evidence suggests that this question should be answered in the affirmative. In one experiment, nonsense words made from uncommon combinations of letters were associated with electrical shocks to the skin during training sessions. Other nonsense words were not paired with electrical shock. Electrical shocks produce a change in the electrical resistance of the skin, which reflects activation of the autonomic nervous system. This change is called the galvanic skin response, or GSR. After a number of pairings of the nonsense words and the shock, the nonsense words came to elicit a GSR—which they had not done originally. Then both the nonsense words associated with shock and those not associated with shock were flashed to subjects in a tachistoscope at an intensity and for a duration such that they could not be identified. Even though they were not identified, a GSR tended to occur following the words that had been paired with the electrical shock. This result means that sufficient information must have reached the subject to alter the response of his autonomic nervous system but not enough to allow verbal identification of the words.

This finding, and others like it, present a difficult problem for psychological theories that draw a distinction between awareness and nonawareness. If a GSR response occurs, and yet the subject reports he does not recognize the stimulus producing it, how is it possible to have an autonomic alerting reaction? Is there a perceptual mechanism that acts to filter or censor the information from the senses and that allows only certain kinds of information to reach awareness? Can stimuli influence unconscious mechanisms in the individual without influencing conscious mechanisms?

Perceptual vigilance and defense

In discussing the effects of punishment on the perception of figures, we pointed out that subjects defended against seeing figures associated with moderate punishment and showed vigilance for figures associated with intense punishment. It is now time to return to these concepts and dig somewhat deeper into this problem.

Both vigilance and defense can be discussed in terms of changes in thresholds. When thresholds for words are lowered, we speak of perceptual vigilance; when they are raised, we refer to it as perceptual defense. The mechanisms underlying both vigilance and defense *could* be operating at a "lower perceptual level," gathering and regulating the sensory data before they reach awareness. We have suggested that these perceptual mechanisms could be controlled or regulated by degrees of punishment alone, but some psychologists believe that the controlling factors are more likely to be more permanent constellations of personality characteristics in the person.

On the one hand *repression* is simply a name that describes the tendency not to remember certain information. Most personality theorists believe that the material below awareness can affect our lives in many different ways. On the other hand, repression is also a term describing a mechanism in psychoanalytic theory. In this type of theory, repression is a defense mechanism used to guard awareness from intrusions of painful memories. Perceptual defense could be the result of a mechanism like repression that operates to scan incoming sensory messages. The potentially threatening or painful perceptions would be prevented from reaching consciousness.

Both perceptual vigilance and defense depend upon the assumption of several levels of mental and perceptual life. This assumption is a common one for personality theorists, but it remains rather foreign to other psychologists. The data from future experiments will help us decide whether it is necessary to assume several levels of mental processes.

SUGGESTED READINGS

Dember, W. N. *Visual perception*. New York: Wiley, 1964.
Hochberg, J. E. *Perception*. Englewood Cliffs, N.J.: Prentice-Hall, 1964.
Leibowitz, H. *Visual perception*. New York: Macmillan, 1965.
Weintraub, D., & Walker, E. L. *Perception*. Belmont, Calif.: Brooks-Cole, 1967.

7

Basic theories of learning

It is difficult to imagine anything we do that has not been influenced by learning of some kind. Even the activities used to satisfy bodily needs, such as eating and drinking, are satisfied in ways that stem largely from early experiences and training. People living in other cultures satisfy their needs in ways that often seem strange to us. The Chinese cannot understand how Europeans and Americans could ever eat spoiled milk (cheese), whereas we are repelled by the thought of eating rotten eggs. A Moslem would rather die of thirst than drink wine or beer, which are prohibited by his religious creeds. Foods and drinks are considered pleasant or unpleasant, good or bad, acceptable or not, because of learning. Psychologists want to understand the empirical relationships between environment and behavior and to learn the rules that govern changes in our behavior which result from changes in experiences.

In this chapter we shall present the theories which were developed to explain changes in behavior accomplished through learning. Learning is inferred from changes in performance. However, all changes in performance do not necessarily reflect changes in learning. Behavioral patterns often change when we are tired or because we are under drugs or medication. These are changes in *performance* and, although they are interesting, they do not represent changes in learning. Learning refers to changes in performance of a rather special kind.

To define learning is by no means easy. Several considerations should be kept in mind when *learning* is to be inferred from behavior. The following suggestions have been made (Underwood, 1949, pp. 340, 341):

1. The performance change (from which learning is inferred) must result from practice.
2. The response measured must show some kind of increment or improvement with practice.
3. At least two observations of performance must be made, since learning is inferred from a *change* in behavior.
4. Learning is the acquisition of new responses or the enhanced execution of old ones.

The important distinction between learning and performance will become clearer as the chapter progresses and as we attempt to see how different psychologists treat them. As you will soon realize, there are many different types of learning theories. All share a common heritage of associationism, which refers to the idea that elements of behavior become more closely tied together through learning. Most learning theories have developed rules, which are more or less complex, describing relationships among the elements of behavior, usually stimuli and responses.

BACKGROUND OF ASSOCIATION THEORY

It is impossible to understand the current status of learning theories without some idea of how they evolved to their present forms. One of the main influences upon American learning theorists stems from philosophy. The British Associationists are the men to whom psychology owes its debt for the ideas from which *rules* of learning have come. Other influences on learning theory can be found in the pragmatic and functional philosophies. The American view of learning resulted from a need to deal only with observable behavior, from the widespread effects of the work of Ivan Pavlov, from the orientation to behavior problems provided by the evolutionary views of Darwin, and from the advances made in the physiological study of the brain and the body.

The British Associationists

In the 18th and 19th centuries, philosophers were interested in the origin of knowledge. Where does our individual knowledge come from? Do we inherit knowledge? Are we born with innately given knowledge? Long ago, Socrates argued that knowledge of the natural laws was within each of us, a notion he illustrated by eliciting information from an uneducated slave whom he questioned about the Pythagorean theorem. The German philosopher, Kant, also argued for knowledge that seemed to come through other than direct experience. Arguing on the other side, some philosophers maintained that people are born with no inherited information and that the mind of man at birth may be compared to a blank slate on which experiences are written. This group of philosophers denied that any knowledge was innate; they believed all knowledge must come to us through sensory information provided by the receptors.

Much of the work of the British Associationists involved the analysis of their own mental experiences. This is what has been termed "armchair psychology," or "introspection," since the person just sits back and tries to examine his own experiences. The problem with this approach has been that different people at different times and in different places arrive at different conclusions about their experiences. However, the British Associationists concluded that visual perception resulted from the assembling of all of the individual sensations arising at the moment. The individual sensations, called sense data, are the bits of colors, light and dark, edges, and contours that can be found in our visual fields at any moment. When one looks at a tree, for example, one sees greens of different shades and brightnesses, blue patches from the sky showing through the green, as well as patches of brown and black. The tiny, *pure*, and uniform patches of color in the total visual field—"microsensations" —were taken as the sense data from which complete perceptions were compounded.

The problem for this group of philosophers was that of determining how sense data are combined to make a meaningful, regular, and consistent world. Their solution to the problem may be summed up as *mental chemistry;* they said that the perceptual world was constructed out of basic sensory elements. According to the views of the British Associationists, objects may or may not exist; we only *know* about sensory *impressions.* In fact the Bishop of Cloyne, George Berkeley, went so far as to maintain that there is no objective world and that which we call an *object* is merely an *idea* in the mind of God.

Our debt to the British Associationists does not stem from their concern with the philosophical problems but from their attempts to work out rules of association by which elementary sense data form "ideas" (objects in the perceptual world). The rules developed by the philosophers of the British Associationist movement were a mental chemistry. These rules varied somewhat from one philosopher to another, but they were in general agreement about the effectiveness of two factors in forming associations: *contiguity* and *frequency*. In the philosophers' terms, sensations that occur close together temporally or spatially in a perceptual field tend to become associated (contiguity). The more often sense data occur together, the stronger the association between them (frequency). Learning theories were constructed in light of these two rules of learning, but they rejected the philosophic aspects of the British Associationist theories.

Influence of American behaviorism

In the early 1900s physics and chemistry were making tremendous advances, because they were able to make precise measurement of their objects of study. Learning theories developed with the view that psychologists could have the same success as physicists and chemists if they could avoid all things that were not objectively definable and measurable. Thus the trend in American psychology was away from the mentalistic concepts used by the British Associationists and toward measurable *stimuli* and *responses*. These were definable in strict physical terms. The stimulus could be defined in mass and acceleration for mechanical stimuli or in other physical units for visual and auditory stimuli. Responses could be measured in terms of muscle movements or in countable acts. For example, the number of times a rat presses a lever can be objectively measured. The trend was to take the subjectivity out of psychology and to make experimental manipulations that would be open to examination and replication.

American psychologists who emphasize the importance of being able to objectively measure the *stimuli* and the *responses* of an organism in a learning situation are known as *behaviorists*. Because behaviorists developed rules of learning that were similar to those formulated by the British Associationists, the term *behaviorists* usually implies a psychologist who adheres to some form of associationistic learning theory.

Behaviorism has dominated the thinking of the psychology of learning. In fact, the only areas of psychology not greatly affected by association theory are Gestalt psychology (treated in the previous chapter) and the personality theories based on the work of Sigmund Freud. However, it should be pointed out that there is no one universally accepted behavioristic theory. There are many types of learning theories that are both associational and behavioristic.

Influences from biology

At the time formal theories of learning came into prominence, scientists were very much aware of man's place in, not apart from, the animal kingdom. Darwin's work made popular the argument that man represented merely one point of evolutionary development. Early psychologists were aware of man's continuity with the other animals and justified the experimental study of animal behavior as one way of gaining new insights into the behavior of man. Darwin's doctrine of natural selection focused the scientific world's attention on the importance of behavioral and physiological competence in dealing with an uncertain environment. At the same time the American physiologist, Cannon, and the French physiologist, Bernard, had made popular the concept of homeostasis. Homeostasis refers to the tendency of the body to maintain a constant and generally favorable internal environment (see pp. 358-359). The effect of these ideas can be seen in the prominence of *biological usefulness* as the most important measure of the correctness or success of behavior. Behavior can be biologically useful either in advancing the causes of the individual e.g., eating, elimination, etc.) or of the species (e.g., sexual behavior). While people tend to explain behavior in terms of these biologically significant goals, how these general (almost *philosophic*) goals influence the actions of an individual remains to be explained.

The conditioned reflex

The Russian Nobel Prize winner Ivan Pavlov contributed to the behavioristic movement in the United States through his studies of conditioned reflexes. The basic functional unit of the nervous system was thought to be the reflex. Pavlov summarized the reflex as follows:

> An external or internal stimulus falls on some one or other nervous receptor and gives rise to a nervous impulse; this nervous impulse is transmitted along nerve fibers to the central nervous system, and here, on account of existing nervous connections, it gives rise to a fresh impulse which passes along outgoing nerve fibers of the active organ, where it excites a special activity of the cellular structures (Pavlov, 1927, p. 7).

This acount of the reflex shows the mechanical, telephone-like concept that Pavlov held of the nervous system. He distinguished two kinds of reflexes. First, there were permanent connections built into the organism. We could think of these as unlearned, innate reflexes. Second, there were the temporary connections that came about through the association of a neutral stimulus with the first kind of unlearned reflex. This new connection was the conditioned reflex.

There are many different kinds of reflexes available to the organism, but most of Pavolv's work was with the acquisition of alimentary reflexes. These reactions primarily involve the autonomic nervous system. He also studied "defense reactions" (escape or withdrawal) of the body to painful or destructive stimuli. His work with the alimentary reflex in which saliva is reflexively secreted to food is most widely known today. A picture of a dog in an experimental situation used for the conditioning of the salivation response is shown in Figure 7-1.

In Pavlov's work we find one of the earliest examples of a laboratory learning situation. The dog stands moderately restrained in the apparatus. The equipment allows meat powder to be introduced into the animal's mouth. By means of a surgical procedure done earlier, a tube has been implanted in the dog to allow observation and measurement of the saliva excreted from one of the glands in the mouth. Through an innate reflex, a flow of saliva is always produced by the meat powder. Pavlov discovered that if he repeatedly presented a sound (bell, buzzer, or metronome) just before the introduction of the meat powder, the sound alone would come to elicit a flow of saliva. This kind of learning is called *classical conditioning*. In it an otherwise ineffectual stimulus becomes one that can elicit a specific response. In the saliva experiment the learned response of salivation is very similar to (but not identical with) the natural salivation occurring to the meat powder. Because of the great similarity of the learned response to the natural response, classical conditioning is sometimes thought of as a simple substitution of the sound for the meat powder. However, since the salivation in the two cases *is* different, it is unlikely that classical conditioning can be understood this easily; the unconditioned reflex involves salivation with chewing, while the conditioned reflex involves salivation without chewing, for example.

Figure 7-1
Dog in the type of conditioning apparatus used by Pavlov.

From the model of learning created by Pavlov certain terms have come to be accepted as part of the language of psychology. The meat powder used to elicit the reflexive flow of saliva is the *unconditioned stimulus (US)* because it always leads to the salivation response and, presumably, without prior learning. The salivation itself is the *unconditioned reflex (UR)*. Today the *UR* is more often called an unconditioned response. The stimulus that does not produce a response like the *UR* (salivation) before training but that does so after training is the *conditioned stimulus (CS)*. The response that is acquired through training is the *conditioned response (CR)*. Figure 7-2 presents the model for classical conditioning. The terms can be used to describe any learning situation in which a response similar to the *unconditioned response (UR)* is conditioned to another stimulus *(CS)* previously ineffective in producing the *UR*.

We should note that the classical model of learning is a switchboard type of association theory. The *CS* and *CR* come to be associated so that the *CS* is more and more likely to produce the *CR*. This associative tendency is one of the vital features of all learning theories. In all of them, things become bonded together, or associated. In some theories stimuli become associated with other stimuli; in other theories stimuli and responses become associated; and in still others the association is between responses. In any case, learning theories all involve some kind of association principle whereby one activity becomes connected with another activity in a more or less permanent manner.

Two types of learning

Traditionally, two general types of learning situations have been distinguished:

1. *Classical or Pavlovian conditioning.* In this type of training, a *CS* is presented just before a *US*. The *US* is always given, and consequently the *UR* is elicited on every trial. The *CR* develops as a response occur-

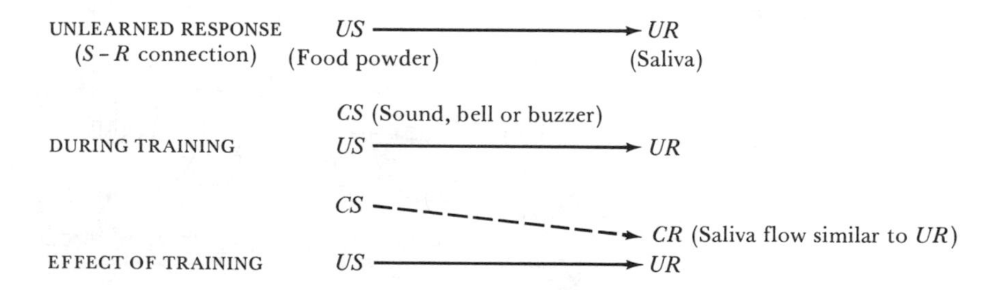

Figure 7-2 *Symbolic model for Pavlovian, or classical, conditioning.*

ring after the *CS*, but before the application of the *US* or as a response to the *CS* on "test trials" when the *US* is omitted.

2. *Instrumental Conditioning.* In many situations the animal or person makes a response that alters the situation. That is, the response is *instrumental* in changing the situation. For example, an animal can press a lever to produce a food pellet that would not have been supplied if the response had not been made; or an animal can make a response to eliminate, or postpone, an otherwise scheduled electric shock. In all instances in which the behavior alters the scheduling of rewards, punishments, or their likelihood, the learning situation is termed *instrumental conditioning* or *instrumental learning.* Most psychological laboratory experiments employ the instrumental form of conditioning.

Summary

Learning theories were molded into an associative pattern by the philosophic traditions of the British Associationists and the physiology of Pavlov. From Pavlov's work we inherited a model for learning (classical conditioning) and a specific set of terms still used in the study of learning (e.g., unconditioned stimulus, *US,* and conditioned stimulus, *CS*).

From the evolutionary movement prominent at the turn of the century came both a stress on the biological utility of behavior and a justification for the use of animals in studying the learning of new responses. At this point we are ready to examine some of the types of theories of learning that developed in America largely in this century.

THEORIES OF LEARNING

Before considering the more recent refinements of theoretical approaches, we shall first present Edwin Guthrie's views of the association process, then the reinforcement theories proposed by Thorndike and more elaborately by Hull, and, finally, the position of Edward C. Tolman.

Guthrie's position: simple contiguity

There could be no better introduction to the behavioristic learning theories than the position of Edwin Guthrie. Like many psychologists, he defined stimuli as follows: "Stimuli are changes in the world order to which sense organs or receptors respond by exciting impulses in sensory nerves" (Guthrie, 1935). This means that physical changes must be effective in altering the state of the nervous system to serve as a stimulus for learning. Not all physical changes become registered as changes in the activity of the nervous system, and Guthrie recognized this in his definition. His emphasis, however, was on the stimulus as a change in the physical environment that is observable and of such a nature that a number of observers would agree upon it.

Guthrie defined a response as specific movements, whether of somatic or autonomic muscles, and he pointed out a distinction that we would do well to remember. This is a distinction between *movements* and *acts.* Movements are the contractions of somatic and autonomic muscles, whereas acts are movements that are considered in relation to the goals attained by the movements. Walking into a classroom, reaching for a pen, and opening a notebook, for example, are acts rather than movements. When we are concerned with the outcome of a series of movements, and consequently we talk of the movements in terms of their results, then we are talking about acts. Guthrie believed that it confuses our understanding of the problems of learning if we try to create laws of learning for *acts.* He preferred to think of learning as the association of stimuli with movements.

All learning theories attempt to connect observable stimuli with measurable responses through certain rules of association. For Guthrie there is only one rule and it is taken directly from British Associationism: *contiguity.* When a stimulus occurs at the same time as a response, a maximal association is at once made between the two. On this basis, all we must do for learning to occur is to arrange for a stimulus (*S*) to occur when a given response (*R*) is going to take place. When the *S* is presented again, the *R* should follow.

At this time it may be useful to introduce the use of *probability* as it relates to a *response.* Probabilities are numbers ranging from 0 to 1.0 that describe the likelihood that a designated response will follow a designated stimulus. In some ways it is like a proportion. If a stimulus is presented 100 times and the designated response occurs 50 times after the stimulus, this proportion would be: 50/100 or 0.5. If the response occurred 60 times after the 100 stimulus presentations, the proportion would be 60/100 or 0.6. If it occurred after every stimulus presentation, the proportion would be 100/100 or 1.0. If it never followed a stimulus, the proportion would be 0/100 or 0.0.

Probabilities are different from proportions in that proportions are constructed by tabulating known events whereas probabilities look to the future. They provide betting odds on what will happen. When one flips an honest coin, the probabilities of a "head" and a "tail" are identical: 0.5. It is impossible to know which will occur on a given flip, but heads and tails will come up equally often in a very long series of coin tosses. While there is an indeterminateness about an individual event, the characteristics of the total distribution of events are specified by the probabilities.

Usually probabilities of the possible events occurring in a situation add together to reach 1.0. Calling the probability of heads p and of tails q in the coin-toss example,

$$p + q = 1.0$$

and if a fair coin is used,

$$p = 0.5, \quad q = 0.5$$
$$0.5 + 0.5 = 1.0$$

If the probability of an event occurring is given as p, one can designate the probability of its not occurring as q. Since the event will occur or it will not, $p + q = 1$. By algebraic manipulation, $q = 1 - p$. This merely means that the probability of an event's not occurring is equal to what is left after the probability of its occurring is subtracted from 1.0.

Subscripts in parentheses are often used in working with probabilities. For example, in Guthrie's theory, $P_{(m)}$ could be used as a term describing the probability of a (particular) movement's occurring after a stimulus with which it has been paired. Since Guthrie specified that the association occurred on one trial—that is, all at once—before the stimulus was paired with the movement, the probability of the movement would be zero.

$$P_{(m)} = 0$$

After a single pairing, this would change to

$$P_{(m)} = 1.0$$

The probability concept is not essential to Guthrie's theory but it will be useful later in this chapter, and Guthrie's theory provides a simple model in which $P_{(m)}$ is either 0 or 1.

Obviously, Guthrie's simple model does not seem to work most of the time. There are many times when movements occur in the presence of a given stimulus and yet do not occur at the next presentation of the stimulus. Most of our adult learning seems to require many training trials, that is, lots of practice. Certainly Guthrie was aware of this apparent contradiction between his theory and the actual conditions of learning in real life. How is this contradiction resolved? Consider yourself at any instant in time. There are millions of different stimuli impinging upon your receptors. Not only do these stimuli come from the object world around but also from the inner world of organs and glands. Hunger, thirst, muscle tension, and internal emotional reactions all contribute to the total stimulus pattern which is, itself, constantly changing. If a stimulus is presented to us twice in succession, it will not occur in the same total stimulus context on each occasion. In fact no stimulus can appear twice in the same total stimulus context. Any new stimulus situation can only be similar to, not identical with, ones of the past. Normal learning requires a large number of trials because of the complexity of the stimulus pattern. The appropriate stimulus figure must be isolated from the ground of other irrelevant stimuli through repetition.

Another reason that adult human learning requires practice and cannot be acquired at once is that most responses that we want to learn involve a sequence of movements. Remember: Guthrie believed that movements, not acts, are learned.

The learning of a sequence of muscle movements depends upon maintaining a complete sequence. There are stimulus effects for each movement we make. These effects include the new position of the body, the tension in muscles, and perhaps the effects of glandular secretions. All of these factors contribute to the total stimulus context to which individual movements are associated. It is important for the sequences of complex behavior to remain in a constant order.

In practical advice to parents, Guthrie suggested that if they want their children to learn to hang up their coats when coming inside, the parents should not have them go back to the chair in which they flung their coats to pick them up and hang them in the closet. Rather, the children should be made to put on their coats, go outside, come in again, go to the closet, hang them up, and then close the closet door. If this is done, each movement produces stimuli for the next movement in the sequence to be learned.

Whether we acquire a given response pattern gradually by learning the individual responses of the whole pattern one at a time, or whether we learn each of these small responses all at once as Guthrie suggested, is still a controversial matter.

Guthrie's learning theory requires the immediate association of movements with the stimuli which elicited them. The stimuli must be regarded as compounds of many different types of sensory stimulation, including the sensory feedback from previous movements. Therefore, if a sequence of movements is to be learned, the entire sequence should be kept intact. The basic rule of learning is *contiguity*. Nothing else is needed. We shall see that this view of learning by contiguity alone is quite distinct from the group of theories which postulate that a reward or *reinforcement* is essential for learning.

Reinforcement and learning

Psychologists' use of the word *reinforcement* may at first seem somewhat different from its use by the man on the street. Reinforcing a crumbling wall means to shore it up, to strengthen it. When we speak of reinforcing a response we think of strengthening the association between a response and its stimulus. This is reflected as an increase in the probability that the response will occur in the future under appropriate stimulus or environmental conditions. This strengthening of associations through reinforcement is a basic feature of several theories of learning. Reinforcements usually are presented after the responses that are to be learned. Most psychological theories speak of them as stimuli but, as we shall learn, this need not be the case. Therefore, it is best to think of reinforcements as "events" occurring after responses that alter the prior response probabilities.

Thorndike and the law of effect

Let us consider the contributions to modern learning of Edward L. Thorndike, a famous learning theorist and educator. Thorndike felt that repetition was an important factor in the acquisition of responses. Previously, the popularizer of behaviorism, John B. Watson, held that repetition was necessary for learning, and as we have seen, it was one of the two principles that stemmed from British Associationism. However, Thorndike believed that more than repeated occurrences of stimuli and responses was necessary for an association to be built up between them and that motivation and reward played important roles in learning. For efficient learning, motivation must be present at least to the extent that rewards will be satisfying to the organism. Thorndike proposed three laws of learning:

1. The law of exercise
2. The law of effect
3. The law of readiness

As a function of all three laws, connections or associations are formed between observable stimuli and observable responses. The first law states that the more times stimuli and responses are paired, the stronger the association between the two would be. When psychologists use the terms association or connection they refer to the phenomenon that links a particular stimulus with a particular behavioral response an organism makes as a result of exposure to that stimulus.

The laws of effect and of readiness are closely related. The readiness law merely states that for rewards to be effective the animal must be physiologically prepared for them. Food will be useful as a reward only if the animal is hungry. A lollipop serves as a reward to a small child, but it will not be very effective if the child has just finished a box of chocolate cream candies. If the organism is ready for a certain kind of reward and that reward is given after every response that is paired with a certain stimulus, then, according to Thorndike, the connection or association between the stimulus and response will be made faster than if the reward is not given.

For Thorndike, reward meant a stimulus that produces a "satisfying state of affairs" in the organism. By this he did not mean that we need to resort to an evaluation of the subjective mental experiences of the animal to determine what would constitute a reward. Thorndike said that a "satisfying state of affairs" could be inferred from the behavior exhibited by an animal. Those things which an animal approached and with which he maintained contact could be presumed to be rewards. However, with this basis of determining which objects would serve as rewards, one would have to test each and every object to determine whether it could serve as a rewarding stimulus. Later on we shall see that a number of ideas have been advanced that attempt to specify reinforcing or rewarding conditions so that their effects may be predicted ahead of time. Many of these concepts will be discussed throughout the chapter.

The law of effect is different from Guthrie's theory in that the *effects* of the response determine the extent to which it was learned. If the effect of the response was to produce a "satisfying state of affairs" for the organism, then the strength of association between the preceding stimuli and the response was increased. If we can think of those stimuli which produce a "satisfying state of affairs" as rewards, then Thorndike's law tells us that rewards act as the agents which strengthen the associations between stimuli and responses.

The theories of Guthrie and Thorndike are contrasted in Figure 7-3. It should be noted that the effects of a reinforcement work backward in time. The reward strengthens an association between a stimulus and a response that have preceded the reward. Just what the mechanism is that allows this backward effect of rewards on prior events is not certain, although many psychologists postulate the existence of *memory* traces of stimuli in the nervous system. The physiological effect of reward could be to act on the neural traces of preceding events. Yet, the problem is one that is very much alive in psychological research, because the physiological mechanisms of learning are still obscure.

Extended reinforcement theories: Hull and Spence

Reinforcement theories came to dominate experimental psychology in the 1950s. They became elaborate in their intricacies and formal structure. Today, these theories have only limited following

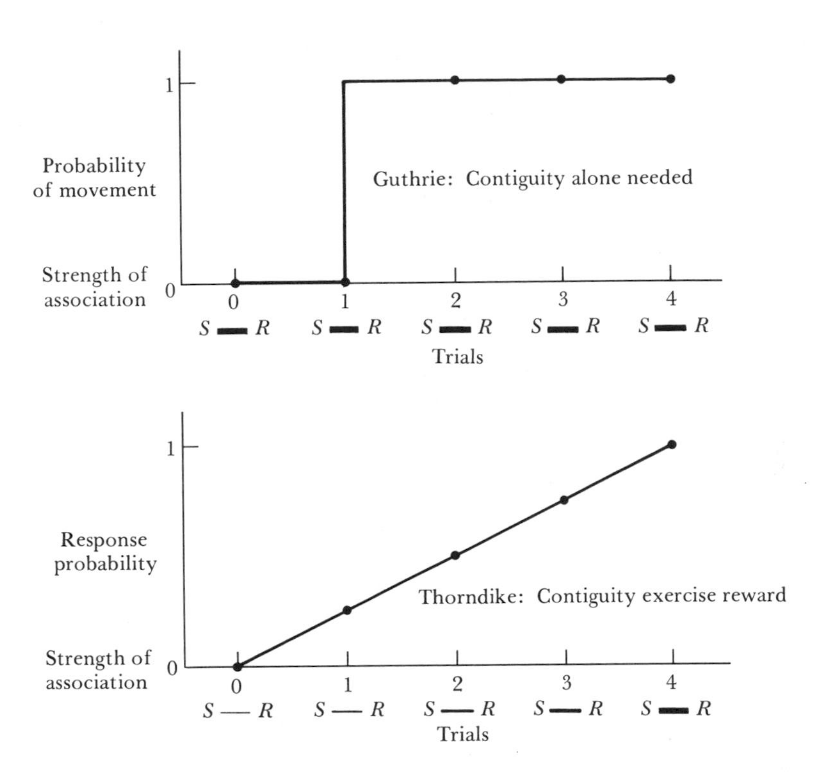

Figure 7-3 *These graphs illustrate the differences between Guthrie's and Thorndike's theories. In the upper graph the probability of a movement (given a particular stimulus situation) is plotted over four training exposures. The initial point, training trial 0, represents the pretraining condition where* $P_{(m)} = 0$. *At trial 1, the association is complete,* $P_{(m)} = 1$. *It remains this way on subsequent trials. In the lower graph, response probability P(R) is plotted against the same training situation. Note the slow growth of P(R), reflecting the law of exercise. The presumed strength of the S-R bond formed during training is given below each training exposure. The width of the bar connecting S and R indicates the associative strength. The larger the bar, the greater the bond.*

among active researchers, but they have a place in the history of psychology and also serve as useful summaries of many experimental contributions. The formal systems of reinforcement theory came to their apex through the work of Clark L. Hull, Sterling Professor of Psychology at Yale University, and one of his former students, Kenneth Spence, who was associated for many years with the University of Iowa. Their formulations of the laws of learning remain the closest approximation to a formal deductive theory in psychology.

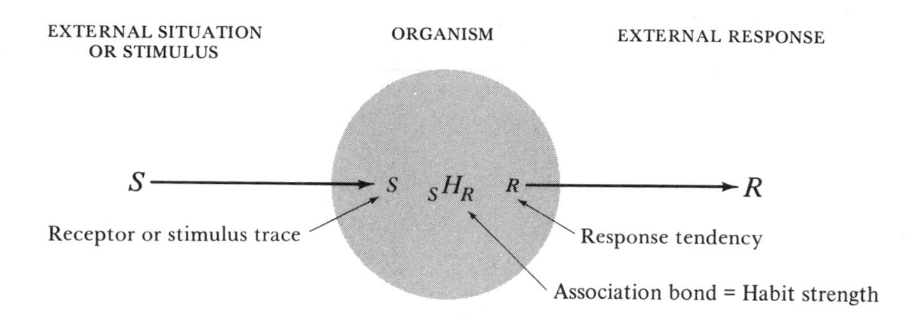

Figure 7-4 *Modified representation of stimulus and response variables in Hull's theories.*

UNLEARNED BEHAVIOR In Hull's system there is a recognition of the importance of unlearned stimulus-response associations. Few learning theories attempt to provide a place for such unlearned responses, and this is due to some extent to the earlier behaviorists' rejection of any kind of inherited characteristics. Yet, learning is a superstructure built upon inherited connections. The nature of inherited response patterns was formulated on the basis of association doctrine; they were thought to be unlearned *S-R* connections. Hull developed an elaborate symbolism for his theory, and in it the symbol $_SU_R$ stands for the species-specific, stimulus-response connection. *U* was an abbreviation for unlearned. The $_S$ and $_R$ represent the stimulus and response, respectively.

Symbolically the learned association between stimuli (*S*) and responses (*R*) is $_SH_R$. The connecting link *H* should be thought of as an abbreviation for habit or habit strength. Changes in $_SH_R$ constitute learning in Hull's system. In Figure 7-4 the distinctions between the various internal and external stimuli responses are illustrated.

LEARNING AND BIOLOGICAL NEEDS Hull and Spence, like Guthrie, made a distinction between learning and performance. Many factors can affect performance, but learning itself ($_SH_R$) is influenced only by one factor in Hull's theory: the number of times the particular stimulus and the particular response occurring together (contiguity) have been followed by a reinforcement. You will find that the word "reinforcement" is often used by psychologists like the word "reward" although Hull's "reinforcement" is quite different from Thorndike's "reward." Reinforcement is defined in a particular way by Hull, and we must be careful to understand what this definition means. To do this properly we shall approach the definition through a brief historical comment.

DEFINITION OF REINFORCEMENT Hull believed that all behavior has its origin in those biological needs which are most demanding in early human life and in the lower animals. Yet very few of the many patterns of action we exhibit as adults seem to be directly related to the fulfillment of these bodily needs. To be sure, we eat and drink and sleep; but the ways, times, and places in which we fulfill our needs are not dictated by the biological conditions themselves. The means to biological fulfillment are social acquisitions that differ from one person to the next and from one culture to the next. Still, Hull believed all complex adult behavior to be indirectly based on our biological needs.

One insight into how adult behavior may be based on biological needs may be gained when we look at Hull's principle of reinforcement. Reinforcement is like Thorndike's reward in one way; it was formulated as a *stimulus* that has the ability to alter the probabilities of a response. Hull postulated that *reinforcing stimuli were those which reduced stimuli uniquely associated with the biological drives.*

A biological deficiency in the organism produces a state of *need.* This can be operationalized in an experiment by depriving an animal or person of food or water over a period of time. One essential characteristic of the need is the pattern of internal stimuli that is always associated with this kind of deprivation condition. The stimuli uniquely associated with a specific need are called *drive stimuli,* S_D. It is only when these drive stimuli are diminished that the animal is reinforced. Whether the animal experiences a "satisfying state of affairs" is immaterial.

Drive stimuli may result from a dry throat due to thirst or stomach contractions due to hunger. In fact, they could be signals in the nervous system arising from hypothalamic centers or other centrally located neural systems. Reduction of S_D, reinforcement, is usually accomplished by the common method of feeding the hungry animal or watering the thirsty one. The definition of reinforcement is flexible, however, and does include the occasions when S_D are reduced by unnatural means. One could reduce the stomach contraction component of hunger S_Ds by filling the stomach of an animal with nonnutritive substances. To the extent that the stomach contractions (S_D) are reduced by the inert bulk inserted into the stomach, reinforcement would be produced.

REINFORCEMENT AND LEARNING For Hull, learning depends on reinforcement. Neither contiguity nor frequency of S and R are sufficient in and of themselves. Hull's basic rule of learning is that a response is associated with a stimulus trace to the extent that the response has been followed by a reduction of the drive stimuli. While the definition may seem a little elaborate, it is nonetheless clear.

The learning rules for Hull can be written as follows: *A stimulus in the environment (S) is presented to the organism; this causes a neural trace in the organism (s). This trace then becomes conditioned to a response tendency (r) occurring simultaneously with the trace if followed by a stimulus with reinforcing properties.*

The growth of habit strength is a function of the number (*N*) of reinforced pairings of *S* and *R*. *No other factors influence the growth of learning.* Hull wrote this in equation form:

$$ {}_{S}H_{R} = 1 - 10^{-.0305N} $$

This equation implies that as *N* gets larger the successive increments to ${}_{S}H_{R}$ get smaller. It indicates that when we learn a response to some stimulus, the first few trials build up habit strength faster than do later ones.

Figure 7-5 presents the typical growth curve of ${}_{S}H_{R}$ as determined by the number of reinforced pairings of *S* and *R* and Hull's theoretical equation.

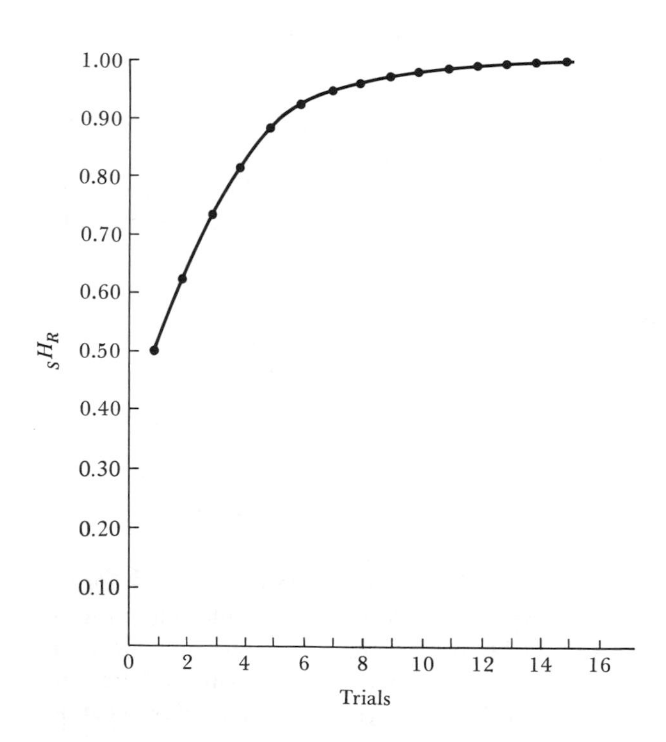

Figure 7-5 *Representational curve of ${}_{S}H_{R}$ as number of trials increases.*

According to his theory, we now know all the rules necessary to describe the learning process but not all the rules that go into determination of final behavior. We must be aware of the distinction between learning and performance. Which factors operate on what an organism has learned so that this learning is evident or not evident in performance?

DRIVE AND PERFORMANCE First of all, we must look at the role of motivation in performance. Thorndike argued that unless an animal is motivated, it will not learn. In his laws of readiness and effect we note the explicit common-sense notion that an organism must be physiologically ready for a reward for it to be effective in producing learning. Hull indirectly asserted the same thing when he stipulated that drive stimuli must be reduced for reinforcement to occur. But, in addition to the effects of drive stimuli on learning, Hull maintained that a general concept of drive was necessary in order that the animal alter his behavior and demonstrate what it has learned. As we have seen, Hull assumed that each different biological need produces a unique pattern of S_D. He also assumed that every need contributes in the same way to D (drive). Drive, then, is a general concept.

Drive serves to energize behavior. Habit strengths formed in reaction to many stimuli guide behavior. Presumably no behavior at all will occur unless there is a sufficient level of D to produce behavior. Drive does not direct behavior, it acts to arouse and intensify it—like an amplifier of our habits. It does not selectively energize the person toward one or another response. The direction of behavior depends on the relative strengths of the stimulus-response associations formed in the past and aroused by the external situation and the drive stimuli present at the moment. Drive operates in conjunction with habit strengths to produce the observable behavior.

The energizing effects of drive are made explicit in the formal context of Hull's theory by the relation:

$${}_SH_R \times D$$

All habits active at any moment are multiplied by drive. As we shall see in the next section, other variables also stand in this multiplicative relation to learning (${}_SH_R$) in the final determination of behavior.

OTHER VARIABLES INFLUENCING PERFORMANCE Drive is not the only multiplier of ${}_SH_R$. The value or desirability of the goal stimulus (K), the intensity of the external stimulus paired with the response (V), and drive (D) all multiply the quantity ${}_SH_R$ to obtain a new number called the *reaction potential* (${}_SE_R$).

$${}_SE_R = H \times D \times V \times K$$

All of these other factors have an energizing effect upon reaction potential, but none so much as D. Hull made explicit the differential qualities and specifications of each of these variables, but they are not vital to our presentation of the basic model. However, it is important to remember that the two most important contributors to ${}_SE_R$ are ${}_SH_R$ and D.

What is this ${}_SE_R$? First it is a numerical quantity like ${}_SH_R$, D, K, and V. This number represents the tendency to make the response *in the theory*. It is strictly a theoretical, or conceptual, variable, useful only in so far as the theory is concerned. It is only the product of the various numbers multiplied together. It represents an intermediate step toward the prediction of the response. It is only an intermediate step, because other variables of behavior must now be considered before the response prediction can be formulated.

RESPONSE INHIBITION It takes energy to make any response. It costs us something in fatigue to do anything at all, and at times it seems as though the muscle fatigue is concentrated in some region of the body. One example would be the localized fatigue of the hand after continuously taking notes for an hour. After any task we have been working on for some time, there is a tendency to want to do something else. However, only part of the explanation of this tendency to change our behavior can be attributed to muscle fatigue *per se*.

Hull would explain the muscle-fatigue effects and the psychological-fatigue effect by two different inhibitory mechanisms. First, there is reactive inhibition (I_R), which is the theoretical counterpart of muscle fatigue caused by the response. The second is conditioned, or learned, inhibition (${}_SI_R$). The two combine to form an inhibitory potential (I_R). After a series of responses, there is this aggregate tendency not to repeat the R again. The conditioned inhibition (${}_SI_R$) is akin to habit strength (${}_SH_R$) in that it is learned and does not dissipate with mere passage of time. The fatigue component does become reduced with time. The aggregate of inhibition detracts from ${}_SE_R$. After the inhibition effects have been substracted from ${}_SE_R$ the new quantity is the effective reaction potential, ${}_S\bar{E}_R$.

$${}_S\bar{E}_R = {}_SE_R - \dot{I}_R$$

Both the inhibition variables are experimentally defined by the amount of work required in making the response. But we are not yet in a position to predict behavior. We must first consider the phenomenon in which a person's responses tend to show fluctuations from one situation to the next and from one time to the next.

BEHAVIOR PREDICTIONS The effective reaction potential is not considered to be constant but rather to fluctuate in an unsystematic fashion. The momentary value of ${}_S\bar{E}_R$ fluctuates and the effects of these fluctuations must be considered in predicting behavior. By mathematical manipulation it is possible always to subtract the oscillation effect (${}_SO_R$) from ${}_S\bar{E}_R$. From this subtraction a new term is defined, *monetary reaction potential* (${}_S\dot{\bar{E}}_R$).

$$ {}_S\dot{\bar{E}}_R = {}_S\bar{E}_R - {}_SO_R $$

Behavioral oscillation does not have any important ties to experimental observation. It is a concept that lives entirely in the theory world of Hull; but it can be thought of as a device that adds in theory the spontaneous fluctuations repeatedly found in neural and muscular systems of the body.

The momentary reaction potential, ${}_S\dot{\bar{E}}_R$, is the end product of the formulas of Hull used in the prediction of behavior. If it is greater than some necessary threshold (${}_SL_R$), then the specific behavior will occur. If the ${}_S\dot{\bar{E}}_R$ is less than threshold, the response will not occur. If several ${}_SH_R$'s are activated in the same situation, that which is associated with the greatest ${}_S\dot{\bar{E}}_R$ will take place. A diagrammatic summary of the Hull variables is presented in Figure 7-6.

The quantity of the ${}_S\dot{\bar{E}}_R$ is used to predict:

1. The probability the response will occur ($P_{(R)}$), based upon how much of the distribution of ${}_S\dot{\bar{E}}_R$ exceeds ${}_SL_R$.
2. The response amplitude.
3. The response latency (the time it takes the response to occur).
4. The number of trials for which the response will continue to occur after the reinforcement is no longer given after the response. This period of "no reinforcement" for the trained response is called the *extinction period.*

All of these measures are used by psychologists to assess performance. For Hull, they are a function of the ${}_S\dot{\bar{E}}_R$ as derived from his theory, which is presented schematically in Figure 7-6.

SPENCE'S CONTRIBUTION Spence made many contributions to the development of Hull's theory through the publication of ingenious experiments and theoretical papers as well as his own personal interactions with Hull. Perhaps his greatest contributions were the creation of separate formulations for classical and instrumental learning situations and his modification of the theory to account more adequately for the effects of the incentives used as reinforcements.

Spence's recasting of learning theory eliminated many inadequacies of Hull's theory. Through the years it was found that many facts of behavior were not predictable from the earlier formulas. The result

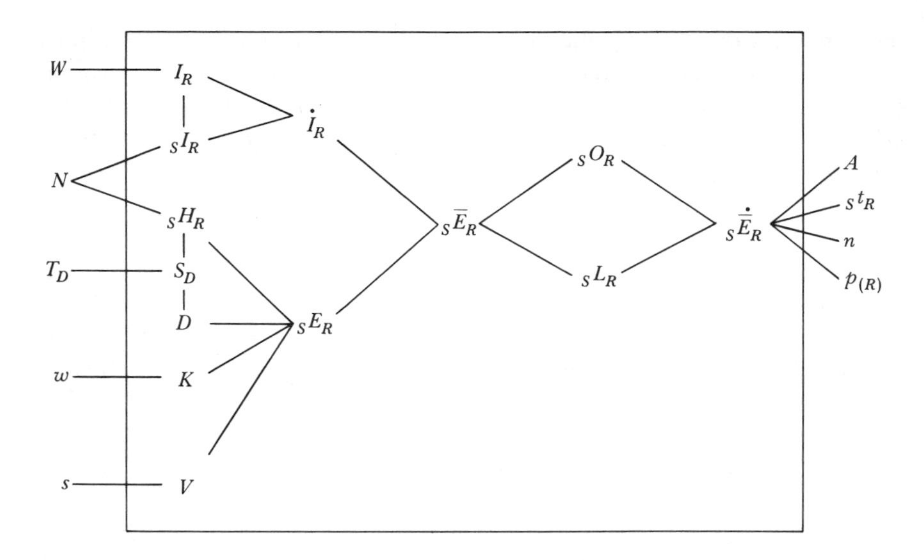

Figure 7-6 *Schematic representation of Hull's theoretical variables. Left: antecedent measurements from which properties of first-order variables of theory are inferred (center box). Right: variables measured on response side. Second- and third-order variables resulting in momentary reaction potential are illustrated inside the box. Symbols used are as follows: W = effort involved in making response; N = number of responses; T_D = length of deprivation, usually food or water in animal experiments; w = magnitude of reward; s = physical intensity of CS; A = amplitude or size of response; $_St_R$ = time after CS required for response to occur (response latency); n = number of responses emitted when reinforcements are no longer given; $p_{(R)}$ = probability of response. (Adapted from Edward L. Walker with permission.)*

of Spence's work is *two* models of learning. One is applied in classical conditioning situations, in which the animal is trained to make a conditioned defensive response such as lifting a paw when it is shocked, when a *CS* is presented. In such situations learning to respond to the *CS* is determined by the variables given in the formula.

$$R = D \times H - I_n$$

where

D = function of the strength of the painful stimulus (shock)
H = joint function of strength of the shock and number of training trials when shock has been used
I_n = function of number of training trials on which *CS* was presented but the animal was not shocked

On the other hand, learning to make a specific response for a positive incentive is supposed to follow quite different rules. The formula governing this kind of learning is

$$R = f\ (D + K) \times H - I_n$$

where

H = function of number of training trials received by individual whether reinforced or not

f = function of

D = drive level

K = magnitude of reinforcement and number of reinforcements

I_n = function of number of times response has not been followed by a reinforcement, given a number of reinforcement trials

If this formula is compared with Hull's, a number of differences can be observed, principally reflecting additive rather than multiplicative relationships between drives and incentives, and the nature of the inhibitory variable I_n. Inhibition of a response is thought to occur when an animal fails to receive a reinforcement in the goal area after having received them there in the past. This produces a frustration effect, which acts to inhibit the response.

The improvements made by Spence are important, because they allow much greater accuracy in the prediction of behavior. Of course, the line of theory building established by Hull and Spence is but one of many possible formulations of the learning processes.

Expectancy theory

So far we have presented the theories of men who have viewed behavior as connections between stimuli and responses. Not all learning theorists look at learning from this same vantage point. For example, Edward C. Tolman argued that we learn the relationships among the stimuli around us. Tolman's name has long been associated with "expectancy theories of behavior." He believed that learning consists of mastering relations between stimuli in our environment. We learn *cognitive maps* of our surroundings. In these maps we learn various routes. These routes lead to further stimuli, which have different values to the person or animal. In Tolman's theory our responses are determined by expectancies that given routes found in our cognitive maps will lead to differentially valuable stimuli.

In this view people follow the routes that will take them to goals which are important and desirable for them at any instant in time. The actual movements involved in getting to the goals are not in and of themselves essential to Tolman.

ARE RESPONSES LEARNED? In Tolman's emphasis upon cognitive learning we find the positive aspect of his work. Viewed from the other side of the fence, however, expectancy theories are an attack upon the foundations of *S-R* association theories. The *S-R* association is the heart of the theories propounded by Guthrie, Thorndike, and Hull, as well as by other behaviorists. Tolman suggests that theories should deal with learned associations *between stimuli,* or *S-S* associations. Which view is most useful?

In one experiment rats learned a maze problem for a food reward. After the animals had learned the desired response, cerebellar lesions were made to produce gross impairments in motor performance. The idea was simply that if responses were learned, then artificially created disturbances of the responses should disrupt what has been learned. The specific question was, could animals with such severe motor debilities still find their way to the goal compartment? They did. Tolman's argument was that the rats could not have learned the maze problem *as a series of motor responses* as Guthrie might have argued, since the mechanisms they would have used to learn these responses were severely disrupted by the lesions. Thus, superficially at least, the animals seem to have learned a cognitive map of the environment rather than to make specific responses. The *S-R* theorists, however, maintained that since many of the muscle movements required to run the maze were common to both the pre- and post-operative phases of the experiment, the results do not provide a conclusive contradiction to their position.

IS REINFORCEMENT NECESSARY? The expectancy theory of Tolman differs from the theories of Thorndike and Hull on the question of the need for reinforcing events in learning. Tolman argued that *S-S* associations are learned through contiguity alone and do not depend on reinforcements. For instance, we *know* the drinking fountain is out the door, to the left, and down the hall about 15 feet. We may know this even though we have never had occasion to drink from it. However, this learning will never become evidenced through performance unless we are motivated to drink. One way to test whether a person has learned where the drinking fountain is located would be to make him thirsty. We observe the subject's reactions when motivated to obtain water. Does he go out the door, turn left, and make a beeline for the fountain as he would if he had a cognitive map that included the fountain? Or does he go out and begin searching in a trial-and-error fashion to find a fountain as he would if he did not know where it was? Tolman's idea is that motivation acts to select which route is followed, and, therefore, what behavioral act occurs.

An experiment with rats was performed in an attempt to illustrate that reinforcement was not necessary for learning. Three groups of animals were given experience in a complex maze. The animals were deprived of food during training. One group of animals was always rewarded with food when they reached the goal box (HR group). Another group, equally hungry, was never fed in the goal box (HNR group). The third and crucial group was equally hungry and was not rewarded with food in the goal box until the eleventh day of training (HNR-R group). The question was this: Would the performance of the critical group (HNR-R) suddenly improve to the level being exhibited by the HR group? The experimenters believed Hull would have predicted a slow learning curve to be exhibited by the HNR-R group with the addition of the food reward, whereas Tolman would have expected the animals to show a sudden improvement because at this point they would start to *use* the map of the maze they had built up by their previous aimless wanderings.

On the day following the introduction of food the animals of the HNR-R group showed performance at least equal to that of the group that had always been reinforced by food at the goal box. In other words, learning became evident to the observers only when the animals were motivated to show what they had learned (see Figure 7-7). Tolman believed that this is the *paradigm* for all learning. For him, sensory (*S-S*) associations are *learned.* These associations among sensory events become combined into internal, cognitive maps of the environment. The maps include areas that represent potential goal objects as well as routes. When the situation makes one goal desirable, animals get there by the shortest route. If this short route is blocked or altered, we still can find the goal by following alternate routes developed in our cognitive maps.

Tolman believed that the behavior of a rat in a maze could be used as an example of the important determinants of all behavior in rat and man. In 1937 he wrote as follows:

> . . . everything important in psychology (except perhaps such matters as the building up of the superego, that is, everything save such matters as involve society and words) can be investigated in essence through the continued experimental and theoretical analysis of the determiners of rat behavior at a choice point in a maze (Tolman, 1938, p. 34).

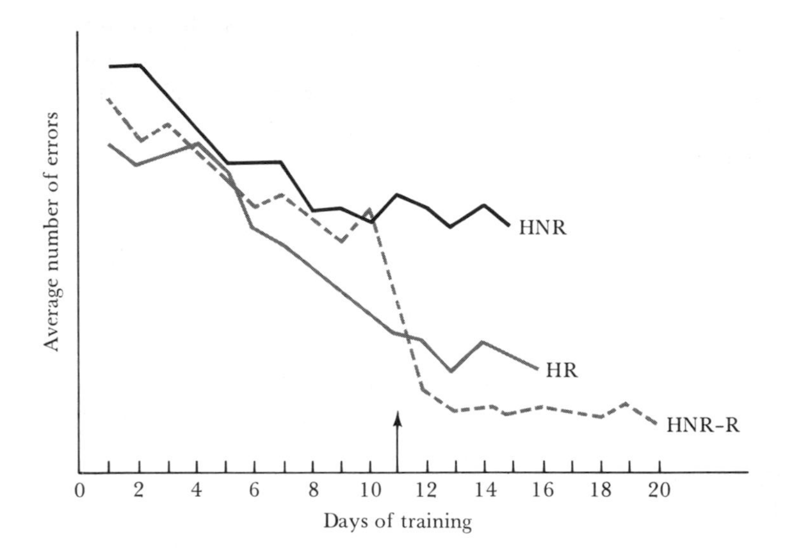

Figure 7-7 *Graphic representation of performances of three groups of animals in Tolman and Honzik experiment.* HNR*: animals hungry but never given food in goal box.* HR*: animals hungry and always given food in goal box.* HNR-R*: equally hungry animals not given food in goal box until eleventh day and thereafter. (Adapted from E. C. Tolman and C. H. Honzik, Introduction and removal of reward and maze performance of rats.* Univ. Calif. publ. psychol., *1930, 4, 257–275.)*

In developing his theory Tolman identified three types of variables the use of which remains much the same today as it did in the 1930s.

1. *Independent variables.* These are the factors that are manipulated by the experimenter in designing and running the experiment. They are ones in which the experimenter has a particular interest, and which he can *control.* If an experimenter is interested in the effects of the amount of reward upon learning, he might give different groups of subjects different numbers of food pellets for each correct response and compare the learning scores of the animals in the groups. By so doing he would be manipulating the "independent variable" of reward (incentive) magnitude. Independent variables are those facets of the situation which are systematically altered so their behavioral effects can be determined.

2. *Dependent variables.* These are the measures made of performance. In the example in which reward levels are altered for correct responses,

the number of correct responses made by the animals would be a dependent variable. Dependent variables are those measures made by the experimenter to determine the outcome of the experiment.

3. *Intervening variables.* These are theoretical in nature. They refer to those factors *presumed by the theory* to be affected by the manipulation of the independent variables and which produce those results obtained and measured as dependent variables. Theoretical variables differ, of course, from experiment to experiment and from theory to theory. For example, we believe that food deprivation (an independent variable) acts upon the animal by increasing the internal "hunger state" (an intervening variable).

Often these terms are used as a shorthand for describing experiments, but the real contribution of Tolman's work lies in the emphasis placed in cognitive aspects of behavior.

The extent to which our cognitive maps range over a great number of environmental stimuli is an important attribute of our personal development. The greater the range, the wider will be our perspective. As children, our cognitive maps are limited. As we grow older, go to school, meet new people and situations, our range of hypotheses about the world becomes extended. In general, we tend to value the person who has a broad range of associations. As we grow old, the range may grow narrower again. This narrowing of the cognitive map is often identified with senility. But there are other times when our maps become restricted too. Under conditions of marked stress, a constriction of our cognitive maps often occurs. When a person returns (regresses) to a mode of behavior that is more appropriate to an earlier age, we find a similar reduction in range of associations. When a person adopts a very limited set of behavior (fixation), this may be identified with a corresponding limited map. Tolman has suggested that the cognitive-map concept might be valuable in understanding such behavior patterns.

Operant conditioning

The enthusiasm for formal theory construction is not shared by all psychologists, even those working in the area of learning. Major contributions to the area of learning have been made by many individuals, for example, B. F. Skinner of Harvard, whose work is of a much different sort than that which has been so far discussed.

Skinner is convinced that psychology should concentrate its efforts upon the accumulation of knowledge through experimentation rather than in the construction of theories. Theories are often justified by the fact that they lead protagonists and antagonists to do experiments to support their positions. But Skinner believes that experiments designed to test predictions from a specific theory are wasteful. He would prefer to explore the changes in responses that result from changes made in the situation.

ELICITED AND EMITTED BEHAVIORS Since for Skinner the appropriate study for psychologists is the relation between situational and response changes, it is important to study the characteristics of learning situations. In general, Skinner distinguishes two types of learning. One is represented by the classical conditioning situation of Pavlov. Typically, a stimulus to which a response would be conditioned (*CS*) is paired with a stimulus that always *elicited* a response. We call this innately effective stimulus the *US* and the associated response the *UR*. Pavlov argued that the *US-UR* association was reflexive in that the *US* always affected the organism in such a way as to evoke the response. These responses are termed elicited responses. As a general rule, he believed the study of elicited responses to be less important for understanding complex behavior than the study of responses that are not reflexively evoked.

One paramount feature of naturally occurring behavior is the large number of responses for which there seems to be no eliciting stimulus. The responses an animal or person produces that are not unequivocally tied to certain stimuli are called *emitted responses or operant behavior*. They constitute a second type of learning. The essential observation about operant behavior (emitted behavior) is that it can be made more likely to occur in the situation by appropriate use of reinforcement.

It is possible for an experimenter to watch an animal and reinforce certain behavior through devices controlled by a push-button or other switch. The button could be connected to a food-releasing mechanism in the box, which delivers a food pellet to the animal. With experimenter-operated devices Skinner can train a pigeon in what appears to be marvelously complex behavior in a matter of minutes. Behavior is shaped toward the desired response by a process called *successive approximation*, or sometimes called *shaping*. To train a pigeon to turn around, a reinforcement is given when the first small turning movement is emitted. This response usually will occur again soon. This time the reinforcement is applied after the animal has turned a little farther. After a while, the reinforcing stimulus is presented only after a half or three-quarter turn is made. A few minutes later reinforcement is given only when a full turn is made. The whole training process usually takes but a few minutes and testifies to the efficacy of properly controlled reinforcements for learning.

REINFORCEMENT EMPIRICALLY DEFINED Earlier we emphasized the distinction between Thorndike and Hull in their use of the word "reinforcement." Thorndike spoke of a "satisfying state of affairs," whereas Hull referred to a reduction of S_D (drive stimuli). There still is no universal agreement on a definition of reinforcement. Many learning specialists have settled for a rather restricted definition, which could be termed an *empirical definition*. This restricted definition merely says that a reinforcement is a stimulus that, when presented after a response, will make the response more likely to occur the next time the person or animal is in the same situation. Reinforcement is defined as the event which will produce an increase in probability that the reinforced response will occur in the future. This type of definition could present the difficult job of identifying which stimuli will act as reinforcements in a complex situation. In general, the defining of reinforcement seldom bothers those concerned with operant conditioning for the simple reason that these psychologists take a very practical approach. They use stimuli that work, i.e., those stimuli which *do* alter response probabilities, and let it go at that. Later on we shall return to the issue of what reinforcements and rewards are, but this is not a matter of concern in the present context.

Reinforcements are used to guide and shape emitted behaviors. The operation is simple. The experimenter waits until the response to be studied is emitted. Then a reinforcement is given promptly. The response tends to occur more and more frequently as reinforcements continue. Thus the behavior of the organism is shaped by the experimenter through his method of distributing reinforcements. The experimenter is passive until the response is produced by the subject. When the particular response does occur, the experimenter becomes active and produces the reinforcing stimulus as quickly as possible following the response.

THE OPERANT CONDITIONING BOX Skinner strongly believes that statistical reports of group behavior are too often misleading and that behavioral measures should be regular and reliable reports of the activities of individuals. The data obtained from *operant conditioning boxes* (sometimes called *Skinner boxes*) seem to fit his requirements best. The basic requirement of any operant box is that there must be a lever that can be depressed by the animal. This depression activates mechanisms which deliver food or other reinforcements. Naturally, the bar or lever in the box does not elicit an immediate pressing response, but through accidental contact with the bar it will be depressed and a reinforcement given to the animal. Then this bar-pressing response will become shaped by subsequent reinforcements administered by the subject without interference of the experimenter. A photograph of a typical operant conditioning box is presented in Figure 7-8. Animals are usually trained, under a food or water deprivation schedule, with food pellets or small amounts of water as incentives or reinforcers. Automatic response-recording devices are connected to the box so that a continuous recording of the depressions of the lever can be made. The recording device moves a pen or writing instrument across paper at a constant rate. As the bar is depressed, the pen moves higher on the paper. If no responses are being made, the pen will make a horizontal line. The more responses made, the faster the line will ascend. A record obtained from an animal in an operant conditioning box is presented in Figure 7-9.

For Skinner, there are two sufficiently reliable measures of behavior and both of these can be represented in cumulative recordings. One measure is the rate of responding, which is indicated by the slope of the line as it ascends swiftly or slowly. The other is the number of responses that will be produced by the subject after no more reinforcements are applied. This is usually referred to as the number of responses from the last reinforced response to that time when the animal fails to respond.

Schedules of reinforcement

In training an animal, reinforcements can be given every time the animal makes the desired response, or no reinforcement can be given following any response. On the other hand, we might ask about the effect of not reinforcing every response but reinforcing some fraction of the responses. Would the animal make fewer responses or more responses? Would it take longer to train the animal? What would happen if we stopped reinforcing the animal entirely after training it on a schedule when we have rewarded the response only at periodic intervals?

Given the empirical definition of a reinforcement, we can investigate the effects upon behavior of applying a reinforcer after each and *every* response, *continuous reinforcement,* or after only some of the responses, *intermittent* or *partial reinforcement.* There are, of course, many ways we could apply a partial-reinforcement schedule; for example, we could reinforce alternate responses or reinforce the bar-press response every 4 minutes. There are four principal partial-reinforcement schedules that have been studied.

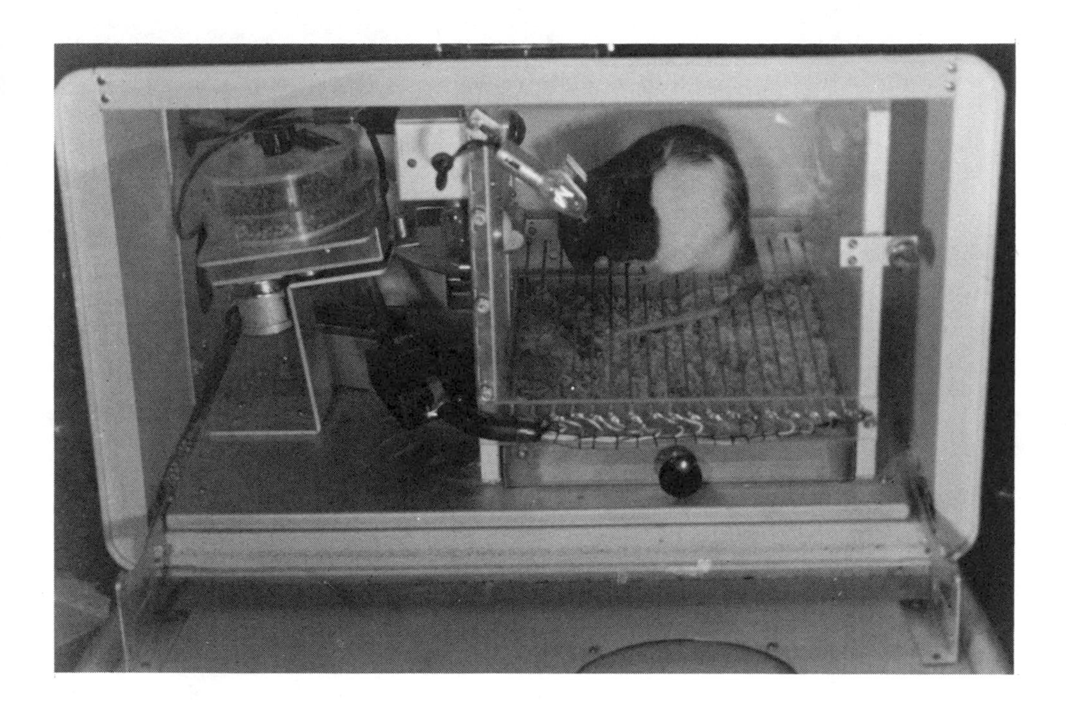

Figure 7-8 *Rat in operant conditioning chamber depresses short bar in wall; this activates feeding mechanism and causes food pellet to drop into receptacle in chamber.*

1. *Fixed Ratio (FR).* A response is reinforced upon completion of a fixed number of responses counted from the preceding reinforcement. The word *ratio* refers to the ratio of responses to reinforcement. With

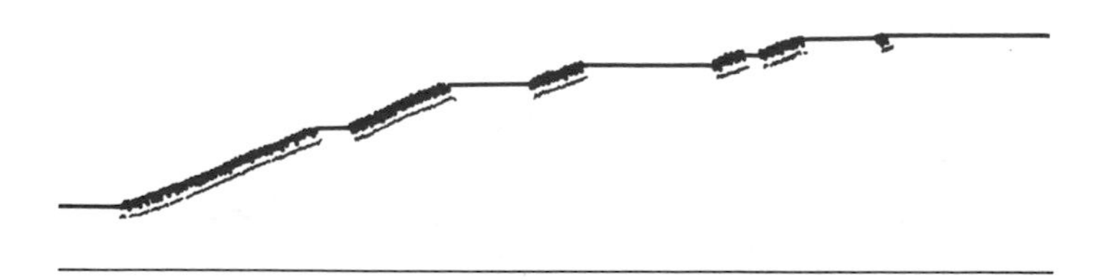

Figure 7-9 *Sample record of animal under continuous reinforcement in conditioning chamber. Each time bar is depressed, recording mark is made slightly higher on the paper. The faster the rate of bar-pressing, the steeper will be the slope of the record.*

an FR-10 schedule, for example, 10 discrete responses must be made by the subject to produce a reinforcement.

2. *Variable Ratio (VR).* Similar to fixed ratio except that reinforcements are scheduled according to a random series of ratios having a given mean and lying between arbitrary values. With a VR-10 schedule the subject must make 10 responses *on the average* to produce a reinforcement. Sometimes only 4 responses need be made to produce a reinforcement, whereas at other times as many as 12, 14, or 16 responses may be required to obtain a reinforcement. The only restriction is that over the course of the training period an average of 10 responses is required to obtain each reinforcement.

3. *Fixed Interval (FI).* The first response occurring after a given interval of time, measured from preceding reinforcement, is reinforced. With an FI-5 schedule, the subject receives a reinforcement following a response provided that at least 5 seconds have elapsed since the preceding reinforcement.

4. *Variable Interval (VI).* Similar to a fixed interval except that reinforcements are scheduled according to a random series of intervals having a given mean and lying between arbitrary limits. With a VI-5 schedule, for example, the subject might have to wait for 2, 3, 4, 5, 6, 7, 8 or some other interval of time to elapse after a reinforcement before a response will produce another reinforcement. The exact interval is selected randomly and is therefore unpredictable by the subject. Over the course of the training period, the average interval is specified and with a VI-5 schedule this average interval is 5 seconds. With a VI-10 schedule, the average interval would be 10 seconds.

Combinations of these basic types can also be made. All of these intermittent, or partial, reinforcement techniques are in contrast to continuous reinforcement.

FIXED-RATIO SCHEDULES Fixed-ratio schedules produce an almost astounding effect upon behavior. As the ratio of responses to reinforcements increases, the rate of responding also *increases.* An animal can be trained so that it makes more and more responses with fewer and fewer reinforcements.

Training an animal under an intermittent fixed-ratio schedule results in a more rapidly ascending response record than training with continuous reinforcement. Under this type of schedule the animal must produce a specified number of responses before a reinforcement will occur. As the animal moves to higher and higher rates from original training with continuous reinforcement, the *rate* of responding increases. Figure 7-10 shows rates of responding for three different fixed-ratio

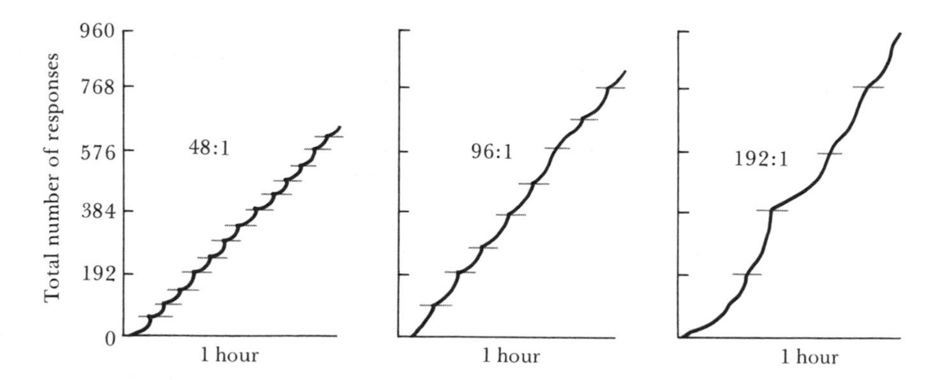

Figure 7-10 *Rates of rat response on three fixed-ratio schedules. (Adapted from B. F. Skinner,* The behavior of organisms. *New York: Appleton-Century-Crofts. Copyright © 1938 by Appleton-Century-Crofts, Inc. All rights reserved.)*

schedules. The rate of responding is greatest in the ratio of 1 reinforcement for every 192 responses.

After each reinforcement (represented by a horizontal line on the curve), response rate slows down. This results in a scalloplike section of the curve between reinforcements. In part, this represents the time taken by the subject to ingest and chew the food—but something else is going on too. For example, it should take no longer for the animal to ingest the food on one schedule rather than another. The food is the same size. At the greater ratios the period between the reinforcement and the beginning of the new response period is greatest.

When the response acquired with a fixed-ratio schedule is no longer reinforced, the curves reveal that the decrease of the response rate comes about through progressive lengthening of these plateaus of no responding. When the animal responds, it responds at a high rate but the periods of responding do not last long. This is illustrated in records obtained from rat research with the Skinner box as presented in Figure 7-11.

One of the reasons for the high response rates obtained by the use of fixed-ratio reinforcement schedules may be that the rate of response itself is being reinforced. During the fixed-ratio schedules the animals tend to be responding at a high rate when the reinforcement occurs.

FIXED-INTERVAL SCHEDULES Fixed-interval reinforcement refers to the administration of the reinforcing stimulus following a response that occurs after some definite period after the last reinforcement. For ex-

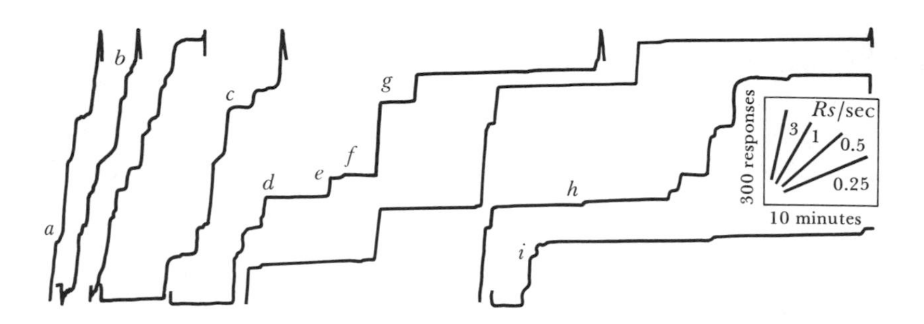

Figure 7-11 *Cumulative records of rat undergoing extinction following training with fixed-ratio (60:1) schedule. Top of left records are continuous with bottom of right records. Note that periods when no responses are made are longer during extinction, but that otherwise rate of response remains high. (From C. B. Ferster and B. F. Skinner,* Schedules of reinforcement. *New York: Appleton-Century-Crofts, Inc., Copyright © 1957 by Appleton-Century-Crofts, Inc. All rights reserved.)*

ample, a reinforcement might follow the first response to occur after a period of 1 minute from the preceding reinforcement. A minimum period of time must have elapsed, and a response must be made by the animal. Generally, lower rates of responding are found with the fixed-interval than with the fixed-ratio schedule, and the longer the period of time between reinforcements the lower will be the rate of response. As with the fixed-ratio schedules there are also lapses in the response rate after each reinforcement, which produces the scalloplike effect in the recorded records.

VARIABLE-INTERVAL AND VARIABLE-RATIO SCHEDULES These two more complicated schedules can change the response rates. The exact effects of the variable-interval and -ratio programs of reinforcement depend to a great extent on the past training histories and prior number of reinforcements given under different schedules. Generally, we may say that some of these manipulations result in response rates that do not show the marked pauses following reinforcement of the fixed schedules. High response rates can be maintained throughout the training of the subjects.

General summary of the findings in experiments in which various schedules of reinforcement have been used would look something like this:

Acquisition: Continuous reinforcement creates faster learning of the response than intermittent reinforcement.

Response rate: Faster rates with fixed-ratio schedules than fixed-interval schedules. Rate on fixed-interval schedules dependent on frequency reinforcement.

Resistance to extinction: Intermittent or partial-reinforcement schedules produce greater numbers of responses during extinction.

Extinction

Extinction periods refer to times during which no responses are reinforced on any basis. The response ultimately becomes "extinguished" through a lack of reinforcement. The number of responses emitted by subjects after all reinforcements have been stopped is the subject's *resistance to extinction.* The greater number of responses emitted, the stronger the resistance.

An animal's resistance to extinction can be increased through intermittent- or partial-reinforcement schedules beyond that which can be obtained through training with continuous reinforcement.

Why do the partial-reinforcement schedules affect the subjects so that they emit much greater numbers or responses when reinforcements are eliminated? Skinner is satisfied to report that they do. His interest is in determining the effect of various training schedules on his two measures (response rate and number of responses to response cessation). However, one explanation of the greater resistance to extinction of animals trained under partial-reinforcement schedules is that the subjects have a more difficult task in recognizing just when reinforcements are eliminated. If animals are trained with continuous reinforcement, the transition is abrupt when depression of the lever fails to produce a reinforcement. When trained under an intermittent schedule, the animals have had experience with situations when the depression of the lever does not result in the appearance of food. If the animal is on a large fixed-ratio schedule (e.g., 48 to 1), it would take longer for the animal to discover the change in conditions. This type of explanation has been generally referred to as the *discrimination-failure* explanation. The animals *fail to discriminate* between acquisition and extinction phases of the experiment.

While acceptable at a common-sense level, this explanation is vulnerable to the objection that it depends too much on thinking (cognition). Some psychologists believe this kind of explanation brings back mentalistic, nonbehavioristic terms to psychology. Many people who do not object to the use of mentalistic concepts in the human are not willing to be quite so mentalistic with the rat or pigeon.

Other psychologists are of the opinion that the results of partial reinforcement in prolonging the period of responding during extinction training can be explained if we view the "response" differently. They say we should look at the response trained under a fixed-ratio schedule as the total series of n responses animals must make between reinforcements. Then, during extinction, the total responses should be counted in terms of the number of "packages" of n responses emitted.

Still another way of explaining the partial-reinforcement results is through the concept of secondary reinforcement. If the bar-press response has acquired secondary reinforcing properties, then each bar depression adds to the habit strength of the bar-press response. Because of the high response rates, animals under the intermittent schedules have built up greater habit strengths than the animals that receive primary reinforcements more often. Greater habit strength should lead to greater resistance to extinction.

There are data to support and refute all of these interpretations. We cannot say which explanation will be best in the long run. At this time it may be safest to side with Skinner, who simply reports the data and leaves the interpretation to the future.

Discrimination and the stimulus control of behavior

When one is training or testing animals in operant procedures, it is often desirable to establish conditions in which one stimulus situation signals the availability of reinforcements while another stimulus situation signals that no reinforcements will be given. The terms used to describe these signals are called by special names.

An S^{Δ} (*S-delta*) is used to designate a stimulus in the presence of which responses are never promptly followed, or scheduled to be followed, by a reinforcement.

An S^D (discriminative stimulus) is a stimulus in the presence of which responses are *sometimes* followed by reinforcements, depending upon the schedule being used. In other words, reinforcements are "scheduled" under S^D periods, but the animal must perform the appropriate pattern of responses to obtain them. S^D's *and* S^{Δ}'s come to control behavior through their association with periods when responses are reinforced or not reinforced. Under most conditions, response rates decline in S^{Δ} periods and can vary considerably under S^D periods, depending on the schedule of reinforcements being used in the S^D period.

While the animal must be able to discriminate the S^{Δ} and S^D stimuli, and between the two of them, this method is not often used to evaluate the discriminability of stimuli to the subjects. More frequently, S^D and S^{Δ} signals are used to determine the effects of other variables upon behavior.

The control of behavior by discriminative stimuli (S^{Δ} and S^D) need not be absolute. In fact, the stimulus conditions may have no effect on behavior with the particular schedule under which the animal is performing. In this case the response rate during an S^D or S^Δ period is not different from the response rate under a more general schedule when not in the signaled period. This would indicate that the S^Δ or S^D has no control of behavior. In the other extreme, an S^D or S^Δ can completely determine response rates—in which case the strength of control is considered to be great. Thus the degree to which response rates determine response rates is a measure of the strength of stimulus control.

Conditioned suppression

Some years ago several techniques were developed within the general operant framework in attempts to evaluate the conditioning of emotional reactions to previously neutral stimuli. One successful technique involved the reduction of an established response rate by the presentation of the "emotional" stimulus. The general idea was that the emotion evoked by the stimulus would disrupt and suppress the response rate. Originally this effect, illustrated in Figure 7-12, was called the "conditioned emotional response" or CER. However, the more popular term today is "conditioned suppression."

The term *conditioned suppression* is preferable, because it describes the basic behavioral change being measured—that is, a cessation or reduction in rate of response.

Most commonly the procedure involves a pairing of a noxious stimulus (such as electrical shock to an animal's feet) with a neutral stimulus. After a number of pairings of the neutral stimulus with the noxious event, the previously neutral stimulus is applied to the animal as it is responding for food or another positive reinforcement.

To use the conditional suppression technique a stable rate of response must first be established. This is usually done by placing the subject on a variable-interval schedule for a positive reinforcement. This schedule produces high, stable response rates. Once the response rate has become stable, the pairing of a neutral stimulus with a noxious stimulus occurs using a classical conditioning paradigm. The neutral stimulus is the *CS* and the painful stimulus the *US*. (Using different terminology, the *CS* becomes an S^D for shock.) After the conditioning of the effects of the noxious stimuli to the *CS,* the *CS* is presented at different times when the animal is responding for the positive reinforcements. The measure of response rate occurring after the *CS* is compared to the rate during periods when the *CS* is not being presented. It should be noted that the conditioned suppression technique combines features from both operant and classical conditioning procedures.

Conditioned suppression is often used to evaluate the discriminatory

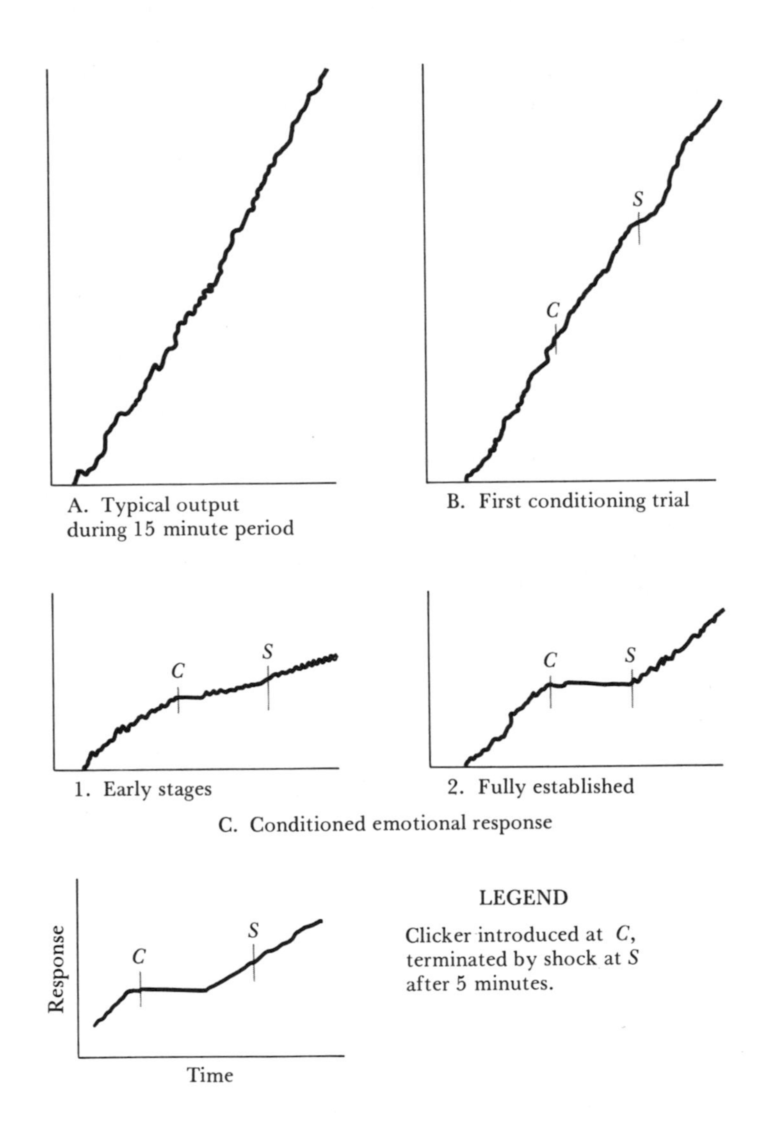

Figure 7-12 *The development of a conditioned emotional response (conditioned suppression).* A: *normal response rate.* B: *effects of first pairing of clicks and shock on response rate. Other graphs show more complete development of conditioned emotional response. (Adaptation of Fig. 2 in H. F. Hunt, and J. V. Brady. Some effects of electroconvulsive shock on a conditioned emotional response.* J. comp. physiol. psychol., *1951,* 44, *88–89.)*

abilities of the subjects. The idea is simple: If the subject cannot discriminate the stimulus, it cannot be used as a stimulus that is effective in establishing response suppression. If the subject can detect it, it can be so used. One approach to determining the range (in frequencies or intensities) of auditory signals to which a species can respond would be to train animals in an operant task and then establish conditioned suppression to tones of different frequencies and intensities. After the association of the tones to noxious stimuli, the tones would be presented as the subject is responding. If the response rate declines (indicative of a suppression), the animal must have detected the signal. Data from an experiment in which this technique was used to determine auditory limits are shown in Figure 7-13.

In the experiment illustrated by Figure 7-13, four segments of records obtained from an animal are shown. The subjects—primitive mammals—were trained to lick a waterspout. Food pellets were given to the animal on a partial-reinforcement schedule so as to produce a rapid licking rate. The hearing tests were imposed upon this high-rate licking response.

When the rate was well established, a tone followed by foot shock was presented while the licking was underway. First the shock produced a reduction in licking, but soon the tone produced the reduction in the interval between the one and the shock which followed. As can be seen in the illustration, tones presented at intensities below auditory threshold did not cause a response suppression (lower left), whereas intensities above threshold did (lower right).

Punishment

Reflection on the usual patterns of social learning leads us to recognize the emphasis placed on attempts to "stamp out" undesirable acts through punishment. When a child does something undesirable, we sometimes resort to a slap, spank, or yell. We previously discussed the law of effect made famous by Thorndike. Originally Thorndike thought of positive rewards as stamping-in *S-R* connections and negative rewards as stamping-out *S-R* connections. Later on the basis of studies in which negative verbal stimuli (rather weak punishments) were used, he concluded that punishment had little effect on eliminating undesirable behavior. For Skinner, responses can be learned by their association with the termination of negative reinforcers—defined as stimuli that adversely affect the rate of responding.

Many things may act to reduce response rates. The presentation of

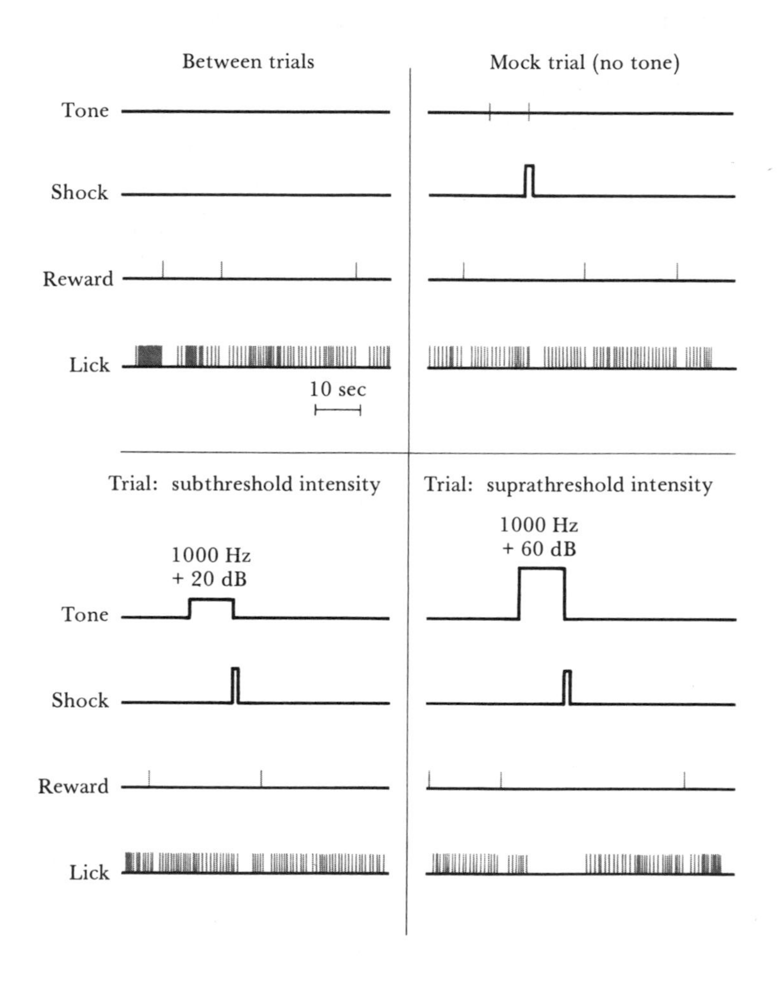

Figure 7-13 *Segment of a typical behavioral record during threshold test trials using technique of conditioned suppression. Time runs from left to right on horizontal dimension; events are represented by short vertical strokes. From top to bottom in each quadrant: tone, shock, reward, tongue contact with lick spout. Note that animal stops licking only after reward, shock, or onset of a suprathreshold stimulus. (Fig. 2 from B. Masterton, H. Heffner, and R. Ravizza, the evolution of human hearing.* J. amer. acoustical soc., *1969,* 45, *968.)*

novel stimuli in the responding situation, motives and emotions of certain kinds, and punishment can act to depress response rates. While a response rate is depressed by punishment, the organism can be trained to emit another type of response. This is the important effect of punishment in Skinner's analysis of behavior. According to this view, if we use punishment at all, we should be careful to train the person or animal in *another (alternative)* way of responding while the rate of emission of the objectionable response is lowered.

Through the number of reinforcements and training schedules a certain *operant strength* is built up in the organism. Skinner defines this concept behaviorally as the number of responses emitted during the extinction period. Punishment acts only upon the response rate, *not* the operant strength of the response. Therefore, even though we punish a response, we would expect the same *total number of responses to be emitted* ultimately. This would lead to the punished animal's responding *longer* than an animal not punished following the removal of the positive reinforcement. To eliminate responses, we must have the subject emit all of the responses that constitute the operant strength without reinforcement. The faster they are emitted during extinction, the sooner the animal will stop making the response entirely. As mentioned above, if we depress the rate by punishment, it will take longer for the animal to reduce the operant strength of the response. In Figure 7-14 we see data from an experiment in which this prolongation of response was demonstrated.

The group of animals punished early in the extinction period show a depression in rate that does not last long. When the punishment is no longer applied (days 2 and 3), we observe the nonpunished animals producing fewer responses than the animals in the punished groups. This summarizes many of the conclusions that have been made about the effect of punishment. Punishment can depress the rate of response, but it does not affect the total number of responses that will be emitted during the extinction training. This should serve as a warning to us. *By punishment it is possible to perpetuate those very responses we wish to eliminate.*

Through the problem of punishment and the effects of intermittent reinforcements we have been moving very close to areas far removed from necessary restrictions of laboratory work.

The teaching machine

One fascinating and important educational innovation that stemmed from operant conditioning is the teaching machine. It is based on the belief that rapid learning depends upon having the student produce a large number of correct responses. The teaching machine was designed to present many short questions, one at a time. The student writes his answers in a

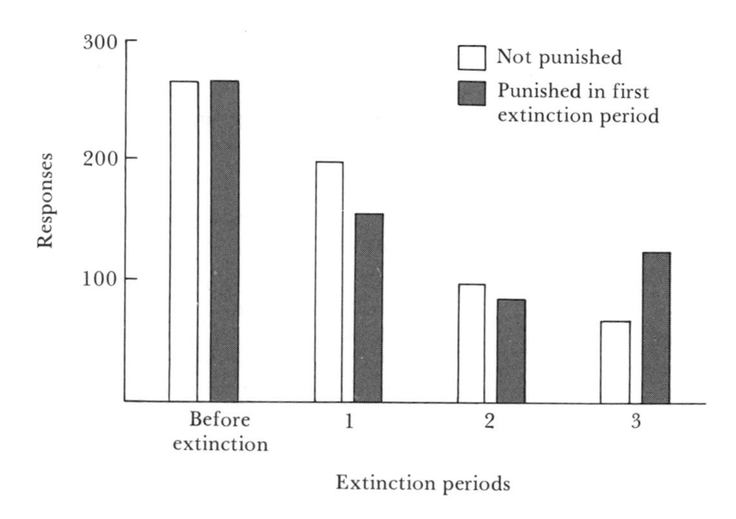

Figure 7-14 *Effects of punishment on extinction. Note that group receiving punishment shows earlier decline in response rate, but maintains a higher rate in third extinction period. (Adapted from E. R. Hilgard,* Theories of learning. *New York: Appleton-Century-Crofts, 1953. Data from W. K. Estes, An experimental study of punishment.* Psychol. monogr., *1944,* 57. *By permission of E. R. Hilgard, W. K. Estes, Appleton-Century-Crofts, and The American Psychological Association.)*

space provided near the question. The material used in the machines is written in a way that makes it difficult for the student to answer incorrectly. A correct response serves as its own reinforcement. Shortly after the student makes his response, the "correct answer" is provided and if his response is correct this event is reinforcing. The sequences of questions represent the "program" of the teaching machine and programs are written to make incorrect responses most unlikely, usually less than 1 percent. The actual methods used to present questions and to record responses are probably immaterial to the effectiveness of the procedure. Computers and other mechanical devices can be used of course, but programs can be made as simple paper pamphlets, too. Once the novelty of the computer approach has worn off, the paper and pencil approach is likely to be as effective a procedure.

It is too early to make any definite conclusion about teaching machines even though most of the preliminary studies and reports have been favorable. Generally, students using the machines learn factual material faster than students working with traditional methods. It is likely that certain kinds of materials are more amenable to presentation by teaching machines than others. Areas of learning in which a student must master a considerable amount of factual material will undoubtedly be put into teaching machine forms first. Areas in which conceptual frameworks must be learned and in which there are alternate interpretations may turn out to be resistant to machine instruction.

Moreover, to write a teaching program for any machine or device requires an immense amount of organization of the material, as well as testing of it to make sure students make few mistakes doing the task. This organization, itself, is of great value to learning. It has been reported that students learn as much sitting passively, making no observable responses, and listening to a program being read to them as when they go through the program, actively making every response.

Behavior modification

The operant movement has caused psychologists and others to be very sensitive to the rate at which responses are made. The simple counting of behaviors—whether desirable ones or not—is essential to understanding any changes that may occur. Baseline rates are discovered, and changes then can be evaluated through the application of operant procedures. Often this can be effectively done in connection with the behavior of children. If a child is exhibiting a dangerous or self-destructive response, the rate of occurrence can be established by counting. The effects of stimuli and reinforcers can be evaluated, and behavior is usually brought under "stimulus·control" by the use of appropriate schedules of reinforcement or discriminative stimuli. Figure 7-15 shows the results of these procedures when they were applied to one particular behavior on the part of a child. The rate of expression of the response was made less frequent through the application of appropriate reinforcements.

This approach to the modification of behavior is not easy. It requires time, patience, and knowledge of the appropriate behavioral techniques. In addition, while it is effective with children with certain types of behavior disorders, it may not be generally effective for all children and for all behavioral problems. Nevertheless, it is an exciting new approach.

Mathematically oriented theories

In ever-increasing numbers psychologists are developing theories of behavior based upon more or less sophisticated mathematical formulations. A complete development of this approach to learning is beyond the scope of this book, but in this section we shall try to provide some understanding of the basic concepts upon

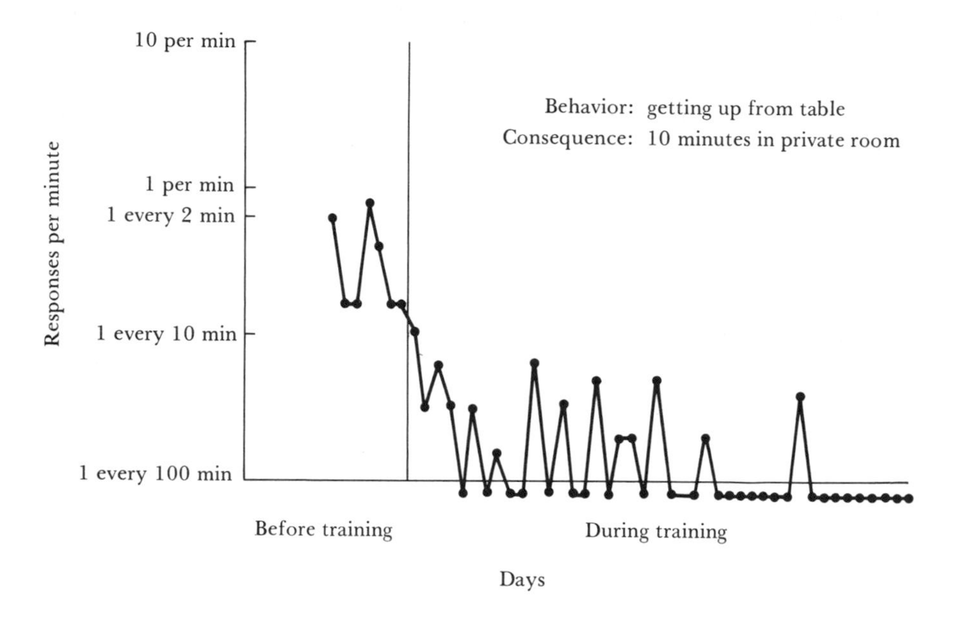

Figure 7-15 *This shows the rate with which a child left the meal table at home before and after a training program was established to lower the rate. Each leaving-the-table response was punished by the child's being placed in a room, alone, for ten minutes. (Figure redrawn from data supplied by Dr. Henry S. Pennypacker.)*

which this work is based, as well as some of the theoretical structure that has been built.

The mathematically formulated learning theories often deal with three types of events: *responses, stimuli, and reinforcing events.*

1. *Responses.* All the behaviors that can be made by a subject in the experimental situation are classified into mutually exclusive and exhaustive categories. Insofar as a theory is concerned, this means that all the varieties of behavior that can be exhibited by the subject are brought under one of the classifications and that there is no overlap in these classifications. Since the experimental situations used by theorists must be capable of straightforward interpretation, response categories such as "a turn into right alley" or "a turn into left alley" of a **T** maze are used. In other words only simple learning situations are used in which the response categories represent "either-or" types of behavior. The classes of available responses are considered to represent a mathematical collection or *set.*

2. *Stimuli.* An organism's stimulus condition is determined by the

nature of its environment and its internal characteristics. All the stimulating conditions, or the environment, may arouse a large number of stimulus conditions, and the collection of all of these constitute a set. The elements of this mathematical set are often called stimulus elements.

3. *Reinforcing events.* It is well known that the probability of a response can be changed by presenting the individual with certain stimuli (for example, food given to a hungry animal). These stimuli are called reinforcements, as we know. For the present purposes, the nature of reinforcement is not important. Once again an empirical definition of reinforcement is our criterion. Reinforcements are presumed to affect the probabilities of elements of the response set given the occurrence of elements from the stimulus set. Once again, the types of reinforcements are presumed susceptible to classification into a set of all such conditions.

LINEAR MODELS In some models the changes in response probabilities are presumed to be a linear function of the probabilities existing on the preceding trial. By this is meant only that the probability of a response, R, is changed (mathematically) by a linear transformation induced by the reinforcement conditions. In other words, if the probability of response R is P_R on trial 17, and if the response is reinforced, the probability of the response's occurring on trial 18 will be increased by an amount predictable from a linear equation of the following form:

$$y = ax + b$$

If P_R is used to represent y on trial 18, it would be predicted as the sum of a constant factor, b, plus a multiplication operation of a upon P_R of trial 17 P. The actual form of the equation depends upon specific assumptions of the mathematical model being used. Thus, on trial 18,

$$P_r = a \cdot P_r \text{ (of trial 17)} + constant$$

While linear models may differ from each other, they all share features which include gradual increments in response probabilities over training, beginning with some starting level (defined by the constant) and approaching 1.0 through repeated applications of the operator a to the previous response probabilities. The operator a can be postulated to have one value when a correct response is made and a different value (or else zero value) when an incorrect response is made. There are many ways in which linear models can be modified by changing assumptions about what governs learning without modifying the fundamental equation.

STIMULUS-SAMPLING MODELS A different type of approach is found in theories that assume learning to be all-or-none associations made between elements of the stimulus set and elements of the response set. Stimulus-sampling models are a case in point. In such models the environment is assumed to supply a set of stimulus elements, but only a portion of this set is available for conditioning on any given trial. This portion is called the *stimulus sample*. This is the stimulus elements that are "available" to become completely associated with any response made with them if it is followed by a reinforcement. The learning, or association, formed on any one trial is complete and absolute.

The performance of the organism depends upon the extent to which the elements of the stimulus set become conditioned to a response. On every trial on which the reinforced response occurs in the experimental circumstances, more stimulus elements become associated with the response. In some models the number of stimulus elements sampled on each trial is assumed to be constant, while in other models different numbers of stimulus elements can be sampled.

The performance of the individual will show gradual increases in the probability of occurrence of the reinforced response, owing to the increasing number of stimulus elements associated with the response—even though the mathematical theory asserts one-trial conditioning between individual stimulus elements and the response. This is so because the stimulus elements sampled on any given trial are likely to be different from those sampled on any other trial. In Figure 7-16 the elements sampled on trial 17 contain a combination of elements previously as-

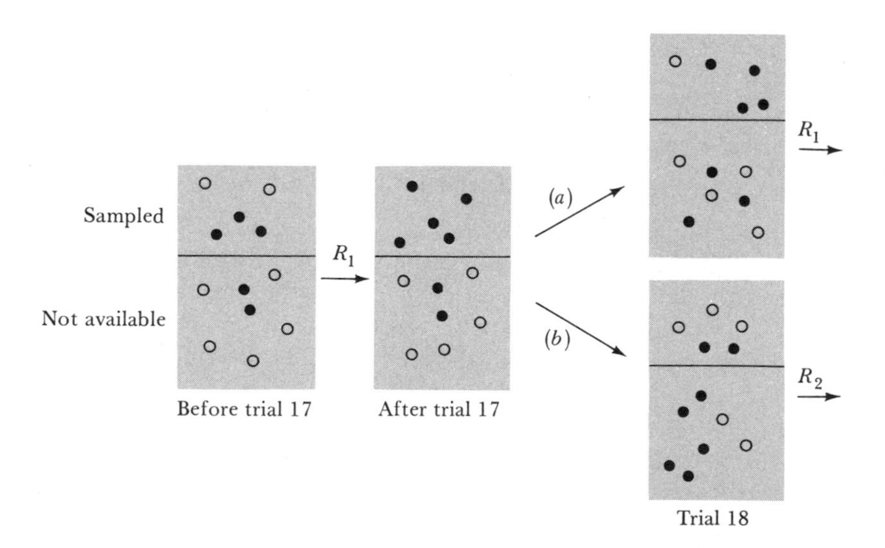

Figure 7-16 *Schematic representation of stimulus-sampling theory. Total set of stimulus elements is represented by rectangle.*

sociated with the response R_1 (filled circles) and those associated with the response R_2 (open circles). Assuming the response R_1 was made and reinforced, all elements sampled on that trial would be associated with this response. Therefore, on trial 18 there would be more stimulus elements available for sampling that have been conditioned to response R_1 than on the previous trial. However, fluctuations in the elements selected would make for fluctuations in the actual response produced by the animal, even though response R_1 was associated with more stimulus elements through the previous reinforcement. Thus in Figure 7-16 two possible sampling outcomes are shown. In one case response R_1 would occur, and in the other, response R_2 on trial 18. This aspect of the theory provides an explanation of the seemingly inconsistent behavior of animals during training.

In the stimulus-sampling model, learning is all-at-once and complete between the stimulus elements sampled and responses. However, behavior need not express the all-or-none quality of learning. Other models can be developed that do lead to all-or-none behavioral changes.

ALL-OR-NONE LEARNING The basic approach to all-or-none learning theories is that the organism being trained to make response R in place of another response moves from an unlearned state to a learned state at some particular time during learning and once in this learned state will never, spontaneously, revert to the unlearned state.

This can be represented by the box shown in Table 7-1. The rows

Table 7-1. **POSSIBLE STATES AND TRANSITIONAL PROBABILITIES FOR SUBJECT ON TRIALS n AND n+1**

		Trial $n+1$	
		L	U
Trial n	L	1	0
	U	c	$1-c$

represent the subject's condition on trial n, while the columns represent the potential states that could occur on trial $n+1$, the next trial. In each cell of the table are provided the transitional probabilities, which describe how likely it is that the animal will move from one state to another.

Since learning is considered in this theory to be permanent, if the animal was in the learned state (L) on trial n, it must also be in the learned state on trial $n+1$. Therefore a 1 is entered in the cell at the intersection of the L column and the L row. This means the probability is perfect that the subject will continue in the learned state. The 0 in the cell marked as being in a learned state on trial n, but an unlearned state on trial $n+1$, also reflects this assumption.

If the subject is in the unlearned condition on trial n, there is some probability that he will shift to the learned state on the next trial. This probability is called c; since the animal will be in either the learned or the unlearned state, the probability that the animal will be still in the unlearned state on trial $n+1$ is $1-c$.

All of this merely states in a clear and unambiguous way that learning is a sudden, all-or-none event and *is* reflected in behavior in this sudden, all-or-none change. But, if learning is all-or-none and if an animal in the "learned state" should never make an error, why do so many learning experiments seem to result in data that show gradual learning curves? There are several possible explanations.

One is that while the transition to the learned state is abrupt it is not absolutely predictable. The transition could occur on any trial with an equal probability—i.e., c. This means that animals in a group will reach the learned state, eliminating their errors, on different trials. By grouping the data obtained from different animals we might be smoothing out the expected all-or-none jumps in behavior. Therefore, it is important to look at the behavior of single subjects and not grouped data in evaluating the all-or-none nature of learning.

Two other potential influences must now be considered. The first is the subject's ability to make correct responses even though in an unlearned state. In a two-choice situation random choices among the two responses will produce a 50 percent correct score. Therefore, a sudden change representing all-or-none learning will represent an abrupt rise in performance from around the chance level of 50 percent to perfect performance. A more complicated possibility would be that there are several stages of unlearning. For example, in an initial stage there may be no possibility of a correct response ($Pc=0$). This could change—abruptly—to an unlearned stage in which some correct responses occurred but did not improve systematically. In other words, the probability of a correct response in the next stage would be constant ($Pc = K$). In the final learned stage, the probability of a correct response would be 1.0 ($Pc = 1.0$). This is one example of a multistage model that exhibits all-or-none characteristics between its stages. The performance of individual subjects can be analyzed so as to detect multistage models without much difficulty.

However, even if individual subjects fail to exhibit abrupt all-or-none learning curves, there is another possible explanation. If animals were learning several all-or-none tasks which were combined into one "problem" by the experiment, the learning of each component would be all-or-none but the effects would be smoothed out, just as when data from different subjects are grouped together. Exactly this type of result has been found. Rats learn an avoidance task in which they go from one side of a box to another when a signal is presented in an all-or-none fashion. The individual learning curves rise abruptly, as shown in Figure 7-17, and can be described as a multistage, all-or-none model. But if a similar all-or-none analysis is made of an avoidance task in which animals shuttle back and forth between sides of the box, the all-or-none quality seems to be lost. However, if one assumes that the two-way avoidance problem is really composed of two, separate one-way tasks, the all-or-none character is restored to the data. These results are shown in Figure 7-17.

It is not possible to tell whether all-or-none learning models will be useful for *all* learning tasks or even a significant number of them. We shall return to this question again in the next chapter when we consider the nature of human verbal learning. At the least, we can say that all-or-none types of learning can be found in many experiments (once appropriate methods of analyses have been found) and that such instances call into question theories that advocate thinking of learning as a gradual incremental process.

Machines and models

Since the beginning of recorded time, man has made images of himself. However, until this century these efforts have been aimed at producing images of the external appearances. Even some of the elaborate creations of the Swiss watchmakers were attempts to create moving images in the likeness of men or animals. Recently scientifically minded craftsmen have attempted to produce models that mimicked the psychological functions presumed to exist in man and animals. Reproduction of appearance has taken poor second place to reproduction of function.

THE SCHEMATIC SOWBUG Tolman designed a schematic animal called a *sowbug,* to help him understand the properties of rats as they made decisions at the choice points in mazes. Presumably, when forced to design a model, even though a schematic model, one must be explicit about

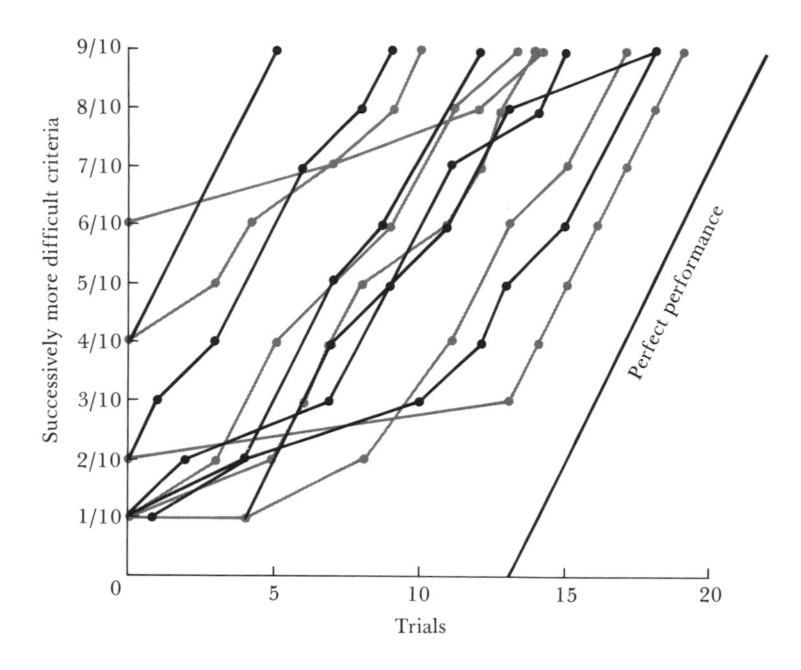

Figure 7-17 *The performance of 12 rats learning a one-way active problem. The* y*-axis gives successively more difficult criteria, e.g., 1 avoidance response in 10 trials, 2 avoidance responses in 10 trials. The* x*-axis displays the beginning number of the trial beginning a block of 10* subsequent *trials. The diagonal line indicates "perfect performance," that is, all responses are avoidance responses. All-or-none learning is reflected by the fact that the animals appear to evidence perfect performance abruptly at some point after making only a few avoidance responses. (Unpublished data from R. L. Isaacson and D. S. Olton.)*

the intervening variables that will be built into the machine. Translating one's theory into a model that works is a way of testing one's theoretical precision, and it may provide fresh insights into behavioral problems as well.

Tolman's sowbug incorporated many of the variables described in the preceding section. The sowbug represents a simple variety of "animal," with one receptor organ at the head and four symmetrically placed motor appendages (see Figure 7-18). The animal would be sensitive to the direction of light falling on the receptor organ, and, in general, the left-hand appendages would be aroused by receptor cells at the right portion of the head. Correspondingly, right-hand motor appendages would be activated by light falling on the left portion of the receptor organ.

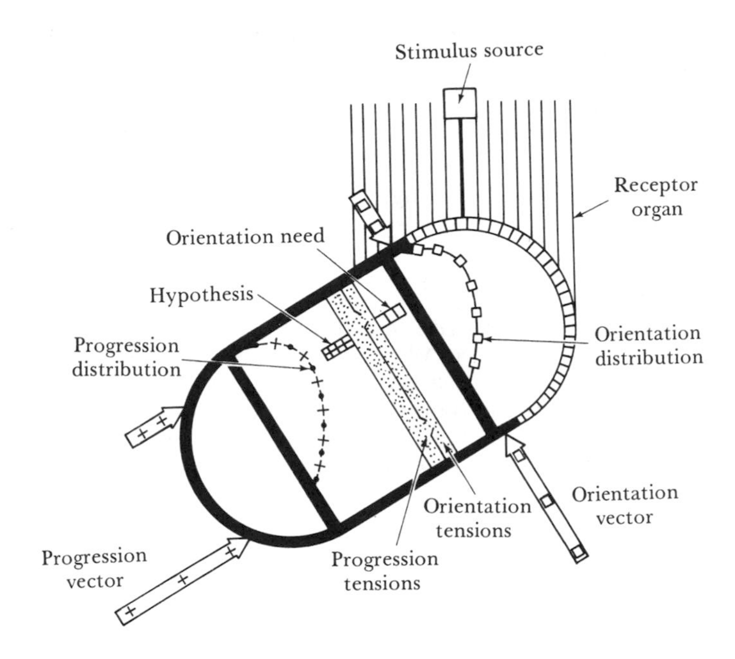

Figure 7-18 *Schematic "sowbug" described by Tolman. (Adapted from E. C. Tolman, The determiners of behavior at a choice point.* Psychol. rev., *1939,* 46, *318–336.)*

This simple mechanism would produce a movement in which the sowbug would orient itself toward any source of illumination. The amount of demand for orientation, a function of maintenance schedule, is an internal variable that would create orienting movements toward the light on some occasions but not others. The effects of previous learning are represented in the *hypothesis area* of the bug.

The *progression distribution* represents the motor tendencies of the bug dependent on the orienting distribution and the hypothesis. Tolman suggested that with a few more assumptions and further complications of design we would have a valuable model of simple animal behavior.

MODELS FROM NEUROPHYSIOLOGY Whereas Tolman proceeded to build his model on the basis of observable data obtained from his research with rats and his theory of behavior, other men have developed models based on data and theory in neurophysiology.

Probably the neurophysiological observation most widely used in connection with model building is the *all-or-none law* of neuronal activity. This law asserts that if a neuron fires, it does so to its maximum potentiality. This is seen as analogous to a simple electric circuit that is either open or closed. If this analogy is valid, could we not build a complete electronic model of a brain and study it as it learns, behaves, and even becomes emotional?

W. Grey Walter discussed the difficulties involved in building a model of the nervous system proceeding from the all-or-none law. After presenting the problems involved in manufacturing even a single artificial nerve fiber, he goes on to say:

> Supposing a sufficient number of these simplest of imitation nerve fibers were constructed, (more) millions of cubic feet of warehousing would be required. . . . At this point we might have to consider cost. A cell with one fiber conceivably made for a dime—in all, say $1,000,000,000. Wiring connection 10^{20} of them, at about two cents each, say $2,000,000,000,000,000,000. Power required would be at least a million kilowatts, even if the transistor crystal were used instead of the prodigal thermionic tube; the human brain runs on 25 watts. The cost would be incalculable. And the comparable cost of producing a first-class living brain? Twenty thousand dollars? (Walter, 1953, p. 117).

Walter estimates the warehouse space necessary for the 10,000,000,000 artificial brain cells at 1½ million cubic feet! For these and other reasons, Walter sees no possibility of producing a working electronic model with anything like a similar number of units. On the other hand, he suggests that an understanding of the functions of the brain may be based not on the number of units involved but on the richness of interconnections between units.

Machines built by Walter support his view that the richness of interconnections must be one of the more important structural characteristics of the nervous systems of man and animals. Figure 7-19 shows his *Speculatrix* on its way "home." Let us reflect upon some of the characteristics that Walter built into this disturbingly "alive" machine.

The machine is very simple in construction. Two cells function as nerve cells. There are only two receptors: a photoelectric cell and an electrical contact serving as a touch receptor.

It is always active, never at rest unless recharging batteries. Since it is always on the move it appears to be exploring.

Speculatrix moves toward lights of moderate intensities. When an adequate light signal is presented, it stops its exploratory operations and moves toward the light source. The photoelectric cell eye at the front of the machine is continually scanning the horizon for light signals. Obstacles and very bright lights are repellent to this device.

When an obstacle is met during the pursuit of an "attractive" light, the light temporarily loses its attractiveness. After the obstacle has been dealt with, the light becomes attractive again.

The "animal" will be attracted to its own lead light reflected from a mirror. It will approach this light, but a circuit in the machine then

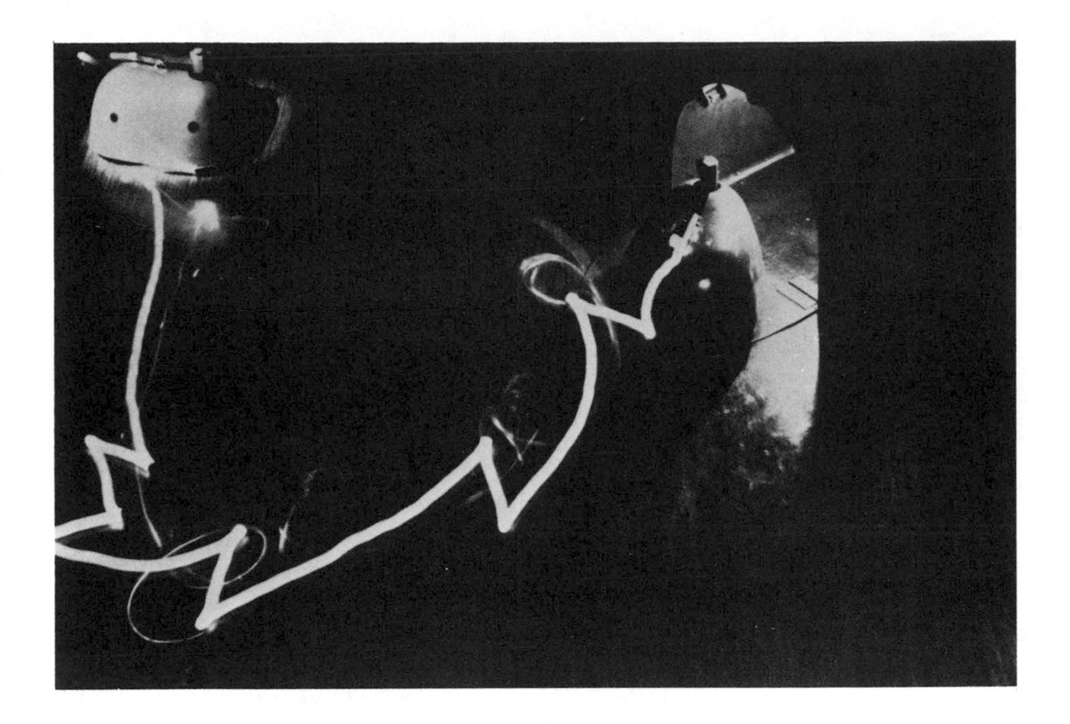

Figure 7-19 *Speculatrix returning to its hutch. (Reprinted from* The living brain *by W. Grey Walter. By permission of W. W. Norton & Company, Inc. Copyright © 1963, 1953, by W. W. Norton & Company, Inc., and Gerald Duckworth & Co., Ltd.)*

extinguishes the light. The "animal" then is no longer attracted to the mirror. But since the photoelectric cell is no longer receiving the reflected input, it turns the head lamp back on. Then the machine is attracted again to the mirror. "The creature, therefore, lingers before a mirror, flickering, twittering, and jigging like a clumsy Narcissus." The machines tend to group together by their tropic reactions to each other's head lamps, unless disturbed by external stimulation. In such a group the individual becomes, alternately, a positive or negative stimulus for others. It acts as an approachable head lamp at one time, but an obstacle at the next.

Walter planned many but not all of the behaviors exhibited by his mechanical prodigies. The headlights were added to inform observers when the steering mechanism was on. Yet these pilot lights made possible the behaviors that could be interpreted as self-recognition and social behavior on the part of a group of the machines.

Many other modifications of the basic machines have been and will be made with the result of greater and greater approximation to animal reactions. They may result in new ideas of how man behaves. Is Walter investigating only what happens in various kinds of models or what *may* be happening in the living brain? As Walter put it: "Of course we are considering both, hoping that the explicit clarity of the first will illuminate the implicit obscurity of the second."

RANDOM-NET MODELS Walter's machines were created with specific interconnections built in among the components. This is the approach used in most electronic devices, radios, television, etc. However, it is possible to arrange electronic components in an unsystematic way—turn the system on and let whatever will happen, happen.

If a large number of electronic elements are wired in an essentially random manner, often the "machine" sets up a pattern of activity that is stable. The pattern that results from the device is not predictable beforehand and probably is not useful in the sense that a radio is useful, but it does have a stability that is difficult to disturb. Removal of some parts fails to disrupt the overall pattern of activity of the system until a very large proportion of the parts have been removed.

Mathematical descriptions of randomly wired systems are sometimes termed *random-net models.* This approach allows the stability of the systems to be described. To what extent can random-net models be useful in understanding behavior?

One way is to help provide understanding of how the brain achieves stable levels of activity in the face of constantly changing inputs. The cortex and certain regions of the brain stem (the reticular formation) have zones in which nerve cells interconnect with each other in ways that appear to have a large random component. In the cortex, this arrangement is called the neuropil and is represented by areas in which axons and dendrites of many cells interweave prolifically. If this system acts like a random network, then the overall activity in the neuropil could achieve very stable activities in the face of a diversity of external stimulation. If enough change is produced by changes of the input to the cortex, then the type of activity will change to a new pattern, which will itself be stable.

The brainstem reticular formation, the other major region that anatomically resembles a random net, may have such an organization to provide a stable form of activity in the face of constantly altering internal conditions. Once again, the entire system would be stable until sufficient internal input changes occur to make a shift to a new stable pattern occur.

Random networks through cortex and brainstem then could provide the means of stability in the face of change. With regard to learning, they could provide a stable background against which alterations occur—or perhaps learning could be expressed in modifications of the stable network patterns. They might also help explain why lesions of the brain so often fail to destroy previously established memories, since removal of many components of the network often fail to disturb the overall activities within. Another way in which this same result could be obtained is by means of holographic representation of past experiences.

HOLOGRAM MODELS Two important suggestions with possible application to brain activities come from the study of holograms, described in Chapter 6 (see pp. 223-224). The first, as we suggested in Chapter 6, is that the construction of the "memory" of images is widespread, occurring everywhere, and therefore would be resistant to damage or lesions of any restricted field. Thus, if memories in general were stored in a hologramic manner, they would show the same resistance to discrete lesions as that provided by the random-net models.

The other suggestive feature of this approach is that holograms could be formed by electrical interference patterns arising from many sources of input to the cortical areas of the brain. The arrival of the information arising in receptor systems over different pathways and mixed with information from the internal organs could produce unpredictable electrical interference patterns at many regions of the brain, and these would then be stored as such.

Both random-net theory and holograms represent interesting new ideas that produce alternative approaches to understanding the operation of the brain. In a way they are like metaphors with which we try to generate better descriptions of our brain and behavior. In a way, all models arc metaphors drawn from the work of mechanics, engineering, electronics, optics, or other fields. To some extent each type of model provides new understanding of behavior, although to date each is inadequate in some degree.

CURRENT PROBLEMS AND ISSUES

Secondary reinforcement

Many technical problems confront each type of learning theory, but these we will leave to the theorists to solve. On the other hand, all theories must face certain difficulties common to all approaches to learning. The following sections will discuss some of these issues of more general interest.

In Western society little of man's behavior aims at direct fulfillment of his biological needs. To be sure, we work for money, which we exchange for the physiological necessities of life. Money is not a primary reinforcement, as defined in most learning theories. In addition only a small percentage of the money we earn goes toward the fulfillment of physiological needs. Millionaires who are assured of enough money to provide handsomely for themselves seem to be motivated to acquire ever more. The fruits of our labor move beyond money alone. Words of praise or esteem and self-realization of success are but a few of the other sorts of goals toward which behavior seems to be directed. These certainly seem to be far removed from the drive stimuli of hunger or thirst.

The learning theorist recognizes that only a few of the actions of modern Western man are guided by hunger or thirst. However, a behavioristic learning theorist believes that the goals of human behavior can be understood through the basic theory that was developed on the basis of direct reduction of biological needs if one introduces the concepts of *secondary motivation* and *secondary reinforcement.* These concepts allow us to extend relatively bare theories to situations in which the reduction of biological needs is not suitable as a condition of reinforcement and consequently to situations more relevant to human behavior.

At the outset we should like to point out that much of the literature of psychology contains references to the concepts of secondary reinforcement and motivation. Secondary reinforcements are stimuli that have been associated with primary reinforcements in the past and have come to possess the ability to increase or decrease response probabilities in their own right.

Animals can be trained to value stimuli associated with reductions of biological needs almost as highly as those natural stimuli which reduce the needs. Chimpanzees will work to accumulate poker chips that are paired with food. The animals are trained with a Chimp-o-mat, into which poker chips are inserted and food is subsequently obtained. They will seek these poker chips, work for them, hoard them—in other words, act toward them as most people act toward money.

Dogs, cats, and rats have also been trained to work to obtain tokens that can be exchanged for primary reinforcements. Furthermore, bar-pressing in an operant conditioning situation can be established solely on the basis of tokens if the animals first learn that the tokens are exchangeable for food. Rats will learn to bar-press for tokens as readily as for food, and they will perform on both fixed-ratio and variable-interval schedules to get them.

The wall of an operant conditioning chamber used in token reinforcement experiments with rats is shown in Figure 7-20. The rat learns to press the lever on the left side of the wall and tokens (small metal balls)

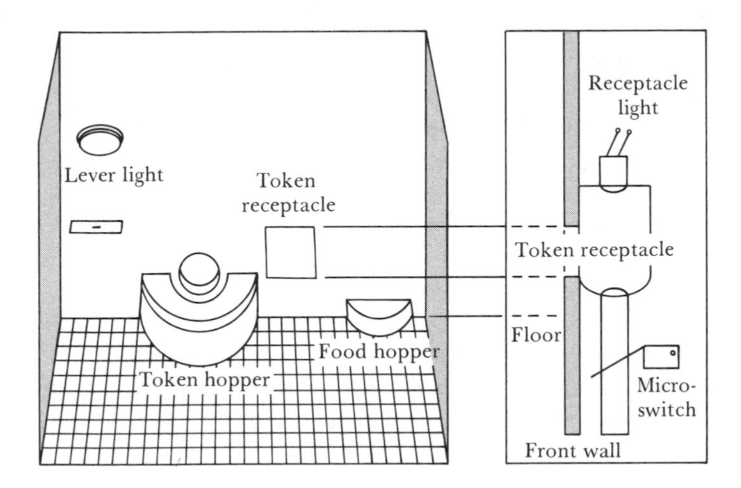

Figure 7-20 *Front wall of an operant conditioning chamber and diagram of the token receptacle. (Reprinted with permission of author and publisher: Fig. 1 from E. F. Malagodi, Acquisition of the token-reward habit in the rat.* Psychol. reports, *1967,* 20, *1335–1342.)*

are delivered to the token hopper. At appropriate times, the tokens can be deposited in the token receptacle for food, which is delivered through the food hopper.

The tokens themselves can be exchanged for food according to various schedules. Thus the animals can be taught to perform on two schedules: one for the delivery of tokens and the other for the exchange of tokens for food. For example, animals could be required to perform on a variable-interval (VI) schedule of bar presses to obtain tokens and then to exchange five tokens for each food pellet on a fixed-ratio (FR-5) schedule.

The nature of secondary reinforcements can be illustrated with further observations about the chimpanzees trained to value poker chips. When a chimpanzee sees a poker chip lying outside of its cage, the animal becomes agitated and tries to find sticks and tools to get the chip inside the cage. The poker chip outside the grasp of the animal is not only reinforcing, but it also has motivational effects. The unpossessed chip acts like a motivating stimulus. The two conditions, poker-chip-possessed and not-possessed alter the chimp's reactions differently.

Some learning theorists view early childhood experience in the light of reinforcement and motivation. Think how consistently a mother is associated with primary-drive reductions in the infant. She is always present when the baby's needs are reduced. On this basis then, the mother should be a secondarily reinforcing stimulus of the first magnitude.

We have discussed poker chips not-in-possession of the chimpanzee. Mother not-in-possession should be a potent condition of secondary motivation for the child. We know that in most homes the child is firmly attached to his mother and is disturbed when removed from her. It is easy to be critical of such a naïve or superficial view, but it does represent a consistent theoretical position. And, it is difficult to find more reasonable and equally consistent ones to supplant it. You might try to design an experiment to show that the child's attachment to his parents is not based upon secondary reinforcement.

Secondary reinforcements can be formed by an association with the primary reinforcements, or they can be formed by association with other previously developed secondary reinforcements or motives. For example, words associated with the mother's approval come to take on their own reinforcing properties. "Good boy," "that's right," "nice going" are examples of stimuli that have reinforcing properties derived from their association with previously established secondary reinforcers. "Bad boy," "oh-oh," or "that's wrong" can be considered as motivational and acquired on the basis of association with secondary or primary motivators. As an example, consider a situation when a child has done something wrong and the mother becomes angry, says "Bad boy," and *leaves the room.* We saw earlier that the mother's absence could be a motivating condition. The words, "bad boy," are now associated with conditions of a negative secondary motivation and may come to have motivational properties themselves.

Is the concept of secondary reinforcement adequate to explain all of those stimuli which act to foster and consolidate new learning for us? Probably not. For one thing, we know that when a secondary reinforcer is no longer associated with the primary reinforcement it quickly loses its reinforcing quality. Yet, secondary reinforcing stimuli such as our parents' approval retain their effectiveness for years after the time when they were related to the reduction of our primary drives.

Another line of work which indicates that traditional views of secondary reinforcement cannot entirely account for an offspring's attachment for its mother is found in the study of various mother substitutes or "surrogates" offered to baby monkeys. The behavior of the baby monkeys could be studied as the stimulus configuration of the mother surrogates was changed. In addition, schedules of feeding (and subsequent reinforcement qualities) could be altered. It was found that there were tactual stimulus patterns (temperature and texture of the surrogate) that influenced the infants' responses to the mother surrogates over and above its need-reducing qualities, although animals somewhat favored surrogates that provided nourishment. A picture of one of the mother surrogates is presented in Figure 7-21.

Figure 7-21 *Mother surrogate used by Harlow. Infant monkey is clinging to surrogate that has more acceptable "skin" qualities. (Courtesy of H. F. Harlow.)*

Reinforcement and reward

There are many controversies about the nature of the reinforcing mechanisms, and they represent an exciting line of investigation in psychology at the present time. As we have seen, through the use of an *empirical* definition of reinforcement, the study of learning mechanisms has progressed in spite of lack of agreement about underlying factors. Let us briefly consider some of the issues behind present discussions about reinforcement.

First, should rewards be distinguished from reinforcements? A distinction can be made between those stimuli which, upon repeated presentation, are met with a reduction in the untrained response and stimuli which are not met with such a reduction. Responses to tokens will become fewer (extinguish) over time if the tokens are not exchangeable for food, whereas the responses to food will persist as long as hunger is experienced. Animals will work simply to produce changes in their environment, such as the introduction of flashing lights or sounds. These responses are reduced over time. It has been argued that the resistance to a decrease in response rates may provide a useful distinction between stimuli acting as *rewards* (to which responses do not diminish) and *reinforcements* (to which they do diminish). This distinction has been useful in characterizing the effects of certain drugs—especially those which block acetylcholine transmission in the nervous system—upon behavior. If such drugs retard habituation (extinction), animals treated with such drugs should show prolonged responding to "reinforcers" but not respond differently to rewards. This result has been obtained. Whether the proposed distinction between rewards and reinforcers will be of more general applicability remains to be seen.

RESPONSE PROBABILITY AND REINFORCEMENT Traditionally, reinforcements are thought of as stimuli that will alter response probabilities when given to the animal after it makes its response. Should we think of reinforcements only as stimuli?

An alternate view would be that a reinforcement is a *response,* but one that differs (in its probability of occurrence) from the one to be trained. The suggestion is that response probability transfers from the more likely one to the less likely one, regardless of the nature of the responses.

The transfer of response probabilities occurs irrespective of the responses involved. It is an idea worthy of more investigation. It argues that only one characteristic of the response is important for reinforcing effects—namely, its probability of occurrence. This stands in contrast to the view to be considered below, that there are responses that by their nature have special significance.

CONSUMMATORY RESPONSES Certain types of specialized responses are associated with the eating of food, the drinking of water, respiration, and other activities that reduce the biological needs of the organism. These are often termed *consummatory responses.* The motor responses that make up the consummatory responses are considered to be "pre-formed" by hereditary mechanisms, since electrical stimulation of the lateral hypothalamus (medial forebrain bundle) can elicit species-specific consummatory behaviors (see pp. 364-365).

It is argued by some scientists that the consummatory responses, themselves, produce the conditions of reinforcement. It could be that the response systems involved are tied into mechanisms of the brain which act to stamp new experiences into memory or that the sensory feedback from the consummatory responses acts to produce these special conditions in the brain. In any case there is evidence that reinforcement can be considered to be the result of *responses* of a special nature and significance to the organism, over and above the mere probability of the response.

Memory mechanisms

For past learning to influence behavior in the future, something of what has been learned must be remembered. "Memory" and "remembering" are very general terms frequently used in loose and vague ways to describe the carry-over of learned information from one time to another. Learning and memory are closely related concepts, but they are not the same. It is possible to learn things that are not remembered at later times. The processes involved in memory are quite different from those involved in learning.

Until now we have not directly approached the topic of memory. One reason is that very little is known about the biological mechanisms underlying memory. Another is that the study of memory for verbal events will be extensively explored in the next chapter; on the other hand, if learning is to be retained by the individual for future use, memory must be involved. To some extent, learning—being a more or less long-lasting modification of behavior—implies memory. How many kinds of memory are there? One, two, three, ten?

In terms of time, alone, there seem to be several types of memories underlying behavioral changes. Tentatively let us consider three types of memory processes. The first would encompass an individual's span of immediate attention, or perhaps lasting a few moments longer. A second type of memory is assumed to hold information from the end of the span of immediate attention to the next few minutes or up to an hour or longer. This can be called "short-term memory." A third type of memory system is often assumed to be a repository for events over long periods of time. Thus the three forms of memory tentatively recognized are

1. Immediate memory
2. Short-term memory
3. Long-term memory

These distinctions will be useful to the extent that they describe different conditions and processes operating over the three time periods. These different underlying processes have been approached through the study of factors that will disrupt memory storage. In the next chapter, we will review studies of verbal learning and memory, including the disruption of both. For the present, we will try to highlight some evidence obtained from investigations that have disrupted memories at the nonhuman level.

Electroconvulsive shock (ECS) and memory

If animals are trained to make a response and afterwards an electrical current sufficient to produce a total bodily convulsion is applied across the brain, the memory for what has been learned in the training period seems to be lost to the animal—provided that the ECS is applied shortly after training. There is some uncertainty as to just how close in time the ECS must follow the training, but certainly it is a matter of only a few minutes for most tasks and may even be less than one second for some. Thus, according to our tentative division of memory into three periods, the shock would disrupt memories in what we have called the short-term storage process. Memories of events occurring earlier than a few minutes before the ECS are unaffected. Long-term memories are also unaffected.

The type of task for which the animal is trained makes a difference as to the interval between training and ECS during which memory can be disrupted. In addition, the interval during which short-term memories are susceptible to ECS begins with the time the animal is removed from the training task and not from the end of training *per se*. In other words, if an animal is trained in a particular situation, it can be left in the situation for several hours after the completion of training and the ECS will still be effective if applied a few moments after the animal is removed from the training environment.

This indicates that the transfer from short-term to long-term memory does not occur so long as the animal remains in the training task. In addition, evidence suggests that the animal's memories of the training situation can be retrieved from long-term memory and restored to short-term memory (susceptible to ECS) days after the training and removal from that situation. This will happen if either the conditioned or unconditioned stimulus (*CS* or *US*) used in the training problem is presented to the animal and followed by ECS. This procedure will eliminate memory of the *CS-US* pairing, which constituted the original training. This observation is difficult to explain, but it may be understood if the *CS* or the *US* is thought of as returning the animal's memories of the specific training to a short-term memory condition, one which is susceptible to disruption by ECS.

While this is undoubtedly an oversimplification, the different effects of ECS upon short-term and long-term memories (as we have used the term) offer one justification for distinguishing between the two types of memory storage.

Chemical disruption of memory

Injection of drugs into the brain through implanted tubes, called cannulae, has provided a new approach to the study of the brain and its relationship to memory. By applying drugs directly to brain tissue, the blood-brain barrier is circumvented. The blood-brain barrier is a mechanism that acts to insulate brain cells from some, but not all, chemicals circulating through the blood stream. Probably the mechanisms of the blood-brain barrier will be found in the supportive glia cells interposed between the blood vessels coursing through the brain and the neurons themselves. The technique mentioned has been used to introduce drugs that inhibit the formation of new proteins in the cells.

In general two types of results have been obtained: (1) disruption of behavior that resembles the disruption produced by electroconvulsive shock and (2) the disruption of memories of longer duration. In the first type of result, the disruption comes about by interference with the short-term memory processes and the transfer from the short-term to the long-term memory condition. In the second type of result, the interference occurs with long-term memory systems themselves.

Drugs that produce interference with memories in the same way as ECS include many antibiotics. These drugs prevent or diminish the rate of combination of amino acids into proteins by the ribonucleic acid systems. When the antibiotics are deposited into the brain—or, at least, certain regions of it—they disrupt the retention of recently learned tasks. Their effects, like those of ECS, begin with the time of transfer of the animal from the training situation and not from the end of training *per se*. It is not known if the antibiotics will produce the disruption of short-term memories when placed anywhere in the brain or only when placed in the limbic system. Moreover, it is not known for certain whether it is the protein-inhibiting qualities of the chemicals that produce the memory impairment or whether the effect is produced by other actions of the drugs. Most, if not all, of the antibiotics used also induce abnormal electrical activities around their sites of introduction in the brain. These localized regions of tissue contain hyperexcitable neurons, the changed activities of which are sometimes called epileptogenic, because the abnormal electrical activities that can be recorded from these sites look very much like the electrical patterns obtained from the area of focal disturbance in epileptic patients. Some studies have found that the severity of the electrical abnormalities produced by the antibiotics is more closely related to the disruption of memory than is the degree to which protein formation is inhibited.

Other classes of drugs can be used to affect memories that have been established for some periods of time. Administration of anticholinesterases —drugs that interfere with the chemicals which normally eliminate acetylcholine from the brain—can affect memories of events that occurred about a week before the drug injection. Moreover, in this case the drug may be given to the animal either through the bodily blood system or through cannulae implanted into the brain. This means that these chemicals can cross the blood-brain barrier. The disruption of memory is specific for events about one week old. Events that occurred at other times, either earlier or later than a week are not susceptible to the disruption. In addition, administration of anticholinergics—drugs that deplete the acetylcholine in the brain—produces the opposite effects. These drugs *enhance* memories about one week old and impair retention of newer memories.

Other types of drugs can selectively impair memories of even longer-standing events. Only the old memories are affected. From all of the evidence, there must be even more than three time periods during which memories of the past can be disrupted. By implication, there must be more than three memory processes involved. As a first approximation, let us consider as a fourth memory state, an intermediate memory, which makes available memories of events from a period of 7 to 8 days, roughly, but which need not achieve more permanent storage. Our tentative list of the forms of memory available will be

1. Immediate memory (span of attention)
2. Short-term memory (minutes to an hour)
3. Intermediate memory (minutes to several days)
4. Long-term memory (permanent)

Functional changes in memory

When we discussed the random-net and hologram models earlier in this chapter, we were suggesting models for brain activities that might provide for the storage of memories of what has been learned. From the broad outlines of these models, the difficulty in finding neurophysiological correlates of either learnings or memory can be seen. Changes in neural activities would be scattered throughout wide ranges of the brain—if not throughout the entire brain—in very different ways at each location. Nevertheless, simpler systems might be used by the brain for the storage of information. Some hint as to the storage systems might be found by probing the brain and its various subdivisions with microelectrodes to determine changes in the activities of single cells related to past experiences or training. This has been done extensively in two regions of the brain: the sensory regions of the neocortex and the limbic system.

When the responses of single cells in the sensory regions are recorded, most of the cells respond to input over several modalities. However, even if a cell responds to different sensory inputs, it will usually respond with a different pattern of activity to each type of sensory input. For example, cells in the neocortex, which receives most of the direct projections from the visual-relay nucleus of the thalamus, respond to visual stimulation and some will respond to auditory or somatic stimulation as well. Of the cells that respond to more than one modality, most have standard and stable patterns of response to each type of input; however, some 12 percent of the cells will exhibit altered patterns of activity if the inputs over the two modalities—e.g., light and sound—are paired for a few trials. The pattern of response to light and sound presented together is different from the response pattern to either alone. After the pairing of the two signals, one or the other of the input signals will produce the combined pattern while the other continues to produce its regular pattern. After the passage of time, usually a few minutes, the "combined pattern" elicited by one of the stimuli will disappear and will be replaced with the earlier pattern of response to the input signal that was found before the pairings.

The fact that some cells of the neocortical sensory systems show transient modifiability offers a possible mechanism for the temporary storage of information. This could represent one type of short-term memory storage. It is not an example of learning in the strictest sense, but it suggests a cellular mechanism that might provide a base for short-term memory.

Cells in the limbic system—or at least certain portions of it—show specialized types of responses during learning. Neurons in the hippocampus, for example, tend to show continued and prolonged change in their rates of activity during periods of behavioral learning. These units continue to respond at faster rates than before training and continue to do so even after the behavioral response has been extinguished. It is doubtful that these cells provide the mechanism required for long-term memory, but they do respond as if they were recording events over periods of time that last a week or more. In this sense, they suggest a brain mechanism that is related to the memory impairments found after treatment with the anticholinesterase drugs.

We are just beginning to establish the correlations among chemical, neural, and structural changes that will provide greater understanding of how learning and memories become encoded in the brain. There is a promising future for research that combines behavioral investigations with the other biological approaches involved.

SUGGESTED READINGS

Allyon, T., & Arzin, N. *The token economy.* New York: Appleton-Century-Crofts, 1968.
Evans, R. I. *B. F. Skinner, the man and his ideas.* New York: Dutton, 1968.

Hull, C. L. *Principles of behavior*. New York: Appleton-Century-Crofts, 1943.

Logan, F. A. *Fundamentals of learning and motivation*. Dubuque, Iowa: William C. Brown Co., 1969.

Mink, O. G. *The behavior change process*. New York: Harper & Row, 1968.

Skinner, B. F. *Science and human behavior*. New York: Macmillian, 1953.

Tolman, E. C. *Behavior and psychological man*. Berkeley: University of California Press, 1961.

Ulrich, R., Stachnik, T., & Mabry, J. *Control of human behavior*. Glenview, Ill.: Scott, Foresman, 1966.

Walker, E. L. *Conditioning and instrumental learning*. Belmont, Calif.: Brooks-Cole, 1967.

8

Verbal learning and memory

The most distinctive characteristic of man is his use of language. Because all languages are learned, it is essential that the student of psychology know the relationships and factors entering into verbal learning and the retention of verbally learned materials. Such knowledge is fundamental to understanding the nature of man himself.

In the preceding chapter, we reviewed some of the prominent theories of learning and behavior. As noted, they are based upon the associationistic doctrine, which stems from the school of philosophy called British Associationism. We shall find that the theories of verbal learning and retention, as well as the experiments generated by them, are also dominated by associationistic theories. There are, however, new trends being advocated in the associationistic theories to explain verbal behaviors. Before beginning our discussion of verbal learning in the adult, let us pause a moment to consider how language develops in children.

DEVELOPMENT OF SPEECH

We are all aware that learning to speak precedes learning to write. A baby takes a long time to master the techniques of vocal communication, and communication with spoken sounds occurs long before communication through written symbols. Historically, written communications probably came long after man had learned how to depict objects symbolically through primitive art forms.

A baby begins learning vocal communications at birth. It is born with the great advantage of being able to make a large number of sounds, a much wider range than that found in other animals. The birth cry is a reflexive response to a sudden increase in the carbon dioxide level in the blood occurring when the umbilical cord is cut. There is a momentary lag before the lungs begin to act. Sometimes newborns have to be encouraged to breathe by a physician's life-preserving swat on the behind. When the baby begins to breathe, it makes its first sounds. Actually, the child makes two broad classes of sounds early in life: those related to crying and a second form related to cooing sounds. The latter develop from the sixth to the eighth week after birth and are elicited by the visual patterns of a familiar face. Many of the early vocal acts, such as crying, are presumed to be reflexive responses to internal bodily changes.

In the first four to five months the infant produces just about all of the speech sounds that have been found in all of the known languages. The infant must learn to *reduce* the number of speech sounds to those used in his culture. Over a period of time, the repertory of sounds a person can make becomes narrowed to the number found in his native language.

When a baby is being fed, held, or cuddled, he produces sounds that are softer (e.g., open vowels) than those he makes when he is deprived of the bottle or physical support (e.g., explosive sounds and grunts). Thus from early in life there is a relationship between the type of sound produced and the state of the organism.

Before six months of age the infant has begun to learn how to control his vocalizations. This means that the muscles of the diaphragm, tongue, and jaws and the parts of the nervous system controlling them have developed to the point where fine discriminative movements are possible.

Babbling and imitation

After the fifth month, babies generally can be heard babbling. Babbling refers to sounds like "uggle-uggle," "erdah-erdah," "bup-bup-bup," and other repetitive noises. Babies babble when alone as well as when with others, and they tend to practice one sound sequence before moving on to another. Babbling affords the opportunity to "master sets" of muscle responses that will comprise the building blocks of later speech.

Babies learn to mimic the patterns of sounds they hear. After sufficient muscular and neural development, speech sounds created by others can be duplicated by the infant. The next step for the baby is to be able to create a pattern of sounds that he has heard in conjunction with a perceptual object. The object becomes associated with the sound created by someone else in its presence. This association provides the basis for the child's vocalization of the sound when the object alone is presented. An illustration of this phase of language learning is presented in Figure 8-1. Here we find the behavioral origins of the verbal acts called labeling.

Labeling and many other varieties of verbal behavior are partially determined through timely reinforcements, and at least some psychologists argue that verbal behavior can be explained through the same kind of learning principles used to account for learning in animals. On the other hand, other psychologists maintain that the rules of learning that have been proposed to account for animal learning are inadequate to account for the complexities of human language learning. The issue is by no means settled. One particularly troublesome aspect of language learning pertains to how the grammar of languages is learned. Another issue involves the inability of animals to learn language as does the human. Both issues will be discussed below. However, if we accept the importance of rewards for at least some aspects of language learning, then the parents' job is to shape the child's verbal behavior so that only those responses remain which are significant in the culture. Watching parents with their children, we can see how sounds are shaped into "language." If the child emits a response that is even a rough approximation to "da-da" in the presence of his father, it is subjected to a good bit of intensive shaping effort. Slowly, the rewarding actions provided by the parents are withheld until "daddy" is a clear response.

Skinner believes that all verbal behavior can be explained by extrapolations from his work with the empirical effects of reinforcements and the unique reinforcement schedules applied to the human infant's vocal responses. Whether or not all of the richness of human verbal

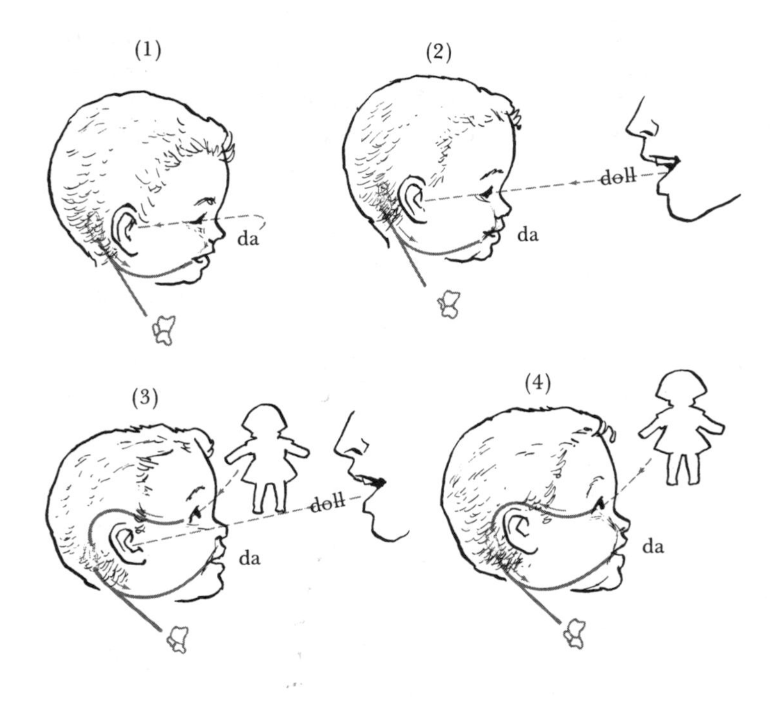

Figure 8-1 *Stages in development of speech in infant. (1): random articulation of syllables; (2): evocation of same elements by speech sounds of others; (3): conditioning of sounds produced by others to object (doll); and (4): sight of doll produces sounds approximating "doll." (From F. H. Allport,* Social psychology. *Boston: Houghton Mifflin Company, 1924.)*

behavior can be explained in terms of simple rules of learning is a question that can not be answered at the present. Yet, there is evidence that the rate of occurrence of specific verbal responses can be increased or decreased by rewarding behaviors on the part of others.

Language learning in animals

Animals of many species communicate with each other. Their communication however, is of a limited nature, usually signalling emotional or motivational states or providing information about changes in the environment that pose a clear and imminent danger. Human speech differs from the vocal communication of animals in that it is more dissociated from the stimuli provoking the utterances and it has a logical quality of its own through which the environment can be analyzed in terms of "parts," which can be regrouped in different sentences. Animal vocalizations cannot be taken apart and regrouped to make equivalent statements. The rules for the order of sounds are acquired early in life, and it may be that a tendency to order significant sounds according to language rules represents a part of man's genetic predisposition to the use of language.

The most recent attempt to understand the ability of nonhuman animals to use language is the continuing study of the chimpanzee Washoe by the Gardners, a psychologist couple. Their experiment differs from previous ones in which chimpanzees have been reared in a household situation in that Washoe has been living in conditions in which the American Sign Language is constantly used and attempts are made to teach them to her. This sign language is based on gestures. The configurations of the fingers and hands make an entire language in themselves, and it is not based on prior learning of another language—as is finger spelling of English, for example.

Previous attempts to teach chimpanzees to talk had not been very successful. After four years of training a chimpanzee could only make less than a handful of recognizable sounds. Washoe can make over 80 different signs after a comparable period. The difference probably lies in the fact that the chimpanzee is not well suited to communicating in human verbal language because of the anatomical construction of its articulatory mechanisms. It is practically impossible for chimpanzees to make the sounds necessary for vocal communication, a handicap not found with the sign language since chimpanzees have great finger dexterity.

Even with the increase in Washoe's physical ability to make signs, she fails to connect them with anything like a sense of grammar. She does connect several signs together, but subjects and objects of verbs are selected without much care and she is not skillful in the use of questions and making negative statements.

Children at the age of two or three talk a lot while alone. They explore language by themselves. Their speech is not random. Words and phrases are substituted into different frameworks. Their private speech is a type of playing with words, but it is not without a role in later language development. Transformations and substitutions within the rules of grammar are produced by the child, Apparently, however, Washoe cannot do this.

In overall perspective, nonhuman animals are limited in their linguistic capabilities over and beyond deficits that can be explained by limitations of speech-producing mechanisms. The nonhuman animal's communications are restricted to information about pressing problems arising internally or externally; they are less abstract and fail to exhibit the orderliness in statement construction that is found in human language.

The acquisition of grammar

The human child is endowed with a readiness to organize spoken communications into an orderly sequence and enjoys making transformations among his verbalizations according to the rules governing these orderly sequences of a language. The question is: How are these language rules learned? The rules differ from language to language and are acquired very early in life.

We have already mentioned that the human organism is especially disposed to the use of language. In fact, some people believe that the child's earliest expressions are one-word sentences. For example, the spoken "daddy" could be an abbreviated form of "Daddy is coming up the walk." Development of more complicated sentences would represent expansions of these simple beginnings.

Even though the child is born with a disposition toward grammatically based expressions, there are different formal grammars in each language, group. How the child comes to master a particular language and grammar is a difficult question, since we do not know the extent to which the child can analyze the grammatical structures he hears (which are mostly those of the adult).

The acquisition of a grammar presents some interesting problems. One of these is that the child must learn rules that are not completely explicable even by adults. Through some method of induction, a usable grammatical matrix is formed. Grammar acquisition represents a specialized form of "rule learning," which has been studied in the adult but only to a limited extent in children.

Spoken communication

The goal of speech is communication of a message from one person to another. We send vocal messages by patterns of sound waves generated by the expulsion of air across the vocal cords and through the oral cavity. No one knows just how many speech sounds the human can make. The set of sounds that are equivalent and can be used interchangeably to transmit meaning are called *phonemes,* and these can be thought of as the units of spoken language. Phonemes differ from one language to another. They are the sounds that differentiate the words or phrases of a language. In English we may consider them to be approximated by the sound of each consonant or vowel. Not all the different speech sounds are phonemes. There are many more distinguishable speech sounds than there are English phonemes.

Phonemes are not the only units of speech. We learn to recognize and use (as units) words, phrases, and sentences. Through learning the language system of the culture, "chunks" of language become available which have some single, unitary quality and function. An analysis of language can be made at the phoneme level or at levels which involve "chunks" made up of many speech sounds and phonemes.

We make speech sounds at a great rate. We produce about 12.5 speech sounds every second when talking. Not all of these sounds carry information of significance for our messages, but they are units that could be used to transmit information. Information is transmitted through the use of sounds, signs, and symbols, which have meaning or which elicit kinds of responses within the perceiver.

It should also be pointed out that the auditory modality is a very rapid system for processing information—faster than the visual system. In addition, it is possible to increase the auditory processing rate by speeding up the rate at which auditory stimuli are presented. This can be done by intensive training in which subjects listen to tape recordings played at faster speeds than those at which they were made.

Children are immersed in a sea of auditory "sentences." Many fewer sentences and other verbal communications are presented visually. This leads to the question of language in the child who has been deaf from birth. Congenitally deaf children *can* learn language skills of an acceptable nature, although much training and patience is necessary. Because of their deafness, they need to be exposed to many well-formed sentences, using vision, since the best method for the learning of appropriate grammar is induction from a large number of examples. Reading and graphic modes of presentation of verbal materials must be used to a much greater extent with the deaf than with people who can hear.

Lip-reading helps the deaf to understand language, but it is inefficient because it provides the possibility of identifying only about half of the phonemes used by the speaker. With experience and training, verbal communication is possible for the deaf. Neither their grammar nor their vocabulary *need* be impoverished.

Studies of retarded and brain-damaged children have shown that speech production is not essential to the understanding of language. Thus knowledge of language can be established in children with an absence of the appropriate sensory input or an absence of response mechanisms. In both cases language capabilities unfold in a biologically determined sequence that is most closely related to the chronological age of the individual.

GENERALIZATION OF RESPONSES TO NEW STIMULI

Of special interest to the use of language is the ability to respond to a number of different stimuli and situations with the same word or label. In other words, the same response is applied to many different conditions. Developmentally, the child can learn that his door is "open" and then come to generalize "open" to other doors, windows, the tops of boxes and trunks, and so forth. Traditionally, when the same response is applied to many objects and situations, we speak of the phenomenon called *stimulus generalization*. The generalization of verbal responses is a special case of stimulus generalization.

Stemming from traditional psychology is a distinction made between stimulus generalization (or as it is sometimes called *primary* stimulus generalization) and "secondary" or "mediated" generalization. The former is based upon a physical similarity among stimuli, whereas the latter is considered to be based upon other factors. Probably this distinction is not entirely justifiable, as we shall see, but its use may provide a reasonable approach to the topic.

Primary stimulus generalization

"Stimulus generalization" describes the fact that stimuli other than the ones used in training often elicit the same response. In general it is assumed that the greater the similarity between the training stimulus and the test stimulus, the greater the generalization that will occur. If we train a dog to salivate to a 1000-cycle tone and after conditioning is well established present a 1200-cycle tone, some flow of saliva will occur. Is this odd? In one way it is, since we have not trained the dog with this new tone at all, and yet there has been a generalization of the response to it. The two tones are somewhat alike. Both are auditory stimuli, and both are about the same loudness. Futhermore, they "sound" somewhat the same, although dogs can easily discriminate between the two tones.

Figure 8-2 shows curves of generalization of a learned response along a visual continuum. The subjects, pigeons, were trained to make a pecking response when a specific color was presented on the pecking-key. The pigeons were evaluated by the presentation of test colors on the key to which they could respond. Visual stimuli nearest the wavelength used in establishing the response evoke the largest number of responses when tests for generalization are made.

However, problems exist for any simple technique used for specifying

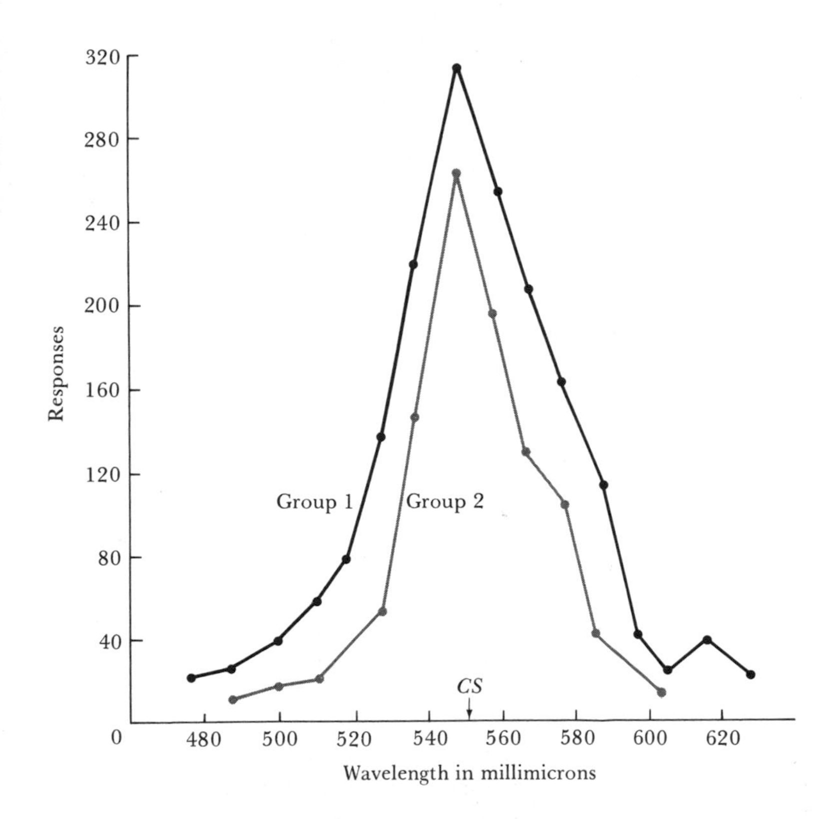

Figure 8-2 *Stimulus generalization along visual-wavelength dimension in two groups of pigeons. Birds were trained to peck key illuminated by wavelength indicated on the* x-axis *by CS; and later tested by key illuminated with different wavelengths. Extent of generalization is reflected in frequency of responses at different wave lengths. (Adapted from N. Guttman, The pigeon and the spectrum and other perplexities.* Psychol. reports, *1956, 2, 451–460.)*

the extent of physical similarities among stimuli. Colors can be similar to each other in hue, brightness, and/or saturation. Generalization can occur along each dimension or along combinations of them. In addition, it has been shown that the slope of the generalization curve for auditory pitch is not uniform. Tones representing "octave steps" from the tone used for conditioning produce greater responsiveness than intermediate tones. This implies that a tone one octave from the original conditioning tone has "more similarity" to it than many tones that are in fact closer to it along a frequency dimension.

At first, one might equate stimulus generalization with a failure in discrimination. Perhaps a dog which salivated to the 1200-cycle tone for some reason failed to discriminate it from the 1000-cycle tone. Yet, while there are instances in which a failure of discrimination can explain some of the experimental results, this cannot be the entire explanation. In a discrimination experiment, subjects who were best able to discriminate between stimuli early in training were the very same ones who showed the greatest amount of generalization later during generalization testing.

Primary stimulus generalization can arise from two processes: (1) a failure of discrimination, discussed above, and (2) a positive tendency to make a response based on a transfer of previous learning (habit strength, or whatever). We have already seen that the discrimination-failure hypothesis is not satisfactory for all cases of primary generalization. With regard to the "positive tendency to respond," Hull and his colleagues, as well as others, postulated a spread of $_SH_R$ from the training stimulus to similar stimuli. It should also be noted that the specific training stimulus is but one component of the training situation. A response can be generalized to other stimulus components, including the training situation, the time of training each day, and the experimenter involved.

The two factors thought to be responsible for generalization assume a passive organism that responds in terms of the applied stimuli and the stimuli of the training environment. However, we know that people and animals organize their own sensory information in accordance with motives, expectancies, and past experiences. In man an important contributor to the active organization of sensory input is language. If two groups of subjects are shown a color intermediate between pure green and pure blue but are given different color labels—"green" or "blue" for the same hue—those given the label "green" will show greater stimulus generalization to the green side of the standard hue than those subjects told the standard was blue. These latter subjects show greater stimulus generalization to hues toward the blue end of the spectrum. The color label given the standard hue disposed the individuals so that different ranges of colors were subject to generalization. Even simple stimulus generalization depends upon how the subjects organize, code, or "screen" the stimuli of the environment. To this extent, there is no such thing as primary stimulus generalization (that is, a generalization based entirely upon the physical stimuli involved).

As mentioned before, phonemes are the basic building blocks of a spoken language. They are those collections of sounds which the hearer considers equivalent for the purposes of his natural language. They differ from language to language. Tests of stimulus generalization across the phonemes of a language indicate perfect stimulus generalization to all sounds within a phoneme's boundaries but an abrupt drop in generalization across a phoneme boundary. Since phoneme boundaries are different from one language to another and are arbitrary to a large extent, this reveals a striking case of the effect of the persón's past experiences upon stimulus generalization.

Mediated or secondary generalization

Consider the following experiment. Subjects are trained to salivate when a red light is presented. This could be done by pairing the red light with the injection of a mildly acidic solution or a food substance into the mouth. In either way a conditioned response to the red light could be established. Now we are in a position to perform the generalization experiment. As a test, we now say "red" or present the written words "red light," to the subjects. Will this cause them to secrete saliva in the same way as flashing the red light did? Will this verbal symbol, which stands for the light used in training, be effective through some kind of generalization?

What kind of explanation can we provide for generalization of a response from a physical stimulus to a verbal symbol standing for the stimulus? One approach would be to suggest that both the red light and verbal "red light" produce a number of responses inside the person and some portion of these are common to both. As the red light came to evoke the salivation response, each of the internal responses became associated with the response. Therefore, when the verbal "red light" was presented, the internal responses held in common with the physical red light were evoked and these produced the overt response. The generalization from the actual red light to the words *red light* is an example of a *secondary* or *mediated generalization*. Mediated generalization must be based on acquired language habits and customs of the society. A Frenchman would not generalize a conditioned response to the word *red* but rather to the word *rouge* after conditioning with a red light as the *CS*.

The notion of internal responses has a long history. In the heyday of American behaviorism, internal responses were considered to be a retreat from true objective behaviorism. Thus responses were often assumed to occur that were "not quite" internal but "almost so." John B. Watson argued that thinking was merely vocal movements too small to be easily observed. To test this theory, muscle potentials in the arm were recorded as people *thought* about throwing a baseball. Some of the attempts to record muscle movements associated with mental acts have been rewarded with some degree of success. Yet it should be obvious that these minute tensions sometimes found in the muscle systems cannot account for the range of mental phenomena in thinking. People without arms can still think about throwing a ball.

Today, many learning theorists conceive of verbal behavior in terms of specific *S-R* connections, although the responses are far removed from possible detection or observation. Some psychologists propose that their neural correlates may someday be found in the brain.

The mediational response

Although different workers have proposed different terms and mechanisms of mediational processes, we shall follow the lead of Charles Osgood and use the symbol r_m to refer to an internal, mediational response. Let us assume that every stimulus object produces two kinds of internal reactions within a person: (1) responses that are closely tied to the stimulus and could not be elicited without the presence of the particular stimulus object and (2) responses that can be detached from the actual presence of the stimulus object. When stimuli other than the stimulus object are presented along with it, they tend to be conditioned to the detachable portion of the reaction to the stimulus object. It must be emphasized that only a *portion* of the total reaction to a stimulus object can be conditioned to another stimulus—that is, the *detachable responses.* It is some part of the detachable reaction of the total response to a red light that becomes conditioned to the words "red light." This part would be the r_m, which produces the behavioral response to the words "red light" following training to an actual red light in our earlier example. See Figure 8-3 for an illustration of this process.

The semantic differential

Osgood has used the mediational response as a way to attack the difficult problem of "meaning." After our discussion of the mediating response we are now in a position to use this concept to gain greater definition and precision in thinking about the relationship between words and things.

If words have meaning because of the elicitation of mediating responses it might be possible to discover the nature of the different kinds of mediational processes elicited by words. One procedure calls for people to rate words (as symbols) on a number of verbally defined scales. The data are then analyzed to determine the number of different independent dimensions needed to account for the ratings of the text words. With this technique, only a limited number of independent scales are needed to describe most of the words tested.

In Figure 8-4 we present a sample of the semantic differential scale used to evaluate words in this way. The dimension with the extremes labeled *good* and *bad* is called the *evaluative dimension.* This dimension

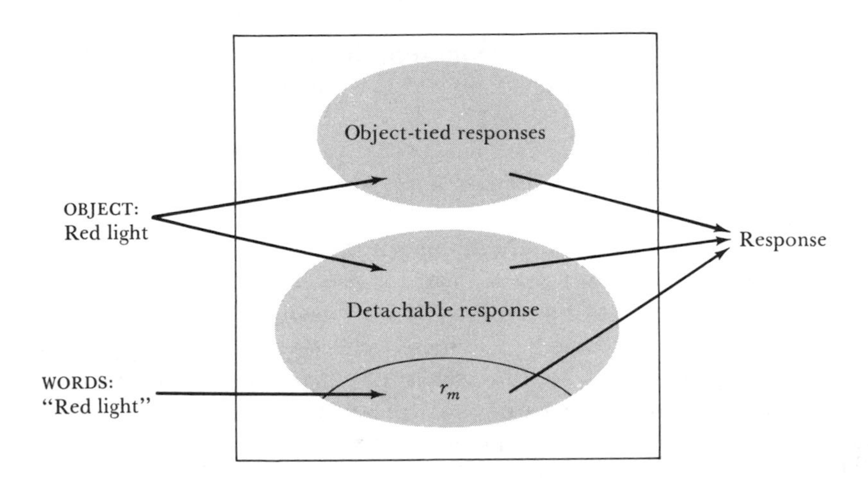

Figure 8-3 *Physical stimuli elicit both object-tied and detachable responses. If the words "red light" have accompanied presence of a red light during the conditioning of a behavioral response, they alone can elicit the conditioned or detachable response (r_m).*

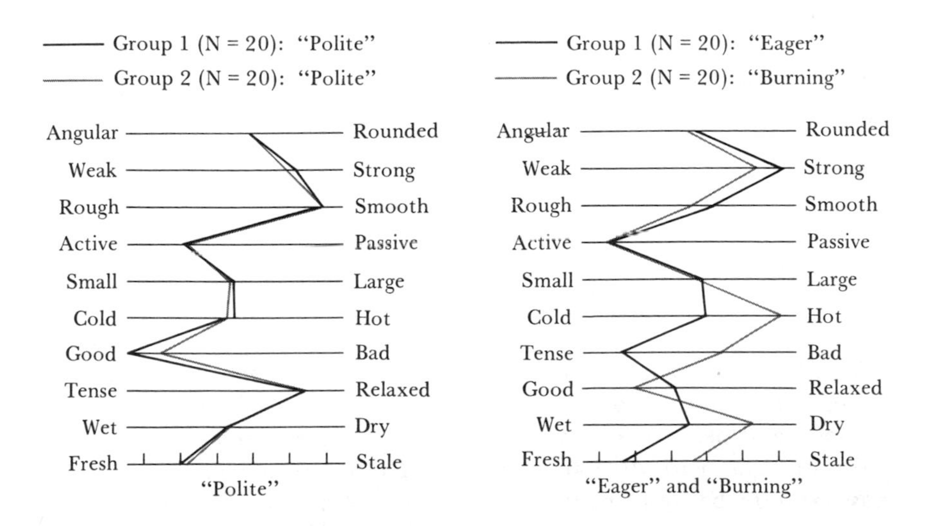

Figure 8-4 *Preliminary forms of the semantic differential for measuring connotative meanings of adjectives. Based on median profiles of two test groups ($n = 20$). (Adapted from C. E. Osgood, The nature and measurement of meaning.* Psychol. bull., *1952,* 49, *197–237.)*

is the most important one for determining the meaning of words. Much of the way we react to words seems to be explained in terms of their "goodness" or "badness." In the figure we find a possible pattern of responses to the word *polite*. The differential patterns of ratings between words on these scales can be used as a very neat and precise method of investigating meaning.

Critics of the semantic differential approach have pointed out that the technique gets at only a part of what is usually understood as meaning. They argued that this technique is only well suited to get at the evaluative aspects of meaning (goodness or badness), or perhaps even the emotional reactions elicited by words, but that it does not attack the problem of the cognitive meaning of words. We should keep in mind that while the good-bad evaluative dimension accounts for a great deal of our reactions to words, it does not account for all. Any word that acts as a label may have an evaluative aspect (its goodness or badness), but it certainly implies other things as well. (To some degree, this objection is met by other factors in the semantic differential, such as "activity" and "potency.")

Other psychologists favor *conditioned images* as a theoretical approach to account for meaning. Images would be a kind of conditioned sensation (specific sensory attributes in Figure 8-4) in the organism.

There are various other ways in which the meaning of words can be studied, and each is more or less useful in specific contexts. Meaning and the meaningfulness of words, however defined, play important parts in the acquisition of verbal materials, and further approaches to the study of them will be considered in this more general context.

THE ACQUISITION OF VERBAL MATERIALS

Since language is a prime example of a learned phenomenon, and one specific to particular cultures, it is natural that much effort has gone into the study of verbal learning, memory, and performance. Historically, modern investigation into these processes began with the lonely efforts of Hermann Ebbinghaus, and it is reasonable to begin with his approach to the problem.

Ebbinghaus and the nonsense syllable

Ebbinghaus was the pioneer in the study of memorizing verbal materials by rote practice. He really was a one-man research team. For the most part he was his only subject. Picture him at his desk memorizing lists of words and testing himself for their retention. He found familiarity of material one very important condition that affected his ability to memorize, and he sought to discover the effect of trying to memorize totally unfamiliar material. Since it was difficult to find verbal material that was unfamiliar, he created his own in the form of *nonsense syllables,* consonant and vowel combinations that are pronounceable yet not words; for example, GOK, MEJ. Such nonsense syllables can be modified and, depending on the requirements of the experiment, can be long or short and can include only consonants or numbers as well. Generally speaking, a nonsense syllable such as TAL has less meaning for a typical subject in a verbal learning experiment than a three-letter word such as BOY.

But even most nonsense syllables are not free from pre-experimental associations. Therefore, the nonsense syllable is an artificial verbal unit that is not totally without meaning but rather has less meaning than do most naturally occurring verbal units. Nonsense syllables are useful because they can be constructed in large numbers to have greater or less meaning (or association value) for the subjects who attempt to learn and remember them.

Most psychologists find it useful to distinguish between the acquisition of verbal responses (learning) and their retention over longer or shorter periods of time (memory). This distinction is important since the two aspects of verbal behavior, i.e., acquisition and retention, are influenced in different ways by many procedural and methodological techniques.

Methods of studying verbal learning

Probably the most common method used to learn verbal materials is the *whole method.* You use it when you memorize an entire section of prose or poetry at once. You study the entire selection. In a verbal learning experiment in which the whole method is used, the subject is presented with an entire passage to memorize. He can be tested on how many words he has learned in a given period of time or on how many minutes it takes him to commit the passage to memory. For example, it has been reported that it took subjects 93 minutes to learn 200 nonsense syllables and only 10 minutes to learn 200 words of poetry with the whole method. As with many experimental paradigms, various measures of learning can be used, such as the time required to learn material to some criterion level of performance, the number of errors made while learning, or the number of repetitions (trials) of the material required for mastery.

When the whole method is used, there is very little that can be done to isolate specific variables which can help us understand the nature of the verbal learning process. We cannot control the effects of the rate of presentation of the stimulus units, the effect of uncontrolled rehearsal of responses, or the effect of learning earlier or later words upon the acquisition of a particular word in the passage. Since these factors make a difference in understanding the processes responsible for the rate of verbal learning, it is necessary to use other techniques in which these factors can be systematically controlled and isolated for independent study.

Sometimes subjects are presented the material to be learned one unit at a time. Single words, nonsense syllables, numbers, or symbols can be shown to the subject one at a time and for a specified duration of time. A device for doing this is called a *memory drum*. The memory drum is built to expose verbal items for varied periods of time. It also controls the length of time of presentation and the time between presentations. A sketch of a memory drum is presented in Figure 8-5.

Using the memory drum, the subject can be asked to demonstrate what he has learned in many ways. If a series of verbal units is presented, the subject can be asked to recall the entire serial list or asked to recall the verbal units one-at-a-time just before each unit is displayed on subsequent presentations of the entire series.

One other common technique presents the learner with the task of learning specific verbal responses to specific verbal stimuli. The subject learns pairs of verbal items. This method is called the *paired-associates technique*. At the beginning of training, the subject is presented with a list of stimulus and response words, one pair at a time. On subsequent trials only the stimulus words are presented, and the subject asked to

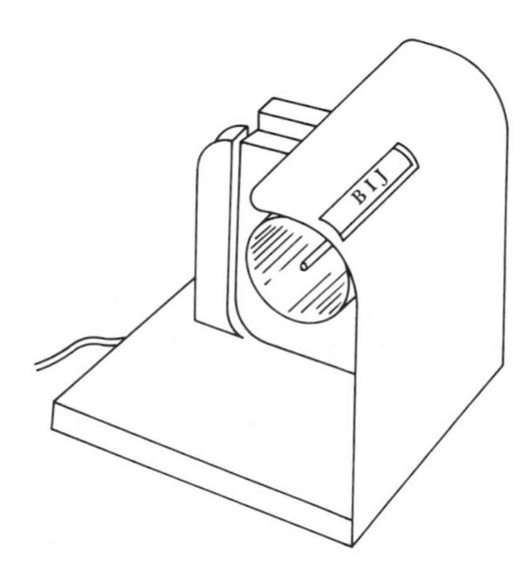

Figure 8-5 *Memory drum used in studies of verbal learning and retention.*

make a response. If the subject fails to respond with the correct "response item," it is presented again so that the subject is once again exposed to the correct stimulus-response pair. For example, a subject may be asked to learn the following pairs of words:

Stimulus words	*Response words*
Apple	Canary
Blue	Table
Wide	Church
Parlor	Milk
Friend	Verb
Curse	Finger
Fly	Motion

On any given trial the subject is presented with one of the stimulus words and must try to respond with the appropriate response word. If the subject's answer is incorrect, he is informed of the appropriate response. Each time the experimenter proceeds through all of the stimulus words, it is counted as a single trial. It is important to remember that the experimenter does not merely go down the stimulus list, from top to bottom, on every trial, or the subject would have only to memorize their order and not pay any attention to the stimulus words at all. By skipping about in the list of stimulus words on each trial, the subject must remember which stimulus word is to be associated with which response word.

Still other procedures exist for the study of verbal learning. In fact, new techniques are evolving all the time. Some of the more interesting include ones in which long lists of words or numbers are presented one after the other and the subject is asked to respond "new" if the item has not been seen before and "old" if it had been presented earlier in the list. This is an example of a "continuous design" in that the learning task goes on through the procedure; there are no specific training and recall periods. Continuous methods can be used in paired-associate learning by repeating the pairs in a long sequence, every now and again presenting only the stimulus item and asking the subject for the response item. Pairs, learned or unlearned, can be dropped or added at any time in the sequence.

Factors influencing learning

In most verbal learning tasks, three components can be identified: (1) stimulus discrimination learning, in which the subject learns about the important characteristic of the stimulus set to be used; (2) "response learning," in which the response terms are acquired and integrated into the subject's response repertoire; and (3) association of the stimulus and response units. This last phase represents the putting-together of the discriminated stimulus and response units in the way specified by the experimenter.

Failure to learn can often be related to a specific failure in one or more of these components of the verbal learning task. In the following sections we will consider the effect of several variables on the acquisition of verbal materials and, where possible, indicate which component of the task is affected by these variables.

MEANINGFULNESS Probably the most important factor influencing verbal learning is the meaningfulness of the material presented to the subjects. This is true for all types of verbal units. For one thing, when very familiar and meaningful verbal units are used, the stimulus and response learning components are negligible.

Meaningfulness has been recognized as an important variable in human verbal learning since Ebbinghaus found some words and nonsense syllables much easier to learn than others. We have already noted that some nonsense syllables are more nonsensical than others. The degree of meaningfulness or familiarity of verbal materials has been assessed in many ways. One technique is to elicit verbal associations of each item of the verbal materials from a group of subjects and to consider the number of associations produced by the subjects in some limited amount of time as a measure of the "association value" of the items. Tables giving the average association values for many verbal units and for nonsense syllables have been published and are available to experimenters.

Some nonsense syllables are more pronounceable than others. The ease with which a nonsense syllable can be pronounced is related to meaningfulness, but the effects of the two factors can be teased apart. It is generally held that the degree of meaningfulness is more important for original learning of verbal materials than the pronounceability of the syllables. It is of interest that the threshold for visual detection is in the opposite direction, with the more pronounceable units being easier to detect than the more meaningful units.

Using words as the verbal material to be learned, the degree of meaningfulness can be estimated by their frequency of occurrence within the natural language. The meaningfulness of a word as measured by the frequency with which it is found in a natural language is also related to the ease with which a word elicits an image. This can be investigated by asking subjects to rate verbal materials on the ease with which images are elicted by the items being studied. By ranking these responses, one can create an image-scale. From recent studies it is likely that an item's image value is at least as important as "meaningfulness"—perhaps it may be even more important. The "concreteness" of the images elicited by words is a most influential variable in retention of previous verbal learning. The meaningfulness or image-evoking quality of a verbal item could be more influential for stimulus or for response items. The use of a paired-associate technique can dissociate these two aspects of a verbal learning task. The more meaningful the item used as a response item and the greater the image value of the item used as a stimulus item the easier learning will be. The differential benefits derived from manipulating these two types of variables on the stimulus and response terms provide further justification for considering meaningfulness and imagery as independent variables that affect learning.

The degree to which the verbal units have some type of organization among them is another important feature governing verbal learning. Organization has been studied by making all stimulus and/or all response terms similar or by having some "system" for the generation of the verbal units. Organization in either sense is beneficial, although if the stimulus items are too similar to each other in paired associate learning, this can cause some retardation in learning.

Completely general conclusions are difficult because of the wide range of experimental variations that are possible. For example, highly similar stimulus and response lists can be created in which the same term can be used as a stimulus for one response and as a response item for a different stimulus item. This produces difficulties in learning situations, as might be expected.

AMOUNT OF MATERIAL TO BE LEARNED Common sense tells us that it takes more time to learn a long list than a short list of items. But it is also the case that as the amount of material increases, the time required to learn a *unit* of material increases as well. As the amount of material increases, the time required to learn it grows disproportionately. This is true both for syllables and for prose. For example, it may take 1.5 minutes to learn 12 syllables, but 6.0 minutes to learn 24 syllables. Doubling the amount to be learned resulted in more than doubling the time required for learning. Thus the time required to learn a unit (single syllable) was increased by lengthening the amount to be learned.

METHODS OF STUDY: WHOLE VERSUS PART Given a passage of verbal materials to be learned, would it be better to break it down into small pieces to be learned separately, and then combine the pieces, or to tackle the whole passage at once? The answer is contingent upon a number of conditions. Generally speaking, the greater the mental ability of the learner, the better it is to study the entire passage. Also, one must consider the length of the passage and the pieces into which it can be subdivided. As we learned in the preceding paragraph, the amount of time necessary to learn a passage is related to the length of the passage. Consideration of the length of the passage, and its possible subdivisions, can help in deciding which technique should be followed.

MASSED VERSUS DISTRIBUTED PRACTICE If you only have so much time that can be devoted to studying a verbal passage, is it better to distribute this time into separate study sessions or to mass your study in one solid interval? While there must be some qualifications, the best procedure would seem to be to mass your studying. To obtain *efficiency* in studying, massed practice on verbal materials will avoid costly warm-up periods and also the time required to get your materials ready for use. However, in learning a motor activity, distributed practice results in so much faster acquisition that it overshadows the inefficient side effects. Distributed practice seems to be advantageous when the learner must master new or unfamiliar responses. In most adult verbal learning the response materials are well-practiced verbal units.

The real interest in distributed versus massed practice comes from the theoretical significance of the effects of the two kinds of practice conditions. In the subsequent sections on the retention of verbal materials these theoretical issues will become clearer.

THE EFFECT OF SERIAL POSITION When verbal materials are to be learned in a constant order, the position in which verbal units occur is an important factor. Items at the beginning or the end of the list will be learned more readily than items in the middle. This serial position effect is illustrated in Figure 8-6, where we can see that it took many more presentations of the list to learn the middle items than those at either end. The favorable effect of coming early in the list is the *primacy effect,* and the beneficial effect of being near the end of the list is the *recency effect.* The recency effect has significance for an interpretation of recent memory; this will be treated on pages 344-345.

Many theoretical interpretations of the serial position effect have been presented. Most of them have one feature in common: the concept of *interference* among the associative connections between the different items in the list. Maximum interference would occur in the middle of the list, because these units would have both forward and backward associations to items occurring earlier and later in the list.

It is possible to overcome the detrimental effects of the middle position. If one, or even a few, of the middle items of the list are made *different* from the rest of the list, the rate of learning of the different items will

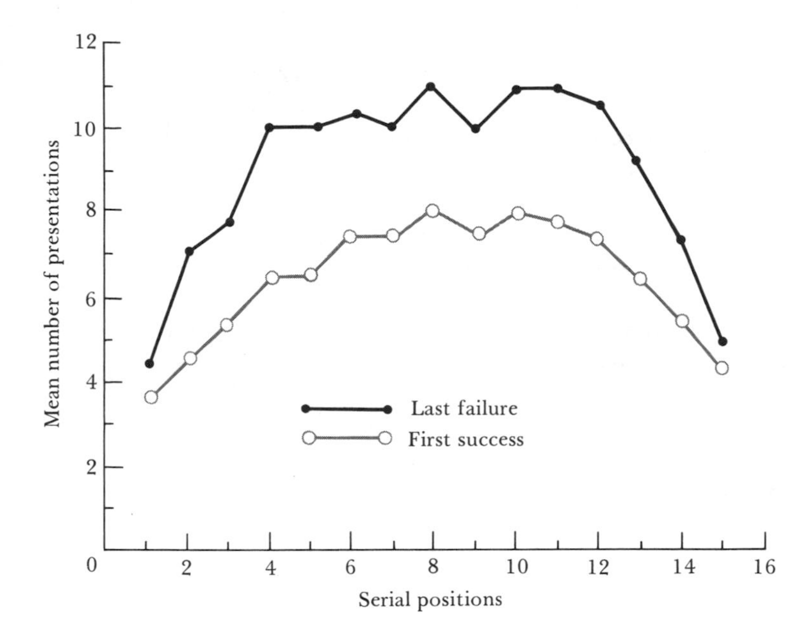

Figure 8-6 *Effects of serial position on number of presentations necessary for learning. Learning was measured by subject's first correct response and his last error. Humps near center reflect the greater difficulty of learning verbal items in middle positions. (Adapted from C. L. Hull et al.,* Mathematico-deductive theory of rote learning. *New Haven: Yale University Press, 1940.)*

be comparable to early and late items. This could be done by printing the selected middle items in a different color or by including a set of numerals in a list of syllables. As the number of special items increases, the effect becomes less evident. Even so, this effect of perceptually emphasizing items can still be observed when 50 percent of the list is differentiated in some way.

The serial position effect brings our attention to the notion of "interference" among verbal units. Interference theory has been the mainstay of verbal learning theory, and we shall next turn to a closer examination of it.

Interference theory

Since Ebbinghaus' work before the turn of the century, the view has been that verbal learning involves the formation, strengthening, and weakening of associations.

Interference among associations has been assumed to be responsible for differential rates of learning and forgetting.

More modern approaches have considered interference but one factor governing the rate of verbal learning. The other factors are thought to be the discriminability of the stimulus elements and the ease of identifying, and making, the responses. These additional factors involving stimuli and responses have led to more use of natural language words and numbers in place of nonsense syllables, since they are presumably readily distinguished and easy to produce before the experiment begins.

It is remarkable that interference theory has never been formulated in a rigid or detailed way, since it has provided a basis for so much research for so many years. Yet it has not been done in a way acceptable to most scientists in the area. Perhaps the informality of interference theory has been responsible for its viability over the years.

Interference theory has been most successful in generating explanations of the retention of verbal materials and of the transfer of learning from one situation to another.

Transfer of training

Many people report that they find French easier after having learned Latin. If the study of Latin does assist the student in acquiring French, this represents what psychologists call a *positive* transfer of training. If, on the other hand, Latin hinders a person's attempts to learn French, this would be a *negative* transfer effect. Of course, Latin may have no effect upon learning French—that is, there may be no transfer effect between them. Transfer of training refers to an effect upon learning a task, B, caused by prior learning of another task, A. The effect may be helpful (positive transfer) or harmful (negative transfer).

TRANSFER IN VERBAL STUDIES One common technique used to study the conditions responsible for positive and negative transfer of training involves changing the stimulus or the response words in a set of paired verbal associates. Experimenters can then study the effect of these manipulations in terms of the effects of different degrees of similarity of the substituted stimulus or response words to the original ones.

From the results of many experiments the following summary statement would seem appropriate: Learning to make old responses to new stimuli produces positive transfer, whereas learning to make new responses to old stimuli is a condition usually producing negative transfer. When one makes old responses to new stimuli, the extent to which the new stimuli are similar to the original stimuli helps produce greater amounts of positive transfer.

Let us assume that a subject learns a list of paired associates similar to the one given below. The letters in the examples are used to symbolize verbal units, such as nonsense syllables.

TASK 1

Stimulus word	*Response word*
A	W
B	X
C	Y
D	Z

We should expect *positive transfer* when in a second task the subject is called upon to learn pairs which keep the same response terms but have new stimulus associates:

TASK 2

Stimulus word	*Response word*
E	W
F	X
C	Y
D	Z

However, if we instead asked the subject to learn a second list like the following, he should show *negative transfer,* because in this he must learn to make new responses to old stimuli:

TASK 3

Stimulus word	*Response word*
A	R
B	S
C	T
D	U

This result probably can be explained on the basis that the response elements had been learned and were readily available to the subjects. The beneficial effect found when old responses are attached to new stimuli depends upon the nature of the responses, themselves. It occurs when the material is not very meaningful or occurs infrequently in the natural language. With meaningful material, the positive transfer may be negligible or even slightly negative. This slightly negative effect with meaningful material would be anticipated, because the first associations could interfere with the new ones if there were no overriding benefit to be derived from having the response set available.

Interference effects upon transfer could be evaluated by having subjects learn paired-associate lists in which the amount of similarity in the stimulus lists and the response lists is varied. Negative transfer occurs in all conditions, but it becomes increasingly more negative when stimulus lists become more and more similar to each other. Again, this would be expected on the basis of interference theory, since increasing similarity would produce more interfering effects due to stimulus generalization.

General factors in transfer

Several factors can be identified that are related to the amount of transfer which will be found among training situations.

LEARNING TO LEARN If people or animals are taught a number of similar problems, they become more and more adept at solving the individual problems. This effect can be demonstrated in the acquisition of learning discrimination problems. This has been demonstrated in monkeys and the data are illustrated in Figure 8-7. As can be seen, the efficiency of the animals improved greatly (in terms of percentage of correct responses) as more and more problems had been learned by the animals. Since each problem required a new discrimination, this effect cannot be based on positive transfer among the stimuli, but on some more general change in the animals. It has been called learning to learn or the formation of a "learning set."

There is no widespread agreement on the explanation of the learning-to-learn phenomenon. Various suggestions have been made, which include the elimination of inappropriate response tendencies so that the animal begins later problems with fewer erroneous responses, and, on the positive side, the development of more effective response strategies.

A similar kind of result has been observed with discrimination reversals. If an animal is trained to respond to a black card and not to a white card, training in reversal would involve rewarding responses to the white but not the black card. A second reversal could be made after the animal learned the first reversal by beginning to reward responses to the black card again. Subsequent reversals could be made along these same general lines. For most species, the animals make many errors in the first few reversals, but when they learn to make reversals quickly, they

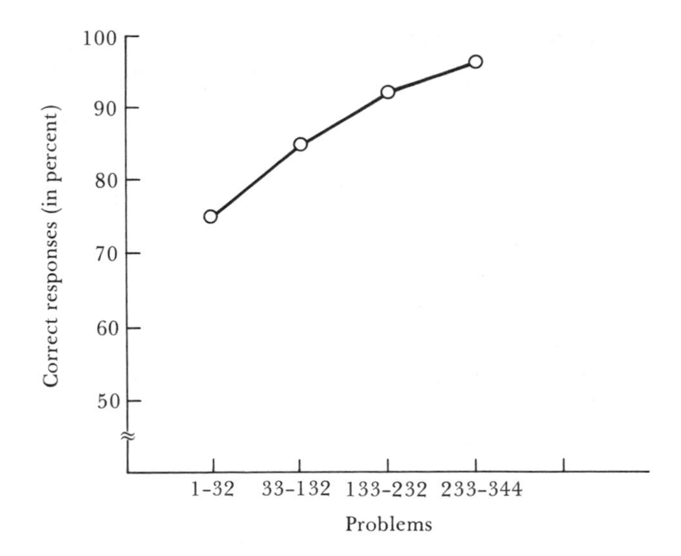

Figure 8-7 *Learning-to-learn. The establishment of a learning set is demonstrated by the increase in the percentage of correct responses made as the animal has more experience with the discrimination problems. (Fig. 3 in H. F. Harlow, The formation of learning sets.* Psychol. review, *1949,* 56, *51–65.)*

sometimes require only one "error" to begin responding to the new positive stimulus.

Overtraining This refers to a behavioral effect produced by continuing training beyond the simple acquisition of the problem. If an animal learns a problem to some criterion, overtraining would be defined as continuing the training after the criterion has been reached. The animal continues to make an already adequately learned response. The same type of approach can be used in human verbal learning, of course.

Overtraining often allows subjects to make alterations in their responses more readily than if training were terminated after reaching a learning criterion. Overtraining probably narrows the number of events to which the person or animal pays attention during performance. The screening of the sensory input becomes focused more and more on a few salient events on a trial and makes changes in the situation more readily detectable.

The overlearning effect is usually evaluated by reversing a discrimination task in which one response is rewarded all of the time and another is not rewarded at all. The effect of overtraining on responses rewarded on an intermittent basis may be more complex, and it is clear that the overtraining effect is found only in some situations and not in all. One speculation about this latter problem—namely, the observation that overtraining affects reversals in some tasks but not in others—may be related to the requirements imposed upon the subjects. If comparison and evaluation among stimuli are required on every trial, overlearning may not facilitate learning of altered response patterns. If, however, the task can be routinized or attention given to one stimulus component, overtraining probably does facilitate change.

WARM-UP AND THE CONTEXTUAL ENVIRONMENT From a person's own experiences, warm-up and context effects can be readily appreciated. It takes a while to prepare for a given type of learning experience, and a reasonable warming-up period tends to facilitate later learning. The more the warm-up experience is like the original learning, the more beneficial it will be.

One curious aspect of the warm-up effect is that it lasts for a longer period of time than might be expected. Some experiments have shown that the effects of a brief warm-up session may last as long as half an hour afterwards.

Contextual effects upon learning may be demonstrated at both the animal and the human level. At the simplest level, they can be described as conditioning responses to cues provided by the environment. Learning a list of stimulus-response words in a particular experimental room causes associations to be made between the room cues and the response items, as well as between the stimulus terms and the response items. These room-response associations can be a source of interference if a new list is learned in the same experimental situation.

Animals form conditioned responses to the room in which they are trained, as well as to the particular signals presented. If an animal has learned a maze in one room, it may not be able to demonstrate this knowledge if the maze is moved to a new room. Probably these contextual cues play a stronger role in early stages of learning than in later stages, but they are related to the relative distinctiveness of the room cues.

Neither the warm-up nor the environmental effects should be surprising when they are considered from the point of view of the brain mechanisms involved. Both tend to provide a consistent background of neural activity upon which the changes produced by learning will be imposed. Changes in neural activity imposed upon fluctuating or unusual neural backgrounds will be less likely to be "learned" or retrieved from memory if already learned.

TRANSFER OF PRINCIPLES To this point only elementary types of transfer situations have been considered. Often we are faced with a more complicated transfer of previously learned materials. For example, using a different variety of tasks, two groups of grade-school boys learned to throw darts at a target submerged in water. Subjects were then divided into two groups. One group was taught the principle of optical refraction through water; the other was not. After this instruction phase the two groups were tested once more, only this time the target was submerged at a different depth of water. The group of boys learning the principle of refraction of the light rays showed more positive transfer of training than the group that had not been so trained.

This study and others indicate more transfer when the subjects know the principle behind the task. Usually this means that one group of subjects has been told certain rules related to their performances or activities. How do the verbal principles of a task come to affect motor performances? What do we mean when we say that one group understands the principle of refraction while the other group does not? (For the present we must stay close to common sense in using words such as "knowledge" and "principle.") We cannot be sure, but in general it is safe to say that transfer of training is facilitated if the principles of the situation can be verbalized by the subjects. At the same time, we should recognize the possibility that principles need not transfer—even though they often do. Principles must be learned in a way which makes transfer to new situations seem appropriate.

MEMORY

Memory and learning are very closely related concepts in the framework of psychology, but, even though closely related, they are also independent in many ways. In a typical experimental study of learning, the *performance* exhibited by the subjects is a result of both the rate of learning and the rate of forgetting. In verbal learning, a single paired-associate combination is almost certain to be remembered immediately after presentation but may become lost from memory within a few seconds, depending upon what occurs after its presentation.

Methods of studying memory

In all experiments on memory, two phases can be distinguished: a training phase and a test phase. By altering the time and/or the experiences of the subjects between the two phases, the effects of many variables upon the retention of the material learned during the training period can be studied.

RECALL Free recall is about the simplest method of trying to determine the retention of previously learned verbal materials. Subjects are asked to recall as much of the training material as possible within some specified period of time.

In a paired-associate learning experiment in which several lists of *S-R* terms are presented to the subjects, testing for retention could be done by giving each subject a list of all the stimulus words and asking for all response terms. This procedure would eliminate the need to remember the stimulus items and provide an opportunity to report several responses to a single stimulus unit—if this had been part of the training task.

Thus, the recall procedure is not "free," but cues (the stimuli) are given for the recall process. For this reason, when the cues are provided during the recall perod, it is called "cued recall" or "modified free recall."

If subjects learn two lists of paired associates with each list having the same stimulus elements but different response terms, the free-recall technique can be further modified. The stimulus elements could be given the subjects, as in modified free recall described above, *and* the response elements for the second list could also be given. The subjects would only be asked to recall the response items of the first list. This procedure would eliminate the need to recall the stimulus units and reduce the possible competition between the two responses to the same stimulus term.

As we have seen, recall methods can vary considerably in modern experimental designs. They can range from totally free requests to remember material to providing one or more components of the previously acquired test materials. Each variant has been designed to explore in a controlled manner certain aspects of memory.

RECOGNITION Recognition tests also can vary. They can be as simple as presenting verbal units one at a time and asking if they had been previously presented or not. The experimenter might repeat certain items in a list and ask subjects to recognize them. Another procedure would be to present a list of verbal items in the test procedure and ask subjects to select those items from the list which had been presented during the earlier training phase. There is also the type of recognition test that is so commonly found on examinations. A question about the training material is asked, and the answer is embedded as an item within other noncorrect items, which are called distractors. This type of recognition procedure is usually called the multiple-choice test.

OTHER METHODS Two other methods are sometimes discussed: *relearning* and *reconstruction*. In the former, the test phase of the retention test involves relearning the material under the original conditions. The difference between the time or number of trials required to relearn the material and the original time or trials required to learn the material is taken as a measure of retention. Since relearning is usually faster than original learning, the difference is often called a "savings score."

With the reconstruction technique, all of the verbal materials originally learned are given to the subjects during the test phase, and the subject need only combine them as they were in the training phase.

These four basic techniques—recall, recognition, relearning, and reconstruction—are used to measure retention. They may also be referred to as measures of memory. This brings up an interesting problem. If the four retention measures are used to assess how much a subject remembers of his original learning, four different assessments could result. Different techniques are differentially sensitive indicators of retention. Material that is forgotten, when measured in one way, may not be forgotten if another technique is used. Think of a speech or poem you once memorized but cannot now recall. It is possible, and indeed likely, that it would take you less time to relearn it now than it took you to learn it originally.

In the past it was popular to compare the several ways in which retention can be tested. Usually recognition was found to be a more sensitive measure of memory than recall. However, there are so many modifications of each technique that an overall comparison is not meaningful. Secondly, the degree to which a recognition procedure (such as multiple choice) is superior to a recall procedure depends upon the similarity of the distractor items. If the distractor items are very similar to the correct item, memory can be demonstrated to be worse with this method than when measured by using a free-recall procedure.

Current research does not seek to find differential memory sensitivity of the two basic methods, recognition and recall; rather, it has investigated the different psychological processes that occur when the two methods are used.

One major distinction between recognition and recall is that the response item need not be retrieved in the recognition task. In addition, the production of the response, itself, is not a factor. If a recognition procedure is used with no distractors, then the task reduces to deciding whether the item has been seen before.

Causes of memory failure

Work in the area of verbal learning and memory has produced two major sources of the failure to remember what has been previously learned. These are *retroactive inhibition* and *proactive inhibition*. These terms have arisen from objective studies of the human memory processes, but, as is suggested by the name "inhibition," they are closely related to specific theoretical ideas about their causes. Many psychologists believe long-standing memories are never really "lost" or forgotten but that they can not be remembered because their expression has been inhibited by interfering associations. Regardless of whether this type of explanation is correct, retroactive and proactive inhibition remain cornerstones in the research on verbal learning and memory.

RETROACTIVE INHIBITION This concept describes one of the major sources of failure to remember verbal materials. Retroactive inhibition refers to a negative effect on the *retention* of a verbal task, learned earlier in the training phase, by other verbal material imposed between acquisition and the retention test. The basic outline of experiments used to study retroactive inhibition is as follows:

	TIME 1 (Training phase)	TIME 2	TIME 3 (Test phase)
Group I	Learn task A	Learn task B	Test task A
Group II	Learn task A	Nothing	Test task A

In this situation the extent to which the retention of task A was less for subjects in group I than for those in group II reflects the debilitating effects of learning the interpolated material of task B. Retroactive inhibition is the term applied to the interference produced by the interpolated task. Several things must be noted about this model experimental situation. First, it is impossible for group II to do "nothing" in time interval 2. They could be rehearsing task A. They could be rehearsing other materials unrelated to task A, or task A, itself. Men and women are always active, and the nature of the activities exhibited by the subjects in group II, in time 2, is bound to be influential in determining later retention. On the other hand, if we do not have an intervening time period for group II, but test them for retention immediately, then we have given them the advantage of a shorter period of time between training and testing. Group I would then be disadvantaged by both interpolated activity *and* a longer time before interval 3. In an ideal experiment on retroactive inhibition we would want to study only the effects of one variable: the interpolated activity.

The disruptive effects of interpolated activity on the retention of verbal materials has been intensively studied. In general the amount of retroactive inhibition increases with the amount of practice on the interpolated material provided by task B. This result might be expected on a common-sense basis, of course. However, further investigations of retroactive inhibition have brought to light new facts about the interruptive effects.

It has been found that there is no consistent relationship between the number of responses from task B produced by the subject when he is being tested for retention of task A and the memory loss produced by retroactive inhibition. Intrusions of words from task B account only in part for the total errors made in task A. These interlist intrusions become greatest with intermediate amounts of interpolated practice (task B).

When task B is very well practiced, the number of intrusions from task B into the retention test for task A becomes fewer, despite the fact that the overall performance of the subjects becomes progressively poorer. The effects of retroactive inhibition on previously learned responses vary over time. Shortly after the intervening task is learned, its effects are greatest. With the passage of time, they become less so, although the change may not be great. This suggests that a part of the retroactive inhibition effect is due to the suppression of previously learned materials. We shall return to this issue after considering proactive inhibition effects. It should be noted, however, that in Pavlov's theory of the conditioned reflex, no conditioned reflex was ever permanently lost. Even after prolonged extinction training there could be a spontaneous recovery of the reflex. Furthermore, in Hull's theory the learning *variable,* habit strength ($_SH_R$), can never be diminished. Other variables might act to suppress behavioral expression of the response, but learning itself was supposed to be a variable that did not diminish.

PROACTIVE INHIBITION The learning of one task affects the subsequent learning of another task. Proactive inhibition is the term proposed to account for the negative effects on the retention of a task by prior learning of another task. Diagrammatically this can be represented as follows:

	TIME 1	**TIME 2 (Training phase)**	**TIME 3 (Test phase)**
Group I (Proactive)	Task C	Task D	Test for D
Group II (Control)	Nothing	Task D	Test for D

The superiority of subjects in group II over those in group I in acquiring task D would reflect the negative effects of proactive inhibition. As with the retroactive-inhibition model, the time interval labeled "nothing" must be qualified. The living organism never does "nothing."

Subjects who have participated in a number of verbal learning experiments tend to forget new verbal material of a similar sort more rapidly than those who have not done so. The percentage of verbal material recalled by subjects who have learned only a few prior verbal lists is much greater than for those who have learned five or more lists of a similar kind. The effect of learning prior lists is a "proactive" effect, since the tasks producing it come before the learning of the task to be tested.

At first, the effects of proactive inhibition seem antagonistic to the formation of learning sets, that is, "learning to learn." Actually, they are not. Learning to learn refers to an effect upon the acquisition of a new problem, whereas proactive inhibition effects refer to a deficit of memory or retention. Subjects who have learned a number of verbal lists actually *learn* new lists (of similar material) faster than do less-practiced subjects. They just retain them less well. These differential effects of the previous learning of verbal units on the learning and retention of later ones is one example of the usefulness of the distinction between acquisition and retention.

The retention of verbal material in everyday life is influenced by both proactive and retroactive inhibitory effects. In everyday life, however, it is impossible to tease apart the two factors contributing to memory losses, and it also is impossible to study them with sufficient precision to understand them adequately. To do so we must turn to laboratory experiments for possible explanations of forgetting and memory more generally.

EXPLANATIONS OF FORGETTING Experimental psychologists involved in exploring the acquisition and retention of verbal material have been torn between interference theories and unlearning theories of forgetting. According to interference theories, decline in memory comes about through factors that interfere with the ability to make the desired response at the time recall is attempted. Interference doctrine says the correct response may not be demonstrated in behavior because of competition from other responses for the stimulus components.

The unlearning hypothesis predicts an actual decline in the memory for the response elements. This decline is thought to occur as a function of time alone, although other factors could hasten the unlearning of the responses. The changes occurring during "unlearning" are general in nature, reflecting a loss of an ability to remember all the elements in the response set previously learned. The battle between these two views of memory is not over. Some psychologists believe that forgetting can be adequately explained by the interference hypothesis alone, and others believe that both unlearning and interference hypotheses are required.

In terms of laboratory experiments, the discovery of proactive inhibition was important in saving the view that forgetting could be attributed to interference effects. Without this concept, all memory losses of the learned materials had to be due to retroactive effects of experiences occurring outside the laboratory between training and testing. Many people doubted that real-world, extra-laboratory experiences could provide enough interference to produce the considerable forgetting that is usually found. Proactive inhibitory effects of previously learned lists of experimental materials undoubtedly contribute the greatest amount of interference with laboratory tasks, and what is left over could well be due to extra-laboratory interferences of a retroactive sort.

However, there is a substantial problem arising from such an interpretation. It is simply that extra-laboratory associations often fail to influence laboratory learning of verbal materials. Subjects in verbal learning experiments seem to be able to set aside previous, extra-laboratory associations while in the laboratory—and vice versa. They isolate the experimental associations from their normal experiences. Perhaps this represents another example of the importance of environmental-contextual cues on learning and memory.

Responses, especially in a laboratory situation, are learned in specific environments, and this context is associated with the responses being learned. Studies on the nature of transfer in verbal learning have shown three sources of interference between paired-associate lists. These are forward associations (stimulus term → response term), backward associations (response term → stimulus term), and contextual associations (environment → response terms).

The retroactive-inhibition paradigm is a special case of the transfer paradigm, and it has been possible to determine the effects of the three components on retroactive interference by evaluation of memory loss when determined by a recall method and by a recognition method.

The logic of this approach is simple: The use of a recognition procedure eliminates the contribution of the "environment-response" component, since the response is provided and the subject must only recognize it. In studies such as that used in retroactive-inhibition experiments, *no retroactive-inhibition effects are found when the recognition procedure is used.* This suggests that the specific associations of original learning ($S \rightarrow R$; $R \rightarrow S$) are not disrupted by interpolated learning, whereas the availability of the "response set" *is.* This supports an "unlearning hypothesis."

The response set is the collection of the responses learned in a particular situation under certain conditions. Response sets are established by contextual cues of the environment, but *many* response sets can be established within the same environment. Instructions to the subjects, recent training trials on a particular verbal list, rewards and payoffs, and other factors all may act to establish a particular response set at a particular time. Interference effects arise from the production of inappropriate response sets.

The question of whether associations are ever eliminated from memory entirely, has not been answered. However, before a definite answer can even be considered we must consider several additional aspects of memory.

TYPES OF MEMORY

From evidence accumulated from several lines of investigation, it seems abundantly clear that several types of memory or memory processes must exist. In the preceding chapter we reviewed some of the physiologically oriented work, which pointed to at least four types of processes: immediate memory, short-term memory, intermediate memory, and long-term memory. In the following sections we shall review data arising from experiments with people that indicate the usefulness of distinguishing among memory processes that are more or less similar to these four memory stages. Before doing so, we should emphasize that there is no universal agreement as to these four particular stages; others may be more useful. Also, the number of stages, processes, or distinctions may vary as a function of the nature of what is learned.

Immediate memory: span of attention

Immediate memory refers to what can be held in the span of attention. Ebbinghaus himself was the first to document the observation that six items—i.e., randomly chosen numbers or letters—could be grasped and retained upon a single presentation. Presenting more than six items added considerably to the number of trials required to master the set of items. Thus the idea was conceived that if the verbal material was less than the span of attention, it could be learned and held in a short-duration memory, all at once; if larger than the span of attention, the learning of the material would require repeated trials.

The absolute size of an individual's span of attention varies from one person to another. It also may be "expandable" to a slight extent through training. In general, the span of attention is thought to be about seven items or "chunks" of information.

Immediate memory and short-term memory processes are often thought to reflect the same underlying processes and are often grouped together. In fact much of what we shall be discussing in the following section on short-term memory will be appropriate to immediate memory. However, immediate memory can be distinguished from short-term memory on the basis of the all-at-once learning that occurs within the immediate memory (span of attention), but not within short-term memory.

Short-term memory

The idea of a short-term memory corresponds to the retention of events that are just beyond the span of attention, but that include traces of very recent events. Short-term memory includes the memories of those things which occurred within the past hour or so.

Experimental evidence of many kinds supports a memory mechanism that is related to very short-term storage of materials. One of the most interesting kinds comes from the effects of information given to a subject over several sensory routes at the same time. For example, different auditory messages can be put into each ear simultaneously. On the basis of an internal priority system, the subjects will attend to the message from only one ear at a time. If, however, the information is not presented too rapidly, and if the subject is allowed a moment or two of "rest," he can often respond appropriately to the message in the ear to which he did not attend. It is as if when the subject is processing the input from one ear, any message arriving from the other will be held in storage for a short while. If attention cannot be directed to it, however, within a few moments it will be permanently lost.

Two things describe short-term memory: a limited capacity for processing information at any given moment and a rapid rate of forgetting.

CHUNKING OF INFORMATION The capacity of both immediate and short-term memory is limited, but the determination of the limits requires some comment. At first, one might suspect that short-term memory is limited to some number of individual letters or numbers. Some further consideration would make this unlikely, as indeed it is. The storage of a set of unassociated, random letters would be harder to hold in memory (or to learn) than the same number of letters arranged as a natural word.

It has been shown that the human being "chunks" incoming verbal information into units in such a way as to keep some type of response unit intact. Three unrelated letters are remembered, or learned, as well as three words—despite the fact that there may be far more letters in the words. People tend to hold a certain number of "chunks" of information in short-term memory. The absolute number of items in a chunk may vary considerably, but as long as it is a "chunk" it will be retained as a unit.

Subjects will use natural chunks of information, if available, but they can be influenced by the way the information is presented, too. If numbers are presented spaced out to form groups of five or six numbers, they will become "chunks" if there are no conflicting reasons to chunk on a different basis.

A number of interesting speculations can be made about "chunking" and short-term memory. For example, it is possible that the limitation in capacity of short-term memory is in the number of chunks that can be processed at any one moment but that the size of the chunk can be quite large.

REHEARSAL Something must happen for it to be retained even for a few minutes or hours. What happens to chunks that reach our span of attention but to which nothing more (i.e., no rehearsal) occurs? One approach to this problem has been to try to prevent rehearsal after a verbal item has been presented. For example, a single verbal item could be presented and the subject engaged in a demanding task for some period of time before he is asked for recall. One type of task often used to prevent rehearsal is that of counting backwards by three's from a starting number provided by the experimenter. For example, the nonsense syllable RTM could be exposed to the subject for a moment and then the number 789 presented. The subject would count backwards by three's from 789 at a regular fast rate until he is asked to recall the three consonants. The counting backwards is presumed to be so demanding as to prevent active rehearsal of RTM during the delay period.

A procedure such as that described produces very rapid forgetting over a few seconds. An example of the amount of forgetting of verbal materials over several different time periods is presented in Figure 8-8. This result is in line with the generally accepted view that rehearsal is vital to retention of verbal materials and also with the view that forgetting is rapid in short-term memory unless rehearsal does take place.

A short-term memory with rapid forgetting is useful in many circumstances. Often we look up telephone numbers that we won't need more than once and that it would be silly to record in a more permanent fashion. On the other hand, there are memories that will be useful for intermediate time periods, such as hours to days, and others for which a permanent storage would be most useful.

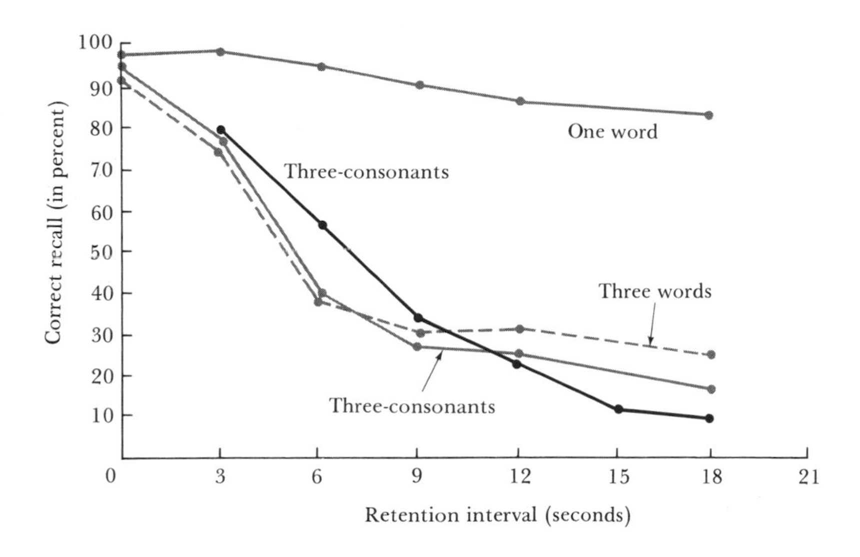

Figure 8-8 *The effect of interpolated activity (counting backwards) on recall of three consonants or three words over various reaction intervals. Data on three-consonant trigrams from Peterson and Peterson, 1959; Murdock, 1961; data on one- and three-word units from Murdock, 1961. (Adaptation of Fig. 1 from A. W. Melton,* J. verbal learning and verbal behavior, *1963,* 2, *1–21.)*

Intermediate memory

This phase of memory refers to retention of verbal material for periods longer than those covered by short-term processes but still not "permanent" or in the longest-term storage.

Probably most of the laboratory learning experiments involve intermediate memory processes, either alone or in conjunction with short-term processes. An example of how the two might work together can be found in research upon the "serial position effect."

If subjects are given a list of items to learn and recall, the first few items and the last few items are best recalled. This enhanced recall of the two ends of the list is called the "serial position effect." An example was shown in Figure 8-6. There are two components of the effect. The ability to recall early items better than items in the middle of the list is called the primacy effect, while the ability to recall items near the end of the list better than middle items is called the recency effect. Each component can be manipulated independently. For example, if the items on the list are presented at a slow rate, the items early in the list are recalled better than if they had been presented at a fast rate. Thus the primacy component can be manipulated by the rate of presentation. Rate of presentation does not affect the recall of the latter items of the list (i.e., the recency component).

On the other hand, if the recall test is postponed for 30 seconds after presentation of the list (and the interval filled with another task), the recency effect is lost but the primacy effect remains unaltered (Figure 8-9). This can be interpreted as showing the effects of two different memory processes: an intermediate memory process for the beginning and middle of the lists and an additional short-term memory process with rapid forgetting of the last items. The last items in the list are favored in recall, since they are stored by intermediate memory *and* in short-term memory processes.

It might be asked why the early items in the list are remembered

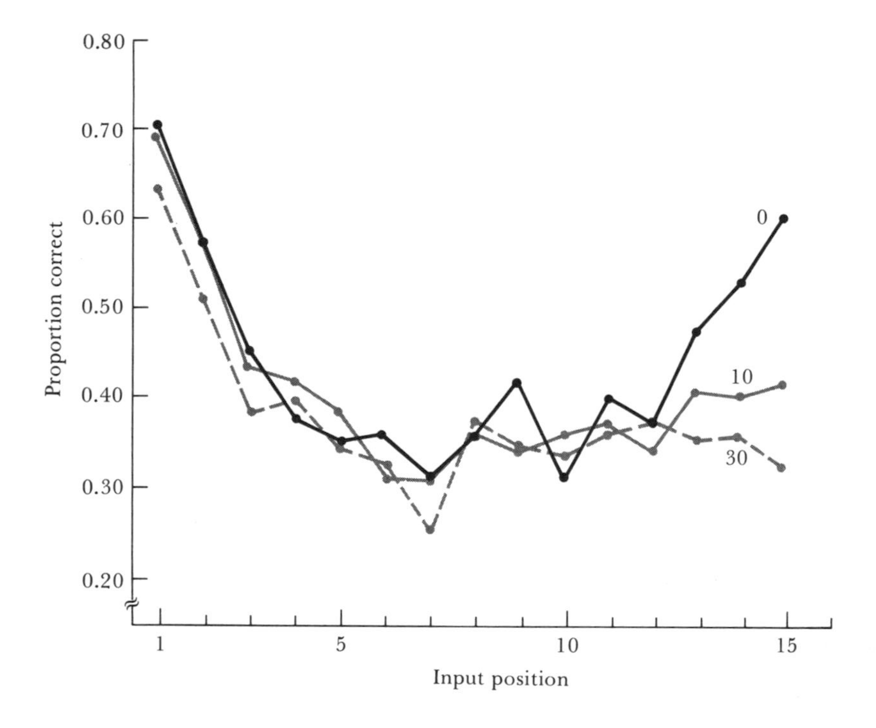

Figure 8-9 *Serial position effects for the recall of verbal items after 0-, 10-, and 30-second delays of the recall test. Note that the recency but not the primary effect is changed by the different delays. (Adaptation of Fig. 2 from M. Glanzer and A. R. Cunitz, Two storage mechanisms in free recall.* J. verbal learning and verbal behavior, *1966,* 5, *351–360.)*

better than the middle items when both are presumably in the intermediate memory stage. The answer is probably that the first items in the list are not subjected to interference from associations from preceding items. The middle items are surrounded by the associations from items occurring both before and after them. Items at the beginning of the list have no, or only a few, preceding items. Evidently interference from preceding items represents a major component in the forgetting of serial lists.

Items in intermediate memory are influenced by many factors, including the length of the lists of materials to be learned and the rate of presentation. Once again, it is as if there is a fixed rate at which memories can be stored and the effects of increasing the rate of presentation or the amount of material produces an overload condition in which material is simply not placed into storage.

Rehearsal is important for items to be retained in either short-term or intermediate memory. Rehearsal is also a necessary condition for the more permanent storage of memories.

Long-term memory

Long-term memory storage refers to the recall of events that occurred beyond the period of seconds, minutes, or hours that were used to describe the less stable forms of memory.

In the previous chapter we discussed some of the physiological mechanisms that might be responsible for these long-lasting memories, and little can be added to that approach. On the other hand, new understanding of the processes of long-term memory storage can be gained from evaluation of the behavioral studies of long-term memory.

Several important distinctions can be made between long-term memory and the other forms previously discussed. These include the types of encoding and retrieval processes involved. As one example, when short-term memories are disrupted by the presentation of similar verbal materials, the greatest confusions arise with similar-sounding verbal units. When long-term memories are involved, confusion occurs between items with similar meaning. In short-term memory, the acoustic aspects of a verbal item are stored, but when rehearsal takes place the rehearsal is in terms of natural language verbalizations. Therefore, long-term memories are encoded by using transformed verbal units.

Rehearsal of verbal materials is similar, usually, to "talking to oneself" in a natural language. This implies an organization of memory based upon language. However, the organization of a language system is *not* the secret to using long-term memories.

IMAGERY AND RECALL The secret to exceptional feats of memory is the construction of a stable framework into which new events or items can be placed. The best framework is one of "images" of concrete places, objects, and things. Centuries ago, orators were trained to increase their memories by establishing a permanent set of images, such as would be made by walking through a series of rooms in a large house repeatedly and distinguishing special objects or features in each room. This series of images was established as the basis for the recall of lists of items in the future. When new lists were to be memorized for short periods of time, the new items of the list were "deposited" in or near one of the objects in the permanent collection. For example, to remember an ordered list of sports equipment, objects would be mentally arranged in the permanent image set, as leaning skis under an arch, putting a tennis ball in a vase, and standing a golf club in a window. Since the orator had memorized the rooms, the objects, and his pathway through the house, he could begin his recall of the objects from any point and reconstruct the entire list. After he was finished with one task, the permanent image structure could be used to provide a new basis for other short-term memories.

At this point we are interested in the fact that images of concrete objects affect storage mechanisms of long-term memory. The more concrete and vivid the images, the better they can be used. Verbal sequence also can be used. A list of verbal terms can be committed to memory and new items associated with each of the older items, but this procedure is much less effective than if the permanent sequence is of high image value.

Earlier in this chapter, we pointed out that the greater the image-evoking quality of the stimulus term, the faster was the acquisition in paired-associate learning. Both results indicate the usefulness of images in retrieving information from storage in memory, whether short-term or long-term. This is probably due to the ease with which storage of images takes place in long-term memory.

ORGANIZATION OF LONG-TERM MEMORIES The capacity to store information in long-term memory is extensive—although probably not unlimited. It is undoubtedly more extensive than any of the shorter-period forms of memory. It is organized in such a way as to make retrieval easier if concrete images are involved, and meaning (rather than acoustic similarities) seems to be significant in the recall process.

Information reaching long-term storage is stored and retrieved in accord with organizational principles. As an example, people asked to remember simple stories remember them poorly over a prolonged period of time. Often only moods, attitudes, or feelings, or perhaps one significant detail can be recalled, and these are incorporated and a new story constructed around this personalized concept. Memories of drawings of figures tend to become more like "familiar objects" if a verbal label of the object can be given to them. Tendencies to overemphasize special details of the figure have also been found. As a matter of custom, the reduction of detail in figures has been termed "leveling" and the overemphasis of a detail has been termed "sharpening."

Weaving related words together into a story radically improves retention of isolated words, and it protects memories of the words from retroactive interference effects. Almost any type of story will do; if the story is remembered the words to be remembered will be remembered.

In most, if not all, verbal learning studies in which a substantial body of material is to be learned, people produce their own strategies for organization and recall. These will vary from person to person, and consequently the storage in long-term memory will be different from one person to another. Since retrieval from long-term storage depends upon arousing the proper organizational system, the processes of retrieval are themselves of critical importance for understanding long-term memory.

RETRIEVAL PROCESSES How often has a word been on the tip of your tongue, but you just can't produce it? Probably quite often. Experimental studies have shown that a person may often know quite a bit about the word that can't be produced—such as its first letter, common associates of it, and even the number of syllables in it—all without being able to produce the one particular word. Some aspect of the stored information has become available, but not all of it.

While we still do not understand the failures that account for the "tip-of-the-tongue" phenomenon, the event does reveal that information stored in long-term memory often is not expressed. Demonstration of memory depends both upon effective storage and retrieval.

Retrieval processes are most important during recall. As mentioned before, a recognition procedure presents the item to the subject—it need not be pulled from a storage system.

When hints or cues are provided to subjects attempting to recall items from storage, significant improvement in retention is found. This is in accord with common sense. What is of importance is that hints or cues are useful only if they were present at the time of learning. If people are asked to memorize a long series of verbal items, presenting another word weakly associated with each to-be-learned word will assist later recall. During testing, if the subject fails to remember a particular word, prompting with the weakly associated word will often allow the subject to remember the correct word. However, if the weakly associated word is not present during learning, prompting the subject with it during testing will not help.

We would expect quite a different result with strongly associated words. The strong associates need not be present during training, since prompting with a strong associate during testing would elicit the correct word as a natural associate and thus the task would be changed from a recall experiment to one in which the subject need only recognize the term.

These results imply that the information reaching long-term storage is not processed much, if any, beyond the form in which it has been presented or rehearsed. Some further changes can occur, as in the leveling and sharpening of details, but the information has been categorized and organized before storage.

RECOGNITION OF LONG-TERM MEMORIES With a recognition procedure an item is judged to be appropriate or not according to some "familiarity" value of the item. Various procedures can be used. Single items can be presented and the subjects asked if it is an "old" or a "new" item. Various forced-choice procedures can be adopted. Four or more items can be given, and the subject asked to pick the correct item.

A simple demonstration might be in order. On page 323 two lists of words were given: a stimulus-words list and a response-words list. To test your memory by recall we could ask: What was the first word of the stimulus list? If you don't remember, a weak associate of this word would be *warm;* if you still don't recall, a stronger associate would be *fruit.* (The answer is *apple.*)

From what has been said before, the weak associate should not have helped unless it had been prominent when you first read the list. The stronger association may have helped.

Now let us consider an example of recognition. On the same page, which of the four words given below was the first word in the response list?

(a) Pilgrim
(b) Canary
(c) Pain
(d) Pear

The answer is (b). Again, the task can be made easier or harder by changing the distractors so as to produce greater or less associative interference, or by choosing all of them from the response-word list or from the stimulus-word list.

In general, recognition requires the evaluation of the degree of familiarity of the item being evaluated. But what kind of model can best describe the familiarity responded to in the recognition task?

One model assumes that if an item has been committed to memory it is always recognized and identified correctly. If memory has not been established, the person guesses among alternatives. This model can be elaborated to include the elimination of obviously false distractors and guesses among the remainder. This type of model that includes a "guess component" is termed *threshold model* or sometimes *high threshold model* of the recognition task.

Another approach considers the probabilities involved and the payoffs involved in making the different possible responses. In other words, it is very much like the signal-detection model described in Chapter 6. It assumes that every stimulus presented has some familiarity value and the subject establishes a criterion value for response tasks in which "yes" signals an old item or "no" signals a new item. When the familiarity value of an item exceeds the criterion a "yes" response is made; if not, a "no" response would be made. As described in Chapter 6, the criterion is established by the values and costs of the responses, among other things.

There are many other models that can be applied to the recognition of verbal items. At the present time, all of the models make very similar behavioral predictions and cannot be distinguished on this basis. However, it seems that under most natural conditions the payoffs for correct and incorrect judgments should be considered in evaluating recognition tasks.

Relations among memory states

It is tempting to think of a progression through the four memory states, that is, from immediate to short-term to intermediate to long-term. Sufficient rehearsal of a memory event in one stage could lead to storage in the next, and failure to achieve sufficient rehearsal would lead to elimination of the event from memory.

This progressive idea of memory is probably much too simple. Certainly immediate memory is the first process activated. However, after that, the short-term memory and the intermediate memory could be simultaneous and parallel systems. In fact, the recency component of the serial position effect demonstrates the summative effect of the two memory processes. Another possibility is that short-term, intermediate, and long-term processes could exist in parallel through training and rehearsal. If the four stages of memory have value for understanding human memory, then the discovery of the transition from one to the next must be worked out in the future.

A caution

We have discussed memory as if the four stages represented separate systems and processes. However, these differentiations among memory stages may be much too simple, too few, and may tend inadequately to separate retrieval from memory storage.

But of all the possibly misleading characteristics of our classifying memory into four stages, the most misleading might be the tendency to think of the four stages as separate neural mechanisms or locations in the brain. We know very little about the workings of the human brain with regard to learning, memory, or retrieval. The behavioral data set targets for future knowledge at which theories of brain function must aim in their explanations, but the behavioral observations do not imply the existence of specific anatomical or physiological events.

OTHER VIEWS OF MEMORY

To this point we have given our interpretation of several important modern directions of research into human learning and memory. These are the directions in which most research is channeled, and for the most part they represent a scientific inheritance from American behaviorism. However, important ideas have been generated by other branches of psychology, and some of these concepts will be outlined below.

Gestalt psychology

When we discussed perceptual phenomena (Chapter 6), we pointed out that Gestalt psychologists attempted to explain perceptual phenomena on the basis of electrical fields located in the brain. Memories of past sensory events were related to the reestablishment of particular brain fields by new conditions. There was strong appeal in their arguing from basic perceptual phenomena. When a stimulus is presented only briefly and the subject looks away at a neutral field, there is a procession of after-images. These after-images resemble the prior stimulating conditions, although there usually are a series of both positive and negative after-images. (In a negative after-image the colors and light-dark relationships are reversed.) In any case the perceptual effects of the preceding stimulus conditions have affected the person so that the effects remain when the stimulus conditions have been altered. This lingering effect is often termed the *trace* of the stimulus. All memories can be thought of as traces of neural events that occurred earlier. Just as perception is altered by forces operating in the electrical brain fields to cause illusions, so memory traces are subject to the same influences. Thus our memories are represented as subject to all of the distorting influences of field phenomena generally. The problem has always been that it is difficult to specify precisely what the distortions of the brain field will be in any but very simple perceptual or memory situations.

A modified approach more in step with current views of the nervous system might hold that the electrical fields are not the important aspects of brain function, and it might emphasize the reverberatory characteristics of loops of neurons. All neural tissue is spontaneously active but also responds to stimulation by a transient resonation of neural impulses through the interwoven network of cells. An external stimulus, such as a flash of light to the eyes, evokes an electrical response in the visual areas of the brain and is followed by a series of transient wave forms originated by the imposed stimulus but produced by the reverberation of neural impulses through many loops of neurons. Perhaps information is encoded by the patterns of reverberatory activities following stimulation. If a particular poststimulus pattern is reproduced, even without the initiating stimulus, this would elicit the response to the stimulus.

An approach like this moves away from the earlier Gestalt view that it is the entire electrical field of the brain that is important and suggests that a form of neural resonance is the information-carrying process. It is, however, similar to the Gestalt point of view in that the emphasis is upon rather widespread forms of brain activity.

Lewin's view

Kurt Lewin was a social psychologist deeply influenced by Gestalt psychology. He postulated that our actions, both mental and behavioral, are caused by "forces" operating within us. These forces are strictly theoretical terms, although they often become very real in Lewin's own conception of psychological issues. They are considered to be the joint effects of the person and the situation in which he finds himself. Memory, for Lewin, was a product of ongoing cognitive activity. To the extent that forces in the person were directed toward past events or objects, they would be remembered. When the forces directed toward maintaining the memory were reduced, the event or object would not be available for recall. One of Lewin's examples was taken from a coffee house in Germany.

The waiters did not write down orders or the amounts each customer owed. These waiters were able to remember everything customers were served, even though hours went by, *up to the point the waiter was paid.* Since the waiter would be responsible for the bill if the customers did not pay, this maintained the "force" necessary for memory. After the customers paid the bill, this force was diminished.

On the other hand, Lewin postulated that strong forces away from events or objects would act to induce forgetting. Examples of this purposeful forgetting could be illustrated by the fact that the name of a "date" with whom you had an unpleasant time is often hard to recall. The frequency with which dental appointments are missed also testifies to the effect anticipated discomfort has upon memory.

Overall, these observations testify to the effects of motivation on the *expression* of memory. The effects of motivation upon memory may be produced in many ways. They could serve to direct attention to certain cues and not others, they could facilitate rehearsal and they could impose a specific organization upon verbal materials. Motivation need not affect the memory processes or retrieval *per se.*

Freud and repression

Even though Sigmund Freud, the founder of psychoanalysis, and Kurt Lewin were contemporaries, each independently developed his own theory of purposeful forgetting. There seems to have been little communication between them. Freud developed a theory of personality based upon his study of people with behavioral problems. Through his method of psychoanalysis, he came to believe that most personality problems stemmed from anxiety. One of the theoretical mechanisms through which anxiety is minimized in the individual is called repression. Repression is a personality mechanism—unknown to the person—which keeps anxiety-laden memories from reaching conscious awareness. However, Freud believed that memories hidden from conscious view by repression could still influence behavior. They could be general or specific memories of previous events or situations. Specific repression would account for the loss of a given fact, for example, the name of a person or an appointment. General repression could eliminate an entire period of one's life from memory.

Once again, the question is difficult to resolve, but mechanisms of memory most likely affect retrieval processes rather than stored memories themselves. This could occur in a number of ways, as in the case of motivation on the expression of memories.

COGNITIVE FUNCTIONS

Psychology aims at understanding all important characteristics of man's behavior. Higher processes, cognitive functions, intellection, and thinking are activities that we count as our highest capabilities—that is, those responsible for the human race. At the same time, we recognize that the ability to think and reason can be a tool for those ends we consider most reprehensible: hate, war, and destruction. Whether applied toward laudable or tragic ends, these higher mental functions can be studied for what they are.

Unquestionably there is a connection between verbal behavior and the higher mental processes. The degree of association, however, has not been clearly established, and it is possible to witness behavior that seems to reflect the activity of higher mental processes without simultaneously witnessing signs of the use of verbal behavior.

Is there a useful definition of what psychologists mean by higher mental processes? Many definitions have been proposed, but each derives its usefulness from the theoretical context in which it is embedded. Generally speaking, however, higher mental processes are inferred from behavior that is not readily predicted on the basis of the environmental (stimulus) conditions presented to the individual or on the basis of the individual's past reactions in similar situations. In other words, if a person reacts immediately and with great regularity to a situation, it is likely that this reaction is one that can be explained on the basis of a previously acquired stimulus-response connection. If behavior is regular and swift in a given social situation, the reaction might be one that has become routine and does not require the use of the higher mental processes. On the other hand, if a response does not occur promptly, we tend to suspect that the response, when it does occur, has been produced by higher mental functions. If one is asked to solve the following mathematical problems, the time required for each will be quite different:

$$2 + 2 =$$
$$718 + 496 + 219 =$$
$$\sqrt{61} + \sqrt{23} =$$

The simple answer of 2 + 2 requires very little time and probably does not require much in the way of higher mental functioning. The response "4" has assumed the character of a simple conditioned response to the stimulus "2 + 2 =."

On the other hand the longer time required to complete the other sums suggests that their solutions involve the use of cognitive functions, even though the final response may be quite uniform among the subjects.

Responses may be a product of higher mental functions at one time and become, through practice, representative of the simpler *S-R* types of response. For example, when one is learning a foreign language, simple responses to questions in that language may require relatively long periods of time. After practice, the responses may become quite automatic. After more practice, quite complicated interchanges in the newly acquired language may occur without delay.

In these examples, delay in response time is used as an indicator of the use of higher mental processes. Another indicator, of course, is variability in responses among different people, coupled with a delay in response. When we try to solve many kinds of problems, there is no one correct answer, and considerable variability can be found. The strategies devised to meet the demands of the day vary from person to person. One way of organizing our daily activities may not be superior to another, but the techniques we use undoubtedly reflect our individual approaches to problems.

The use of higher mental processes is inferred when there is a considerable amount of time between the presentation of the problem and the response, or when there is variability between people in situations, or when it is difficult to determine the single correctness of a given solution. We assume that the time lag between the presentation of a problem and the response represents the time required for the higher mental processes to occur. These processes are thought to be internal activities occurring in the person. Psychologists who believe in association learning theories think of the internal processes as series of *S-R* associations (mediational processes), whereas other psychologists would take other points of view. The well-known operant theorist B. F. Skinner has stated that man is unique only in being exposed to unique schedules of reinforcement—an approach which some people might consider rather dreary. Today, most psychologists emphasize man's verbal capacities as his unique claim to higher functions. The attributes responsible for the verbal behavior include the genetic disposition to produce and understand speech, which involves both specialized sensory and motor systems. Once language has been developed, new horizons in rehearsal and memory-storage systems are opened.

SUGGESTED READINGS

Carroll, J. B. *Language and thought.* Englewood Cliffs, N.J.: Prentice-Hall, 1964.
Ebbinghaus, H. L. *Memory: A contribution to experimental psychology.* New York: Dover, 1964.
Ellis, H. *The transfer of learning.* New York: Macmillan, 1965.
Fitts, P. M., & Posner, M. I. *Human performance.* Belmont, Calif.: Brooks-Cole, 1967.
Manis, M. *Cognitive processes.* Belmont, Calif.: Wadsworth, 1966.
Penfield, W., & Roberts, L. *Speech and brain mechanisms.* New York: Atheneum, 1966.
Slamecka, N. J. *Human learning and memory.* New York: Oxford, 1967.
Smith, W. I., & Rohrman, N. L. *Human learning.* New York: McGraw-Hill, 1970.

9
Motivation and emotion

The concepts of motivation and emotion have been frequently used in attempts to study and explain man's behavior. Motives have been used to account for the direction, the intensity, and the persistence of behavior. The concept of emotion has been used to describe both the mental states implied by words such as anger, fear, terror, love, and happiness, as well as "emotional behaviors" that can be observed in people or in animals. But, what is an emotional behavior? Emotional behaviors are often described as those which reflect experiences in others that signify feelings such as fear. The term also reflects occasions when confused and disorganized behavior occurs under circumstances that would allow the inference of emotional feelings. In this chapter we discuss first the use of motivational concepts in relation to behavior and then turn to an examination of emotions.

MOTIVATION: HISTORICAL PERSPECTIVE

Psychologists tend to use the word *motive* in different ways, depending on their theoretical biases and orientation. There is no universal agreement as to what the word means either at a common-sense level or in a scientific way, except insofar as the term is used in a particular theoretical framework. One attempt to incorporate all that psychologists mean when they use the word *motive* ran to 244 words. However, as a first approximation, we might say that *motives are theoretical concepts used to explain the direction, intensity, and persistence of behavioral patterns.* As long as we keep within a very general framework, this definition will be satisfactory. With it in mind we can move toward an examination of some "motivational phenomena," in particular those which most people would agree represent the operation of a particular motive, such as hunger, thirst, or sex.

Motives are inferred from the observation of behavior. The statement "a hungry man will seek food and eat" implies a considerable number of hidden assumptions; for example, one must assume that the hunger motive *directs* the person toward certain environmental stimuli, that this action will *persist* for some finite period of time, that there will be certain *consummatory responses* when the appropriate objects are found, and usually we must stipulate a qualifying term such as "all other things being equal." By "other things" we mean that this behavioral sequence (seek food, eat) would occur if there were no other more imperative motives functioning at the time. Still, we are not ready to predict actual behavior. The patterns of a man's food-seeking acts depend upon learned techniques for obtaining food. The ways in which consummatory responses are made vary too. The time of day and many other significant variables are influential in predicting what patterns of behavior will occur.

In the history of modern experimental psychology, motivation has been studied by several *general* approaches. In particular, these approaches have attempted to place motives in a wider perspective so that the effects upon behavior of many or all motives can be understood without having to provide a behavioral theory for *each* specific motive. These more general approaches have dealt with motives in biological and philosophical frameworks.

Homeostasis

The concept of homeostasis was propounded by the French physiologist Claude Bernard near the middle of the 19th century and it was used as a basic principle for understanding motivation. Simply stated, homeostasis refers to the body's tendency to maintain a relatively constant internal environment in the face of external changes. Fortunately, the *relative* invariability of the internal environment is usually a favorable one for survival of the organism. For example, when the body's supply of blood sugars becomes depleted, more blood sugars are released from bodily stores to resupply the internal environment. This tendency to maintain a relatively constant internal environment is a result of changes in the internal organs. Homeostasis can be achieved through changes in the somatic muscles too. For example, when the environment gets cold, we huddle and shiver.

The concept of homeostasis provided psychologists with a perspective from which motivation can be viewed. Many early psychologists believed that the homeostatic principle underlies all of man's behavior. Freud and Hull developed quite different theories of behavior, but both views were based on the assumption that our actions can be considered as attempts at the restoration and maintenance of favorable internal states.

Should we, however, view eating as fulfilling homeostatic demands? To be sure, eating provides us with the substances needed to maintain the internal conditions necessary for life. On the other hand, the word "homeostasis" is rather like the word "instinct" in that it is only descriptive and does not provide us with an explanation of the behavior under study.

Need

Given the biological and philosophic orientation provided by the homeostatic principle, the concept of *need* soon came into use. When we are deprived of food, we *need* it. When we are deprived of water, we *need* it. Experimentally, when we deprive an organism of material necessary for survival, we have created a need for that material. This use of the term is relatively unambiguous: *Deprivation produces need.*

Needs are frequently used as explanations of behavior. Some psychologists use the word *need* to explain the direction of behavior; a person eats because he needs food. In the same way a need for food is used to explain *persistence* or *intensity* of food-directed behavior.

However, this use of the term "need" poses two types of problems.

First, not all deprivations of essential substances alter behavior. If animals are deprived of vitamin A or D, for example, we find no evidence of any special change in their behavior directed toward meeting this "need." Secondly, sexual behavior is not essential to the survival of the individual organism and is not based on deprivation. Yet it is based, in part, upon internal physiological changes. Faced with these two types of problems for our definition of *needs,* should we change our descriptive definition to say that only certain biological deprivations result in *needs* that are capable of directing behavior? Should we also say that any physiological change in the organism can become a *need* even though it may not stem from an internal deficit?

These problems of the definition of need have been further aggravated by the adoption of the word *need* by theorists dealing with social motives. Motives such as *need for achievement, need for affiliation,* or *need for power* are defined by operations far removed from those defining biological needs. The result is that today some psychologists believe that the concept of need is of little value for the understanding of behavior and should be dropped from current psychological usage.

While this suggestion may have merit, it is unlikely to be adopted by any large number of psychologists. Rather, we must be alert to the several meanings and uses of the word.

Preferences and appetites

Given a homeostatic orientation, we might expect organisms suffering from biological deficits to become more directed toward foods that contain the materials required by the body. In many circumstances rats will choose a balanced dietary fare from cafeteria-style offerings of many different foods. Some, but not all, bodily deficiencies alter the preferences exhibited for various foods in ways that tend to restore the body's supplies of missing substances. The needs imposed on the animals resulted in specific hunger for the missing substances. For example, casein is a protein very low in the rat's order of food preferences. However, if the rats are deprived of protein for a prolonged period of time, they will come to choose casein in preference to other foods.

While some changes in the kind of food sought can be produced by biological need, not all food preferences can be explained on this basis. Why is it that different people have different tastes in foods? One explanation for taste preferences might be the past association of specific foods with the fulfillment of the hunger motive and the subsequent homeostatic restoration of the body's food supplies. People and animals might prefer tastes that have been associated with nourishment in their past. We might like the sweet taste of saccharine (which has no nutritive value) because sweet tastes have been associated with actual nourishment in the past. We should notice that this explanation attempts to account for preferences on the basis of biological needs and the stimuli associated with them in the past.

This rather appealing approach—based on learning and past experiences—is not adequate to explain appetites for specific tastes and other forms of stimulation. Many forms of stimulation have an appeal to animals and people that can be explained only on the basis of species-specific preferences for these stimuli. These preferences can be modified but probably not completely overcome. For example, from shortly after birth a group of guinea pigs was fed a steady diet of food adulterated with a bitter substance. With nothing better to eat, these guinea pigs learned to associate the unpleasant taste with hunger reduction. Later in life these experimental animals were tested against a control group of normally fed guinea pigs and given a choice between foods with and without this bitter substance. Despite their exclusive experience with the bitter food, the test group did *not* show any greater preference for the unpleasant taste than did the control animals.

In another experiment dogs were raised from birth on a diet of milk. They did not have any experience with the sight or smell of any other kind of food. When meat was first presented to the animals, the smell of it did not produce any salivation. The animals readily ate the meat, however, and after a few experiences of smell, followed by meat, the animals salivated profusely to a meat odor. If one looks at the salivation as a conditioned response in the Pavlovian sense, the smell of meat was an unusually effective *CS*. The establishment of a salivary response to other truly neutral stimuli would have taken much longer to develop. Thus there was something special about the smell of meat that enabled it to become an effective stimulus for the salivary response with great ease.

Response preferences can also affect learning and performance. Learning of a response will be faster if the animal is trained to make a response for which it has a pretraining preference. Training is retarded if the responses involved are counter to pretraining dispositions. Animals and people more readily "give up" or *extinguish* responses that go against their preferences. If children who normally prefer white bread to dark bread are rewarded for selecting dark as opposed to white bread at the dinner table, their behavior can be altered so that they choose dark bread more frequently than white. However, as soon as the rewards are terminated, this behavior will quickly change and white bread will become the favorite once again.

Earlier in our discussion of learning (p. 300), we discussed the reinforcing value of certain consummatory responses. It should be noted that the reinforcement value of consummatory responses is related not only to the type of response elicited but also to the length of time required to make the responses. The longer a rat eats food, the greater the reinforcement value, even though the total amount of food may be unchanged.

One might think that consummatory responses, those which occur when needs are reduced, are only reinforcing if the needs are in fact reduced. However, there is considerable evidence indicating that the consummatory responses *themselves* are reinforcing.

The sexual response may act as a reinforcement for behavior even though it does not continue long enough to produce emission in the male or climax in a female. On an experimental level, male rats will learn to run a maze to engage in sexual behavior with a receptive female even though they are parted from the female before orgasm. Thus they learned the response without experiencing a direct reduction of sexual "need." On an everyday level, sexual petting and "foreplay" can be rewarding even if orgasm is not achieved.

Female rats will learn a bar-press response to achieve sexual contact with males, and their rates of response are determined by the degree of sexual contact allowed. The more intense the sexual contact, the higher the rate.

Some psychologists explain preference behavior and the behaviors not based on need-reduction on the basis of an activity or process within the individual called *pleasure*. When we prefer one object to others, these psychologists infer that the individual expects that object to produce more pleasure, or less unpleasantness, than the other possible choices. This kind of psychological explanation has been with us for centuries and is generally called *hedonism*.

Hedonism

As stated above, the doctrine of hedonism refers to a proposed general tendency for organisms to try to attain pleasure and to avoid pain or unpleasantness.

For hedonists, pleasure is the prime mover of behavior. Many psychologists believe that pleasure and pain do not depend on any association with present or past reactions with need-reduction. According to this point of view we eat candy because it tastes sweet and this is a pleasant taste. Certain types of stimulation are pleasant, others are unpleasant or painful, and others are neutral.

Biological basis of pleasure

In 1954, two psychologists at McGill University, Peter Milner and James Olds, discovered that electrical stimulation of certain regions of the brains of rats produced behavioral effects which indicated that the animals would seek this form of stimulation and choose it over other reinforcements—even over food when they were extremely hungry. Subsequent work has revealed regions which, when stimulated, will produce behavioral effects that appear to be rewarding, punishing, or "neutral" to the animal. The charting of the brain for these types of reactions was a major scientific breakthrough, and at the same time it presented a major problem to theories which asserted that rewards and reinforcements must be related to a reduction in biological needs. With brain-stimulation techniques we find reinforcing effects produced without reduction of biological need. How do the advocates of the homeostatically based theories interpret these results from stimulation of the brain?

Animals prefer electrical stimulation of some brain regions to other forms of reinforcement, but this does not mean it produces "pleasure" in the animal. We can never fully know the subjective experiences of animals or people. One type of explanation of self-stimulation behavior tried to show that intracranial stimulation produced compulsive, automatic behavior patterns, only superficially related to the effects produced by true rewards. However, the great number and variety of tasks in which animals have exhibited preferences for stimulation of certain brain areas over natural rewards makes this alternative explanation doubtful. But we cannot dismiss so easily the arguments that stimulation obliterates unpleasant neural activities or that the stimulation activates the same neural systems that are aroused naturally when needs are reduced.

Both approaches have been suggested as possible explanations of why brain stimulation may produce rewarding effects. On the other hand, both seem to be grounded upon the assumption that behavior is based upon a reduction of unpleasantness or pain. Except for historical reasons related to need-reduction theories of motivation, there is no reason to take such a dim view of behavior. In accord with everyday observation, people and animals are positively oriented and do seek out the pleasurable aspects of life.

This approach—that is, attributing behavior to pleasure or pain—is certainly useful in predicting behavior. But it, too, operates at a descriptive level. It fails, moreover, to satisfy in that it accepts events as either pleasurable or not and fails to explain *why* the events are pleasurable or provide an explanation for the changes in the pleasure produced by a given event. While there is little doubt that people and animals seek pleasurable events and avoid the unpleasant, psychology still must *explain* this form of behavior in terms of principles of operation of the central nervous system.

What about pain? Consider the seemingly prodigious effects of this experience upon behavior. There are few impelling motivational conditions that produce the effects of pain.

Areas of the brain have been found that appear to have punishing or unpleasant effects when electrically stimulated. Areas producing behavior indicative of positive or negative effects when stimulated are shown in Figure 9-1.

Neuroanatomically, pain tracts can be found within the spinal cord and followed to the posterior hypothalamus and the thalamus; however, at this point the trail ends, and no higher representation of pain has been found. Stimulation of the neocortical surface of the brain in the human produces no painful sensations. It is for this reason that some types of neurosurgery can be performed on man with only local anesthetics.

At the level of the posterior hypothalamus, the positive and negative systems come close to each other. Electrical stimulation in this region often produces behavioral effects that are "mixed." Animals work to turn on the electrical stimulation but also work to turn it off. This suggests that as the stimulus is applied its effects spread over an increas-

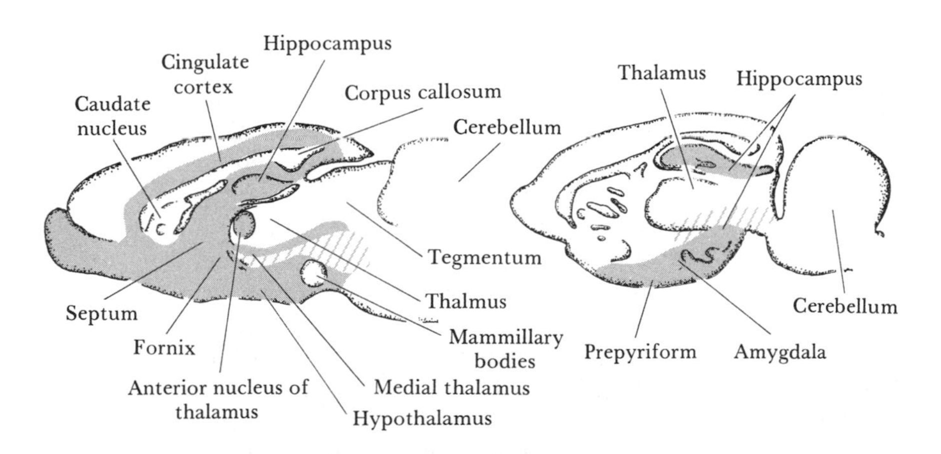

Figure 9-1 *Locations of brain areas which produce positive (lined areas) and negative (stipple) effects when stimulated electrically. (Adapted from J. Olds, Positive emotional systems studied by techniques of self-stimulation.* Psychiat. res. rep., *1960,* 12, *238–257.)*

ing range of tissue from the initial "pleasure" point and affect "unpleasant" points of the nearby pain system. At this time, the animals act to turn off the electrical stimulation.

Pain is by no means a simple psychological problem. Almost always the pain response is coupled with other reactions, such as fear, anxiety, and concern about possible future pain.

In some cases of patients suffering from relentless pain, neurosurgeons have severed certain neural tracts connecting the extreme forward portions of the frontal lobes (called the prefrontal lobes) with other portions of the brain. This operation seems to produce an interesting and, at present, inexplicable result. The patients on whom the operation was performed still report their pain to exist, with the same severity as before the operation, but it no longer "bothers them." The operation seems to free them from domination by the sensation of pain. These results have yet to be satisfactorily incorporated into any theory of behavior.

Pain probably arises from an intricate combination of peripheral and central events. The higher regions of the brain (e.g., the neocortex and thalamus) probably exert regulating influences upon the sensory systems of the spinal cord so that certain signals are interpreted as pain.

"Stimulus-bound behaviors"

The term "stimulus-bound behaviors" refers to acts that are elicited by electrical stimulation of the brain in animals not subjected to any deprivation schedule. These behaviors occur only when appropriate goal objects are present in the environment as the electrical stimulus is applied. Animals will even perform a task that is instrumental in achieving a specific object needed to complete the elicited responses. In this sense motivation for the behavior is created rather than an automatic, stereotyped behavior. The occurrence of stimulus-bound behavior is often interpreted as indicating that the electrode is located in a hypothalamic region responsible for the motor behaviors associated with a specific biological motive.

The behaviors which are elicited by the electrical stimulation of the hypothalamus seem stable but could they be altered? In one study an attempt was made to determine how elicited behaviors could be changed. When the electrical current was applied, some animals tended to perform *one* set of actions, others tended to make another set of behaviors, and still others a third type. However, it was found that it *was* possible to alter the stimulus-bound behavior without changing the location of the electrode or parameters of stimulation. The technique involved was to stimulate the animals' brains for prolonged periods of time (e.g., overnight) without the appropriate goal object for the stimulus-bound behavior being present. Other objects related to different responses were present. Afterwards, the electrical stimulation produced a new stimulus-bound behavior related to one of the objects in the environment during the period of prolonged stimulation. After the change in stimulus-bound behaviors had been made, animals did not return to their former behaviors.

There are good reasons for believing that stimulus-bound behaviors are not similar to normal motivational states. Animals exhibiting stimulus-bound licking of a drinking tube will not transfer to drinking from a water dish. They would be more likely to persist in licking a dry water tube instead. When we remember that electrical brain stimulation produces the behavior only when appropriate environmental stimuli are present, it appears that a condition must be induced in the animals such that a tendency arises to engage in acts that are unrelated to any normal motivational condition. Satisfaction arises from completion of the consummatory response rather than the satisfaction of an induced motivational state. Since stimulus-bound acts can be changed, this means that an association can be made between the brain stimulation and the opportunities to respond that are provided by the environment.

It should be emphasized that not all electrical brain stimulation produces stimulus-bound behavior. There are some brain locations which when stimulated produce positive reinforcing effects, such as those discovered by Olds and Milner, but which do not seem to elicit stimulus-bound behaviors. Perhaps the most common behavioral correlate of positively rewarding brain stimulation is a general increase in activity and exploration.

At the very least, the work on stimulus-bound eating makes it clear that traditional views of the organization of the hypothalamus in terms of fixed centers that have within them prepackaged motivational or response circuits, is inadequate. Evidence from other directions also makes it clear that the hypothalamic systems are capable of differential adjustments to changing circumstances.

Drive

Based upon a theory of behavior that viewed organisms as passive creatures, which became activated only when deprivations produced a homeostatic deficiency, the concept of "drive" was created to account for the energizing of behavior. The organism became energized by "drive" or "drives," which in turn were created by deprivations. In some ways "drive" was used like the term "force" in physics. Both refer to *theoretical terms* that are used to account for movement-creating conditions—for behavior in psychology and for objects in physics.

The prime example of drive as a concept in psychology is that found in Hull's learning theory (pp. 254-263). In that theory, the total amount of drive (D) of the animal is proportional to the total of all deprivations being experienced by the animal. Each habit available to the animal was potentiated by the same amount of drive; it was exactly the same for all habits (${}_SH_R$'s). What this means is that the differences in the tendencies to make a response, the excitatory potentials (${}_SE_R$'s), will be exaggerated by increasing amounts of drive. For example, if we assume two responses of different habit strengths to be possible in a situation (${}_SH_{R1}$ and ${}_SH_{R2}$), different drive levels will differentially affect the excitatory potentials.

If

$$
\begin{aligned}
{}_SH_{R1} &= .2 \\
{}_SH_{R2} &= .3
\end{aligned}
$$

and if $D = 2$, then

$$
\begin{aligned}
{}_SE_{R1} &= {}_SH_{R1} \times D & \qquad {}_SE_{R2} &= {}_SH_{R2} \times D \\
&= .2 \times 2 & &= .3 \times 2 \\
&= .4 & &= .6
\end{aligned}
$$

Difference $({}_SE_{R2} - {}_SE_{R1}) = .2$

This difference between the two excitatory tendencies will be changed if D is increased. For example, if the value of D is increased to the value of 4, the difference in the excitatory tendencies can be calculated as follows:

$$
\begin{aligned}
{}_SE_{R1} &= {}_SH_{R1} \times D & \qquad {}_SE_{R2} &= {}_SH_{R2} \times D \\
{}_SE_{R1} &= .2 \times 4 & &= .3 \times 4 \\
&= .8 & &= 1.2
\end{aligned}
$$

Difference $({}_SE_{R2} - {}_SE_{R1}) = .4$

This "drive approach" to motivation can produce several interesting predictions about behavior. Of special interest are experiments in which the drive level of a person can be evaluated and in ways which do not directly involve changing conditions of deprivation.

Drive and anxiety

According to some psychologists, Hull's notions of drive can be modified so as to include in D individual tendencies to react more or less strenuously to emotional situations. Individual differences in emotional reactivity can be assessed and often are considered to be differences in the "anxiety level" of a person. One attempt to measure anxiety in a way related to drive theory is through the use of a self-report questionnaire. Questions used in one questionnaire were initially selected by clinical psychologists so that answers to them reflected the subject's internal anxiety levels. Assuming that anxiety-test scores indicate the individual's emotional responsiveness, and a person with a higher anxiety score will have generally a greater drive level (*D*) than subjects with low anxiety-test scores, scores should allow prediction of the differential behaviors of groups of people with high and low test anxiety.

In a simple situation which involves only one response ($_SH_R$) the greater the level of drive (*D*) the greater the response should be. This result has been frequently observed. For example, subjects were trained in an eyeblink conditioning experiment. Puffs of air (*US*) are delivered to the eye at two different intensities and are paired with a previously neutral stimulus (*CS*). As training progresses we can observe the increased tendency for the *CS* to elicit the eyeblink response. The data are presented in Figure 9-2. Subjects with high anxiety scores show a greater

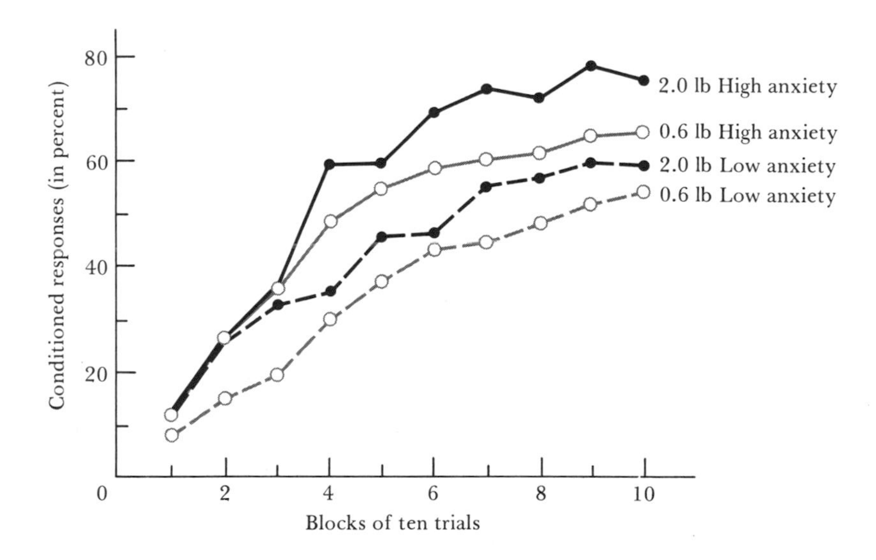

Figure 9-2 *Performance in eyelid response conditioning as a function of US intensity (in pressures) and position of subjects on anxiety scale. (Adapted from K. W. Spence and Janet A. Taylor, Anxiety and strength of the UCS as determiners of the amount of eyelid conditioning.* J. exp. psychol., *1951,* 42, *183–188.)*

percentage of conditioned responses than those with low anxiety scores *for a given pressure of air puff*. We observe two factors influencing performance: the anxiety level of the subjects and the strength of the puff of air used to condition the response.

When more than one response is involved, high drive level can interfere with performance, since the difference between excitatory potentials becomes greater as drive increases, as we have learned.

This approach was tested in an experiment in which subjects had to learn two kinds of lists of paired associates. One list was prepared so that the correct responses were readily available, since they had had relatively high habit strengths before the experiment. For this list, high drive helped acquisition of the list. The other list was constructed so that the correct responses had lower habit strengths than incorrect responses. On this list subjects with high anxiety (drive) were poorer in acquisition. Therefore, the effect of drive upon performance depends upon the strength of the response to be learned, relative to the strengths of other possible responses in the situation. When the correct response is nearly dominant in the situation, drive will facilitate performance. When this response is weak relative to other responses, high drive will interfere with performance.

Since everyone's drive level is, to some extent at least, a unique property of the individual, it is difficult to formulate any general statement about whether a person should take steps to increase or decrease his drive level before an examination. For individuals with normally high drive or anxiety levels, it would probably be best to try to reduce anxiety by going to a motion picture the night before the examination, trying to relax, and to think of other things. For individuals with normally low drive or anxiety levels, steps should be taken to raise drive level. Black coffee and jangling nerves may actually improve the performance of a person with a low drive level. We should remember that this discussion of drive level and examination performance has assumed learning to be constant for all individuals. We should recognize that examination performances are jointly determined by drive and learning.

The notion of a general drive resulting from any and all conditions of deprivation or related operations has gradually been disappearing from psychology. There are many reasons for this, but prominent among them is the fact that the different manipulations used to alter drive tend to produce unique changes in the individual. Food deprivation changes the animal's responsiveness to smells, tastes, activities, and experiences in a way different from that produced by water deprivation or sexual arousal. As an example of the more specific approach that is now most common, we will discuss three separate biological motives later in this chapter.

Arousal theories

The concept of arousal refers to the degree of mobilization of the body's activities. Low arousal conditions would be ones of relaxation, sluggishness, or even sleep. On the high arousal extreme, we have all those conditions in which the organism is "energized," "intense," and perhaps even "on edge." Note how we have used more or less familiar words to indicate a continuum of arousal from low to high. Note also the assumption of *continuous* progression from low to high arousal conditions.

Since verbal descriptions of arousal are subject to interpretation in different ways by different people, psychologists working with the relationship between arousal and behavior have turned to other ways to define arousal conditions. The most common is the use of physiological variables. These include heart rate, blood pressure, the electrical resistance of the skin, and other measures that will be discussed in more detail later in the chapter.

The assumption of a continuum of arousal from low to high means that arousal conditions can vary from low to high along a single "arousal" or "activation" dimension. An organism is assumed to move in one direction or another along this dimension as circumstances, past experiences, and genetic constitution dictate. Arousal is represented as a single quality, and if a person is in a state of high arousal, the physiological and behavioral significance of that state will be the same regardless of the conditions that produced it. Therefore, arousal is like "drive" in this regard. Drive and arousal are both general concepts and their effects upon behavior are independent of instigating conditions. High drive or arousal could be produced equally well by food deprivation, water deprivation, pain, or sexual stimulation.

Arousal is different from drive in that it reflects the mobilization of the organism; this may be independent of deprivation conditions or other traditional drive-inducing variables. Arousal can be heightened by the occurrence of unexpected events or by electrical stimulation of portions of the brain-stem reticular formation, for example. It is also operationally defined in different ways—namely, through measurement of specific physiological reactions.

Arousal theories were related to motivation and emotion by the assumption that different kinds of behaviors were optimally suited to different arousal states. If the animal or person is too much or too little aroused, behavior becomes inefficient. The concept of arousal was further strengthened by the discovery that stimulation of the brainstem reticular formation could lead to an apparently generalized condition of activation. However, as research progressed, the notion of a unitary arousal system has been abandoned for many reasons, some of which will be mentioned below.

Problems with general arousal theories

Of the difficulties presented by a global arousal theory, the following seem most significant.

The physiological variables used to measure arousal often fail to give similar indications of the arousal state. Heart rate may increase, and yet skin resistance may remain unchanged. Correlations among the various physiological measures used to assay arousal are often low or nonexistent—which would mean they are measuring different things.

Moreover, not only do the physiological variables reflecting arousal often fail to relate to each other but they also often fail to relate to behavior. As one example, the drug atropine produces an EEG pattern similar to that found in sleep or drowsiness, but behavior seems well-organized and the animal alert. This is a dissociation of a physiological indicator and behavior. As another example, during sleep, a highly aroused EEG pattern can be recorded during certain times (during that stage of sleep when rapid eye movements are found—REM sleep). In this case the organism is asleep and behaviorally quiet; yet, an activated physiological index is reported.

Other examples of the dissociation of physiological and behavioral phenomena could be given, but perhaps more important is the observation that shows that the reticular formation of the brain stem, presumed to be the neural substrate of arousal, is not, itself, a unitary system. This structure is made up of many subsystems, some producing increased arousal and some producing decreased arousal. These subsystems have different neurochemical transmitters associated with them. Stimulation of the *same* anatomical location with one neurotransmitter (norepinephrine) will produce increased EEG arousal, but stimulation with another (acetylcholine) will produce decreased EEG arousal. Also related is the discovery that EEG arousal and behavioral activation are subserved by different subsystems of the reticular formation. Destruction of the reticular formation can be so specific as to produce an animal that is behaviorally unresponsive to stimuli that produce extensive arousal of the brain as measured by the EEG.

Another problem has to do with the peripheral portions of the autonomic nervous system that are involved. Since the physiological measures associated with low arousal are those mediated by the parasympathetic branch of the autonomic nervous system and those associated with high arousal are typically associated with sympathetic activities, it would be tempting to think of arousal as merely reflecting a continuum from parasympathetic dominance to sympathetic dominance. The situation is not this simple. During conditions of very high arousal both branches of the autonomic nervous system are active, even though the parasympathetic effects are masked by the reactions of the sympathetic. The hidden, strenuous reactions of the parasympathetic division can be discovered through the use of drugs that block the sympathetic system.

Perhaps the most important criticism of any theory assuming a "general arousal" state which is produced by any means is that arousal, like drive, tends to be specific to the circumstances producing the arousal. A cat sitting motionless before a mouse hole, watching for its prey, is not in the same condition as a cat fleeing from a dog—even though both situations are marked by intense internal arousal. Most psychologists agree that an understanding of the emotional and motivational systems involved will best be accomplished through study of the specific mechanisms involved for each motivational condition. Studies of the arousal systems have turned more and more to the study of specific forms of arousal associated with a particular motivational state.

THE BIOLOGICAL MOTIVES

The biological motives can be inferred from observations of behavior directed toward particular goal objects, from verbal reports, or from certain physiological conditions of the body. For example, we may wish to accept verbal statements about being hungry as a measure of hunger. These statements may represent a conscious awareness of a desire for food. On the other hand biological motives can influence behavior without reaching conscious awareness, and it may be impossible to determine the conscious awareness of a motive in some people, just as is the case with the use of animals.

Some psychologists study the physiological basis of our awareness of motives, others study the brain areas concerned with the initiation and cessation of eating and drinking, and some study the mechanisms underlying motivated behavior patterns. In the next several sections we will consider how the biological motives of hunger, thirst, and sex affect behavior, and then examine how peripheral bodily factors implement these motives before considering the mechanisms of the central nervous system responsible.

Hunger

It is in some ways remarkable to believe that a person can be aware of changes in the condition of his stomach. We have learned about the functions of sensory nerves in general, and there are sensory nerves from the stomach that project to several areas of the brain. But knowledge of the anatomical presence of nerves running from the stomach to the brain does not imply that activity in these tracts signals conscious awareness of hunger.

PERIPHERAL MECHANISMS Undoubtedly, the original investigators, Cannon and Washburn, were excited when they found that a subject's report of hunger pangs correlated with the contractions of his stomach. In their experiments subjects swallowed a balloon which could be inflated in the stomach. Pneumatic equipment was arranged to record each contraction of the stomach. Since reports of hunger followed the stomach contractions, it was inferred that contractions had *caused* the conscious experiences.

This correlation does not tell the whole story, however. In some diseases it becomes necessary for a surgeon to remove the entire stomach. Many reports have indicated the removal of the stomach does not reduce the awareness of desire for food, nor does it eliminate appropriate food-seeking responses. Experimentally, no loss in the effectiveness of food incentives has been found in stomachless rats. We can say only that stomach contractions may be a sufficient condition for conscious feelings of hunger, or of hunger-motivated behavior, in otherwise intact animals. Certainly awareness of hunger must result from other causes too.

Stomach contractions can be inhibited by a hormone secreted from a portion of the intestines just below the stomach. This hormone, like all hormones, is circulated through the blood to its target organ.

Two aspects of stomach contractions and other peripheral factors must be considered: (1) those factors responsible for the initiation of motivated activity and (2) those responsible for the cessation of the activity. Stomach contractions are not essential to the initiation of eating, and their cessation is not responsible for the cessation of eating or for the feeling of satiety. Distention of the stomach has a negative influence upon eating only when the stomach is severely extended. These phenomena have been studied by implanting a tube directly into the stomach, bypassing the mouth and throat. Foods or nutritive substances can then be pumped directly into the stomach. If this is done before feeding, it is called "preloading" the stomach of the animal. Moderate preloading of the stomach with food before a meal has no effect upon the amount of food eaten at the animal's mealtime. Preloading the stomach with high-caloric materials that have little bulk does not reduce the animal's feeding behavior even when the preloading is about 200 percent of the animal's daily caloric requirements. If the high-caloric stomach loading is continued for weeks, however, the animal will gradually reduce the amount of food eaten at meals.

This suggests that the cessation of eating is determined primarily by signals arising from the mouth as food is ingested. The animal gauges the appropriate amount of food required to maintain itself, and once this amount is established, it remains relatively fixed. The means by which the animals evaluates food value through oral taste factors is not yet understood.

The fact that animals will, ultimately, reduce their food intake with stomach loading prior to meals suggests that two food-regulation systems may exist. The first is one that controls eating on a day-to-day basis, and a second exerts a long-range influence on food intake that is based upon eating's long-range effects on the body.

Food introduced directly into the stomach does have incentive value to the animal and will act as a reinforcement. It is not, however, so effective a reinforcement as indentical food that has been eaten. Artificial distention of the stomach, say with a balloon, does not serve as a positive reinforcement and it is, if anything, aversive to the animal. Animals can be trained to press a lever in an operant chamber to obtain delivery of nutritive substances to their stomachs via implanted tubes, and they can learn to press an appropriate number of times to maintain a satisfactory diet. Perhaps even more surpising is their ability to adjust their rates of response to maintain appropriate nourishment when the nutritive substances placed in their stomachs are diluted. The animal must eat a greater quantity of food to maintain the same amount of caloric input. This adjustment in bar-pressing rate is almost immediate in response to the dilution and thus stands in sharp contrast to the results obtained from the stomach-preloading experiments in which a longer period was required for the adjustment of oral food intake.

There is a great deal of evidence to the effect that the blood of a hungry animal is different from that of a satiated animal. However, the absolute blood sugar level in arteries and veins has not been found to correlate with behavioral indices of hunger. It has been discovered, however, that the *ratio* of blood sugar in the arteries to blood sugar in the veins is so correlated. When the difference in glucose levels between the arteries and veins was small, human subjects had stomach contractions and reported sensations of hunger. When there was a good deal more sugar in the arteries than the veins, the subjects did not show these characteristics. These differences between glucose levels in arteries and veins have been interpreted as reflecting degrees of utilization and availability of body sugar. When the artery-vein glucose ratio is high (*S*s sated) this is believed to reflect a greater availability and utilization of sugar in the blood.

However, even with this relationship between blood sugar and "hunger," we should be careful not to attribute all sensations of hunger to these artery-vein sugar differences. Most likely it is but one of many factors contributing to our awareness of a need for food.

We should also recognize the need for a mechanism by which we become cognizant of these differences in artery-vein sugar levels. It is not enough to know of these blood differences; we must find how the central nervous system becomes aware of them. We must find receptor mechanisms sensitive to these changes in the composition of the blood.

CENTRAL MECHANISMS It is likely that cells sensitive to glucose levels in the veins and arteries are located in the hypothalamus. Cells in this brain area of the mouse pick up gold-thioglucose (glucose with a sulfur link to gold). This compound is taken into cells in much the same manner as is plain glucose. Once in a cell, however, the cell dies because the gold is toxic to the cells, and it is possible to examine the brain of the mouse *post mortem* to find areas of maximum glucose absorption and subsequent cell death. Destruction seems to be centered in the ventromedial nucleus of the hypothalamus. If we observe the mouse after an injection of gold-thioglucose that destroys this hypothalamic area, we find the animal becoming more and more obese. Data from many studies have shown that destruction of this area of the hypothalamus by any means will produce obesity. A picture of one of these extremely obese—but otherwise normal—animals (called hyperphagic) is presented in Figure 9-3. The hyperphagic effect caused by the gold-thioglucose deposited in the hypothalamus is but one of the bits of evidence relating the hypothalamus to the biological motives.

HYPOTHALAMUS CENTERS The existence of centers in the hypothalamus that control food and water consumption has been known for many years. Studies of the central nervous system areas related to food intake, as well as areas related to other motives, involves the use of restricted lesions or stimulation—either chemical or electrical—of the brain. For many years it has been possible to make small lesions in the brains of experimental animals to evaluate their effects upon behavior. As we found with respect to the role of peripheral factors in hunger, different mechanisms are responsible for the initiation and for the cessation of eating. When the center in or near the ventromedial hypothalamus is destroyed, the animals will not stop eating. It is as though a mechanism that normally acts to stop the ingestion of food is removed. The ventro-

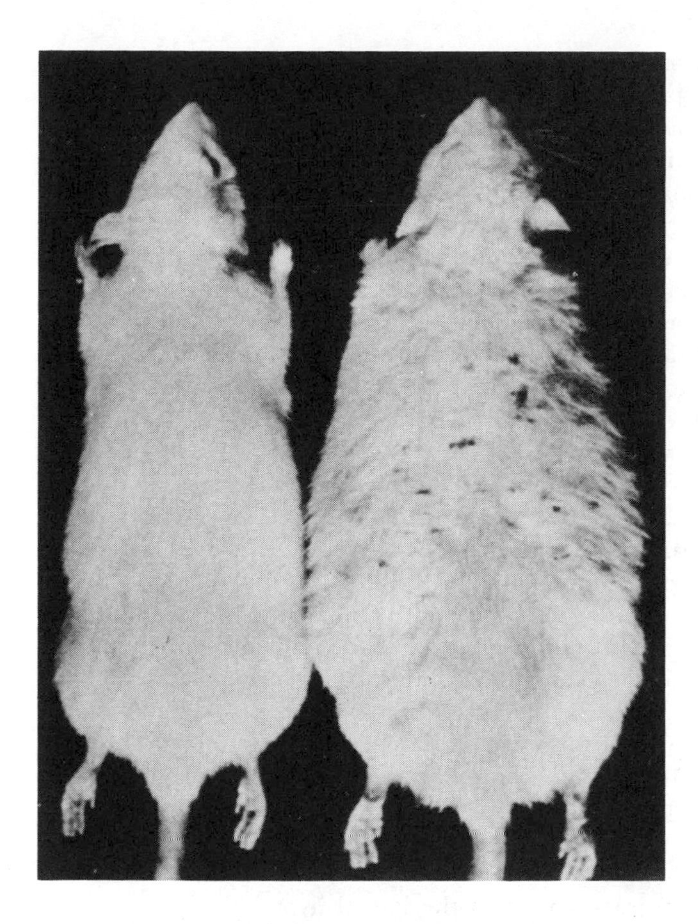

Figure 9-3 *Comparison of normal rat (left) with one made hyperphagic by lesions in the hypothalamus (right). (From Fig. 6 in A. W. Hetherington and S. W. Ransom, Hypothalamic lesions and adiposity in the rat.* Anat. rec., *1940,* 78, *155.)*

medial region is thought to be a "satiety center." Lesions placed more laterally in the hypothalamous produce animals which do not eat, and which will starve to death unless special care and retraining are undertaken. This more lateral hypothalamous area can be thought of as a center that acts to modulate the initiation of eating: a "feeding center."

One effect of the lesions in the ventromedial nucleus of the hypothalamus (the satiety center, which normally "turns off" eating) is a change in an animal's sensitivity to the tastes of foods. As we have learned before (p. 164), taste signals leave the tongue and mouth over three cranial nerves, but they influence behavior in accordance with the motivational state of the organism. It might be expected that the lesions that produce overeating could produce changes which make the pleasant taste of food even more desirable, but the hyperphagic animals are more sensitive to *both* favorable and unfavorable adulterations of their food.

The obese animals with lesions of the ventromedial nucleus will actually stop eating foods adulterated with a bitter-tasting substance at smaller levels of adulteration than will normal animals.

There are still many poorly understood aspects of brain lesions that cause animals to become hyperphagic. For example, these animals will not work to provide themselves with the extra food needed to remain obese. If required to operate a lever in an operant conditioning chamber to obtain food, the animals with hypothalamic lesions will maintain themselves at normal weight levels.

Lesions of the hypothalamus just outside the ventromedial nucleus produce animals that fail to eat *or* drink. There are several interesting aspects of the lateral hypothalamic lesions that will be covered in greater detail when we discuss thirst.

Electrical stimulation of the lateral hypothalamic areas sometimes elicits eating during the stimulation, even if the animal is thirsty and in the middle of drinking when the stimulus is applied. The reason the word "sometimes" is used in the preceding sentence is that the stimulation must be applied to just the right anatomical location to produce the eating during electrical stimulation. Much wider areas of the lateral hypothalamus, however, can be stimulated to produce greatly increased food intake *after* the stimulation has stopped. Increased food consumption can be found for several days after a single session in which electrical stimulation was applied to the lateral hypothalamus.

Since the terms and results of lesions or stimulation of the lateral hypothalamus may be confusing, the following chart summarizes the major points.

Table 9-1. **THE HYPOTHALAMUS AND FEEDING**

		Effects	
Hypothalamic area	*Name*	*Lesion*	*Electrical stimulation*
Ventromedial nucleus	Satiety center	Hyperphagia	Reduced eating
Lateral hypothalamic area	Feeding center	Aphagia	Eating—immediate or delayed

CHEMICAL SYSTEMS RELATED TO HUNGER Even though the hypothalamus clearly contains regions of importance for the regulation of eating (and other biological motives), it is not the only portion of the nervous system concerned with this biological motive. In one sense all of the brain is involved in motivated behaviors, but some regions are more direcly concerned with them than are others.

One recent approach to the problem of how direct a relationship brain systems have to hunger or thirst has been to stimulate regions of the brain directly with chemicals related to different neurotransmitters. The two chemicals most commonly used to stimulate the brain are norepinephrine and drugs that act like acetylcholine. Norepinephrine stimulation has been found to elicit increased eating when injected in many portions of the limbic system. Cholinergic stimulation fails to elicit eating, but it does influence drinking. It should be mentioned that if the norepinephrine is injected into the body in a general way—and consequently must cross the blood-brain barrier imposed between the blood stream and the central nervous system—appetite and food intake are depressed. Depression of appetite and food consumption also is a common result of taking the amphetamine drugs that are often used to reduce appetites (as well as act as a stimulant). These drugs stimulate the norepinephrine systems in the posterior hypothalamus and probably the "satiety centers." The reason that direct brain application of norepinephrine increases food intake while systemic application of the same drug inhibits eating is unknown, but the process implicates adrenergic neural systems coursing through the limbic system in the regulation of eating.

In overall perspective two antagonistic central nervous systems are related to food intake. Both are relatively diffusely represented throughout the limbic system but become funneled through, and focused at, the level of the posterior hypothalamus. At this location, the more medial systems, represented especially in the ventromedial nucleus, are concerned with the cessation of eating, while the more lateral systems are concerned with the initiation of eating. One might speculate that the norepinephrine used is likely to be the neural transmitter in the lateral systems, since direct application of this chemical induces increased eating. Further, the medial system may use a closely related, but different, transmitter, such as might be formed when norepinephrine is altered as it crosses the blood-brain barrier, since systemic administration of norepinephrine produces reduced food intake.

While the feeding systems are scattered throughout the limbic system, motivational systems can be found through most brain regions, even though their influences may be subtle and more difficult to discover. For example, the neocortex plays a role in the recovery of eating after lateral hypothalamic damage, but this can be discovered only by removing neocortical influences after the recovery has been accomplished. If the neocortical influences are abolished in animals who have been subjected to the lateral hypothalamic lesions and have begun to eat once again, complete aphagia will be effected once more.

Thirst

The body is largely (70 to 75 percent) water, and it maintains its internal water balance within quite narrow limits. It quickly and effectively reacts to too little water or too much water. Either condition serves to activate mechanisms that will move to restore the appropriate water balance.

We tend to think of the motive "thirst" as those feelings we experience when we say we are "thirsty"—that is, a dryness of the throat and other related sensations. Quite naturally we think of the reason for the sensations as being simply a water deficit. However, neither dryness of the throat nor the amount of water depletion can account for all that is meant by "thirst," as we shall soon learn.

PERIPHERAL FACTORS Most accounts that considered peripheral factors as the cause of thirst have assumed that a dry mouth was *the* important signal for thirst. Historically, a theory popular around the beginning of the 19th century held that the dryness of the throat was secondary to the thickening of the blood due to dehydration. More recent formulations have turned this around, arguing that as a body becomes dehydrated, water is removed from other tissues so as to produce a constant amount of water in the blood. Preserving the constancy of the water level of the blood at the sacrifice of other tissues could produce a dehydration of the salivary glands, among other glands and tissues, and contribute to the dry throat. But can dryness of the throat and mouth account for "thirst"?

The dryness of the mouth and throat is partly determined by the secretion of saliva. Elimination of the salivary glands does not eliminate thirst nor does the cutting of the nerves over which signals of throat-dryness reach the central nervous system. In addition, wetting of the mouth actually produces only the most transient alleviation of thirst. Probably the most conclusive argument against the "dryness-of-the-throat theory" comes from animals in which a tube has been placed into the esophagus so that any water they drink goes through the mouth and throat but never reaches the stomach. Consequently it cannot serve to alleviate the dehydrated state of the body. Such animals drink well beyond the normal amount consumed for a given period of water deprivation. If thirst were signaled by the alleviation of throat dryness, the animals should stop when a normal throat wetness had been achieved.

For all of these reasons, and others as well, it is necessary to abandon theories based only upon signals arising from the mouth and throat as a basis for the phenomena considered to represent signs of thirst.

There are several stable correlates of dehydration. One is an increase in the concentrations of various electrolytes normally found in the body's fluids. As water is depleted, there will be more electrolytes per unit volume of the fluids. Secondly, cells throughout the body become dehydrated and, to some extent, physically deformed. Receptors sensitive to the electrolyte densities of the fluids could exist in the body, but it is likely that the more effective signal for thirst would arise from the dehydrated state of individual cells. In addition, dehydration is signaled through a reduction of the volume of blood serum in the body. This in turn reduces the fluids lying between and among the body's cells. The signals indicating the blood volume and the state of dehydration that are significant for thirst probably arise from neurons located within the central nervous system, and it is to these more central factors that we now turn our attention.

CENTRAL FACTORS The cells of the central nervous system that are most responsive to changes in the internal composition of the body are located around the ventricular canals, deep within the middle portions of the brain. One can think of these cells as being receptors sensitive to changes in the blood and the cerebrospinal fluid. In the case of thirst, the cells that signal changes in the densities of electrolytes in the blood and blood volume itself are located near the ventricles in the anterior hypothalamus. In response to dehydration, the hypothalamus exerts at least two types of influence upon behavior. In general they relate to the animal's two reactions to water loss: (1) conservation of the water remaining in the body and (2) drinking. The first influence is through the secretion of a hormone formed in a portion of the hypothalamus, transmitted to a portion of the pituitary gland, and then released into the blood system. The second type is based upon the regulation of drinking. This second reaction is comparable to the regions of the hypothalamus that regulate food intake.

The hormone called the antidiuretic hormone (ADH), which is released through the pituitary gland, acts to control the permeability of the membranes of small tubules in the kidney to electrolytes in the blood plasma. During periods of dehydration, more ADH is secreted than normally and the urine becomes more concentrated, thus preserving water for the body.

The locations in the hypothalamus in which the ADH is actually formed and the pathways to the pituitary over which it is transported for release have been fairly well established and are different from the hypothalamic regions concerned with drinking. The independence of the ADH sites and the drinking sites has been established by experiments in which electrical stimulation of the hypothalamus has been used to produce drinking, a heightened increase in urine concentration due to greater ADH, or both. While some sites produce both when stimulated, most sites produce either one or the other effect. The fact that the two effects can be dissociated indicates that the two types of effects are mediated by separate neural systems.

Electrical or chemical stimulation of the lateral hypothalamus will induce drinking behavior in nonthirsty animals. In many species the areas in the lateral hypothalamus that induce drinking when stimulated are in the same region as the centers for food intake, although in other species, such as the goat, they are separable.

The chemicals that are effective in eliciting drinking are those which stimulate cholinergic systems of the brain. Adrenergic stimulation is without effect upon drinking, as was mentioned before in connection with hunger. As with norepinephrine and hunger, cholinergic stimulation over wide ranges of the limbic system produces drinking. The neural system controlling water-intake becomes anatomically restricted in the lateral aspects of the hypothalamus.

If cholinergic systems that converge in the lateral hypothalamus are responsible for the initiation of drinking, what mechanisms are responsible for the termination of drinking? A few reports have been made of the discovery of regions responsible for the cessation of drinking, but they have been rare. With thirst, we have the peculiar situation that anatomical sites have been discovered that initiate water intake, but those which mediate the cessation of drinking are poorly located at best.

It is unlikely that changes in the blood volume or concentration of electrolytes in the blood can cause drinking to be stopped. Animals stop drinking water after periods of time that are in direct proportion to how water-deprived they were when they started drinking. Moreover, they stop drinking long before the water they have consumed can possibly cause alterations in the blood system. Moreover, the distention of the stomach cannot be used to signal the amount of water consumed, because appropriate amounts are consumed when nerves from the stomach are cut and in people without stomachs. What remains is the conclusion that the amount of water drunk is somehow metered in the mouth and/or throat and is related by the brain to the degree of water deprivation even though the cues arising from the throat are not important for the initiation of drinking.

THE LATERAL HYPOTHALAMIC SYNDROME After lesions have been made in the lateral hypothalamus (in those regions at which electrical stimulation initiates drinking), the animals quickly become aphagic and adipsic—that is, they neither eat nor drink. However, at least to some extent, recovery can take place after these lesions are made, provided that the animals are kept alive by feeding them through tubes carrying the food directly into the stomach. Given this life-preserving care, the animals will begin to show a recovery sequence, which is quite stable from animal to animal; consequently, the entire progression from the adipsic and aphagic condition to "recovery" has come to be known as the "lateral hypothalamic syndrome."

The recovery follows the following sequence:

Stage 1. Complete aphagia and adipsia. Animals will die in this period unless food and liquids are provided, usually by stomach tube.

Stage 2. Adipsia with some food intake. In this period of recovery, animals will eat highly desirable, wet foods but will not eat dry food.

Stage 3. Adipsic but will eat wet but less palatable foods. At this time, the animals' most difficult problem seems to be the inability to drink. They will accept less than the most desirable foods but also need to have the food made wet for them to eat.

Stage 4. Recovery. At this final stage, animals will eat dry food and will drink of their own accord. However, the recovery is incomplete in certain ways.

Stage 4 of the lateral hypothalamic syndrome is only a relative recovery. The animals do drink, but only to wet their mouths so as to provide moistness during eating. In other words, they come to exhibit drinking at meal times and this maintains them. They do not properly adjust their drinking to the degree of water deprivation, which means that they have recovered only one aspect of water regulation but still lack the complete, normal drinking response to deprivation. These "recovered" animals also show altered responsiveness to unpleasant tastes; their eating is still more easily disturbed by unpleasant tastes.

Recovery from lateral hypothalamic lesions depends upon the integrity of the neocortex. Removing neocortical influences through one of several possible procedures results in a reinstatement of the complete lateral hypothalamic syndrome.

There are some similarities between the course of recovery from lateral hypothalamic lesions and the development of eating and drinking in the infant. On the basis of these similarities, it has been argued that the hypothalamic lesions produce a regression of eating and drinking behavior to that of an earlier period in life. This interpretation is related to observations of the results of brain lesions in the frontal neocortex of adults that seem to reinstate earlier behavioral reactions lost many years before. Nevertheless, while this is an interesting suggestion, it remains only a suggestion and does not help us understand the mechanisms underlying a "regression," if it does follow brain lesions.

Sexual behavior

Reproductive behaviors hold special interest to all of us, for many reasons—one of which is, of course, that if it were not for these behaviors we would not be here. Sexual activities, treated as a motive, differ from hunger and thirst in that they are not the result of a deficiency motive. People can survive without engaging in sexual acts. Sexual activities assist the species to survive, not the individual, but it is the individuals who must cooperate in achieving perpetuation of the species. Moreover, most people who "cooperate" in sexual behaviors, today, are not motivated toward increasing the number of people in the world.

Nature, in her wisdom, has created two sexes and cooperation between members of each must occur for new offspring to be created. The reproductive behavior of each sex varies in response to different internal mechanisms.

PERIPHERAL FACTORS Probably the most significant factor affecting sexual behavior is the contribution made by the sex hormones. In men the hormones are somewhat simpler than in women. One major male hormone, testosterone, is secreted by cells in the testes.

Even before birth, testosterone is secreted from the embryonic testes and actually produces changes in the make-up of the brain in some, if not all, animals. After birth, administration of this hormone can produce effects such as accelerating sexual development, e.g., allowing copulation to occur earlier in the hormone-treated animals than in untreated animals. Sexual potency can be restored in animals of some species by administration of testosterone after sexual activity has diminished with senility.

Castration—removal of the testes of the male—produces a drop in sexual activity in certain animals, but not all animals. In man, there are reports of continued, apparently normal, sexual activities after loss of the testes. Loss of the testes is generally more debilitating early in life (before puberty) than it is later.

In females, the hormone picture is vastly more complicated. Hormones related to reproductive behaviors are secreted in several places, including the ovaries and the pituitary gland, and fluctuate in a near-monthly rhythm. The two major groups of hormones secreted by the ovaries, the estrogens and progesterone, are related to sexual receptivity in females. As these hormones reach their greatest levels, near the time of ovulation, the female is most receptive to the advances of the male. Castration of the female usually produces an immediate cessation of sexual receptivity in all female animals with the remarkable exception of the human. Only in women is sexual activity continued after removal of the ovaries. The same continued sexual interest is found in women after the ovaries have become "senile" and no longer produce their hormones, i.e., after menopause.

Birth control pills are a combination of estrogens and progesterone that interrupts other hormones responsible for ovulation. The "pill" thus supplies artificial levels of these normally occurring hormones and makes pregnancy all but impossible. The supplementary use of estrogens is also helpful to women when the ovaries stop operating at menopause. Small amounts of the estrogens are often helpful to women who develop physiological or psychological disorders at this time of life.

EXTERNAL STIMULATION Sexual behaviors differ from other of the biological motives in that they are profoundly influenced by environmental stimulation. Sights, smells, and tactual stimulation all can act to arouse the sexual motive in animals and in people. This is found with other motives, too, such as when feelings of hunger occur when one sees a picture of a grilled steak or when one smells freshly baked bread. But sexual behaviors are more dependent upon environmental conditions than are hunger or thirst.

In Chapter 3 we reported the observation that release of hormones in female doves can be stimulated by having the doves watch a strutting male dove. These visual cues must be quite subtle, because observation of a castrated male dove fails to alter the hormone levels of the female. Tactual stimulation of the genital areas of some species of animals is sufficient to produce ovulation and make them ready for copulation, although females of most species are "receptive" only during portions of the monthly menstural cycle. This receptive period, termed the estrus period, or being "in heat," is often produced in experimental studies by the administration of estrogens.

The sexual behavior of people is different from that found in other animals in many respects. These include, in addition to those previously noted, the fact that at least some women are receptive to men at all times of their monthly period. Sexual activities are not limited to periods of heat. In addition, recent studies of the physiological reactions of the uterus have shown that that organ shows contractions which become more frequent and more intense as sexual arousal increases. What is of special interest is the ways in which these uterine contractions can be affected. Reading sexually oriented materials is one effective technique, and this is not too surprising in view of the fact that suggestive books sell very well. However, books dwelling on romantic themes are more arousing to women than are pornographic materials; at least in terms of this one measure of sexual arousal, romantic stories are the most effective verbal stimulus. Although the data are not conclusive, it seems that men are aroused more by pornographic-type materials than by stories of romance, and this suggests a rather clear difference between what sexually motivates men and women.

CENTRAL FACTORS Most of the individual motor movements of which sexual behavior is composed are organized within the spinal cord and can be elicited from animals without any brain tissue remaining above the upper spinal cord. However, as with the other biological motives, the main region for integrating these individual components into a more or less complete behavior pattern is the hypothalamus.

Two different regions of the hypothalamus concerned with sexual behavior have been discovered. One of these is closely tied to the pituitary hormone systems, which regulate the testes or ovaries. Lesions in these areas produce changes in sexual behavior that are correlated with changes in hormone levels and physical changes in the gonads. Lesions in other regions of the hypothalamus produce alterations in sexual behavior *without* correlated changes in hormones or gonads.

Unfortunately, while the latter effects have been found in the anterior hypothalamus in some species, there are other species in which the location of the regions controlling sexual behaviors are found in other places in the hypothalamus. Therefore, it has not yet been possible to reach firm conclusions about the anatomical systems that are involved with the two "sex regions" of the hypothalamus.

Once again we would do well to think of the hypothalamus as a zone in which neural systems pertaining to sex converge from other, higher brain areas. The limbic system has within it neural systems that affect sexual activities, or components of sexual behaviors, when they are stimulated or destroyed.

Sexual behavior can persist despite many kinds of damage to the nervous system. Blindness, deafness, elimination of tactual input, and large lesions of the neocortical mantle all may fail to eliminate sexual behavior. This is not to say that these damaged regions or systems are without effect on sexual behavior. All of these types of damage undoubtedly produce limitations in the range of sexual activity, if not in the form of their expression.

A summary of central factors in motivation

Hunger-, thirst-, and sex-motivated behaviors are all intimately related to mechanisms of the hypothalamus. The hypothalamic regions closely related to these motives have been called "centers"; this led to the view that these areas were specialized zones acting with autonomy in governing these motives. Some people have suggested that each biological motive may have an "on" and an "off" center in the hypothalamus. This is, however, not an accurate representation of the organization of the brain. To be sure there are limited regions of the hypothalamus that influence motivated behaviors in specific ways, but these areas are not merely "on" and "off" centers. They control behavior in complicated ways, and each motive has somewhat different types of controls exerted by hypothalamic regions.

In addition, the hypothalamic zones related to the biological motives are far from autonomous. They are under the continual influence of the internal environment, the sensory systems, and the higher forebrain systems, especially the limbic system.

Throughout the hypothalamus, nerve fibers descend from the limbic system (and from other forebrain areas), which could be affected by lesions or stimulation in the hypothalamus. Therefore, it is difficult to attribute the behavioral consequences of any treatment—lesion or stimulation—only to those cells in the area of treatment. Fibers going down to the cord or up to higher forebrain regions, or originating in cells at a considerable distance from the treatment, may be affected and participate in producing the behavioral changes.

Of special significance for behavior is a large system of small fibers that course along the base of the brain, through the lateral hypothalamus and the midbrain, called the *medial forebrain bundle.* This system contains fibers from the limbic system and from midbrain areas that are joined by fibers going into and out of the hypothalamus. It is the medial forebrain bundle that, when electrically stimulated, produces the effects which seem to be rewarding to the animal. Since this system passes throughout the lateral hypothalamus in a diffuse manner, it is often difficult to differentiate its behavioral contributions from those produced by cells located in the lateral hypothalamus.

Even though the limbic system and the hypothalamus seem to be closely related in directing motivated behaviors, this does not mean that neocortical influences can be ignored. The limbic system does not operate by itself any more than the hypothalamus does. All types of sensory influences, as well as the activities of the neocortical systems, monitor, regulate, and direct the limbic system. The activities of the neocortex—insofar as they are related to verbal behaviors and "thinking"—can operate to inhibit or enhance motivated behaviors.

EMOTION: HISTORICAL BACKGROUND

The word *emotion* comes from two roots, one meaning to upheave or to shake and the other, from the same root as the word "motive," meaning to move. Both roots are important for the way "emotion" is considered and studied today. On the one hand, emotion refers to those intense reactions signaled by great upheavals of the body and disruption of ongoing behavior; on the other hand, the emotions can direct behavior toward specific goals.

Two very difficult problems face the student of the emotions from the start. The first is that past efforts directed toward understanding the emotions have often been variously aimed. For example, some have tried to provide an account of the conscious experiences found during emotional periods. Other people have tried to explain emotional *behavior,* and still others have investigated nervous system activities during emotional reactions. Different theories have tried to explain quite different facets of the emotions, and this frequently has led to confusion and conflict. The second problem is the determination of how many emotions must be considered by any theory of the emotions.

The second question—How many emotions are there?—is not easy to answer. Certainly there are some emotions that most people who share a natural language system tend to acknowledge. Most of those who share the English language would recognize love, hate, fear, and a few other terms, perhaps, as describing commonly experienced emotions. But what about jealousy, grief, mother-love, and anxiety? Even though people might agree that these feelings are "emotional experiences," it is doubtful that there would be agreement on what experiences are being described. The emotions experienced by any single person are highly individual matters, difficult to describe, and that each person has many types of emotional reactions. Nevertheless, it is possible to make progress in the study of the emotions through careful study of emotional reactions, experiences, and the physiological correlates of emotion, despite the great diversity in emotions that we must anticipate.

In the late 1800s, William James argued for a theory aimed at explaining the awareness of the emotions. He believed that the perception of an "exciting event" came first. This perceptual act produces bodily reactions, both of the somatic muscles and the internal organs, and these reactions are perceived as the emotion. Therefore, this theory described the experienced emotion as the product of reactions of the body. Because a Swedish scientist, Lange, independently presented a theory much like that propounded by James, it is now referred to as the James-Lange theory of the emotions.

The major position offered in opposition to the James-Lange theory is one named after its two proponents: the Cannon-Bard theory. It is also known as the "thalamic theory." Cannon and Bard argued that the bodily reactions *and* the emotional experiences were a result of neuronal discharges from the thalamus. From the thalamus, the downward discharges (into the spinal cord) produced the internal bodily reactions, while the upward discharges to the neocortex and other forebrain areas were responsible for the emotional experiences.

Differences among the emotions would arise from differences in the patterns of internal bodily reactions according to the James-Lange theory, but they would arise from different patterns of thalamic discharges according to the Cannon-Bard theory.

Many experiments were undertaken to establish which theory was correct. One approach was that of studying the emotional reactions of animals and some patients in whom the sympathetic branch of the autonomic nervous system had been removed surgically or "blocked" by drugs. Blocking of a neural system with drugs eliminates synaptic transmission of nerve impulses. The sympathetic branch of the autonomic nervous system was chosen because it is the system that produces the major emergency reactions. In general, the results showed no loss in emotional reactivity after these procedures were performed. Those who agreed with the James-Lange theory then argued that the sympathetic discharges were necessary for the original learning of emotional experiences but, once established, the experiences could be produced by other means. This in turn elicited a new period of experimentation in which the surgical or chemical procedures were accomplished early in life. However, these procedures are either difficult to accomplish in the young animal or difficult to control, as in the case of drugs. Moreover, either procedure produces its own peculiar effects on the developing organism, which makes the results difficult to interpret. Therefore, no "critical experiment" has been done to discriminate between the two theories even though many have been attempted. However, to save the James-Lange theory, it has been necessary to modify it so as to make the internal events of the body play a role in the development of emotional experience but not in the experience of emotions in the adult.

The Cannon-Bard theory, too, was far from acceptable in its initial form. It had at least to be modified to a "hypothalamic theory." Most of the characteristics of the thalamus—as it was supposed to affect upstream forebrain regions and downstream spinal mechanisms—are much more adequate as descriptions of the hypothalamus than the thalamus. The Cannon-Bard theory also encountered the same difficulties as those which ascribed motivational processes to various hypothalamus "centers."

THE PHYSIOLOGICAL STATES

What happens to the body during periods of emotion? The reactions most often described are those in which the sympathetic branch of the autonomic nervous system comes to predominate. This is an oversimplification of events, since there is often increased activity in the parasympathetic branch, as well, and at times there are alternations of dominance between the two branches. But the predominant effect is a sympathetic reaction during periods of intense emotion. Heart rate and blood pressure go up, and other signs are presented that indicate mobilization of the body's resources for emergency reactions. These sympathetic effects all can be elicited by stimulation of the posterior hypothalamus. This portion of the brain has been thought of as the brain's point of coordination for the sympathetic branch of the autonomic nervous system. The anterior hypothalamus from which parasympathetic effects are elicited through stimulation has been considered a region for coordination of parasympathetic effects.

It should be noted that this "fore-and-aft" distinction in the hypothalamus is another version of a "center" theory and should be considered with the reservations held about all such theories.

But even as a description of some of the events produced by stimulation of the hypothalamus, the posterior-sympathetic, anterior-parasympathetic distinction can be improved upon by recognizing that more happens through stimulation of the anterior or posterior hypothalamus than these autonomic reactions. The terms *ergotropic* ("work-oriented") and *trophotropic* ("rest-oriented") have been suggested as terms that are more descriptive of the effects of stimulation of the posterior and anterior hypothalamus, respectively. Stimulation of the posterior, ergotropic region increases sympathetic autonomic effects, increases *somatic* muscle tone, gears the sensory systems for a more intense bombardment of information, and stimulates some endocrine glands, especially the adrenal glands.

Stimulation of the rest-oriented, trophotropic system produces greater parasympathetic activity and reduces somatic muscle tone, changes the endocrine balance, and prepares the animal for less intense somatosensory information.

Tuning of the body

A shift toward an ergotropic balance represents a shift toward greater arousal and activation, whereas a shift toward a trophotropic balance represents a tendency toward decreased activation. Establishing these balances in one direction or another can be thought of as "tuning" the body. How the body is "tuned" through the hypothalamic systems determines the types of reactions to stimulation. The same stimulus can produce quite different reactions at different times, depending upon how the hypothalamus is tuned when it is applied.

Years ago while studying conditioning in dogs, Pavlov found that a painful stimulus could be used as a conditioned stimulus (*CS*) for a salivary response to meat powder. When applied in the conditioning situation, the painful stimulus did not produce the normal responses to a painful stimulus. The animal did not seem bothered by the painful *CS* when it was a signal for a positive conditioned response. According to the tuning theory, the training situation and the learning task had created a trophotropic balance. This had prepared the animal for trophotropic reactions and this type of reaction was, in fact, elicited by the painful *CS*. If an ergotropic balance had been established and the same stimulus applied, a normal "pain" response would be elicited.

The reactions produced by any stimulus depend upon the readiness of the animal to respond in trophotropic or ergotropic directions. This tuning can be established by many techniques, among which are previous training and experiences in the situation, drugs, and other manipulations, including the types of sensory information arriving from the body.

The information arising from the somatic muscle systems influences the state of the hypothalamus. The administration of drugs that block the junctions between nerves and somatic muscles (paralytics) produces an extremely trophotropic bias. The paralysis produced by such drugs reduces the sensory information arising from the somatic muscles and leads us to the suggestion that the normal role of this type of sensory information is to create an ergotropic balance. In the situations in which the somatic input is decreased by partial paralysis or other techniques, brain waves reflect rhythms that normally indicate a relaxed, inattentive condition. It is more difficult for a person in a relaxed posture to become angry; if a military posture is maintained, it is more difficult to become sad or depressed. Altering muscle tone through instructions or training in muscle relaxation given to human subjects, or by clinical means in experimental animals, can exert profound effects upon emotional reactions. In one animal experiment, for example, electrical stimulation in the hypothalamic region produced an aroused, aggressive animal that would bite the experimenter or anyone else nearby. However, if the ergotropic balance was reduced by administration of drugs that reduced muscle tone, the animal no longer reacted in this aggressive way and would often merely retreat to a corner of the experimental chamber or simply wander around when the same brain stimulus was applied. Some school teachers have discovered that it is possible to reduce the intensity of emotional reactions of young children by having them assume a posture incompatible with their emotional state. If a child is aggressive and destructive, teachers often try to induce a relaxed posture, elicit smiling, or induce happier body postures. If the child is crying, they try to create postures or activities that are antagonistic to crying.

Activity in the ergotropic regions is associated with the neurochemical norepinephrine. Apparently this drug is an important transmitter substance for the highly aroused activities associated with this system, which suggests that the levels of this drug available in the brain are related to emotions and moods.

Neurochemistry of moods

The neurochemical hypothesis of moods has been formed on the basis of many types of experiments in which moods and feelings have been found to be related to the level of norepinephrine in the brain. When a person is depressed, a deficiency of norepinephrine would be expected, whereas feelings of elation would be associated with an overabundance of this chemical. This idea came in part from experiments with animals in which a depression in behavior was induced by the tranquilizer reserpine. This drug decreases norepinephrine in the brain. However, there is also evidence that deficiencies of other neurochemicals, especially serotonin, can produce a mood depression.

One problem for theories of mood based on norepinephrine availability is that direct injection of this chemical into the brain does not create a "manic" or elated state. Sometimes quite the opposite is found. Another problem stems from the fact that significant differences are found among animals treated with drugs that alter the available norepinephrine in the brain.

Probably the levels of certain neurochemicals found in brain tissue *are* related to moods and feelings, but we are a long way from understanding the relationship in any degree of completeness. Moreover, we must learn more about the differences found among individual animals —and people—in their reactions to drugs that alter the brain's levels of neurochemicals.

Bodily reactions

During emotional reactions, there is an enhancement of ergotropic activity and up to this point we have not considered any differentiation in the bodily reactions produced by the specific emotional behavior being expressed.

At a common-sense level we would expect differences in the body's reactions to different emotions. Elation and aggression are both associated with increased ergotropic reactions, but we would anticipate large differences in the internal states associated with each.

For many years, however, many psychologists, physiologists, and other scientists thought that the autonomic nervous system could respond only in a very diffuse fashion. At the extreme, this would mean that there might be only a "more" or "less" response within the autonomic nervous system and that no differentiation of emotions could be expressed through the organs controlled by that system. However, this has been shown to be inaccurate by recent studies by Neal E. Miller and his associates.

In these investigations animals were studied while under the influence of a paralytic drug (a neuromuscular blocking agent) so that the activities of the somatic muscle system could be reduced or eliminated. The animals were conscious but unable to move. (The paralytic drug does not affect the internal organs.) The paralyzed animals were trained to make responses with these internal organs by providing "rewards" in the form of electrical stimulation of the pleasure centers of the medial forebrain bundle that was discovered by Milner and Olds. Results showed that many single components of autonomic reactivity could be conditioned, which would not be possible if the autonomic nervous system always acted in a global or general way—i.e., as a unit. For example, the experimenters were able independently to condition changes in blood pressure, heart rate, the filtration rate of urine in the kidneys, and the blood flow through the stomach, among other reactions mediated by the autonomic nervous system. In a study of special interest, the blood flow to the ears could be conditioned so that more blood went to the left ear than the right when this pattern was rewarded.

These experiments illustrate that the autonomic nervous system is capable of mediating internal reactions of great specificity, but the information gained does not indicate whether the autonomic reactions are this specific during emotional reactions. The specificity of reactions for different emotions can be evaluated only through comparison of the reactions that occur during emotional periods.

Measures of emotionality

The reactions of the body to emotion can be recorded in many ways. Some of the most frequently used methods are described below:

1. *Changes in heart rate.* Through the methods developed to record the electrical potentials generated by the heart (electrocardiograph or

EKG), the heart rate can be recorded. Increased ergotropic dominance tends to increase the heart rate through the sympathetic branch of the autonomic nervous system; whereas increased trophotropic balance tends to slow the heart rate, because of activation of the parasympathetic division of the autonomic nervous system.

2. *Blood pressure.* There are two aspects of blood pressure: (1) the diastolic phase, in which the heart muscle expands so that blood can enter the heart from the veins to be pumped out during the next contraction, and (2) the systolic phase, in which the heart muscle contracts and the blood is pumped into the arteries of the body. Blood-pressure measures of either the force of the contraction (systolic) or the expansion (diastolic) phase can be used as an index of emotion. The difference between the two blood pressure measures can also be so used.

3. *Blood vessel size.* The diameter of the blood vessels can be measured as a sign of emotion. As activity in an organ system increases, the blood vessels supplying that system increase in size to allow greater blood flow. Emotional reactions have been evaluated by the differences in blood supply to different portions of the body. There are significant differences involving the peripheral blood supply that are readily observable during reactions to stress. During intense exercise, for example, some people turn a bright red color and others turn pale. In both cases extra blood is being supplied to the muscles, but in the first type of reaction there is a correlated increase in blood distributed to the skin and in the second type blood is diverted from the skin by a constriction of its blood vessels.

4. *Changes in the skin.* Skin changes during emotional periods fall into three general types: (1) palmar sweating (2) electrical resistance of skin, and (3) an electrical response produced in cells of the sweat glands. The response of each is, to some degree, independent of the responses in the others. With greatly increased ergotropic activity, the sweat glands produce sweat, and to discrete events, a discrete electrical response. At the same time, the overall skin resistance becomes less.

5. *Urination and defecation.* Frequency of urination and defecation has been used to measure emotionality in studies of smaller mammals, such as rats and mice. Most often these measures are used when the experimental animals are placed in a standard testing situation. These measures came to be used as indicators of emotion on the basis of observed increases in rates of urination and defecation when the animals were under stress. The selection was also based upon the fact that if ergotropic activation becomes great enough, the bowels and bladder are voided in all animals, including man.

6. *Muscular tension.* Muscle tension is also measured to evaluate emotional levels—as might have been anticipated on the basis of our earlier discussion of the relationship between sensory input from the muscles and tuning of the hypothalamus.

7. *Gastrointestinal activity.* At least in some people pronounced changes in the stomach and intestines can be found during emotional periods. The type of reaction that occurs depends upon the specific situation, the particular individual, and the activities going on in the stomach as the emotion occurs. During prolonged periods of stress, the secretions of the internal organs change toward a greater overall level of acidity. This is considered to be a factor in the development of ulcers in the gastrointestinal tract.

8. *Respiration.* Although changes in respiration are related to emotional reactions, the respiratory response is not simple—nor is the relationship of any component of the respiratory response to any emotional reaction. In breathing there are two forces involved in making air move into and out of the lungs: an abdominal contribution and a rib-chest component. Under normal circumstances the separate contributions to breathing are balanced. During an emotional period, one or the other or both may be changed. The breathing cycle has periods of inspiration (breathing in) and expiration (breathing out), with pauses between each. Each can be altered more or less independently during emotional episodes.

Given these eight categories of measures of the emotions, what can be concluded with respect to reactions the body exhibits during emotional periods? The first problem confronted by a student of the emotions (and one of the major problems) is that these measures do not correlate well with each other—except during periods of the greatest and most intense emotional reactions. If one were to set out to measure the degree of ergotropic activation of a given person or that produced by a certain situation, which measure should be used? Which would be the best indicator? What would happen if several measures were used and each gave a different index of arousal level? There is no one best measure of activation, and different measures often give divergent results.

Differences found among the various measures of the degree of activation (or ergotropic balance) can arise from a number of causes. These include the possibilities that all of them are unreliable measures of anything, that each person is different in his reactions, that each emotional reaction is unique, and so on for many more possible explanations. The approaches to the diversity found among people and among measures of emotionality have taken two principal directions:

(1) investigations of the patterns of emotional reactivity found within a particular individual, and (2) investigations into the patterns of reactivity elicited by particular situations.

Intensive studies of individuals have revealed that a person maintains a pattern of autonomic reactions to stress that is fairly stable over time. The patterns were derived from an analysis of many measures of emotionality while the subjects were repeatedly tested over fairly prolonged periods. The pattern of reactions for an individual did remain stable for a period of months, although the patterns of reactivity among subjects varied widely. This means that during a given period of life, individuals will tend to react in a consistent fashion to many emotion-producing situations. The actual pattern exhibited—e.g., increased heart rate, no change in blood pressure, change in skin resistance, no change in sweating—will be specific to the individual and be a result of his own past experiences and genetic inheritance.

Given these observations, the evaluation of specific situational effects must be of great magnitude, large enough to overcome the differences found among the reactions of individual subjects. Several attempts have been made to show differences in the physiological reactions produced by the emotions of anger and fear. Situations and circumstances can be arranged so as to induce either anger or fear in subjects and to allow the simultaneous recording of physiological indices of the emotional reactions of the body. In both anger and fear, the main observation was that ergotropic activation predominated, even though with some variables the two situations could be distinguished. The use of drugs that separate the effects of the hormone epinephrine from the closely related norepinephrine has allowed researchers to find that the experiences of anger and fear are related to differences in the secretion of the two hormones. Anger and aggression directed toward others are associated with enhanced secretion of norepinephrine, whereas fear and depression are related to enhanced release of epinephrine.

Overall, few systematic differences have been found between the upheavals of the body, both somatic and autonomic, that are associated with different emotions. The capacity for fine-grain control of the organs is available and is reflected in the differences found among people as they react emotionally to stress. Nevertheless, the individual patterns of reactivity are not perfectly stable, and change does occur over periods of months. How then can emotional experiences be so different, varied, and yet relatively stable? One answer to this question comes from studies in which the cognitive aspects of brain activities are given a more important role in determining the experienced emotion.

COGNITIVE DETERMINANTS OF EMOTION

If emotional experiences can be thought of as having two components—(1) the excitatory, arousal component we have described as resulting from a balance favoring the ergotropic systems and (2) a cognitive interpretation of the bodily arousal—the observation that the ergotropic reactions are rather general in scope has led to the view that the *specificity* of the emotions arises from the second or *cognitive* component.

Experiments to test this theory were based on the assumption that cognitive activities would be especially important determinants of emotion when an ergotropic reaction occurred for which no ready explanation was available. In a series of ingenious studies, Stanley Schacter has induced ergotropic arousal through the use of epinephrine injected into the blood stream. Some subjects were warned about the autonomic and somatic effects of the drug, others were not, and still others were led to expect erroneous symptoms following the injection. The subjects then were given different social experiences with a "stooge" in an experimental room. Some of the experiences were designed to induce euphoria and others to induce anger. The results of the experiments show that the social circumstances to which the subjects were assigned did indeed determine the emotion experienced by the subjects, as measured both by the subjects' verbal reports and by observation of their behaviors. From this type of experiment, using many types of social and environmental manipulations, it has become clear that even though the ergotropic reactions that accompany the emotions may be quite general, the cognitive factors of the situation and the person can add the specific qualities that allow emotions to be identified and labeled in accordance with language and custom.

To this point, we have concentrated upon the emotional reactions and their internal correlates. It now will be useful to consider some conditions that initiate emotional experiences and behavior.

Frustration-induced behavior

There are some circumstances in which the problems presented by the environment are too much for the organism to deal with effectively. What happens then? An inability to cope with the demands of the situation produces an emotional reaction, but it may turn the behavior sequence away from its normal goals. N. R. F. Maier believes that some behavior is not goal-directed at all. He believes some responses become *fixated* through frustrating emotional circumstances. Once a response becomes fixated, it will occur again and again quite apart from any effects produced by the responses. Only through special retraining procedures can this fixation be altered.

In a typical experiment rats are trained to jump to a given pattern in a window of a Lashley jumping apparatus (which is illustrated in Figure 9-4). Cards are placed in the two windows of the jumping stand. There are different figures on each card. The animal is forced to jump from the stand to the platform behind the windows. The windows can be fixed so that a card can be locked in place or just lightly held so that it will be knocked down by the rat's jump, allowing the rat's entry to the platform. If the animal jumps and strikes a window with a card locked in place, it falls into a net below. If the animal jumps at a window that is blocked by a lightly held card, it lands easily on the platform behind it. Usually the animals are trained while on mild food-deprivation schedules, and food is available on the platform behind the windows.

Let us assume that the card with a triangle painted on it is always locked in place and a card with a square painted on it is held in place only lightly. The cards are placed in the right or left window on a random basis. The animals soon learn to jump to the card with the square on it. By doing so, they gain entry to the platform and do not bump their noses and fall into the net below, as happens when they jump to the card with the triangle.

The next step is to change the situation by randomly locking the cards in place so that there is *no solution* to the problem. Now a jump to either card may or may not pay off. Half the time a jump will result in a bumped nose and a fall. What happens to the behavior of the

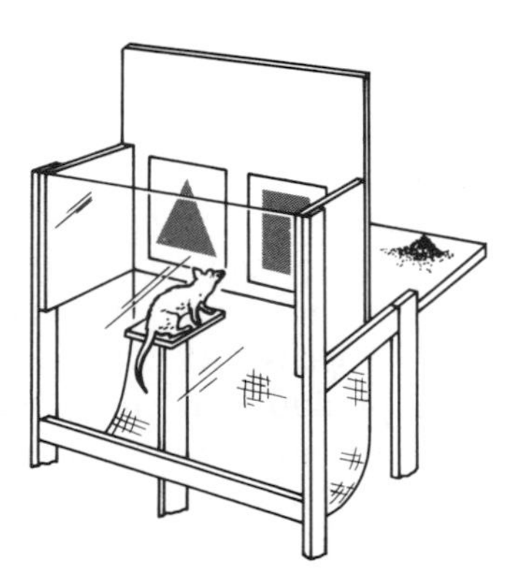

Figure 9-4
One form of the Lashley jumping stand.

animals? Quickly the animals adopt an invariant position response. For example, an animal will jump toward the right window on all trials. This is the *fixation* of a response. It occurs on every trial and in a stereotyped fashion. If an animal has fixated a jumping response toward the right window, and the left window is completely open, the rat will lean out toward the open window, sniff at it, then jump at the closed right window on trial after trial. The argument is that frustration (in this case the insoluble problem) leads to response fixation, and this fixation serves no goal. When an individual's frustration tolerance has been exceeded, there is a complete loss of adaptivity as stereotyped behavior is initiated.

Many things may lead to the frustration-instigated fixation of responses. In the jumping-stand experiment above it was the introduction of an insoluble problem. In other instances frustration-instigated fixation could be caused by punishment, anxiety, a series of business failures, disappointments in love—in short, any severe emotional reaction. Maier uses the term *frustration* somewhat more broadly than many psychologists do who restrict the term to instances in which an individual is thwarted in attaining a specific goal.

The fixated responses discussed by Maier are similar to those exhibited by mentally disturbed individuals who exhibit compulsive behavior. Anyone may show fixated behavior when frustrations have temporarily exceeded tolerances; but the compulsive person evinces fixated, stereotyped responses day in and day out, relentlessly. Both temporary and permanent fixation responses are a phenomenon that we cannot deny.

Information and uncertainty

Under normal conditions, an individual processes information from the environment by using guidelines based on past experiences that are related (1) to the behavioral sequence that is active and (2) to expectations about the environment. The situation can have a greater or smaller amount of uncertainty. For example, sitting in class listening to a lecture on psychology produces specific expectations about what will occur during the hour. Usually, expectations about the situation are largely confirmed and only relatively minor unexpected events occur. In other situations, such as going out with a new date for the first time, expectations may be less certain. When expectancies are not confirmed, i.e., when the unexpected occurs, the emergency (ergotropic) systems are engaged. The interpretation of the emotional reaction may be influenced by the social and environmental circumstances surrounding the disruption.

In a way the dashing of expectancies represents a loss of control by the person. Control, in this context, would refer to the development of efficient plans and expectancies about what will be happening. When disruption occurs the plan must be reevaluated, since it has failed to accomplish its task. This disruption produces a greater or smaller engagement of the emergency reaction systems and produces, at least temporarily, a condition of uncertainty. The person attempts to incorporate the unexpected events producing the uncertainty by expanding and altering existing plans, and he begins to seek through his sensory systems new information that may be of help.

If the expected is always that which is experienced, steps can be taken to provide new experiences. Certainly to have every expectation fulfilled would be a boring situation, and the use of drugs and psychedelic colors and lights may represent attempts to provide new, unexpected experiences in an easy way. Such devices would represent a readily available method to relieve the boredom produced by a highly routinized life program.

Notice, however, that when *action* is taken to expand the number of experiences, we have returned to a motivational context. The person has been motivated in the sense that a goal-directed course of action has been initiated and maintained, aimed not toward fulfillment of a biological motive but toward enriching perceptual experiences and perhaps also toward achieving plans that provide better control and comprehension of the environment.

COMPETENCE AND EXPERIENCE Not only are all animals spontaneously active, but they are also motivated to experience change and to attain some degree of mastery over their environment. Rats and higher animals will learn to press bars to produce changes in the lighting in their home cages. Monkeys will learn new responses when rewarded only by the opportunity to look into the laboratory from their cages. They also work increasingly complicated puzzles merely for their own sake. Children given choices among games of different levels of complexity choose those which are just beyond their present capacities. The tendencies of man to tackle problems and challenges without other apparent rewards is well known.

The term "competency motive" has sometimes been used to describe behaviors directed toward achieving greater commerce with, and control over, the environment, when these actions are not based upon tangible rewards. The conditions leading to these competence behaviors are closely related to emotional reactions that arise from the failure of present plans or from the tedium of having too little in the way of the unexpected occur. At this point, the concepts of emotion and motivation tend to merge.

CONCLUSIONS

The union of the emotions and motivation represents really only a portion of the real merger among mechanisms that are responsible for the behaviors and experiences described as learning, memory, sensation, perception, and the other categories of psychological processes we use to fractionate behavior so as to make our study of it easier and more systematic. All behavior, however, reflects a continual merging of information from the external world and the internal environment—from the past, the present, and anticipations of the future. Our distinctions among behavior processes are artificial and reflect our inability to cope with behavior in all its complexities. Each person is an individual, operating in his own ways to achieve his goals and to find his way in our world.

SUGGESTED READINGS

Fowler, H. *Curiosity and exploratory perspective.* New York: Random House, 1965.

Fuller, J. L. *Motivation: A biological perspective.* New York: Random House, 1962.

Gellhorn, E. (Ed.) *Biological foundations of emotion.* Glenview, Ill.: Scott, Foresman, 1968.

Gross, C. G., & Zeigler, H. P. *Readings in physiological psychology: Motivation.* New York: Harper & Row, 1969.

Jose, H. R. *Emotions.* Dubuque, Iowa: William C. Brown, 1966.

Appendix A
Comments on theories in psychology

Most *people* are interested in observing and analyzing their own behavior as well as the behavior of others, and they use the information they have acquired about the behavior of others for many different purposes. These activities are quite different from the professional activities of psychologists, who study behavior from a *scientific* viewpoint.

Let us now contrast the layman's and the psychologist's observations of behavior. The layman who successfully uses his own "psychological" knowledge often cannot express exactly *how* or *why* he is able to do it. He may have learned how to deal with people in some situations, but he has not learned how to state his findings in terms of precise principles or techniques that are transferable to other situations and to different people. Scientific information must be communicable. The nonscientific, private information of the layman generally is useful only to him. Its privacy may often stem from the fact that it represents and depends on one individual acting as an observer and interpreter.

Scientists depend upon information obtained from experiments that (1) allow precise determination of factors controlling behavior and (2) can be trusted to yield the same results every time the experimental conditions are repeated; that is, they must be reliable. Such information can be called *data.* Psychologists use this word to refer to observations that come from acceptable processes of collecting information. Observations that are not reliable cannot be used as data, since they measure nothing.

FACTS AND THEORIES OF BEHAVIOR

The justification for the cliché, "Psychologists seek the facts of life," comes from the interpretation of the word *fact.* If we agree that data are reliable observations and records that come from well-controlled and repeatable experiments, then what is a *fact?* A fact is something more than data. Data are always limited to the situations in which they are collected. If a hypothesis is tested in many situations, with subjects of different types, then on the basis of these additional data we might be moved to accept the hypothesis as being of wide usefulness. Facts, to the psychologist, are general statements about behavior that have been supported by data collected in many kinds of situations. They are hypotheses that have been accepted as generally useful and significant.

In modern science, hypotheses become confirmed facts only after repeated collection of data. Hypotheses are most often simple statements of relationships between variables. One way of viewing a *theory* is to think of it as a set of interrelated hypotheses. Psychological theories can also be defined as a collection of statements—verbal, mathematical, or symbolic—from which predictions of behavior can be made. When a theory has been supported by data from many experiments, it is considered a fact. Newtonian theory in physics has come to be accepted as fact; synaptic transmission of impulses between the nerve cells in the brain—which only 60 years ago was a hotly debated hypothesis—is also accepted as fact.

One of the most important features of a theory is that its statements act jointly to predict behavior. Since psychologists are interested in the prediction of behavior, their whole enterprise centers on the development of useful theories. Their goal is to produce theories about human behavior that attain the same factual status that Newtonian theory has in its application to physical objects.

A simple theory of behavior might be something like this: As a response is repeated by an organism in a specific situation, a tendency builds up in the organism to make the same response in similar situations in the future. Let us complicate our theory somewhat by assuming that the organism must be motivated to make any response in the situation. In this case, suppose that motivation can be defined as the specified number of hours of food deprivation. Let us further assume that the longer the time without food, the greater will be the tendency to make the response. This is an inadequate theory of behavior, to be sure, but let us examine what we have.

The tendency to make a given response in a situation is determined by two factors: motivation and the frequency with which the response has been made in the past. The prediction of the response cannot be made if we know only one of these variables; both the motivation and the number of past responses must be known. To test this theory, we would experimentally manipulate one or the other or both of these variables and note whether our predictions are borne out by the resulting data. If the theoretical predictions are fulfilled in all the test situations, the theory will be useful enough to be acceptable.

Most theories in psychology, as well as in other sciences, have arisen as attempts to explain a great deal of existing data, as well as to predict the discovery of new data. In this sense theories are summaries of accumulated information, which provide sources for developing additional facts about behavior.

There are many ways to describe and analyze experimental data, just as there are many ways to design an experiment. Not all are equally useful or appropriate to test a particular hypothesis. There is no one book to read, and there is no one academic course that will prepare a person to be a good researcher or scientist. As in most areas, experience and scholarship in the area of specialization will lead to a competent level of ability in experimentation. But both ingenuity and creativity are also necessary for significant research contributions.

EXPLANATIONS OF BEHAVIOR

Psychologists want to explain human behavior. In predicting behavior we take information already at hand and look toward the future. Given certain behavioral data and a theory, we then expect (predict) certain other behaviors to follow. We expect these other behaviors because the theory tells us what to expect. It is theory that makes our present observations the precursors of the future.

The essential role of theory in predicting behavior is illustrated in Figure A-1. Here a horizontal line represents the separation of the theoretical world of variables, concepts, and theoretical constructs from the real world of observations and data. In the world of theory there are rules whereby combinations of certain concepts lead to certain other concepts, or permit them to be inferred.

In a simple experiment using biological motives, we could have a theory that relates food-seeking to a state of hunger. If we want to predict how fast an animal will run down a long passageway for food, we might predict that the hungrier an animal is, the faster his running speed will be.

Hunger, the motive factor, is a theoretical concept. We can never see hunger directly. It is something inferred from observations made in the real world. We could infer the presence of this *motive construct* from observing the number of hours the subjects have been without food. In doing so, of course, we must state the relation between the intensity of the motive and the number of hours without food.

To make a prediction of behavior, deductions must be made from the theory. The theory might state that when biological motives are aroused, the organism will attempt to satisfy this motive. It might go on to state that the greater the biological motive, the greater attraction food will have. We test the deduction made from the theory by looking for data in the real world. We could measure how hard an animal works

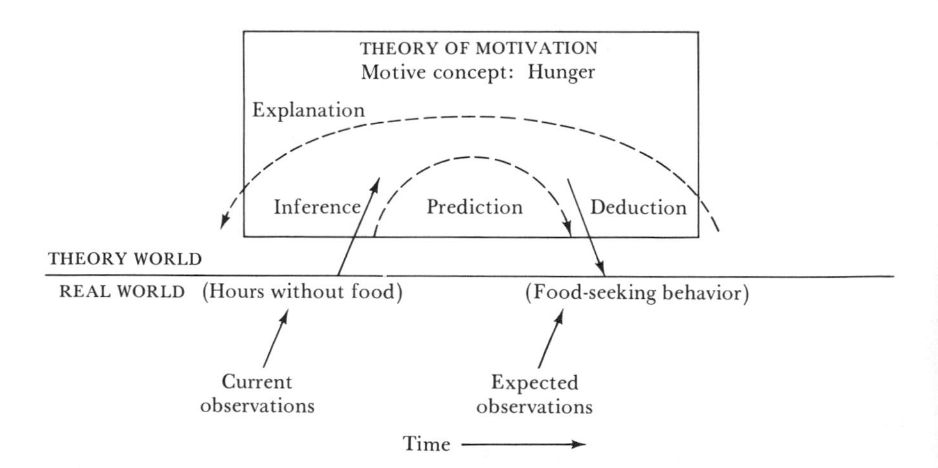

Figure A-1 *Schematic representation of the role of theory in the explanation and prediction of behavior.*

to obtain food, how much punishment it takes to deter his food-seeking behavior, or whether he chooses food in preference to water or a sexual partner. These represent predictions generated by the general theory of motivation and by our current knowledge that the animal has, in fact, been deprived of food for a certain time.

Explanation, on the other hand, follows a similar pathway through the theoretical and the real world, but in an opposite direction. Suppose we notice an animal exhibiting persistent food-oriented activity. Why does he do this? We would accept the explanation that this behavior is attributable to hunger, provided that (1) we have a theory that relates hunger to food-seeking and (2) we learn that the animal had been previously deprived of food.

SUMMARY

We have completed a full circle. We began by discussing the views of the layman about psychology and how the psychologist looks for firmer ground and better observations than the layman does before he develops theories to explain events. The scientist wants well-controlled and highly reliable data and is not satisfied with a few observations made under uncertain circumstances. Once he has made his observations, the psychologist looks for consistent, repeatable relationships among them; we have used the word "fact" to describe such firm relationships. Goaded on by a need to understand behavior, scientists develop theories or interlocking sets of hypotheses about behavior that, if useful, will allow the *prediction* and explanation of behavior. Not all theories work well; only those theories which work best are retained in science.

Theories that are useful in predicting behavior are the goal of psychology. Theories are not necessarily true or false; they are more or less useful for explaining and understanding behavior and are evaluated pragmatically according to their usefulness.

Appendix B
Statistical analysis of data in psychology

We live in a world of numbers. We use them daily as identification symbols, tools, and sometimes even weapons. We each have a social security number, and we each use numbers in shopping, figuring out our bank balance, writing addresses, and countless other ways. Nevertheless, the appropriate use of numbers in science requires thought and consideration. Throughout our education we have learned how to manipulate numbers according to the rules of mathematics, but we always must consider what the results of our manipulations mean.

When numbers are used as identification symbols, as in the social security system, the numbers are simply a name written in a different language. We could add them, subtract them, and multiply them, but these operations would make little sense. The sum of the social security numbers 343-34-4067 and 386-28-4567 carries no greater meaning than would the addition of Harry Smith and Joe Doaks.

Numbers are also used to describe the order of a set of things. If the players on a football team were lined up from lightest to heaviest, the number 1 could be assigned to the lightest player, the number 2 to the second-lightest, the number 3 to the third-lightest, and so on.

This technique, of course, tells us about the relationship among subjects, but again it does not allow us to manipulate the numbers through addition, subtraction, and so forth. For example, if the lightest football player weighed 160 pounds, the second-lightest 164 pounds, and the third-lightest 180 pounds, we could not say that player 1 plus player 2 equals player 3.

Often, however, we use the kind of numbers that do make sense when manipulated mathematically. In dealing with weights, for example, 1 pound plus 2 pounds does equal 3 pounds. Numbers that can be used in common mathematical procedures all have some reference point, like zero. If there is an absolute reference point, it does make sense to consider some number as being twice as large (times 2) as some other number. If there is no such reference point, then saying (player) 2 is twice (player) 1 is senseless.

Numbers are ideas. As such, they should be applied only with a full grasp of what they signify and how they can be manipulated in the context in which they are being used.

In psychology, numbers are most frequently used in describing data obtained from experiments. For example, if we were to evaluate the effect on intelligence of a preschool educational program, the data obtained from the subjects would be expressed in numbers that represent the intelligence quotient (I.Q.) scores derived from some standard test. If we were to study the effect of LSD on visual perception, the data obtained from subjects probably would be numbers representing the ability of the subjects to make fine visual discriminations. Almost always, the data from psychological experiments are expressed directly by (or are quickly transformed into) numbers. It is at this point that we must consider carefully just what these numbers mean. Once we have the significance of the numbers clearly in mind, then we may proceed to use them in testing hypotheses and establishing facts of behavior.

There is a universal need to be able to summarize data so that they can be more readily grasped and more meaningfully used. This summarization requires descriptive statistics. Usually we wish to describe at least two characteristics of the data (numbers) coming from an experiment: (1) the central tendency and (2) the variability of the data.

MEASURES OF CENTRAL TENDENCY

A *measure of central tendency* is a combined score, a number that tells us something about the characteristics or the level of performance of a group under observation. It is the best single measurement of the set of data collected from observing the group. The most commonly used measure of central tendency is the *mean,* the numerical average of the scores obtained from each subject in the group. To obtain the mean, the *sum* of all the scores is divided by the total *number* of scores involved.

Psychologists also utilize other measures of central tendency. One such measure is the most frequently obtained score in a group, the *mode*; another, the *median,* is that score which separates the upper from the lower half of the group when all the scores have been placed in order from highest to lowest. Thus in the series of numbers 6, 5, 5, 4, 3, 2, 1, the number 5 would be the mode, but 4 would be the median.

Which of these three estimates of central tendency—the mean, median, or mode—is the best to use depends upon the characteristics of the data. Where the number of cases is large, the mean score is often the most appropriate. When the number of cases in a group is small, the median is sometimes preferable. An important advantage of the mean, in general, is that it, unlike the mode and the median, is an algebraic value that can be utilized in any further algebraic operations the investigator may wish to employ.

MEASURES OF DISPERSION

Knowledge of a measure of central tendency gives us some information about a group of numbers. Often, however, we also want information about the dispersion of the numbers about their central tendency. For this we need to use *measures of dispersion.* These measures indicate *distribution*—the arrangement or allocation of numbers assigned to individuals in a group. In discussing a distribution, for example, we can give the *range* of the scores. The range is obtained simply by subtracting the lowest from the highest score. We also can calculate statistical estimates of the amount of dispersion of the scores around the mean of each distribution. Some of these measures are called the *average deviation, standard deviation,* and *sum of squared deviations.* Statisticians have specific rules for determining these measures as well as for describing the shape of distribution. These rules go beyond the scope of our present inquiry, but the student should be aware that these three measures of dispersion, like the mean, are the result of algebraic calculations.

NORMAL DISTRIBUTION

A normal distribution has highly desirable mathematical characteristics and, when plotted on a graph, takes on a bell-shaped curve, often called a *normal curve,* as illustrated in Figure B-1.

If the data collected in psychological experiments approximate a normal distribution, a description of the dispersion of the scores about the mean can be given by a statistic called the *standard deviation.* When data approach a normal distribution and when the mean and standard deviations are stated, we then know the complete distribution. This is a great saving in description. By two numbers, the mean and the standard deviation, we provide as much information as by presenting all the individual scores that go into the distribution.

INFERENTIAL STATISTICS

Statistical description helps us to do more than summarize data; it allows us to evaluate hypotheses about behavior. As a general strategy in behavioral research, some population of subjects, be they people or mice, is determined as the appropriate target population. By *population,* we mean the entire group of organisms about which we wish to make some conclusion. If this group is too large to be studied in its entirety, samples of the population must be obtained. For most experiments, we must attempt to find a smaller group that is representative of the larger population.

There are many ways of trying to establish a truly representative population. The best is to select a so-called *random sample* from the larger population. But practical considerations often prevent the use of this

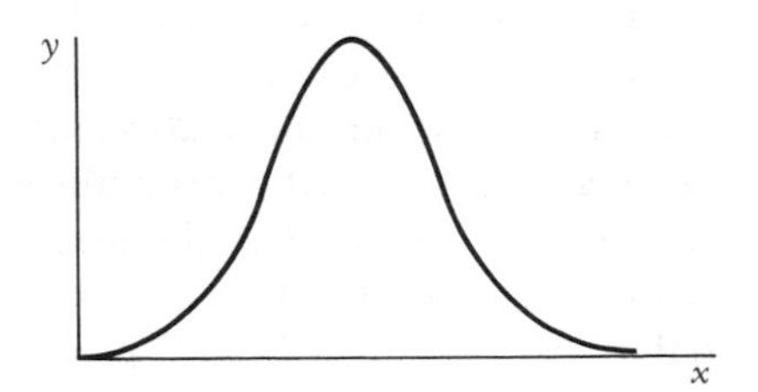

Figure B-1 *A normal distribution. Mathematically, this distribution describes a relationship between two variables. Often, frequency distributions approximate this relationship. For frequency distributions, scores are plotted along the* x-*axis and the number of individuals acheiving each score are plotted on the* y-*axis.*

method, and other means of finding a sample of subjects must be found. However, these substitute techniques of finding samples from a population are often quite useful. College freshmen and sophomores probably are not good representatives of the entire "population" of all people, and conclusions derived from studies involving them as subjects should be interpreted accordingly. By the same token, animal experiments should not be generalized beyond the species or strain used.

Once a sample has been obtained, it is divided into two or more portions, once again—as much as possible—without bias. The one sample now becomes two or more samples, each of which should be equally representative of the population. Each of the new samples from the population is now given a specific treatment.

For any particular experiment, we can postulate at least two possible outcomes: a positive outcome or affirmation of our original hypothesis, or conversely, affirmation of the null hypothesis. Originally, we predict that the subjects in one group will behave significantly differently from those in the other groups. The null hypothesis, on the other hand, postulates that the groups will behave in essentially the same manner, and the difference among their behaviors will be only that normally expected to arise from the selection of our samples.

We know that in selecting samples—particularly if the sample is small in proportion to the total population it represents—there are bound to be some differences owing to purely chance factors that may have nothing to do with our hypothesis. People in one test group may be smarter than those in the other groups, no matter how randomly the samples are chosen. However, we can calculate the probable range of such misrepresentation that might have arisen through selection of the samples. If the difference among the mean scores obtained for the groups in our experiment is large in relation to the *standard deviations* of the samples, the null hypothesis can be rejected. If the null hypothesis is to be disproved in favor of a positive hypothesis, the differences among the groups must be greater than those predicted by the null hypothesis. It is worth noting that all research aims at disproving the null hypothesis, rather than at proving the test hypothesis.

The following experiment demonstrates the effects of taking samples from a population. Take 20 small pieces of paper and write numbers on them according to the distribution of scores given in Figure B-2. On one piece of paper write the number 1; on another, write the number 7. Continue to work alternately with the scores at either end of the distribution; there will be two pieces of paper with the number 2 on them, and two pieces with the number 6. Place numbers on the remaining pieces of paper according to the frequencies shown in the figure. Then place the 20 pieces of paper in a box or hat so that you cannot see the numbers,

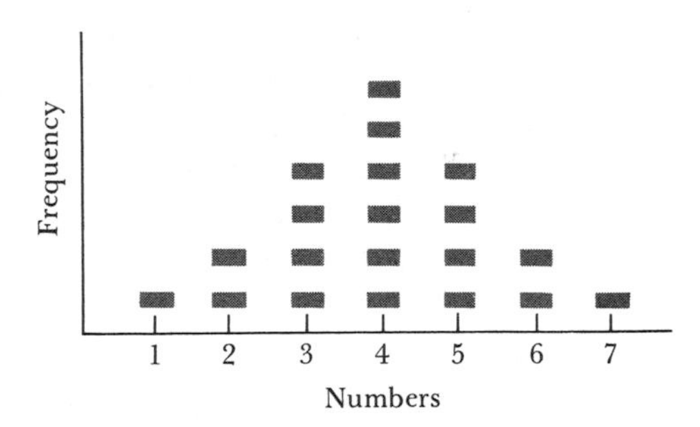

Figure B-2 *Example of distribution of a "population." Deviation of sample mean from population mean will decrease as the size of the sample decreases.*

and mix them thoroughly. Now draw out a sample consisting of three pieces of paper and note the average of the numbers on the three papers. Place the papers back in the box and mix them again. Now continue to take additional samples of these papers, three each time, and jot down the average in each case. Note the fact that the means of the samples of three papers differs from the mean of the entire population of the 20 slips of paper, often by a considerable margin. Now increase the size of your sample by drawing four instead of three slips of paper each time, and again note the averages obtained. If you continue to increase the size of the sample you take when reaching into the box, you will find that the means of the selected sample get closer to the true mean of the population as the samples get larger.

The null hypothesis merely asserts that any differences among the scores of the groups come from this kind of chance fluctuation—that is, the difference is due to the "luck of the draw" in obtaining the sample. We usually try to determine if the null hypothesis can be rejected, because it is simpler to test for the absence of a significant difference than to test for the affirmative hypothesis.

Two kinds of mistakes can be made in interpreting the results of experiments: The null hypothesis can be accepted when it should be rejected; or, conversely, it can be rejected when it should be accepted. Given the means and measure of dispersion among the data (standard deviation) of our groups of subjects, it is possible to estimate how likely it is that the difference between means of the groups was obtained as a result of chance factors, alone. These estimates come only from information from the mathematics of probabilities and depend in part upon the extent to which the data obtained in the experiment approach well-known distributions such as the normal distribution.

The results of a psychological experiment are often reported by use of a statistic that estimates the likelihood that the difference among the groups can be explained by sampling fluctuations. Some names of statistics for the evaluation of the differences between groups are the *t* test, the *F* ratio (or *F*) and the chi-square (χ^2). For each of these, it is possible to find the probability that the null hypothesis should be rejected. For example, you may read a report of an experiment which says that a difference between the scores of subjects in two groups in the experiment was significant beyond the .05 or .01 (5 or 1 percent) levels of confidence. This means that the difference in the scores of the two groups was large enough to justify rejecting the null hypothesis because only 5 times in 100 attempts or 1 time in 100 attempts would drawing two samples from a single population give a difference as large as or larger than that found in the experiment. This statement is justifiable, of course, only after the experimenter has made assumptions about the distribution of the underlying population from characteristics found in the data of the two groups. Thus from these characteristics he must first determine how different the groups were likely to be under *chance* conditions—that is, were the null hypothesis to hold true. Here, since the chances that the groups differ only because of sampling effects are remote (that is, 5 in 100 or 1 in 100), we say the difference is *significant,* meaning that it is unlikely that the null hypothesis is valid. The .05 and .01 levels of confidence are frequently, but not always, employed to satisfy the test of a "significant difference." The specific level of confidence or the criterion for significance chosen in any given experiment depends on the degree of risk of being wrong in rejecting the null hypothesis which the experimenter wishes to employ in drawing a conclusion.

CORRELATION METHODS

Often it is desirable to express the results of an experiment in terms of the relationship between two measurements made upon the same group of subjects. This can be done through giving a *correlation coefficient,* a statistic that expresses the degree of relationship between two sets of measurements.

The relations between two groups of measurements also can be presented graphically as a *scatter plot.* Numbers representing measures of one characteristic of the subjects are given on the ordinate, or *x*-axis, and numbers representing measures of the other characteristic of the subjects are plotted on the abscissa, or *y*-axis. A point on the plot is determined by the two respective scores representing each subject.

For example, consider an experiment in which we wish to relate the amount of "exploratory behavior" shown by animals to the amount of a hypothetical hormone **X** in their blood. First, we allow each animal to explore a box with a checkerboard floor for ½ hour and count the number of squares it enters. Then we take a blood sample from the animals and make a biochemical analysis to find the level of hormone X in each subject. For each animal, we have two measures: (1) the amount of exploratory activity represented by squares entered in ½ hour, and (2) the amount of the hormone X present in 1 cubic centimeter of the animal's blood.

Table B-1 presents the results of our hypothetical experiment. The first

Table B-1. **HYPOTHETICAL DATA RELATING AMOUNT OF HORMONE X PRESENT IN THE BLOOD AND AMOUNT OF EXPLORATORY BEHAVIOR SHOWN BY ANIMALS**

Animal	*Amount of hormone (in arbitrary units)*	*Number of squares entered in exploratory period*
Q	7	6
R	6	4
S	10	7
T	4	3
U	7	4
V	4	5
W	9	7
X	12	8
Y	8	3
Z	8	6

measure for each animal is given in one column, and the second measure for each animal in the other column. The same results are plotted in a scatter plot in Figure B-3. By looking at this figure we can see that there appears to be some relationship between the two sets of measures. The relationship is not perfect; if it were, the data would fall in a straight line.

Calculating the correlation coefficient for these data produces a numerical result of +.74, which indicates numerically the degree of relationship present in our data. In this case a rank-order correlation was used, because it best fitted the characteristics of our hypothetical data. There are many types of correlation coefficients that may be used, depending upon the nature of the variables being evaluated.

Because of their mathematical nature, correlations (short for correlation coefficients) range from −1.00 through zero to +1.00. A correlation cannot be lower than −1.00 or greater than +1.00. The minus and plus signs are arbitrary and indicate only the direction of the relationship. In our example, large scores on one rating go with large scores on the other rating; thus the correlation is *positive,* as indicated by the +.74

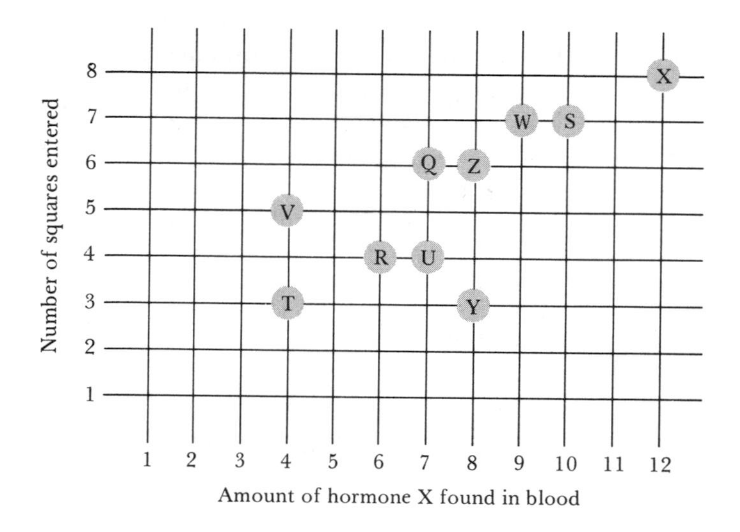

Figure B-3 *Table B-1 drawn as a scatterplot. The letter designating each animal is encircled at the intersection of its hormone level and the number of squares it entered in the exploratory period.*

value obtained. If we had measured the tendency of the animals to remain in one place, that is, the tendency *not* to explore, and compared this measure with the blood levels of the hormone, then we would have had a *negative* correlation, or −.74, since high levels of hormone would correlate with low scores for the tendency of the animals to stay in one place. The meaning of the results would be the same, however: animals high in the measured hormone move around more in our maze than do animals low in measured hormone. The sign (positive or negative) of a correlation has nothing at all to do with the strength or degree of the relationship between the two measures.

The degree of relationship is conveyed by the extent to which the absolute value (disregarding the + or −) of the correlation approaches 1.00. The closer the correlation is to 1.00, the greater the degree of association between the two sets of scores. A correlation of +1.00 or −1.00 represents a perfect correlation between the two variables. A correlation of +.74 indicates the same degree of association as does a correlation of −.74. Figure B-4 shows scatterplots of various degrees of correlation. The reader should note that the more the scores tend to cluster along a straight line, the greater is the size of the correlation coefficient.

Just as with differences between the mean scores of groups of subjects,

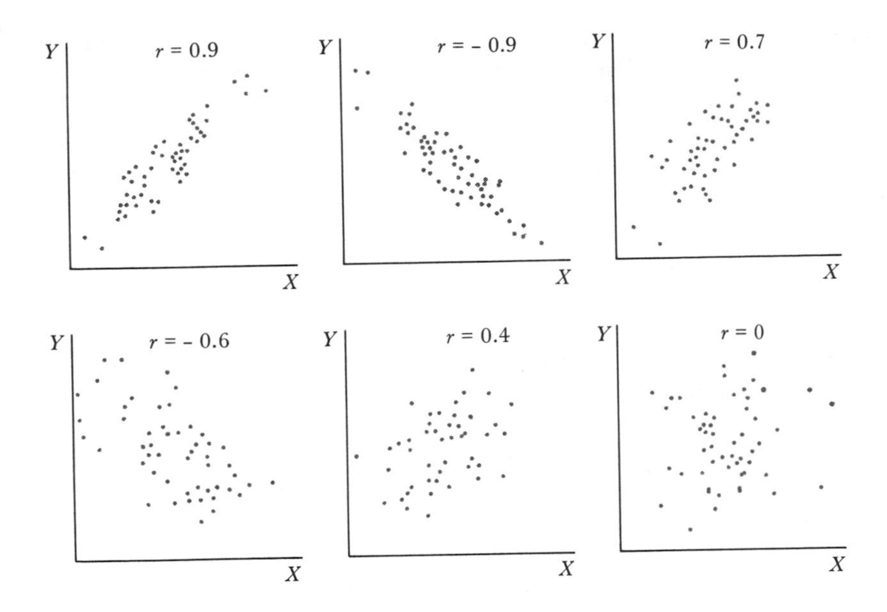

Figure B-4 *Scatterplots of different degrees of relationship expressed by the associated correlation coefficients.*

it is possible to determine correlation coefficients that represent a degree of relationship not likely to occur through fluctuations in the samples—that is, it is not due to chance factors. In the case of correlations, the null hypothesis states that the obtained correlation was due merely to a peculiar stroke of chance in sampling from the two populations. From characteristics of the samples which are plotted on the *x*- and *y*-axes, it is possible to estimate the probability that the null hypothesis is incorrect and that there *is* a relationship between the two sets of measures.

CORRELATION AND PREDICTION

A perfect correlation allows perfect prediction of one measure or score from the other measure or score. If the correlation between exploratory activity hormone level had been $+1.00$ or -1.00, we could have predicted either of the ratings from the other. A high degree of correlation allows us to make predictions that are far better than chance.

Predictions arising from correlations often are made about groups of people, frequently in applied situations such as personnel selection or the prediction of academic success. With relatively high correlation coefficients, people high on one measure will tend to fall into predictable ranges on the other variable. Without a perfect correlation, however, some exceptions will occur. Success in college achievement correlates approximately +.30 with scores obtained from the entrance examinations. This means that those who have low scores on the examination will tend not to do well in college and many of them will be asked to leave college. This is a statistical prediction that has been repeated many times. The information gained from the tests can be used in counseling prospective students and in selection by educational institutions of the students who will best benefit from their programs.

This use of correlational data obtained from the performance of groups of people presents conceptual and ethical problems for science and society. If an organization can improve its efficiency, even by a moderate amount, by selecting individuals who have personality characteristics correlated with success in the business, is it justified in giving personality tests to job applicants to screen out persons who do not have the characteristics? Some of these persons, perhaps quite a few, will not even be given the opportunity to try the new job. Is the use of knowledge of statistical characteristics of a population justified when applied to individual cases? From a pragmatic, statistical point of view the answer is "yes," since more correct judgments are made than wrong ones.

What must be remembered is that a significant correlation can be obtained by using a large group of subjects even though the absolute size of the correlation is quite small. This means that the use of a test that correlates moderately with job success will increase the efficiency of job selection. The predictions will, however, be far from perfect. Many people near the "poor end" of the test scale could in fact be successful at the job, while many people near the more favorable end could fail. A low but significant correlation indicates that there will be many such errors of this kind. Nevertheless, the use of the test as a criterion for job selection will yield more successful predictions than would be possible if the tests were not used.

In one sense, less than perfect correlations reveal our lack of knowledge about a phenomenon. If we know that one personality characteristic correlates moderately, but far less than perfectly, with success in a business or profession, then knowing more about the characteristics of success would allow us to make the predictions approach a correlation of 1.00. Then it might be possible to apply the discovered method of prediction in both the group and the individual cases.

References

Beach, F. A. The descent of instinct. *Psychology review*, 1955, *62*, 401–410.

Guthrie, E. R. *The psychology of learning*. New York: Harper & Row, 1935.

Hebb, D. O. *The organization of behavior*. New York: John Wiley & Sons, 1949.

Hebb, D. O. *A textbook of psychology*. Philadelphia: W. B. Saunders, 1958.

Herrick, C. J. *Neurological foundations of animal behavior*. New York: Holt, Rinehart and Winston, 1924.

Hirsch, J. Behavior-genetic, or "experimental," analysis: the challenge of science versus the lure of technology. *American psychologist*, 1967, *22*, 118–130.

Kennedy, W. A. Van de Reit, V., & White, J. C. A normative sample of intelligence and achievement of Negro elementary school children in the southeastern United States. *Monograph in social research and child development*, 1966, *28*:6.

Koffka, K. *Principles of gestalt psychology*. New York: Harcourt Brace Jovanovich, 1935.

Lorenz, K. A. The evolution of behavior. *Scientific american*, 1958, *199*, 67–78.

Maturana, H. R., Lettvin, J. Y., Pitts, W. H., McCulloch, W. S. Physiology and anatomy of vision in the frog. *Journal of general physiology*, 1960, *43*, 129–175.

Meehl, P. E. Schizotaxia, schizotypy, schizophrenia. *American psychologist*, 1962, *17*, 827–838.

Olds, J. & Milner, P. M. Positive reinforcement produced by electrical stimulation of septal area and other regions of rat brain. *Journal of comparative and physiological psychology*, 1954, *47*, 420–427.

Pavlov, I. P. (G. V. Amep, trans.) *Conditioned reflexes*. New York: Oxford University Press, 1927 (Dover, 1960).

Savory, T. H. Spider webs. *Scientific american*, 1960, *202*, 115–124.

Shearer, M. L., Davidson, R. T., & Finch, S. M. The sex ratio of offspring born to state hospitalized schizophrenic women. *Journal of psychiatric research,* 1967, *5,* 349–350.

Taylor, M. A. Sex ratios of newborns: associated with prepartum and postpartum schizophrenia. *Science,* 1969, *164,* 723–724.

Tinbergen, N. *The study of instinct.* New York: Oxford University Press, 1951.

Tolman, E. C. The determiners of behavior at a choice point. *Psychological review,* 1938, *45,* 1–41.

Underwood, B. J. *Experimental psychology.* New York: Appleton-Century-Crofts, 1949.

Walter, W. G. *The living brain.* New York: W. W. Norton & Company, 1953.

Watson, J. B. *Behaviorism.* New York: W. W. Norton & Company, 1924 (Phoenix, 1935).

Index